GOVERNMENT FACTORIES AND THE ORIGINS
OF BRITISH REGIONAL POLICY
1934–1948

Government Factories and the Origins of British Regional Policy 1934–1948

Including a Case Study of
North Eastern Trading Estates Ltd

HERBERT LOEBL

Visiting Lecturer
Department of Industrial Administration
The University of Newcastle upon Tyne

Avebury

Aldershot · Brookfield USA · Hong Kong · Singapore · Sydney

Published by

Avebury

Gower Publishing Company Limited
Gower House
Croft Road
Aldershot
Hants GU11 3HR
England

Gower Publishing Company
Old Post Road
Brookfield
Vermont 05036
USA

British Library Cataloguing in Publication Data
Loebl, Herbert
Government factories and the origins of
British regional policy 1834-1948: including a
case study of North Eastern Trading Estates Ltd.
1. Regional planning - Great Britain - History
2. Great Britain - Economic conditions - 1918-1945-
Regional disparities
I. Title
330.941'082   HC256.3.

ISBN 0 566 05343 8

Printed and bound in Great Britain by
Biddles Limited, Guildford and King's Lynn

Contents

List and location of figure and tables

Foreword

S. R. DENNISON

In his Preface, Dr. Loebl writes that he was associated for many years with companies located at the Team Valley Trading Estate and that he became interested in the history of the Estate through a study of industries established in the North East by refugees from Hitler's Europe (many of whom, incidentally, were 'encouraged' by the authorities to go there). There is rather more to it than that, for Dr. Loebl was himself a refugee, coming to Tyneside as a boy of 16. His father and uncle established a business on the Estate and Dr. Loebl himself became the principal founder of two manufacturing companies at Team Valley which have developed into significant high-technology businesses.

I mention this because his first-hand knowledge and experience, and his many contacts, are important elements in helping to make this study definitive and authoritative, especially in the use and interpretation of the archival material on which it is based.

He thus sheds new light on many matters which were previously ill-understood or neglected, even by those (including myself) who had made some, though necessarily less intensive studies, of this topic.

But his analysis is of wider interest than merely to the specialist. His case study of the Team Valley Estate contributes to a much better understanding of the basic problems it was intended to alleviate and of the attitudes of government to economic depression in the older industrial areas.

His main theme (to which the case study is an essential adjunct - the two are highly complementary) is the development and implementation of policies, from the tentative pre-War attempts to alleviate local unemployment by what were regarded as unorthodox (and possibly dangerous) 'experiments' to the post-War efforts to achieve a 'balanced distribution of industry' by means of full-blooded central government control.

He has explored a mass of contemporary material, including the relevant Cabinet and departmental papers, the files of the Commissioner for the Special Areas of England and Wales, the archives of North Eastern Trading Estates, as well as published works, including the writings of politicians and their biographers.

The story is indeed labyrinthine, with political decisions arising from an often confused complex of events and ideas, with individual personalities exerting great influence, e.g. Neville Chamberlain on pre-War Special Areas policy and Hugh Dalton on the evolution of post-War Development Areas policy during the War.

As Dr. Loebl states, I was myself involved as a member of the War Cabinet Secretariat - though only marginally - in the discussions leading the the 1944 White Paper on Employment Policy and the formulation of the post-War policies for controlling the distribution of industry. I can confirm that his use of the sources is impeccable and that I find nothing in his interpretation with which I would disagree.

In the depression years before the War, one vital element was the failure to understand that the problem was rooted in structural change in industry, resulting in the decline of the staple industries and creating a need for new industries to develop in their place - an essential basis for economic development and growth. Along with this went failure to distinguish between structural change and the effect of cyclic fluctuations, which could either partly mask the need for change or make the problem worse. The confusion remains; it is compounded by the spread of simplistic neo-Keynesian dogmas.

There was also little appreciation or knowledge of the factors on which the establishment and development of new enterprises depended. Dr. Loebl's discussion of the part played by finance is particularly apposite here. But, perhaps above all, there was a lack of clear formulation of the 'proper' functions of government in economic affairs.

The result of all this was the adoption of a number of expedients (including, of all things, Land Settlement, which had many advocates) designed to alleviate unemployment in the worst-affected areas.

Whatever success the Team Valley Estate achieved in the pre-War period needs to be seen in this context; as Dr. Loebl shows, it was due more to local initiative - supported by the first Commissioner for the Special Areas - rather than to any action by central government.

The post-War story was little better. In spite of ambitious plans for the 'balanced distribution of industry', the aim was ill-defined and perceived immediate needs were allowed to dominate over longer-term structural considerations. There was also a conflict between the aim to provide factory space as quickly as possible within the available resources and the creation of employment in places where new opportunities were thought to be necessary but where land was not immediately available.

Post-War government policies have not prevented the re-emergence of the pre-War problems. Although in a somewhat different form, they have the same basic causes. The 'great divide' between North and South (in Britain, not in the sense of the Brand Report, even if there are parallels) has reopened. Again, there is little understanding of the real nature of the problems, with a good deal of exaggeration both of their magnitude and the possibility of solutions by government action.

One detects few signs that politicians and others are fully acquainted with the experiences of the past 60 years. Yet they are highly relevant and there are many lessons to be learned from the formative period of regional policy. It is foolish to look into crystal balls when books can be read, and Dr. Loebl provides us with a major text.

S.R. Dennison

Preface

The author was associated for most of the years from 1939 to 1980 with manufacturing companies located at the Team Valley Trading Estate, the first government-financed Trading or Industrial Estate in Britain. He became interested in the history of the Estate through a study of the industries established in the North East of England and Cumbria before and after the last War by refugees from Hitler's Europe (*).

That study involved an examination of the origins of the Team Valley Estate only in so far as it helped to understand the background of the settlement of refugee industries. The approach of the 50th anniversary of the Estate provided a good reason for studying the history of government-financed factories on trading estates and smaller sites in the North East in some depth.

It soon became evident that their origins could not be understood except in the context of early British regional policy, because the provision of factories for rent represented the main government action under the policy within the regions, both before and immediately after the last War.

The original intention was to study the whole period since the establishment of the Team Valley Estate, but given the need to link the early history of government-financed factories in the North East with the evolution of regional policy, it was not possible to cover such a long period in a single work.

This study is limited, therefore, to the years up to and including 1948. The reasons why that year may be considered to mark the end of an era are briefly touched upon in the Introduction.

So far as the Trading Estates Corporation is concerned, however, much
has happened since 1948 that would have to be related in an official
history.

The development of regional policy in Britain was intimately linked
with the evolution of economic, social and political attitudes. The
earliest period was perhaps the most interesting. In the old industrial
areas, the effects of the world-wide business recession triggered by the
Wall Street crash in 1929 combined with structural problems of long
standing to cause difficulties of unprecedented scale and complexity.
Fundamental changes in political and economic thinking were needed, but
governments were not ready. Public opinion eventually made intervention
unavoidable, and once it had begun, it increased by its own momentum.

The main principles of regional policy since 1945 - 'the stick and the
carrot' - have not changed, but the political will with which the
'stick' was applied began to falter in the late 1950s. The size of the
'carrot' has varied; in recent years it has continued to become smaller.
Other factors have tended to diminish the effectiveness of regional
policies, particularly the concentration of the high technology and
defence industries around London and in the South East and the
attraction to industry of the Channel Coast after Britain joined the
European Communities in 1973, to name but two of the most significant.

The continuing secular decline of the traditional industries of the
North East had not yet been made good by the rather undirected
restructuring efforts since 1936 when the region was again plunged into
a serious unemployment crisis in the middle of the 1970s. Although the
recession has eased, the decline of employment in the traditional
industries of the North East is now irreversible. The newer industries
are prospering - as they did in the depression years before the War -,
but they employ relatively small numbers of people.

The present crisis has reopened many of the questions which were
discussed in the 1930s: the wide difference in unemployment between the
North and South of the country; the ability of market forces on their
own to improve industrial structures and redress regional imbalances;
the role of the State in assisting structural change; the effectiveness
of public works and government contract preference schemes to reduce
unemployment; sources of finance for start-up industries; the potential
of areas of high unemployment to help themselves and the role of
development and enterprise agencies in local efforts. Even the problem
caused by advances in technology is not new: it was the main cause of
unemployment in the coal mining industry, the largest employer in the
North East, in the decade before the last War.

A repeat run may also be discerned in particular local attempts to
improve the employment situation: the encouragement of unemployed men
and women to start businesses, the counselling of small firms to ensure
their survival and the search for new products for small firms to
manufacture were some of the ideas tried out 50 years ago.

It must be observed, however, that the social and economic effects of
the present crisis cannot be compared with those of the early 1930s. The
structural improvements achieved by regional policy and the development
of indigenous industries, as well as the provisions of the Welfare
State, have cushioned the effects of the crisis. Within the context of a

major - almost worldwide - structural change in industry and a high national average unemployment rate, the situation in the Development Areas is not seen by the government to require special attention. Indeed, some measures were introduced in 1984 which aimed to reduce the cost of regional assistance.

It is hoped that this study will be of interest to those concerned with the economic fortunes of less favoured regions as well as to the general reader, and that the source material provided - some of it new - will encourage further work on early regional policy.

Herbert Loebl

Newcastle upon Tyne, May 1987.

(*) Loebl, H., 1978, Government-financed Factories and the Establishment of Industries by Refugees in the Special Areas of the North of England, 1937 - 1961, unpublished M.Phil. Thesis in the University of Durham.

Acknowledgements

My thanks are due, in the first place, to Professor John Goddard of the University of Newcastle upon Tyne for encouragement to proceed with this study, to Professor Norman McCord and Dr. David J. Rowe for help and guidance during the years I was engaged on it, and to Emeritus Professor S.R. Dennison for suggesting publication and writing the Foreword.

I am grateful to the Department of Industry for authorising the English Industrial Estates Corporation - the organisation which absorbed North Eastern Trading Estates Ltd - to make freely available to me all their records. I am particularly indebted to Mr. Kenneth John, lately secretary of the Corporation, for his interest and help, and for his concern for the preservation of the Corporation's records. As a result of this concern - and of the cooperation of Dr. W.A.L. Seaman, lately Chief Archivist of the Tyne & Wear Archives -, some 1,200 boxes of records were transferred to the Archives in 1982, where the task of cataloguing and rearranging the material was undertaken most competently by Mr. Roger Sims.

I have been able to submit parts of this study for criticism and suggestions to a few people who were personally involved in the events described in it. The late Emeritus Professor G.H.J. Daysh - whose distinguished connection with the North East coast had spanned almost 60 years - helped me a great deal. My thanks are due to Col. R.M. Percival, the first secretary of North Eastern Trading Estates Ltd in 1936, Mr. Walter Bevan, lately chief executive of the English Industrial Estates Corporation who joined North Eastern Trading Estates Ltd in 1937, and Mr.James Anderson, lately deputy chief executive of the Corporation.

Sir Raymond Appleyard, son of the late Major-General K.C. Appleyard, chairman of the founding Board of North Eastern Trading Estates Ltd, was good enough to read parts of the manuscript and I am grateful to him for a number of valuable suggestions.

Mr. Garry Philipson, lately chief executive of Aycliffe & Peterlee Development Corporation, enabled me to interview two members of his staff who provided important information. Mr. R.J. Fothergill helped me greatly with the collection of information from the surviving records of the early tenants of the Team Valley Trading Estate. Mr. F.W.D. Manders advised me on the geographical definition of the North East. Dr. F. Robinson xdrew my attention to and lent me the Pepler & MacFarlane Report. I am grateful to them all.

I have received help from many other people, but I would particularly wish to thank the following:-

Miss Ivy Black	lately Records Officer, English Industrial Estates Corporation
Dr. Martin Jones	lately at the Department of Economics, University of Durham
Mr. J.D. Crabtree	lately Principal Planner, Aycliffe & Peterlee Development Corporation
Mrs. A. Dewar	formerly draughtswoman at the Royal Ordnance Factory, Aycliffe
Mr. K.D.Hodgson	Manpower Services Commission, Training Division, Newcastle upon Tyne
The Controller and Staff	Public Record Office, Kew, Richmond
The Staff	Tyne & Wear Archives, Newcastle upon Tyne
The Librarians and Staffs	University Library, Newcastle upon Tyne Central Library, Newcastle upon Tyne Central Library, Gateshead, Local Studies Section Literary & Philosophical Society, Newcastle upon Tyne.

I am indebted to the Rt.Hon. D.P.T. Jay and to Emeritus Professor S.R. Dennison for permission to use biographical material from Who's Who and to Sir Raymond Appleyard, Sir Robin Chapman Bt, Lady K. Forster, Viscount Ridley, Sir Ronald Stewart Bt and Lord Westwood to use material from Who Was Who . I thank Lady Forster for permission to reproduce the letter from the late Sir Sadler Forster to The Times of 26 July 1935 and Mr. H.J.H. Sisson for a brief biography of his late father, Mr.H.A. Sisson.

Permission to reproduce extracts from Crown documents has been received from the following and is gratefully acknowledged:-

Publications Division (Copyright), H.M. Stationery Office, Norwich
The Copyright Officer, Public Record Office, Kew
The Departmental Records Officer, Historical Section, Cabinet Office.

H.L.

Geographical area

As frequent reference is made in this study to the North East region of England, to the North East coast, or simply to the North East, it is necessary to define its extent.

In the period covered - and until 1974 -, the region which included the North East of England was designated the Northern Region, comprising the counties of Northumberland, Newcastle upon Tyne, Durham, Cumberland, Westmorland and the North Riding of Yorkshire.

In pre-second world War official papers, the industrial areas of the region were often loosely called 'Durham and Tyneside', or more comprehensively - because parts of the Tyneside conurbation were within the County of Northumberland -, 'Northumberland and Durham'. The City of Newcastle upon Tyne itself was often treated - for census purposes, for example - as a County Borough within Northumberland, in spite of the fact that it had been a county since 1888. It was included, therefore, in either of the designations mentioned above.

Since the problems of the North East were predominantly those of its depressed industrial areas - which in some parts coincided with its congested and deprived urban areas -, the references to the North East are intended to be restricted to such areas within the region: that is, to the Tyneside, Wearside and Teesside conurbations and to the coalfields of Durham, and - to a lesser extent - of Northumberland. These were the areas in which most of the basic industries of the North East were situated: coal, steel, shipbuilding and heavy engineering. It was the secular decline of these industries since the end of the first world War and the difficulties in effecting structural adjustments which represented the regional problem.

The Local Government Act 1972 created new entities: parts of Durham and Northumberland were combined with the City and County of Newcastle upon Tyne to form the County of Tyne & Wear; the Teesside area of County Durham and the North Riding of Yorkshire became the County of Cleveland, and the former Counties of Cumberland and Westmorland were amalgamated to form the County of Cumbria.

In a further reorganisation in 1982, Cumbria was attached to the North West Region. The new North East Region now comprises the administrative Counties of Northumberland, Tyne & Wear, Durham and Cleveland.

Where published official documents relating to labour and employment statistics are used, the extent of the area covered is always indicated. The unpublished data collected for this study, however, is restricted to the Employment Exchange and Office areas in the North East proper (listed in Appendices 28 and 32). These cover the pre-1974 counties of Northumberland (incl. Newcastle upon Tyne), Durham and a few places in the North Riding of Yorkshire.

There were only minor changes in the Employment Exchange and Office areas in the North East between 1936 and 1948: Berwick and Helmsley (in North Yorkshire) were added and Shiremoor was removed. In order to facilitate the comparison of pre- and post-(second) world War figures for the insured population and unemployment, the 1948 Employment Areas have been used both in Appendices 28 and 32.

Abbreviations

DOCUMENTS AT THE PUBLIC RECORD OFFICE

BT	Board of Trade
CAB	Cabinet Files
CC	Cabinet Minutes and Conclusions, 1919-1939
WC	" " " " , 1939-1945
C	" " " " , 1945 -
CP	Papers submitted to Cabinet, 1919-1939
WP(G) or WP(P)	" " " , 1939-1945
CM	" " " , 1945 -
DA	Cabinet Committee on the Reports of the Investigators and Commissioners for the Special Areas
DA [ID]	Inter-departmental Committee attached to DA
ECA	Economic Advisory Council
Lab	Ministry of Labour
T	Treasury

DOCUMENTS AT THE TYNE & WEAR ARCHIVES

TWA	. Tyne and Wear Archives

DOCUMENTS AT THE ENGLISH INDUSTRIAL ESTATES CORPORATION
in the process of being transferred to the Tyne & Wear Archives

EIEB	Minute books of the Boards of Directors
EIEM	Microfilm file on the early tenants
EIE	Miscellaneous documents

OTHER ABBREVIATIONS

BOE   Bank of England
CSAEW   Commissioner for the Special Areas of England & Wales
HC Deb   Hansard, series 5, House of Commons Debates
HL Deb   Hansard, series 5, House of Lords Debates
HMSO   Her Majesty's Stationery Office
RID   Reports of Investigations into Industrial Conditions
          in certain Depressed Areas, 1934, Part II, Durham &
          Tyneside
RCDIP   Report of the Royal Commission on the Distribution of
          the Industrial Population, usually referred to as
          'the Barlow Commission', after its chairman,
          Sir Anderson Montague-Barlow
RCDME   Minutes of Evidence taken before the Royal Commission

ABBREVIATED IDENTIFICATION OF BOOKS, REPORTS AND OTHER PUBLICATIONS

For items listed in the Bibliography, abbreviated
identifications are given in the references. These precede the
fuller identification in the appropriate section of the
Bibliography.

Conventions

Alternatives are used for the following terms:

GOVERNMENT-FINANCED FACTORIES

> Where documents of the post-War period refer to 'Treasury-financed factories', this term is used here. Both terms normally refer to new factories rather than to Royal Ordnance and other wartime factories, although the Teasury paid for the conversion of such factories to peacetime use, where necessary.

DEPRESSED AREAS

> The relevant legislation designated the depressed areas of the North East of England as 'Special Areas', and later, as 'Development Areas'. They are often referred to simply as 'the Areas'.

NORTH EASTERN TRADING ESTATES LTD

> In order to save frequent repeats, 'the Trading Estates Company', 'the Estates Company', or simply, 'the Company', are used.

TEAM VALLEY TRADING ESTATE

> For the same reason, the Team Valley Trading Estate is referred to as 'the Trading Estate', the 'Team Valley Estate', the 'Team Valley', or simply 'the Estate'.

Additional Conventions:

OTHER ESTATES COMPANIES AND TRADING ESTATES

A lower-case first letter used in 'company', 'companies', 'trading estate(s) companies' or 'trading estates' signifies that other estates companies or trading estates - government-financed or private - are meant.

COMMISSIONER FOR THE SPECIAL AREAS OF ENGLAND AND WALES

While there were two Commissioners, one for the Special Areas of England and Wales, the other for the Special Areas of Scotland, the term 'Commissioner' is always used in reference to the former. Where the Commissioner for Scotland is meant, this is clearly indicated.

LETTERS FROM THE COMMISSIONER

With a few exceptions, the references to letters from the Commissioner imply the Commissioner's office. The name of the officer writing the letter is given in the reference, if known. The dates alone are almost always sufficient for identification purposes.

REFERENCES

No references are given when the information in the text is sufficent to find the document or quotation. The date of a Parliamentary debate and the name of the speaker mentioned in the text, for example, will identify the relevant passage in Hansard with little search. Sometimes a reference is provided either on the first occasion a speaker is mentioned or where the matter is of particular importance. The date of Board meetings of the Company mentioned in the text will identify the extracts referred to in the Board Minutes.

UNDERLINING

Underlining replaces italics. It is used to indicate publications, books, foreign words as defined in the 1979 edition of Collin's English Dictionnary, and to facilitate reading. Underlining within quotations is always to be understood as having been done by the author.

WORDS IN BRACKETS WITHIN QUOTATIONS

These have been added by the author in order to facilitate reading, and on a few occasions, as comments.

Introduction

1. The old industrial areas of Britain suffered a greater economic decline in the inter-War years than the rest of the country and the crisis reached disaster proportions in some areas after the start of the business recession in 1929. Governments not only failed to accept the possibility of permanent secular decline of the basic industries of these areas, they were trapped within an economic orthodoxy that originated before the first world War. According to this, it was almost axiomatic that intervention would fail to improve the situation in the depressed areas and might have an adverse effect on the economy as a whole. When intervention eventually became politically unavoidable, rapidly effective means to improve the situation were not readily to hand.

The need for new industries was recognised, but while indigenous development had been discussed by the Economic Advisory Council in 1931 [1] and was encouraged in principle, it was accepted that new industries would have to come mainly from outside the depressed areas. But neither inducements nor any restrictions on industrial location beyond those of local planning regulations were politically conceivable at the time. In any event, a statutory location policy would have taken time to enact and would have worked too slowly for the needs of the affected areas.

The first regional measure, the Special Areas Act 1934, was a minimal response to public opinion, which demanded some action to reduce the heavy unemployment and social distress in the Areas. Although billed as a new approach to the problems of the depressed areas, the government was anxious that there should be no departure from its non-interventionist policies. The main provisions of the Act reflected its limited aims: to improve existing social and welfare structures, and to enhance and coordinate public and private aid to the unemployed.

Within these confines, the two Commissioners appointed to implement the Act were encouraged to experiment. Circumstances arose in 1935 which enabled the Commissioner for the Special Areas of England and Wales to test the limits of his remit by proposing government-financed trading estates, where small factories would be available for rent. The government accepted this proposal, mainly for electoral reasons. The first of these estates was at Team Valley, Gateshead, in the North East of England, a region then containing some of the most depressed areas in the country.

The establishment of this estate represented the first small act of intervention by any British government to promote industrial activity in a particular place. While the government remained committed, in principle, to a policy of non-intervention, it can be seen with hindsight that the authorisation of the Team Valley Estate marked the precise point in time when reliance exclusively on market forces to correct local structural problems was reluctantly abandoned.

The significance of this step was recognised at the time: an official at the Board of Trade, in a brief on the Team Valley Estate some 18 months after it was authorised, described this first government-financed trading estate as 'a most interesting experiment in practical state socialism ... It is a complete breakaway from the orthodox laissez-faire attitude of governments relating to the location of private industry' [2].

Moreover, this intervention marked the point of no return. In the few years that remained before the second world War, intervention in the depressed areas steadily increased: two more government-financed trading estates - in South Wales and in Scotland - followed within a few months; in May 1936 the government provided partial guarantees for loans to new and small firms in the Areas; in May 1937, the amendments to the 1934 Act introduced financial inducements - including government loans - to persuade industry to move to or set up in the Areas, and government-financed factories in particularly depressed areas beyond the practical catchment areas of the government-financed trading estates; when it was proposed in 1938 to terminate the Special Areas legislation, intervention would continue by the provision of government loan finance. The second world War greatly increased government intervention in industry in general and the post-War plans foresaw a great increase in intervention in the formerly depressed areas - formerly, because the War had temporarily restored full employment. The achievement of government aims would rely to a significant extent on government-financed factories.

Intervention and government-financed factories have been closely interrelated during the period covered by this study, and as the government lost its economic virtue at Team Valley, the early history of intervention and of this 'most interesting experiment' can now be seen to be seminal.

Little was expected from this first step - which owed a great deal to electoral considerations -, so that the early modest success of the Team Valley Estate caused surprise and satisfaction. The speed with which the

2

initial phase of the scheme was completed confounded those who were opposed to public works as partial cures for unemployment partly because of the long time lags often involved. The contrasting experience at Team Valley was almost entirely due to the unusual form of organisation established to build the Estate.

While in the time available before the War the impact on the industrial structure of the North East was hardly noticeable and the employment created by these factories was small in relation to the magnitude of the continuing unemployment problem, a number of important conclusions emerged: for example, that light industries could, in fact, succeed in an area with a tradition of heavy industries. Perhaps the most significant realisation was that, even in a period of continuing - if easing - depression, the ready availability of small modern factories to rent stimulated at least some new economic activity which might otherwise not have been undertaken.

The novelty of these conclusions must be stressed: while small, privately-financed modern factories available for rent had been in great demand in and around London since the end of the first world War, the early experience at Team Valley indicated new and fruitful opportunities for public intervention in the older industrial areas, where private factory estate developers had declined to invest.

These considerations greatly influenced government policy for the formerly depressed areas after the second world War: in contrast with the tentative nature of their establishment in 1936, an important role was assigned to government-financed factories in the reconversion of industry from war to peace and in the efforts to prevent the re-emergence of serious unemployment in the Areas in the post-War world.

The early history of regional policy in Britain cannot be understood without an examination of the changes in the political and social climate which led to the abandonment of long-established economic doctrine and to a reappraisal of the role of State intervention in declining industrial areas. It is one aim of this study to trace this evolution during the years 1934 to 1948, particularly as it affected the North East of England.

An account of the main events in the history of the Company which developed the Team Valley Estate is certainly of intrinsic interest; but it also serves a wider purpose: it shows that at almost all significant stages in the Company's early history, the government and the civil service were faced with unfamiliar problems and the need to make policy decisions of a novel kind.

Before the last War, these had to be based on concepts which governments of all political shades had rejected up to then and which were concerned with activities hitherto associated with private commerce. Thus, the early experience of the Company reflected the attitudes of government on new territory.

When the State assumed new responsibilities after the last War, government and the civil service had become used to and experienced in intervening in industry and commerce to a greater degree than ever before. Nevertheless, the nature and scale of the intervention posed new problems: while pre-War governments arguably intervened too little in the economic affairs of the North East   - and then at arm's length through Commissioners -, the post-War Labour Government intervened directly, urgently and in detail. Since government-financed factories were seen to be a key element in the implementation of the post-War employment policy for the Areas, the level of intervention had profound consequences for the Estates Company. It led to a struggle with the Board of Trade over the question of responsibility for control of factory and tenant location in the North East and the extent of development. At the same time, it demonstrated the limits of the effectiveness of government in achieving industrial ends, as well as the pitfalls of central planning and day-to-day control.

There are good reasons for treating the year 1948 as the end of an era: the sudden termination of the post-War advance factory building programme caused by the Dollar Crisis and mounting inflation in 1947, and the loss of the remaining vestiges of independence of North Eastern Trading Estates Ltd on 30 April 1948, marked the end of the formative years of regional policy in Britain on the one hand, and of the rapid post-War growth rate in the number of government-financed sites and factories in the North East and other formerly depressed areas, on the other. The last measure of that era, the Town & Country Planning Act 1947, introduced the formal location of industry policy which had eluded the promoters of the Distribution of Industry Act 1945.

There were parallel developments in South Wales, the South West of Scotland and - on a smaller scale - in West Cumberland. The experience gained at Team Valley helped to reduce the negotiation and foundation phases of the Welsh and Scottish estates companies. The policy aspects of this study apply equally to them and to West Cumberland. But since it was impossible within one work to cover either the specific problems of all the regions containing the pre-War depressed areas of Britain or the histories of their government-financed estate companies, this study deals with the North East of England only.

Neither the formative history and early record of government-financed factories in the North East nor their interrelation with regional policy appear to have received much detailed attention in the past. This study aims to bring these topics together and to examine them in the context of the changing economic, political and social environment of the period.

The events which will be examined in this study occurred within five distinct periods:-

-   the year 1934, in which a regional policy in Britain began with a series of reports on each depressed region, leading to the 1934 Special Areas Act;

-   the years 1935 - 1939, i.e. the years before the War, in which the first government-financed factories in the North East and in other depressed areas were authorised, constructed and tested; two further significant regional policy measures were adopted in the middle of this period,

-   the War years up to 1943, which were relatively passive ones for the Estates Company;

4

- the years 1943 - 1945 in which the post-War policy for the depressed areas evolved. This period saw the momentous White Paper on Employment Policy in 1944 and the Distribution of Industry Act 1945 which fundamentally changed the role of the Company;

- finally, the post-War years to 1948 in which the 1945 Act was implemented, leading to the loss of the Company's autonomy. During this period, the legal framework for a location of industry policy was embodied in the Town & Country Planning Act 1947.

2. The terms 'Regional Policy' and 'Location of Industry' are used frequently in this work and must be defined.

The Industrial Transference Board (1928) is seen by some as the first regional policy instrument [3], albeit a negative one. It was based on the recognition of a problem in the coal mining industry and, therefore, of those areas where this industry employed a significant proportion of the insured workers. The further recognition of the preponderance - and similarity - of structural problems in the older, heavy industrial areas of Britain - most of which were located on the periphery of the country - led to an association of regional problems with such areas, even if there were other types of areas with quite different problems, for example the Highlands of Scotland on the one hand, and the Greater London area - which suffered from over-rapid growth and congestion -, on the other.

How slowly the concept of regional policy developed may be concluded from the fact that the Report of the Royal Commission on the Distribution of the Industrial Population used the term 'regionalism' as late as 1940, when it meant to convey what would be called 'regional policy' today.

The term 'regional policy' is now used to describe the means adopted to correct structural imbalances within certain regions and between regions. Odber [4] and others have maintained, that there has never existed a regional economic policy in Britain; instead, there were 'piecemeal plans for increasing employment in particular areas' [5]. This observation applies even to the policies of the post-War Labour Government. After the end of the period of post-War prosperity in the early 1960s, governments did little more than respond to problems of regions like the North East as they arose, with the object of preventing unemployment from rising to unacceptable levels. The view as to what constituted such levels varied, but it was accepted that they would be higher than the national average. Except for a period after 1965, when some attempts were made to establish both national and regional planning, regional policy in Britain has had mainly an employment and social aim. This may be because a convincing economic case for regional policy has never been made out [6].

Regional policy was implemented from 1945 onward mainly by measures intended to affect the location of industry and for this reason, regional policy and location policy are often used synonymously. Location policy is now generally understood to be one of the means by which an - ideally, much broader - regional policy is achieved, although historically, the concept of location of industry policy, i.e. the persuading or inducing of industry to move into economically depressed areas, preceded that of regional policy.

The term 'regional policy' is used in this study, therefore, in the sense in which it corresponds to its limited objectives in Britain. Insofar as the term 'location of industry' rather than 'regional policy' was used during the period covered by this work, it will be found here.

3. Stilwell [7] has asked, at what point do the several forms of regional inequalities constitute a problem , and once a problem has been identified, does its solution require a specific intervention?

In parts of the North East after 1929 the answers would have been painfully obvious without any economic analysis at all: the industries which had for many years employed almost half the working population of the region were either closing down or were - and had been for some time - in a parlous state.

The economic crisis which affected the North East Coast and other similarly-placed regions of Britain after 1929 was of a dual nature: it comprised both a deep structural component and a severe cyclic one. Changes in world trade unfavourable to the North East were beginning to become apparent before the first world War, but as the main industries of the region continued to prosper, this did not cause the concern it deserved. Since the industries of the North East were resource-based, it is unlikely, in any event, that the region could have carried through a process of diversification without outside help, which could have come only from the State. The post-(first) War years had been marked by secular decline. After 1929, the combined effects of cyclic recession and secular decline created problems unprecedented in scale and complexity. The question arises, why did governments not intervene earlier and more decisively in the depressed areas?

In the first place, no British government had ever been faced with a problem of the same magnitude. With unemployment in the whole country higher in the 1920s than before the first world War - a situation which was aggravated by the return to the Gold Standard in 1925 on a pre-(first)world War parity -, the problems of the North East and other depressed areas after 1929 continued to be seen as resulting from the severe disruption of trade, at least until these areas failed to recover in line with the rest of the country. But even then, governments remained wedded to an orthodox economic doctrine according to which market forces should not - and, indeed, could not - be tampered with, a view which was widely accepted.

Even before the start of the world trade recession in 1929, the problem had assumed a different scale and persistence from those to which economists, Committees of Enquiry and Royal Commissions had addressed themselves since the 1880s.

Periods of trade recession and unemployment were features of industrial countries almost from the beginning of the industrial revolution, but since they occurred in economies which were generally expanding, they were normally of fairly short duration. It was only in the depression of the 1880s that the problem of the unemployed began to figure prominently in public discussion. At that time, unemployment was considered 'mainly as a "social" problem arising out of the normal working of the economic system, rather than as a defect in the functioning of the economic mechanism itself', and was often linked, therefore, with 'questions of charity and Poor Law relief, with the main emphasis being placed on the character deficiencies of the unemployed worker' [8]. Moralistic attitudes towards the unemployed were still in evidence 60 years later ⌊9⌋.

The Minority Report of the Royal Commission on the Poor Laws of 1909 noted that the average citizen of the middle or upper classes took for granted the constantly recurring destitution among wage-earning families due to unemployment as part of the natural order of things and 'as no more to be combatted than the east wind' [10]. The chief innovation proposed in the Minority Report was for the government to set aside part of its normal capital appropriation for use in financing public works on a contra-cyclical basis when unemployment rose above the 4% level. On the basis of this idea it reported that 'it is now administratively possible, if it is sincerely wished to do so, to remedy most of the evils of unemployment'.

Winch [11] has shown why this announcement was highly premature. Beveridge [12], in a book published in the same year as the Minority Report, came to a pessimistic conclusion: that 'unemployment cannot be eliminated without an entire reconstruction of the industrial order ... within the range of practical politics, no cure for industrial fluctuations can be hoped for; the aim must be palliation'.

As late as 1920, Marshall, the foremost British economist of his day, had expressed his agreement with Say's Law, according to which over-production was impossible, because, under certain assumptions, a market was as big as the volume of products offered in exchange. Although he allowed that there might be unemployment in _particular_ industries which did not adapt to fashion or demand, he opposed any short-term remedies to deal with unemployment, such as direct government intervention to help industry or indirect intervention in the form of tariff protection; these remedies would impair the long-term ability of the system to grow and adapt. The proper remedy, and, by implication, the sole task of government, was to 'establish a general monetary framework favourable to the stability of the price level' [13].

Hobson [14] had earlier ·(1887) refuted Say's Law and saw a profound reason for the malfunctioning of the economic system and the resulting unemployment, but as he put forward his ideas in a political rather than a purely economic context, he was not influential. Pigou (1913) saw the rigidity of wages, together with trade fluctuations, as the sole causes of unemployment ⌊15⌋.

But because structural problems of the magnitude suffered by the North East and similar areas of Britain and the nature of the unemployment resulting from it had not been experienced before, economic theories of the past proved unhelpful, even if policies continued to be based on them.

The Liberal Party had been discussing the abnormal unemployment in Britain since the end of the first world War in a series of summer schools which started in 1923. They formulated a pragmatic philosophy of State intervention which attempted to steer a course between _laissez-faire_ individualism and collectivism. At the heart of these proposals was a large-scale public investment programme. In an article in the _The Nation_ in May 1924, entitled 'Does Unemployment need a drastic remedy?', Keynes came out decisively in favour of such a programme. He proposed that it should be financed by the Sinking Fund, which was normally used to make substantial annual repayments of the National Debt. In 1928, the Liberals published **Britain's Industrial Future** , which proposed a 'vigorous policy of national reconstruction and development' to be financed by a National Investment Board. The policy involved greatly increased public investment in roads, housing, electricity, waterways, telephones and agriculture. The objective was to cure the 'abnormal unemployment of a quasi-permanent character' that had developed since the end of the (first) world War.

These ideas recurred in the Liberal election manifesto in 1929. Winch [16] has pointed out that 'for the first time a major political party was proposing to treat unemployment on a scale and in a manner comparable to War'. Each year, £100 million was to be spent on capital expenditure which, it was claimed, would eventually provide employment for one and a half million workers. The goverment was sufficiently concerned about the electoral impact of the Liberal proposals that it published a White Paper refuting their reasoning [17].

Even before the first world War, there were some who had argued against public works remedies, because, in their view, the effect of an increase in public spending on employment would be offset by the decrease in private spending caused by the increase in taxes. Pigou, who followed Marshall in the Chair of Economics at Cambridge, had countered these arguments in his inaugural lecture in 1908, but they were increasingly accepted by the Treasury after the first world War. Winch [18] has observed that 'the official Treasury position on public works as a solution to unemployment in the latter half of the twenties was one of growing coolness. By 1929 coolness had hardened into the dogma known as the "Treasury View"'.

The classic statement of 'the View' was given by Churchill in his 1929 Budget speech. After reciting the sums spent on various public works schemes, he claimed that, as a cure for unemployment, the results were disappointing. They were, in fact, so meagre 'as to lend considerable colour to the orthodox Treasury doctrine, steadfastly held that, whatever might be the political or social advantages, very little additional employment and no permanent employment can in fact and as a general rule be created by State borrowing and expenditure' [19].

The Treasury was more concerned with external confidence and stability than with unemployment and its moral and political implications. There was not apparent, in any event, the political will in the 1920s to shift priorities from so-called sound finance to social ends. But accepted economic virtue apart, balanced budgets were seen to be crucial to the defence of Sterling after the return to the Gold Standard in 1925. The cost of any State intervention in the economy would make the defence more difficult, if not impossible.

Recent work by Peden [20] has shown that the 'Treasury View' cannot be summarised in simple terms. Unlike economists, the Treasury had to operate in a political and administrative context. There were, moreover, several factions within the Treasury and there appeared to be developing a slight shift away from 'the View' in the early 1930s. But when Sir Richard Hopkins gave evidence to the Macmillan Committee on Finance and Industry in 1930, 'the View' had evidently not yet changed very much:

while claiming that the Treasury was not opposed to public works in
principle, but only to the Liberal schemes in practice, he explained why
it was difficult to identify, plan and carry out schemes involving a
large capital expenditure. Such schemes would, in any event, have
negative effects on the economy: the additional bureaucracy required by
any increase in State intervention would create an adverse public
reaction; the rate of interest would rise, leading to a 'despondency on
the part of general business'; prices would rise in Britain in relation
to those of foreign competitors and thereby damage the export trade; the
increase in the demand for resources engaged in particular capital goods
industries like road building would lead to 'a singularly lopsided form
of prosperity ... which could not possibly be permanent' [21]. In other
words, public works were likely to be both inflationary and
diversionary.

The Treasury had begun to distinguish, however, between public works
which were mainly designed to relieve unemployment and those which would
result in revenue production or were of public importance. In terms of
employment, the former had proved disappointing, as Churchill had
claimed in his Budget speech in 1929: in the seven years to 1931, an
expenditure of £700 million had at no time produced more than 100,000
jobs [22]. In the depressed areas, moreover, the problem was twofold: no
conceivable public works schemes would automatically provide orders for
the industries most affected by decline, and even if this was accepted,
schemes of economic value could not always be readily identified. There
was, indeed, the paradoxical situation 'that the places where public
works or capital expenditure are needed on economic grounds are the
growing, prosperous areas and not the depressed areas' [23].

In 1937 the Treasury summarised the general policy of the government
since 1931 as 'the endeavour to create and maintain conditions in which
trade and industry can be carried on profitably and employment and the
purchasing power of the community can expand' [24]. The main features of
the policy were: financial stability, brought about by a series of
balanced budgets - 'which has given business confidence, the mainspring
of any economic recovery' - and cheap money. Other policy features
included tariffs to help the steel industry and bilateral arrangements
with the Dominions and other countries which would increase the export
of coal. These had a useful but small effect on employment. There was
also a major housing programme in progress which, in the North East, had
resulted in an increase in employment in the building industry from
33,740 in 1924 to 71,560 in 1934 (see Appendix 1). The Treasury was
evidently baffled by the fact that the goverment's policies 'had led to
success in the country as a whole, but not in the Special Areas'.

It did not require much economic analysis to see that the depressed
areas of Britain needed new industries. Local opinion on Tyneside had
recognised this since 1926 [25] and the Economic Advisory Committee had
discussed how to obtain them in 1931. But since the creation of such
industries was not within the competence of government and a shift of
industries from the more prosperous parts of the country to the
depressed areas was inconceivable at the time, a greatly increased
public works programme was believed to be the only direct means at the
disposal of government to mitigate unemployment in the Areas, even if
this would have little effect on the structural problem.

But rather than expand public spending during the recession, the May Committee was set up in 1930 - at the suggestion of the Liberals, who had become concerned by the rise in social expenditure - with the task of finding ways of cutting expenditure and income to balance the budget at a lower level.

Two answers to the question raised now emerge: governments of the period were relatively impassive in the face of the disastrous levels of unemployment in the North East and other similar areas after 1929 because of an unwillingness - in an increasingly crisis-ridden world - to depart from the economic and financial status quo, and because they did not know, within the accepted tenets, how to deal with an unprecedented situation.

By 1931, the economic and financial situation of the country had become so serious that few would have considered it an auspicious moment for experiments, even if a coherent body of alternative economic theory had been available and accepted. But such an alternative was not expounded - by Keynes - until 1936 [26], and far from becoming an instant vade mecum for economists and governments alike, it proved initially to be highly controversial.

Although international trade remained far below its 1929 level, the recession eventually began to abate and, helped by the abandonment of the Gold Standard in 1931, the country as a whole began to recover relatively rapidly between 1932 and 1934. For budgetary reasons alone, this would have made it easier for the government to intervene in the depressed areas within the tenets of economic orthodoxy. But another factor made intervention politically unavoidable: the recovery of the economy had little effect on the depressed areas, and in the most affected parts recovery was not possible, because industry had died. The resulting social distress - vividly described in three special reports in The Times in March 1934 - disturbed public opinion in the rest of the country, where people were beginning to think again in terms of prosperity. At this point, the government took a series of steps which were to lead to intervention, although initially within narrowly defined limits.

After describing the situation in the North East, this work gives an account of the origins of this intervention, which took one particular form: the provision in the depressed areas of - mainly small - factories for rent. They represented both a classical public works programme 'of public importance' and, perhaps, a revenue-earning one in the longer run - even potentially one with unusually high multiplier effects -, but at the same time, a first, small - if unplanned - step towards structural change.

The events following from this first intervention and from the great political, economic and social changes brought about by the second world War are recounted in subsequent chapters, in which the history of the Trading Estate Company is interwoven. The results both of the pre-War and post-War intervention and the achievements of the Estates Company are critically evaluated.

REFERENCES AND NOTES

[1]   For example, by the Economic Advisory Council, meeting of 12.2.1931, CAB 58/2. See also preparatory memorandum from Board of Trade, which concluded that 'local self help and initiative must be the keynote of any effort to bring new industries into the depressed areas', CAB 58/12, ECA, (H) series, 136, and support for this view in a memorandum by H.D. Henderson, CAB 53/14, ECA, (S) series, 5.

[2]   BT 104/27, note for Parliamentary Secretary, Board of Trade, 10.3.1937.

[3]   McCrone, G., 1971, p.92, calls it 'the first step towards a regional policy in Britain'. The Northern Regional Strategy Team, 1975, included the Industrial Transference Act 1928 in its summary of regional policy legislation.

[4]   Odber, Alan. J., 1965, p.330.

[5]   Cole, G.H.D., in introduction to Fogarty, M.P., 1945.

[6]   Op.cit.3, pp.47,48.

[7]   Stilwell, Frank, J.B., 1972, p.7.

[8]   Winch, Donald, 1972, p.52.

[9]   For example, Chamberlain speaking of the need for a spiritual regeneration in the depressed areas, HC Deb 293, 1996, 14.11.1934.

[10] Quoted in op.cit.8, p.60.

[11] Ibid.

[12] Quoted in op.cit.8, p.61.

[13] Op.cit.8, p.56.

[14] Ibid, pp.57,58.

[15] Ibid, p.62.

[16] Op.cit.8, p.128.

[17] White Paper, 1929.

[18] Op.cit.8, p.112.

[19] HC Deb 277, 54.

[20] Peden, G.C., 1984.

[21] Evidence quoted in op.cit.8, p.120.

[22] Feiling, Keith, 1970, p.24.

[23] T 172/1828, Sir Warren Fisher in a note to the Chancellor of the Exchequer (Chamberlain), 26.1.1936.

[24] T 172/1828, unsigned and undated memorandum 'Restoration of Industries in the Special Areas', probably notes for a parliamentary speech by Chamberlain, ca. 8.3.1937.

[25] Tyneside Industrial Development Board, 1950.

[26] Keynes, J.M., 1936.

PART I: DEPRESSION IN THE NORTH EAST

1   The origin of the crisis

Any account of the beginning of government intervention in the North
East of England in the the 1930s must start with an examination of the
problems which made it necessary. In this chapter, the causes are
examined of the economic decline of the region and the severe depression
after 1929; the industrial situation and some aspects of the depression
will be outlined in subsequent chapters.

The industrial problems of the North East - as, indeed, those of all
the older industrial areas of Britain - were due not to one crisis, but
to the coincidence of two: the secular decline of the traditional
industries of these areas and the world-wide economic recession between
1929 and 1933/34.

The recession was generally thought to be no more than one phase in
the alternating movements of prosperity and depression known as the
Trade Cycle, the validity and immutability of which was widely accepted
before Keynes challenged the views of his generation. Although unusually
severe and with special features of its own, it was expected to be of a
temporary nature, as had been the case with previous trade slumps.

The decline of the traditional industries of the North East was a
different matter: by 1929, it had been going on for a decade, and had it
not been masked by the demands on these industries during the first
world War, it would have been evident sooner. The decline was generally
considered to have had two principal causes: changes in the pattern of
world trade and advances in technology.

Ever since the end of the first world War, unemployment in the North
East had been heavier than in the country as a whole. The best that

could be expected from a turn of the Trade Cycle was a return to levels of unemployment in the period immediately before 1929.

In a summary of the economic background of the recession by the staff of the Economics Department at Armstrong College (now the University of Newcastle upon Tyne) in 1935, the situation before 1929 was assessed as follows [1]:-

> The world as a whole was in a prosperous condition between 1926 and 1929. The ravages of the Great War appear to have been more than made good. Between 1919 and 1925, world production had increased to a greater extent than world population. By 1928, depreciating currencies had been stabilised and an international Gold Standard restored. There were some disquieting features and some problems still unsolved, but of the general prosperity there was no question.

So far as Britain was concerned, this view did not go unchallenged: W. Arthur Lewis, writing in 1949, believed that 'there was not even an interlude of prosperity; throughout, there was a high level of unemployment ... which was between two and three times as high as the pre-(first) War expectation of "normal"' [2].

Britain apart, the peak of prosperity was reached in other countries in 1929. The sudden break in the boom, of which the half-expected crash of the American stock market was but the signal, led to financial and political crises in all parts of the world and was followed by the most severe business recession in history.

The most serious result of the recession was widespread unemployment. In Britain, over one million people were out of work even before the start of the recession. By the end of 1932, the figure had risen to three million. The position in other countries was generally worse or even much worse. Britain was hit less hard precisely because she had not participated in the upswing so marked in other countries - particularly in the USA - between 1925 and 1929. But the general trend in Britain masked the effect of the recession on the older industrial regions.

The causes of the recession were complex, but there was a consensus that the centre of the depression was the United States of America, in the sense that most of what happened elswhere could be explained in terms of its economy. One of the reasons for this was that the USA was the largest consumer of primary products in the world. But the American national income contracted by 38% between 1929 and 1932, and 15 million people were out of work. American lending, which had contributed much to world prosperity in the 1920s, declined by 68% in the same period. Lewis sees the sequence of events leading to recession in the international sphere as 'the contraction of lending, the fall of prices, the contraction of trade, and the monetary crisis' [3].

Agricultural prices fell more rapidly than those of manufactured goods, and some analysts believe that this - and the fall in the price of other commodities - was at the core of the recession. The social and political impossibility of adjusting internal prices and costs to the unprecedented fall in external prices led to the breakdown of the international Gold Standard - re-established with much difficulty a few years before. While its suspension enabled individual countries to escape partially from difficult adjustments, it proved no solution to the real problem. As more and more countries devalued, the relative advantage of the early devaluers disappeared and world trade failed to expand. The departure from an international Gold Standard made possible widely varying recovery policies, but it also strengthened the retrograde tendency towards economic nationalism. On the other hand, the effect of exchange restrictions by countries still nominally adhering to the Gold Standard tended further to restrict the volume of international trade. There was widespread international economic disharmony and no attempts were made to maintain an international monetary standard.

In the North East, the exceptionally serious cyclic depression was superimposed on a structural problem of long standing: the overwhelming importance of a small group of heavy industries: coal mining, iron and steel, shipbuilding and repairing, shipping and port services.

Unless otherwise stated, the data on the output of these and other industries in the North East and the employment figures discussed in the following (and in the next chapter) have been taken from the work of the economists at Armstrong College cited in [1] above.

These industries had been in decline for many years, yet their importance was such that 64% of the insured population of the North East was still engaged in them in 1924. As they employed mainly men and boys - only in electrical engineering was the percentage of women and girls higher than 10% - the percentage of insured male workers depending on them was greater, therefore, than 64%.

Four of the industries in the group - coal mining, iron and steel, engineering, shipbuilding and marine engineering - accounted for 60% of all insured workers in 1924. They were not only in structural decline, but, like other capital goods industries, particularly sensitive to the Trade Cycle.

The decline of the group as a whole was such that the percentage of insured workers in it dropped from 64% in 1928 to 48% in 1938. Only the chemical industry grew rapidly in the period (see Appendix 1), but it was the smallest employer by far of the group. There was an apparent growth in some sectors of engineering, but this masked a serious decline in general engineering.

The pattern of world trade, on which the North East depended so heavily, had been changing since before the first world War, but the change had not been reflected in the industrial activities of the region. Most of the traditional industries were still making good profits and there appeared to be neither any reason for concern, nor was there a mechanism by which new industries could have been introduced, even if the need had been foreseen. The first world War had masked the problems because of the heavy demand for armaments and ships, even if the loss of export markets had led to a fall in the demand for coal.

The world trend towards national self-sufficiency in primary products accelerated after the first world War and this had serious consequences for producers in Britain and elsewhere. The main industries of the North East were particularly affected, because they had been substantial exporters. Even in 1929, the coal mining industry in the North East still exported 20.7 million tons, i.e. 53% of its output.

The (Balfour) Committee on Industry and Trade had commented on this trend in 1925 [4]:-

> Taking the world as a whole, the widespread development of home manufactures to meet the needs formerly supplied by imported goods ... is perhaps the most important permanent factor tending to limit the volume or to modify the character of the British export trade. In part, this tendency is a natural and universal one inseparable from healthy economic progress and dating from a period long before the (first) world War.

This tendency became more marked after 1925 and its effect on Britain more pronounced. It became the chief factor in the problems of the depressed areas. The conditions on which Britain maintained the Gold Standard after its restoration in 1925 accelerated the trend and increased unemployment: the Pound Sterling was overvalued and Britain's export prices were too high [5].

Rapid structural changes were not unknown in the industrial history of the last 150 years or so. New invention and the consequent changes in technology, the exhaustion of raw materials in some places and the discovery of new sources in others, changes in population and markets, political and tariff changes were some of the factors which had caused problems to established industrial areas in the past.

It is difficult to see how the North East - with its resource-based industries - could have responded to the challenges posed by the changed pattern of world trade, except by greater efficiency and by investing in entirely new industries. Where new technology was introduced - for example, in the coal mining industry -, unemployment resulted and no steps were taken to provide alternative employment. There was little light, diversified manufacturing, which elsewhere became the breeding ground for new enterprise, as Dennison has pointed out (see [11] below). The adaptation process required in the North East and in similar regions of Britain was of a fundamental nature and it is doubtful whether it could have been carried out without outside assistance, that is, assistance by government agencies.

Another factor in the situation was the growth of the population in the North East since the first world War. The statistics for Northumberland and Durham for the years 1923 - 1937 are given in Appendix 2. In spite of the fact that 265,041 people had emigrated from the two counties during this period, the population declined by only about 30,000. Relatively high unemployment figures were recorded even before 1929. In 1931, the economists at Armstrong College estimated the surplus of male workers to be 80,000, but it soon became evident that this forecast had been too optimistic: even when the main industries of the region were working again to near capacity in 1938, there was a surplus of about 100,000 workers [6].

Technical changes led to higher productivity and, therefore, to a decline in the demand for labour. It has already been observed that this was to become an important factor in the largest industry in the North East, i.e. in coal mining and, to a lesser degree, in steel-making. This aspect will be discussed in more detail in the next chapter.

The dependence of the region on a small number of heavy industries - the origins of which were largely due to geographical and geological factors - has already been noted. Given this limited range of industries, the problems of the North East may also be looked upon as having resulted from over-specialisation.

The Royal Commission on the Distribution of the Industrial Population (Barlow Commission), which will be referred to later in this work, examined this aspect of the industrial situation in the North East and similar areas of Britain and reported that 'the grouping together, or concentration within a particular area, of enterprises engaged in a particular industry is claimed by leading industrialists to carry with it definite industrial and commercial advantages' [7].

After reciting these advantages in some detail, the Barlow Report continued [8]:-

> On the other hand, high specialisation has its drawbacks. The more highly specialised an industrial area and the skill of its workers, the more difficult it becomes to adapt it to occupations of entirely different types and ... when an area ... for international or others reasons encounters a severe and prolonged depression, the consequences to the workpeople and, indeed, to the population of the area as a whole are likely to be disastrous. At no time has this been more vividly demonstrated than during the last two decades, when certain industrial areas of the country ... suffered intensely because of the steep decline of industries on which for many years they had concentrated.

Fortunately, the Barlow Commission underestimated the adaptability of labour in the North East. While the favourable evidence in the pre-War years had related mainly to juvenile labour [9], later experience, and particularly the second world War, proved to be conclusive in this respect.

A summary of the employment in the 23 fastest-growing industries in the years from 1923 to 1937 is given in Appendix 3. In Northumberland and Durham, employment in these industries had grown by only 4.1%, compared with 32.2% in London and the Home Counties. It may be asked why the North East did not more rapidly develop industries of the lighter type, which had largely accounted for the increased employment in and around London. The Barlow Commission examined the reasons for the tendency of these industries to prefer a location in, or on the fringe of large towns or industrial areas and it concluded that, among a number of other factors, the nearness of a large market was the most important [10].

But this was not the only reason why regions like the North East failed to generate new light industries. The Barlow Commission underestimated the disadvantage arising out of the industrial structure of such regions. Dennison [11] has pointed out that the preponderance of a few heavy industries and the specialisation which follows from this militated against the growth of new industries:-

> Where the industrial structure of an area is one of limited industries, probably all connected with each other, ... there is

19

a small probability of there being diversification and the
development of new industries from old; specialisation of an
area has the danger of involving no, or few second lines of
defence in the event of a decline in the chief industry. Where
there is a more diversified structure, however, there are more
possibilities of internal readjustment to a decline in a
particular branch of industry. On the one hand can be cited the
derelict mining villages in Durham and South Wales as examples
of the complete failure to develop new industries to take the
place of old, because they were areas of one dominant industry,
and on the other, there is the case of the newer industrial
areas of the South, experiencing a continuous process of the
emergence of new forms of economic activity.

This finding was confirmed and extended 30 years later by Segal [12]:
peripheral regions, with a past specialisation in mining and heavy
industries tended to have characteristics which militated against
entrepreneurship and new company formation.

It was precisely for this reason that the diversification of the
industrial base from within the depressed areas would prove to be so
difficult, if not impossible, and why the government would be advised in
1934 that it would both have to provide help within the Areas and adopt
measures which would bring new industries from outside.

2   The industrial situation

Any examination of the small number of industries which determined the economic fortunes of the North East must start with the coal mining industry, which had played an important role in its economic life since the beginning of the industrial revolution. Even in 1929, the industry still employed 30% of the insured population of the region. (see Appendix 4).

In spite of the growth of industrial activity, the demand for coal in Britain had remained stationary since before the first world War. There were two reasons for this unfavourable trend: economies in the utilisation of coal and growing competition from oil and electricity.

In the North East, the output of coal had been falling ever since 1913. The decline of such a key industry was bound to have more than a marginal effect on the the economy of the region. But even if demand and employment had remained steady, there would have been a growing surplus of labour in the mining villages because of an increase in the population.

The reduction in employment was far greater, however, than the fall in output. Between 1923 and 1937, employment had fallen by 34% but output only by 13%. It is clear that changes in the manner of producing coal had a much greater effect on employment than the business recession.

The most important of these changes was the progress of mechanisation. This was not uniform in the coal fields of the region. While the percentage of coal cut by machine in Northumberland had increased from 55 in 1929 to 81 by 1933, in Durham it had reached only 33 in that year. But a time when almost all coal would be cut by machine was foreseeable.

Unemployment also resulted from the abandonment of uneconomic mines. Between 1929 and 1933, the number of mines in Northumberland and Durham decreased from 368 to 327. Had it not been for the Coal Mines Act 1930, more mines would have been closed.

In some localities, the abandoned mines had been the main, or even the only source of employment. No steps were taken to provide alternative industries or any other form of paid occupation and the people in these places faced great hardships.

There was a considerable difference in demand in different coal fields in Britain. In South Yorkshire and Nottinghamshire, for example, there was sufficient expansion of coal production to maintain the volume of employment even in the face of progressive mechanisation. The coal fields with sea access, on the other hand - like those of Northumberland and Durham - , were severely depressed because they depended on exports for a large part of their market. But the export demand had been falling ever since 1913; between 1929 and 1934, shipments of coal to the four major markets - Germany, France, Belgium and Italy - had dropped by 50%. During the same period, there was a sharp decline in local demand, mainly due to the recession in the iron and steel, shipbuilding and heavy engineering industries. This decline was not made good by any improvement in the coastwise trade to the power stations in the South of the country.

A specially difficult situation existed in South West Durham, an area with a relatively small population: until 1825 it was largely a marginal hill-farming area with a few very small pits, where the surface was scratched for landsale coal. The coming of the railway in that year opened the district for large-scale mining. The coal measures contained some of the finest coking seams in the country and the product was in great demand in Britain and overseas. Expansion was rapid and in the latter half of the 19th century and the early years of the 20th, South West Durham enjoyed great prosperity. Men came from all parts of Britain in search of work. The influx of population completely changed the pattern of settlement. The large majority of the newcomers were housed in entirely new settlements at the pit heads - mere collections of houses which lacked every amenity. The almost ruthless exploitation of the shallow, easily-worked seams led to the exhaustion of a large part of the coalfield in a relatively short time. By 1910, the westernmost part - where the seams were nearest the surface - was nearly worked out. Water seepage from the abandoned workings gradually made its way eastwards. The costly pumping operations, coupled with the exhaustion of the better seams, led to the close-down of the majority of the mines at the end of the 1920s.

The virtual end of coal mining in most of the South West Durham coalfield meant the loss of almost the only source of employment. The area was now carrying a population completely out of proportion to its resources and mass unemployment resulted for most of the period between the two world Wars.

Nevertheless, 34% of the insured population in the North East as a whole was still engaged in the coal mining industry in 1924. By 1934, the figure had dropped to 26%. The reduction among boys was 50%, reflecting the decline in recruitment.

But if there were more people unemployed in the coal mining industry than in any other, the shipbuilding industry showed the most dramatic slump in output and the highest percentage of unemployment of any major industry in the North East.

In order to make good the losses in ships sunk by German submarines, the industry had greatly expanded during the first World war. Since the end of that War, there had been a decline in the proportion of the world's ships being built in Britain, and in the proportion of British ships built in the North East. Even in 1929 - a relatively good year by post-(first) World war standards - unemployment in the industry had reached 20%. In that year, North East yards launched 679,000 tonnes. In 1933 it was a mere 37,000 tonnes, rising to 67,000 tonnes in 1934. The figures do not include naval construction, which had been small and irregular in occurrence since the end of the first World War: the average annual naval tonnage launched in the period 1931 - 1934 was only 6,000 tonnes, compared with 66,000 tonnes for the years 1907 - 1913.

The unemployment created by these devastating falls in activity was concentrated in a small number of riverside towns and the industrial and business life of those which depended mainly on shipbuilding virtually came to an end. In an attempt to avert the bankruptcy of the industry, a rationalisation scheme was introduced, which resulted in the closure of many yards. Some would never reopen , others would restart only when naval re-armament began in the late 1930s .

When Palmer's shipyard at Jarrow closed, unemployment in the town reached 80%. There was no alternative employment and the disadvantages of specialisation were demonstrated in the harshest way. The march of the Jarrow men to London became a symbol of the misery of much of the North East, and Ellen Wilkinson, the Member of Parliament for Jarrow, wrote a book about 'The Town that was murdered'.

The situation in the other two major industries - iron and steel, and engineering - was more complex: steel production in the North East - concentrated mainly on Teesside - had actually risen by 23% between 1929 and 1937, but the output of pig iron had dropped sharply. At the same time, productivity in the industry was improving - as in the coal mining industry - by the adoption of new processes. This led to a decline in employment. Considering the high tariffs the industry still needed for protection against foreign imports, it was essential for the trend to continue. At the same time, the employment in the iron and steel industry was only 22% of that in coal mining and the 8,000 men shed by the industry between 1924 and 1932 were absorbed by the growth of constructional engineering on Teesside and at Darlington. Teesside benefited from the fact that there was no coal mining there.

In engineering, the situation was even more complex, because of the wide range of activities classified under this industrial heading.

In 1929, approximately 59,000 people were employed in general, electrical, marine and constructional engineering, the making and repairing of motor vehicles, cycles, aircraft, carriages and carts, railway carriages, waggons and tram cars. By 1932, the number had fallen to 32,000, a drop of 46%. What was worse, the reduction in employment in these industries was between two and three times greater than in the country as a whole. By 1934, the number employed in the categories enumerated increased again to 41,000, but this was still far below the 1929 figure, which was, in any case, 10,000 below the number of insured workers in the industry.

Not all these trades moved in the same direction: electrical engineering, motor vehicles, cycles and aircraft, railway carriages, waggons and tramcars were each employing more people in 1934 than in 1929. Their employment, in aggregate, increased from 8,800 in 1929 to 10,400 in 1934, an increase of 18%, compared with a national increase of only 3%. This growth in employment would have given more satisfaction, if the numbers involved had been more than a small proportion of those engaged in engineering.

This, unfortunately, was the trend in engineering generally: the trades which prospered were relatively small employers, while the larger ones languished. Although exact figures for general engineering are not available because it is a category which included a very varied assortment of work, including some of the region's specialist activities like locomotive building and armaments, the industry was a large employer. Over the six years from 1929 to 1934, it experienced an average unemployment rate of 34%, rising to 46% in 1932.

It is not intended here to examine all branches of engineering in detail. The examples discussed above indicate the complexity of the picture. The severity of the recession in the industry as a whole is indicated by the unemployment figures.

Since frequent reference is made in this work to the official unemployment figures, their meaning and significance will be discussed in Appendix 5.

It would be misleading to give the impression that the situation of the declining industries represented the whole picture in the North East. A list of industries which had expanded their employment between 1924 and 1934 is given in Appendix 1. The list provides some interesting conclusions: the majority of the expanding industries employed relatively few people, even if their percentage growth was impressive. The exceptions stand out: building and public works, transport and communications, the distributive and miscellaneous trades, including local government, the hotel and catering trades. These four industries or services accounted for 80% of the growth in employment in the 20 industries listed in the Table.

The most dramatic growth in employment in the decade to 1934 was recorded in the Building and Public Works industry. This was mainly due to the expenditure of public funds by central and local government. While slum clearance and housing policies were likely to safeguard the continuation of activity for some years, the level of employment depended largely on national economic and social policies.

The expansion of the other three industries in the major growth group ensured that unemployment in a big centre like Newcastle upon Tyne rose less rapidly during the depression years from 1930 onwards than the national average.

It is to be noted, however, that the group showing this large absolute expansion in employment did not include a single manufacturing industry.

24

The lag in this sector indicated how badly some stimulation ·and growth were needed in order to make up for the decline of the traditional heavy industries of the North East.

By the end of 1934, when the economy had largely recovered - although exports only fitfully so -, the comparison between the unemployment in the North East and the country as a whole showed that changes highly unfavourable to the North East had taken place during the business recession. Unemployment in Great Britain between 1923 and 1929 had varied from 9% to 11% and on the North East Coast from 13% - 16%. During the recession years the gap had widened, as the graph in Figure 1 indicates:-

Figure 1
Comparison of Unemployment in the
North East with the National Average
1930 - 1934

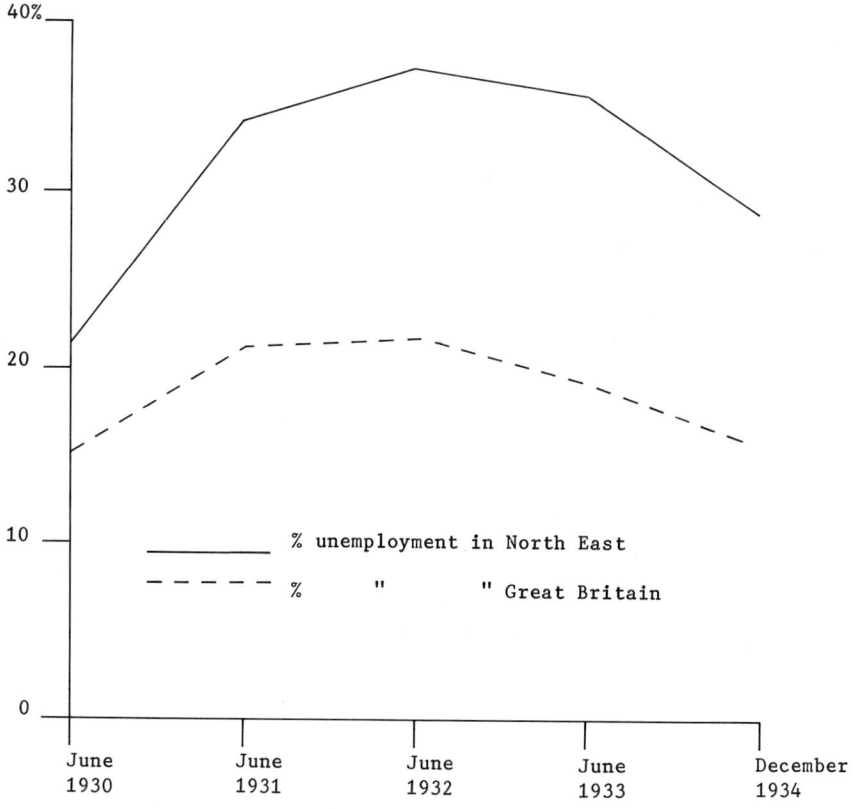

Source: Armstrong College, 1935, p.17

25

The economists at Armstrong College were forced to come to the following conclusion:-

In a period when the recovery from the depth of the world depression might have been expected particularly to benefit the export industries of the North East Coast, the percentage of unemployment remained almost twice as great in this area as in the country generally. These facts indicate that during the world depression important internal changes in industrial Britain were going on and that the North East Coast will, when the depression ends, be left with the very serious social and economic problems presented by a large, permanent and disproportionate amount of unemployment.

3 The social effects of the crisis

It will be shown in II/1 that regional policy in Britain began as the direct result of the social consequences of the crisis. The origins of the policy cannot be understood, therefore, without an appreciation of the effect of the crisis on ordinary people.

While government intervention was triggered by the distress in County Durham, the situation was no less disastrous in other depressed areas, and only slightly less so in those other parts of the country where the business recession had caused exceptionally high unemployment. To the people affected, economic theories seemed wildly irrelevant and the apparent heartlessness or helplessness of governments in the face of so much misery eventually became intolerable to large sections of those who lived in happier parts of the country.

The social effects of the crisis were both visible and hidden: visible, because mines, shipyards and factories were closed and derelict. Many shops were shut and unemployed men and youths were standing about on the streets. Hopelessness and deprivation could be seen everywhere. J.B. Priestley described the unemployed in some of the towns he visited as 'men wearing the drawn mask of prisoners war' [1]. The Bishop of Winchester came away from a visit to the North East with 'the ineffaceable impression of men suffering through being overwrought and worn out by anxiety' [2].

But the hidden effects were even more damaging. The majority of the unemployed had been out of work for long periods, a minority for up to eight years. Worse even than poverty and the lack of adequate nourishment, long-term unemployment had a corroding effect on people:-

Prolonged unemployment is destroying the confidence and self-respect of a large part of the population, their fitness for work is being steadily lost and the anxiety of living always upon a bare minimum without any margin of resources or any hope of improvement is slowly sapping their nervous strength and their power of resistance [3].

A report by the Pilgrim Trust in 1938 confirmed the grave effects of long-term unemployment [4]:-

The depression and apathy which finally settles down in many of the homes of these long-unemployed men lies at the root of most of the problems which are connected with unemployment. It is one of the reasons why they fail to get back to work. It is one of the reasons why the majority 'have not the heart' for clubs or activities of other kinds, and it is one of the reasons why their homes seem so poverty-stricken.

On 20, 21 & 22 March 1934, The Times published reports from a special correspondent it had sent to County Durham under the title 'Places without a Future'. These reports aroused public opinion so strongly at last that the government could not ignore it. Before the year was out, the first Act of Parliament dealing with the most depressed areas of Britain was on the statute book. This unexpected consequence of the reports by The Times and the events leading up to the Act will be discussed in II/1.

The reports painted a sombre picture of the situation. The special correspondent noted that 'there was anger and resentment against the South, because it was felt that the South governed in ignorance'. His own response echoed local feeling: 'there are parts of Durham where one feels strongly and sometimes angrily that London still has no conception of the troubles of the industrial North' (20 March 1934).

The leading article in The Times of 20 March 1934 - the issue which opened the series - saw 'a background of bare justice behind the unyielding Socialism which spellbounds Durham Man today, because he thinks he can see no proof of genuine consideration from any other quarter'.

The correspondent found ample reason for the hopelessness of the men and youths:-

In nearly every part of the country, the steady reduction in the unemployment figures has emboldened hope of better times ahead. Yet in places where the pits are not only closed but abandoned, the works not only closed but dismantled, it is difficult to see any ground for hope, because there is no industry left there for recovery to vitalise (20 March 1934).

There appeared to be no prospect of any effective reduction in the number of unemployed; no hope of a revival of the export of coal; no immediate hope of a revival of shipbuilding and no hope of any large industry moving into the distressed districts. It was this hopelessness which was the most serious aspect of the crisis.

If the position was bad for the men, it was worse for boys and girls. Many of them had never done a day's paid work in their lives and they saw no prospect of finding work in the foreseeable future.

Large numbers of people, particularly young people, were leaving the places where they were born. The break-up of families and of the tightly-knit mining communities caused much hardship and heartbreak.

Britain was still one of the world's richest countries and it is hard to believe that the correspondent was describing conditions in parts of this country when he reported on the conditions in the mining villages and towns where the majority of men were unemployed:-

> Friends or relations cannot help one another because all are straitened in the same way. Everything superfluous has been pawned and the necessities of life are worn out. In Jarrow, even some of the pawnshops have closed. Clothes are from charity, underclothes were rare. Men are not starving but they are permanently hungry. Malnutrition among children was rare, but teachers report the sort of apathy resulting from insufficient food and of the wrong sort. Fathers and mothers went short to ensure the children did not suffer (21 March 1934).

Unemployment benefit - cut in 1931 - was restored under Part II of the Unemployment Act 1934, so that payment to a single man under 21, for example, was increased from 15/6d to 17/-d, (i.e. from 77.5p to 85p) per week. For the majority of the unemployed, however, benefit had long ceased; instead, they received so-called 'transitional' payments. This was money paid out to those who were unable to make at least 30 contributions to Unemployment Insurance during a previous two-year period. The money came out of a special account of the Unemployment Fund and was administered, under the Unemployment Insurance (National Economy) (No.2) Order 1931, by the Councils of Counties or Boroughs. But payment was subject to a test of need. A circular issued by the Ministry of Labour on 10 November 1931 dealt with the position of applicants owning any small assets: 'it would be difficult to reconcile a practice of recommending transitional payments to such persons, irrespective of the general circumstances of the case [5].

The test became known as the 'Means Test' and, while the circular made it clear that there could be circumstances where the income value of capital assets need not necessarily prevent the payment of transitional relief, the test procedure caused great resentment and bitterness among the unemployed. It was felt to be unfair in its application, particularly by taking into account small savings.

The Means Test and the Dole formed a common subject of conversation among the unemployed. They did not look upon transitional payments as poor relief, but as money to which they were entitled in the same way as unemployment benefit.

Irregularities in the administration of transitional payments by Durham County Council - in favour of the unemployed and at the expense of the State - led to the appointment of Commissioners to take over the administration in 1932 [6].

The poverty resulting from prolonged unemployment imposed a heavy burden on the local rates. The cost of public assistance in County Durham in 1933/1934 was greater than that of all other general county purposes put together. 80% of the money disbursed under this heading was spent on so-called outdoor relief, i.e. on relieving hardship among the able-bodied. Even after taking into account a special distressed areas grant from the Exchequer, the public assistance cost in County Durham was almost six times greater in 1932 than the average in England and Wales. Given that 76% of the dwellings in County Durham had a rateable value of £10 or less [7], the burden fell on an increasingly smaller number of ratepayers.

The high local rates constituted an almost unsurmountable barrier to economic recovery and the government eventually had to implement a scheme which would more fairly share the burden beween the prosperous and the distressed areas of the country.

It was one of the tragedies of the depression years that people had been advancing more rapidly than their environment in the years before the crisis struck. While men and women had received a better education and acquired more skills - leading to higher expectations -, too many of them lived in overcrowded conditions and in the ugly surroundings created by defunct industries. Many had worked in industries which had not changed their methods for a generation or more and now there was no work at all for a large number of people.

The Times correspondent made a dramatic plea for government action:-

No hope exists for thousands of men and boys ever to lead a normal working life again, unless drastic, specially directed action can be taken ... Can we be satisfied that every nerve is being strained to lift these people out of the pit of permanent worklessness? ... Perhaps all the reserves of a democratic government are not yet exhausted (21 March 1934).

It will be shown in II/1 that the government reacted almost immediately to the outcry caused by the reports in The Times and took the first, hesitant steps that began a slow but fundamental change in the fortunes of the depressed areas of the North East and elsewhere in the country.

It must be noted again, however, that the aim of the first regional policy measure was to mitigate the social consequences of the economic crisis. If regional policy in Britain has never amounted to much more than an employment and welfare policy since its inception more than 50 years ago, one of the reasons may well have to be sought in its origins.

4 Some measures of social relief

The articles in The Times brought home to the country - perhaps for the first time - the full extent of the misery of the people in parts of the North East. They raised a groundswell of sympathy and concern. Even before, many private and public bodies as well as individuals had felt the need to do something to ameliorate the conditions of their less fortunate countrymen. Of all these relief efforts, the most notable were schemes for the adoption of particularly depressed places, or of families and individuals who lived there. These schemes took all kinds of forms, for example

> the adoption by more fortunate families of those less fortunate, the adoption by a county, a town, a church or an association in the more prosperous parts of the country, or by the staff of a government department or a business firm, of a town or village in the (depressed) areas, or of financial support of a particular kind of institution or activity in the Areas [1].

But only the more powerful adopting bodies could hope to achieve anything significant within the depressed areas, such as the establishment of new industries. Others would have to set themselves more limited objectives; the most useful way in which they could help was 'by finding employment in their own districts, facilitating the removal of workers and the settlement of individuals or families in their new surroundings' [2].

An appeal was made to bodies and organisations in the more prosperous parts of the country to consider seriously whether they could not bring practical help to the depressed areas by these means:-

An adoption scheme which finds permanent employment in a new
area brings real relief to individuals and groups and is of far
greater permanent value than the adoption of palliatives such as
the provision of clothes, social amenities or even temporary
work in the (depressed) areas [3].

It would go beyond the objectives of this study to examine the results
of these appeals in detail and a few examples must suffice.

Two County Councils in the South of England made an early
contribution. Surrey Council, under the leadership of Sir John Jarvis,
attempted to assist Jarrow by reviving the steel industry and by
establishing new industries in the Borough, as well as by the transfer
of girls to employment in Surrey. Hertfordshire adopted half a dozen of
the most unfortunate colliery villages in County Durham and established
schemes for poultry keeping and land cultivation there. It also provided
money for occupational centres. The town of Bedford adopted a small
rural township in County Durham and found employment for a number of
men, women, boys and girls, housing the newcomers and providing social
arrangements to prevent homesickness. Later, schemes of adoption were
undertaken by the staffs of many large concerns in London and other
relatively prosperous places, and by civil servants. By September 1936,
no fewer than 70 government offices had adopted distressed villages or
townhips and collected voluntarily some £ 40,000.

Faced with the prospect of unemployment of unforeseeable duration,
many people had left the North East since the early 1920s (see Appendix
2). Up to 1928, migrants had to make their own arrangements for
employment in other parts of the country, or in the Dominions and
Colonies. In 1928, the government set up the Industrial Transference
Board. Its purpose was to retrain the unemployed from the declining
industries - initially from the coal mining industry - and to provide
grants and loans to enable them to move and find employment in the
expanding industries elsewhere. Schemes were introduced later for the
assisted transfer of families and whole households. Transference reached
a peak in 1936, declining thereafter (see Table 18).

Land Settlement was considered an important element in the solution of
the problems of the depressed areas. It occupied a high place in the
thinking of government and of influential sections of the public, until
practical experience disappointed the often exaggerated hopes which were
placed in it.

References to Land Settlement and Transference will be made in II/1
and II/3. Because of their importance in depressed areas policies, some
extended notes are provided in Appendix 6.

None of the measures for social relief taken by public or private
bodies and individuals would remove from the government the obligation
to take steps to help the depressed areas of the North East in more
fundamental ways and on a scale commensurate with the crisis. The first
of these steps will be described in II/1.

5 Regional and local development boards

The relief efforts described in the last chapter attempted to ease the problems of the unemployed. At the same time, much attention was devoted to examining ways of creating new employment. This was seen to depend crucially on the introduction of new industries.

In order to attract such industries from outside the region and to assist the establishment of new indigenous ventures, a number of development agencies were established. The small budgets of these organisations, however, limited their activities to research, publicity and the provision of information. Because some of these agencies played a role in the events which will be related later in this study, an outline of their origins is given here.

The government encouraged the formation of regional and local development agencies, in the hope that their activities would make intervention less urgent or necessary. In the event, these organisations helped to generate the political pressure which eventually forced the government to intervene more intensively than it had intended.

The need for new industries was seen to be the most important issue for Tyneside well before the world business recession. This recognition led to the establishment of the first development agency in the North East [1]:-

In 1926, the Tyneside Industrial Development Conference was formed to consider the problem of industrial development of the whole area. It was a pioneer movement which was followed by a large number of municipalities throughout Great Britain. The pressing need for immediate and consolidated action was recognised over the whole of Tyneside and every municipality and urban council linked themselves together in this important Conference. They were joined by the Tyne Improvement Commissioners, the Newcastle Chamber of Commerce and the Public Utility Companies.

The moving spirit of this organisation was a Col.S. Monkhouse, who was connected with the local Electricity Supply Company. It is now all but forgotten and few records of its activities have survived [2]. The results of the work of the Conference appear to have been small: so small, indeed, that Newcastle Corporation withdrew its support in 1932 [3].

It should not have caused any surprise that, with an annual budget of only £5,000 and in the absence of any supporting government policies, the Conference made little impact.

Nevertheless, the fact that all local authorities on Tyneside were initially willing to take part in the Conference was seen as a great step forward: 'it was recognised that Tyneside was one community from an industrial point of view, and increased employment in any part of the area would be to the advantage of the area as a whole' [4]. This wider view did not survive for long after 1929, when the intensity of the problems in particular localities reestablished more parochial attitudes.

In addition to the Tyneside Conference, local development boards were formed in the early 1930s in Sunderland and on Teesside. An attempt to form a regional development organisation in 1932 - in the depth of the recession - ended in failure: 'in December 1932, proposals were made for the constitution of a North East Development Board, whose activities would cover the district from the Tyne to the Tees. The proposals ... were unsuccessful owing largely to the refusal of the Newcastle Corporation to join' [5]. The Tees District Development Board was prepared to cooperate in making the North East Development Board an effective body, but - like Newcastle - Sunderland, the second largest town in the region, steadfastly refused to join.

The organisation continued to exist on paper. It was closely connected with the Tyneside Conference and used the same offices.

As the government hoped that local and regional development organisations would do some of the work it could not or would not do itself, several efforts were made to bring a wider scheme into existence. Sir Horace Wilson, the chief industrial adviser of the government, visited Newcastle in 1932 and discussed the possibilities with the Tyneside Industrial Conference. He pointed out the advantages of a regional Development Board on the lines of those which had been set up in Scotland, Lancashire and South Wales. At that time, his efforts were not successful, 'and the reason is undoubtedly the lack of acknowledged leadership. Local authorities, of which there are thirteen on Tyneside alone, are frequently jealous of one another and lacking in the spirit of cooperation' [6].

Runciman, the President of the Board of Trade, came to the North East in March 1934 and strongly advised the local authorities on the North East Coast to cooperate. [7]. His advice was eventually accepted: on 26

November 1934, a meeting under the chairmanship of the Lord Mayor of Newcastle 'unanimously decided that the formation of the North East Development Board should be proceeded with' [8]. The Board started operations on 4 March 1935.

While the new Board represented the regional interest as a whole, some overlap with the activities of the existing local development agencies was unavoidable and this led, initially, to some friction.

The start of operations of the North East Development Board was delayed for several weeks because Barclays Bank was not satisfied with the security for the £500 it was asked to advance until local and government finance became available. In the meantime, the Board had to rely on financial support from the local development agencies, and this seems to have caused further friction. The District Commissioner in Newcastle suggested that 'the first task of the Central Board will be to break down this habit (of local bickering) and replace it by one of a joint central cooperation' [9]. In order to achieve this, it was necessary not only to make the North East Development Board financially independent from the local agencies as soon as possible, but also to provide it with sufficient funds to promote the region adequately.

The Tyneside Industrial Development Conference ceased to exist and a Tyneside Industrial Development Board was formed in its place in March 1935. In view of the meagre results obtained by its precursor, this was not achieved without a good deal of debate in Newcastle City Council on the justification for contributing the proceeds of a 1/8d rate. The 1936 budget of the Tyneside Board was less than £3,000, out of which an executive secretary and a small staff had to be paid, as well as the promotional and travelling expenses.

A smaller Board was formed in Blyth and discussions were going on about the formation of a local Board in Berwick on Tweed.

In South West Durham - an area specially hard hit by the exhaustion of the coal field - a Development Board was formed in 1935, but something more than promotion was required and an organisation with more specific aims and powers was set up in 1937 [10].

Although the local authorities were strongly represented, the development organisations also gave opportunities to public-spirited private persons to put their expertise and understanding of the local situation at the disposal of the region.

Inevitably, the local development bodies created additional vested interests, and their efforts to attract new industries to their own localities would cause some problems with the Trading Estates Company later [11].

At least one of the development organisations played a part in attracting refugees from Nazi Germany and other European countries to the North East and assisting them to start manufacturing businesses. Stanley Holmes, the secretary of the Tyneside Industrial Development Board travelled several times to the continent of Europe before the outbreak of the War and made contact with threatened industrialists. He succeeded in attracting a number to the North East, although not all of these managed to escape from Germany in the end. Since industries established by refugees gained some importance, reference to them will be made in III/5 and III/6.

The development organisations had no investment funds at their disposal. The role of readily available capital particularly in the creation of new local enterprises was well understood (see III/4) and the lack of facilities appears to have lost the region some opportunities: 'the Tyneside Industrial Conference has been in contact with a number of promising schemes, the majority, however, have gone to other districts which could provide the financial assistance which the Conference is unable to provide' [12].

In order to help to overcome this difficulty, Col. S. Monkhouse and some prominent Tyneside businessmen set up Northern Industries Development Ltd in 1933, 'to provide necessary assistance to approved new ventures or for the development of undertakings already established and handicapped by lack of capital for expansion' [13]. The company may be considered a small forerunner of a partly government-guaranteed investment company which would be established in 1936 with the object of providing capital for small and new firms in depressed areas (see III/4).

It was gratifying that a region which had become prosperous in the 19th century 'by the enterprise, foresight and courage of individuals, unaided by any government or by the big London Banks' [14], had thrown up at least one financial support venture in the period of its greatest distress. It was, up to then, the most constructive recognition that special steps would have to be taken to assist the diversification of industries in the region.

In the foregoing, only those development organisations were discussed which existed in the middle of the 1930's or earlier. Those founded during the last War will be referred to in appropriate places in the text. Development organisations continue to exist up to the present time and their operations have been greatly extended.

REFERENCES AND NOTES

I/1.   The Causes of the Crisis

[1]   Armstrong College, 1935, p.2.
[2]   Lewis, W. Arthur, 1963, p.41.
[3]   Ibid, p.57.
[4]   Balfour Committee, 1925, p.9.
[5]   Op.cit.2.
[6]   Op.cit.1, pp.17,18.
[7]   RCDIP, 1940, para.176, p.86.
[8]   Ibid, para.178, p.87.
[9]   TWA,1762/4, Report, 'Activities of the Company during the Year to 30 September 1938', Employment, pp. 5,6.
[10]   Op.cit.7, para.102, pp.48,49.
[11]   Dennison, S.R., 1939, p.95.
[12]   Segal, N., 1979.

I/3.   The Social Effects of the Crisis

[1]   Priestley, J.B., 1977.
[2]   HL Deb 98, 965.
[3]   RIDT, 1934, para.17, p.76.
[4]   Pilgrim Trust, 1938, p.148.
[5]   Ministry of Labour, 1932, p.91.
[6]   Ministry of Labour Gazette, December 1932, p.448. The two
      Commissioners were appointed 'in view of the refusal of the
      County Council to administer transitional payments in accordance
      with the requirements of the order'.
[7]   RIDT, 1934, pp.89,90.

I/4.   Some Measures of Social Relief

[1]   CSAEW, 1935, 1st Report, para.155, p.62.
[2]   Ibid, para.157, p.62.
[3]   Ibid, para.158, p.63.

I/5.   Local and Regional Development Organisations

[1]   Tyneside Industrial Development Board, 1950, p.2.
[2]   For example, article 'What the Development Conference is Doing to
       Attract Works', Newcastle & Gateshead Chamber of Commerce, 1929.
       See also Tyneside Industrial Development Conference.
[3]   TWA,589, Newcastle upon Tyne City Council, 1932.
[4]   Op.cit.1.
[5]   BT 104/30, memorandum from the North East Development Board to
       CSAEW, 8.1.1935. See also BT 104/1, unsigned and undated
       memorandum from Commissioner on Industrial Development Councils
       in the North East.
[6]   RIDT, 1934, para.38 (4), p.85.
[7]   CAB 27/577, DA [ID], CP 220 (34), Report, III, 2, 37.
[8]   North Mail , Newcastle upon Tyne, 26.11.1934.
[9]   BT 104/1, District Commissioner at Newcastle upon Tyne (Forbes
       Adam) to Commissioner (Tribe), 9.5.1935. The function of the
       District Commissioners will be explained in II/1.
[10]   CSAEW, 1937, 4th Report, paras.329 - 333, pp.79,80.
[11]   For example, the Tyneside Industrial Development Board did not
       normally pass any enquiries for factories to the Company, see
       EIEB, minute 172, 2.2.1937.
[12]   North Mail , Newcastle upon Tyne, ca.1933.
[13]   North Mail or Newcastle Journal , Newcastle upon Tyne, ca.1933.
[14]   North East Development Board, 1936, Speech by CSAEW to North East
       Development Board.

PART II: THE ORIGINS OF REGIONAL POLICY

1 The 1934 Special Areas Act

In this chapter, the events will be recounted which led to the first Act of Parliament dealing with the depressed areas. Although intended to do little more than demonstrate that the government had not forgotten them, the Act contained within it the seeds of profound changes and it marked the beginning of British regional policy. One of the first - unforeseen - consequences of the Act was the establishment of government-financed trading estates in the depressed areas. The first of these would be at Team Valley, Gateshead. The Act represents the starting point, therefore, of the main topic of this study.

By 1934, the country as a whole had begun to recover from the effects of the world trade recession. Between 1932 and 1934 the Gross National Product increased by 10% and unemployment declined, although it was still greater than in 1929. Like other depressed areas, however, the North East failed to recover in line with the rest of the country, as Figure 1 has shown.

Reference was made in I/3 to a series of remarkable articles published by The Times in March 1934 which painted a harrowing picture of the life of many people in County Durham. In the issue of 20 March 1934, the special correspondent drew attention to the fact that recovery had by-passed at least this part of the country:-

> England is beginning again to think in terms of prosperity and may even deceive herself into imagining that at home, if only she holds what she has gained, everything everywhere is going to come right. That is not so. There are districts of England, heavily populated, whose plight no amount of general trade recovery can cure, because their sole industry is not depressed but dead. It would be a failure of statesmanship to ignore them.

In the last report of the series, on 21 March 1934, the special correspondent made some proposals for action which were supported by the first leader of the same day:-

> The government would do well to choose and appoint one man and send him to study the Durham situation comprehensively for a period of months, and then require him to report his frank recommendations covering as wide a field as he thinks fit. He would need to be empowered to call into consultation, at his discretion, any local authorities, any companies, public bodies or private individuals, and to receive assistance from the Civil Service in disentangling the facts on any particular subject ... Nothing was to be ruled out of his mind ab initio ... If the government were to send one man separately to each of the half dozen areas of Great Britain which present the same phenomena of crushing unemployment and the death of local industry, it would be provided with half a dozen parallel reports from which it would distil ideas for possible action ... It is a task for one man, not a committee.

The Times reports gave Members from Durham constituencies an opportunity to raise the issue of the depressed areas in the Commons. For example, Mr. Lawson (Lab., Durham, Chester le Street) remarked that

> we have suddenly found an ally in an unexpected quarter ... upholding the traditions of a great public journal, The Times has had a representative investigating conditions in those areas, and he has supplied articles which ... almost perfectly mirror the conditions of things in those parts of the land [1].

Such was the extent of the comment that Sir H. Betterton, the Minister of Labour, was obliged to respond [2]:-

> It is a striking and a fortunate coincidence that during the past three days there has appeared in The Times newspaper a series of valuable, informative and wholly sympathetic articles. I have no doubt that they will be read by thousands who will not read the report of our discussion here today. I think the facts ought to be known. I am, very glad that Hon. Members raised this discussion this afternoon.

The publication of the last of the reports coincided with a visit to Newcastle upon Tyne of Chamberlain, the Chancellor of the Exchequer. He made a speech there from which it would appear that he, too, had taken note of the reports: referring to the Unemployment Assistance Bill going through the House of Commons, he said, according to The Times of 23 March 1934, that

> he hoped that one of the first things the Board would do would be to visit some of these areas like Tyneside and see for themselves what the conditions were ... He hoped they would make a general survey of the conditions ... It may be some months before our Bill passes through all its stages and before the Board is set up ... but I want to ask the people of this stricken area to believe that they are not forgotten in London.

In his foreword to a Life of Geoffrey Dawson [3], for many years an influental editor of The Times , the Earl of Halifax observed that 'special weight was held to attach to opinions expressed in its leading articles, on the assumption that these carried some quality of government stamp, if not of approbation'. The idea for the investigation in Durham did not, in fact, come from Dawson, but from Barrington-Ward, the deputy editor [4], and far from being approved, the articles were embarrassing for two related reasons: firstly, because the government was committed to a policy of non-intervention and The Times appeared to advocate a contrary policy; and secondly, because the articles were likely to reopen the political debate on unemployment. Booth [5] has shown that the Bill to which Chamberlain had referred in his speech at Newcastle was intended to take unemployment out of the political arena and put it into an administrative framework.

The articles revealed for the first time to readers in the South of the country the full extent of the distress in parts of the North East. They aroused public opinion to a degree the government could not ignore. It acted immediately and almost exactly on the lines proposed by The Times . The government would be reminded of the role played by The Times on several later occasions [6].

On 26 March 1934, an addendum was made to the draft agenda for a Cabinet meeting on 28 March, according to which the Minister of Labour intended to make a statement concerning 'the derelict' areas.

The Minister informed the Cabinet, again with a clear nod to The Times - both in regard to its main recommendation and to the different levels of distress it had discerned -,

> that for some time he had it in mind that his Ministry ought to take steps to obtain a closer knowledge of those special areas sometimes referred to as 'derelict' areas, as distinct from 'distressed' areas, where the local industries had perished and there was little prospect of providing employment for the inhabitants [7].

The Minister claimed that he had been encouraged to follow up this idea by the speech the Chancellor had made in Newcastle. Unlike the Chancellor, however, he considered 'that it would not be right to await the setting-up of the Unemployment Assistance Board before initiating these enquiries'. He gave an indication of the composition of the enquiries he had in mind and of their terms of reference. The Cabinet agreed to the enquiries but asked that they should be rather informal and that the Prime Minister and the Chancellor of the Exchequer should be included in any consultations in connection with the arrangements. This implied an anxiety that the enquiries should not go beyond certain limits. Chamberlain seemed to confirm this later by suggesting that those making the enquiries should be called 'Investigators rather than Commissioners or anything more formal' [8].

During Question Time in the House of Commons on 12 April 1934, the articles in The Times were again mentioned and the Minister of Labour announced that he was considering 'whether any steps can usefully be taken to obtain further information ... as to the position in these areas'. But he appeared to diminish the urgency of the situation by referring to 'the so-called derelict areas', a blunder which drew a rebuke from The Times the following morning, 13 April 1934: 'this apparent failure to acknowledge the special and urgent need is disquieting. The more the general economic conditions in the country improve, the deeper, by contrast, are the gloom and hopelessness of the stricken areas'.

Neither the Prime Minister nor the Minister of Labour revealed that the decision to appoint Investigators had already been taken, and the strictures of The Times were made in spite of the fact that this decision was known to the Press through a leak, a matter noted with displeasure at the Cabinet meeting on 11 April [9].

The appointment of Investigators for West Cumberland and Haltwhistle, Durham and Tyneside, and South Wales and Monmouthshire was announced in the Commons on 19 April 1934, that of an Investigator for Scotland on 25 April 1934.

The Investigator for Durham and Tyneside was Capt. D.Euan Wallace, a Civil Lord of the Admiralty. While he claimed that 'only certain broad lines were indicated as a basis upon which a general survey of the derelict areas might proceed' [10], Booth [11] has found that the government had, in fact, prepared a remit which tried to steer the enquiries into directions which would not involve any additional intervention and which would lead to conclusions compatible with the philosophy enshrined in the Unemployment Assistance Bill. Chamberlain hoped that the Investigators would include in their recommendations the need for an increase in transference - a well-established policy -, an expansion of the public and voluntary agencies giving aid to the unemployed, and improvements in social provisions, health care and housing.

The Investigators consulted with public and private organisations as well as individuals, almost exactly as The Times had suggested. It has proved impossible to find the Minutes of Evidence, but since it was not, originally, intended to publish the Investigators' reports, the minutes may have been destroyed.

The facts, as exemplified by the unemployment statistics, were stark enough. They are summarised in Appendix 7. In June 1934, 16.1% of the insured working population was out of work in Great Britain as a whole. The figure for Durham & Tyneside was 27.2%. In particular localities, the situation was much worse. In Jarrow, unemployment was 56.8% and in Bishop Auckland 50.4%, to mention only two of the worst. For reasons explained in Appendix 5, these figures understated the problem in relation to the national average. But current figures apart, the outlook for coal and shipbuilding was gloomy, at least in terms of future employment.

Within a few weeks, Wallace and his staff had learned enough to realise that they were faced with a situation unparalleled in British industrial history. They produced concise and clear analyses of the causes of the problems of the depressed areas of the North East and they put forward ideas which would shape British regional policy up to our own day. Some of Wallace's proposals must have gone very much against his own political grain - he was a Conservative Minister - but he appears to have been shocked by what he found.

Wallace reported to Oliver Stanley - the new Minister of Labour - on 27 July 1934. If Wallace had intended to produce a report on which the government could act without too great political and practical difficulties, he had failed by his own admission: 'I recognise that many of my recommendations raise issues which may prove embarrassing' [12].

Wallace did not restrict his enquiries to the derelict areas, although the Minister of Labour had amended the final version of the Investigators' remits so as to make it clear that these areas were the primary objects of the enquiries [13]. But Wallace had found that neither a study of the causes of the problem nor any remedies which might be applied made it possible 'to isolate certain parts of the area ... and to consider them apart from their surroundings' [14]. This extension of the scope of the enquiry was unwelcome to the government and would lead to unforeseen conclusions. Wallace's recommendations, while obliging the government with the conclusions it had hoped for on Transference, went far beyond improvements in amenities and administrative matters. Chamberlain, nevertheless, claimed to be disappointed: 'he had hoped for something bigger in conception' [15]. What he meant was that Wallace's recommendations did not include any dramatic yet acceptable ideas which would instantly lift the morale of the people in the depressed areas, one of the main political objectives of the exercise.

Wallace believed that the key to the solution of the problems of the depressed areas was the introduction of new industries, and, in particular, the establishment of light industries which, 'as a result of scientific development, appear likely to displace progressively the heavier trades ... (and) have a special employment value, since they belong, generally speaking, to the 'large labour and small capital group' [16].

The recognition of the need for new industries was not, in itself, anything novel. Means of stimulating indigenous new industries in the depressed areas had been discussed before. But in examining how new industries of any origin might be obtained, Wallace reached two conclusions of fundamental and far-reaching importance. The first was basic to all his recommendations: he made out an irrefutable case for government intervention in the Areas [17]:-

If it be admitted that the industrial depression and the heavy unemployment in this area are due to causes outside the control of those who reside there, it is equally true to say that there is no likelihood that the same forces which have created the present situation will automatically readjust it, except after a lapse of time and at a cost in human suffering and economic waste which no modern government would care to contemplate. Durham and Tyneside can only escape from the vicious circle, where depression has created unemployment and unemployment has intensified depression, by means of external assistance.

In the political climate of the times, the novelty of this conclusion by a government Minister cannot be overstated. Faith in the self-correcting effect of market forces was still strong and the idea of State intervention remained anathema to the government and to a large part of its supporters in and outside Parliament.

Wallace's next conclusion was to have a profound effect on national policies in the longer-term: he showed that, whatever might be done within the depressed areas, their problems were due in a large measure to the lack of national policies in planning the location of industry and the consequent imbalance in economic activity between different parts of the country.

The problem was of long standing. More than 300 years before, a proclamation by James I had warned about the uncontrolled growth of London: 'the other good Townes and Borrowes of his Kingdom by reason of so great a receit for people in and about the said city are much unpeopled and in their trading and otherwise decayed' [18].

In the context of the depressed areas, the dangers of the unplanned industrial expansion of London and the South East and the drift of the population to the South of the country had been discussed before, for example by the Economic Advisory Council early in 1931, when Attlee - a Minister in the 1929 Labour Government - had proposed some form of national locational planning of industry and had shown why it would be impossible to countenance the indefinite growth of London [19]. Now - only three years later - Wallace came to the same conclusion, probably the first Conservative Minister to do so in a government report [20]:-

It is impossible to promote effective measures for the rehabilitation of any one area without reference to the country as a whole. The first of these questions is the attitude of government towards the location of industry. Any large-scale movement of population involves an immense waste of social capital ... The most outstanding example of the movement of population to a new area is the industrialisation and consequent growth of London. It is, therefore, suggested that the time has come when the government can no longer regard with indifference a line of development ... which appears upon the long view to be detrimental to the best interests of the country; and the first practical step which could be taken towards exercising a measure of control in this direction would be some form of planning of industry.

A summary of Wallace's principal recommendations is given in Appendix 8. Among them, two were to have an immediate significance:

Recommendation 10 called for 'the appointment of a Commissioner to coordinate all activities in connection with government schemes for the rehabilitation of the area'. Wallace proposed that the Commissioner should 'direct and coordinate the work locally, without the necessity of referring any but major questions to London'. The idea was very much in line with the proposal put forward in a leading article in The Times on 21 March 1934 for a 'Director of Operations' who 'would be the channel and instrument of a concerted national effort to rid the land of these terrible pools of idleness ... He would bind together the agencies of relief and amelioration and direct remedial measures with concentrated force'.

Recommendation 2 suggested the formation of an Industrial Development Company for Tyneside. One of its tasks would be the clearing of derelict sites (recommendation 8c).

46

The Investigator reported, furthermore, that he had received representations concerning the establishment of one or more trading estates in the depressed areas on the lines of those at Slough and Trafford Park [21]. These representations will be referred to again in II/2.

The main ideas and some of the principal recommendations of the Wallace Report represented a barely-veiled criticism of the government's non-interventionist stance. Booth [22] has shown how the interventionist tenor of the Report undermined the concept underlying the Unemployment Assistance Bill. The government aimed, therefore, to have the Bill passed before having to deal with the Investigators' reports in Parliament, an aim in which it succeeded.

It may be noted that the outlines of almost all the depressed area policies adopted between 1934 and 1947 were first touched upon in the body of Wallace's report or in its recommendations. Even most of its specific proposals for local action, for example, the construction of a Tyne Tunnel and the unification of the local authorities on both banks of the Tyne, were eventually implemented: the latter recommendation almost 40 years later.

A Committee of the Cabinet - chaired by Chamberlain, the Chancellor - would consider the Investigators' reports after an Inter-departmental Committee had examined them.

The Inter-departmental Committee chaired by Sir Horace Wilson, the chief industrial adviser of the government, reported at the end of September 1934 [23]. As the Committee contained representatives of two government departments known for their anti-interventionist attitudes - the Board of Trade and the Treasury -, the negative views of the Committee on the fundamental changes suggested in the Wallace Report was hardly surprising.

On the location of industry, for example - which was not part of the principal recommendations -, the Committee observed with evident disapproval that 'the implication of this suggestion appears to be that some authoritative body should have power to direct where particular industries or perhaps new factories should establish themselves'.

Wallace had not, in fact, made such a proposal. He had suggested that there were areas - for example, the Greater London area - where the expansion of industry should be controlled. The Committee does not appear to have understood the distinction between telling industrialists where they must not open factories and ordering them to places where they did not wish to go, because it continued:-

Locational control (would mean that) ... some industrial development would be prevented unless a guarantee were given to a prospective manufacturer to compensate him for going to what he might regard as an unsuitable locality. It seems probable, too, that the assumptions of powers to settle the location of factories (except perhaps on defence grounds) would involve the State in embarrassing questions of management.

Regarding one of Wallace's suggestions that the government should support the establishment of a financial organisation which would more effectively help small and new businesses in the depressed areas than the recently-established Credit for Industry Ltd [24], the Committee observed that 'the formation of a new agency with State financial assistance would not possess any advantage', and it was afraid that such a body might 'be left with unsound schemes which others would not touch'. It concluded that 'it seems better to leave this business to private enterprise'.

The Committee was equally negative regarding the clearance of derelict sites, another principal recommendation: 'so far as this proposal is related to government action', it observed, 'it raises the dilemma that either the Exchequer would be financing works which would enure to the benefit of private owners, or the government would assume responsibility for the ownership and the ultimate disposal of such property'.

With the fundamental proposals of the Report ruled out of court, the Committee expressed disappointment with what was left: 'what emerged is unlikely to fulfil the expectations and hopes that have been created, especially in the depressed areas themselves, by the appointment of the investigators'. The conclusions of the Inter-departmental Committee reflected the pessimism characteristic of the government's views on the depressed areas: 'none of the policies are new, none of them can give big results. The situation seems one that can only be dealt with - alleviated would perhaps be a more correct word - by persistent attempts to apply a number of minor remedies of diverse (and perhaps changing) character'.

The Cabinet Committee issued three reports within less than a month. Its views on the fundamentals of the Report by the Investigator for Durham and Tyneside were no more positive than those of the Inter-departmental Committee. In its interim report of 10 October 1934 [25] it recognised, - like the Inter-departmental Committee -, that a policy confined to those proposals which could be carried out by the machinery of government was unlikely to satisfy the expectations aroused by the appointment of the Investigators. The reference to the 'machinery of government' indicated that the government was thinking in terms of administrative solutions rather than of any new, interventionist policies.

Some of the Investigators' proposals might be tried as experiments 'for the important psychological effect they might have in persuading persons in the distressed areas that the government had their plight very much at heart'. This cynical comment provides further confirmation that no fundamental action was intended.

There were two reasons for presenting any proposals in an experimental context: firstly, to provide a rationale for limiting the number and the extent of the depressed areas to be designated. This would save the government from embarrassment 'by demands for financial assistance from other areas which regard themselves as depressed'. Secondly, by stressing the experimental nature of any scheme from the start, the government would be less discomfited in case it had to be abandoned.

Experiments, however, required special machinery which would ensure 'a large measure of flexibility and considerable freedom of action'. This was essential 'to obtain a willingness to experiment with the risk of failure and the need to abandon a line of action'. Such a flexibility could not be ensured by departmental action. The desiderata could best be met by the appointment of Commissioners for the 'initiation, organisation and prosecution of schemes to facilitate economic development and social improvement' in the depressed areas. The Commissioners would be visible proof that something was being done. It will be noted, however, that although the Cabinet Committee accepted Wallace's recommendation to appoint Commissioners, the objectives it had in mind were more limited.

The Commissioners were to devote themselves, in the first place, to work which could not be done under existing powers. They would not be empowered, however, to subsidise ordinary industrial undertakings - i.e. private enterprise -, nor were they to relieve local authorities of any duties laid upon them by Statute, although it was recognised that 'many of the most valuable activities of the Commissioner will be in connection with matters falling in the territory of local authority cooperation'. So far as housing was concerned, for example, the Commissioners would not be able to make any contribution towards costs, but they could help to clear sites on which houses might later be erected by local authorities. The Committee accepted that the Commissioners would need powers to acquire land by compulsory acquisition.

The Commissioners would have a wide discretion in expending funds, which should not be subject to detailed control, so that they would be able to act with less delay than government departments. The Commissioners would be under the control of the Minister of Labour, but the relationship would have to be carefully worked out. Finally, the Commissioners would have agents resident in each of the four areas contemplated, which were later to be called District Commissioners.

On some other matters, the Committee agreed with the findings of the Investigators, for example on training, transference and land settlement, activities which had also met with the approval of the Inter-Departmental Committee.

The second report of the Cabinet Committee [26] was concerned with the delineation of the depressed areas which were to be designated. The Committee expected that there was likely to be 'strong pressure to extend areas to cover other depressed districts', and it considered it to be 'imperative to confine (the areas) to the limits prescribed by the Investigators'. This did not mean that all the areas within these limits would be designated, as the Investigator for Durham and Tyneside had suggested [27]. No powers should be taken to extend the designated areas. Their boundaries could not be enlarged 'without grave danger of having to extend the scheme throughout the country'.

The Cabinet Committee considered other details of the Investigators' Reports and the views on them of the Inter-departmental Committee; its conclusions were almost equally negative and restrictive. One example relating to the North East illustrates the point: Wallace had recommended that the so-called Jarrow Slake scheme should receive grant aid (recommendation 8a). Under this scheme, new docking and other facilities would be created close to the mouth of the River Tyne - and to the locality with the highest unemployment in the region, and perhaps in the country -, which would enable larger ships to use the River than was possible at the time. The Cabinet could not accept this scheme because any 'increase in traffic would almost certainly be at the expense of other east coast ports'. Such a likely outcome would cause political difficulties, i.e. protests from other port owners, no matter how desperate the situation was in Jarrow.

On 30 October 1934, the Prime Minister announced in the Commons that, subject to certain excisions of information given to the Investigators in confidence, their reports would be published after all. The Cabinet Committee had concluded that 'it would be less embarrassing to publish and that there were reasons to believe that the Investigators would welcome this' [28].

The Debate on the Reports took place on 14 November 1934 [29]. The Motion was 'to consider the Reports of the Investigators'. Chamberlain took an early opportunity to say that the government would not accept all their recommendations. He did announce, however, that the government had decided to appoint two Commissioners, one for the depressed areas of Scotland, and one for those of England and Wales, and that they were to be given 'very wide discretion'.

The Commissioners would be allotted a substantial sum to spend at their discretion and an initial amount of £2 million would be paid into a special fund which they would administer. The Chancellor promised the immediate introduction of a Bill to provide the necessary powers. Since there was no legal reason why the appointment of the Commissioners had to wait until the Bill was passed, the Chancellor was able to announce that he had apppointed Mr. P.M. (later Sir Malcolm) Stewart as Commissioner for England and Wales, and Sir Arthur Rose as Commissioner for Scotland. Both had asked to be allowed to work in an honorary capacity. Brief biographies of Sir Malcolm Stewart and his successors as Commissioners for England and Wales will be found in Appendix 9.

The Chancellor made a long speech: it was necessary to convince the people in the depressed areas 'that these reports (of the Investigators) are not going to gather dust in some remote pigeon hole, but that they will be the subject of continuous executive action'. He made much of the need for 'speedy, direct and less orthodox action' and for experiment, but it was all rather vague. The most glaring omission was any indication of how the government intended to obtain more employment in the depressed areas. The Commissioners would not be charged with the duty to relieve unemployment by the provision of work. In this respect, the remit of the Commissioners would be different from that of the former Unemployment Grants Committee. The change reflected the government's negative views on public works, and no other direct means were apparent by which the Commissioners could help to create permanent work.

The government accepted recommendations 6 and 7 of the Investigator on training, Transference, and land settlement schemes. While Transference had been an established policy since 1928, the government now attached great importance to land settlement as a means of mitigating the problems of the depressed areas. The Chancellor had confirmed this in his opening speech in the Debate on 14 November 1934: 'the best hope for people who cannot be employed in old industries or in new ones on the spot and who are not susceptible to transfer elsewhere, must lie somewhere on the land' [30]. The fact that this view was shared by the leaders of the main political parties will be referred to again.

The government was criticised on all sides of the House for having failed to offer any comments on the more fundamental proposals of the Investigators, for example, the control of the expansion of industry in the South East and the Midlands. Chamberlain replied that 'some of the recommendations raise very far-reaching questions of policy which could not be decided by reference merely to particular and limited areas', while others would require further investigations [31]. He may have included the industrial development company proposed by Wallace among the latter, but no evidence has been found that the government followed up the idea at that time.

But even if the government had agreed to initiate a location of industry policy as the Investigator for Durham and Tyneside had suggested, it would not have had any significant effect on the depressed areas for some years. The government was under pressure, however, to achieve some improvements in the Areas as soon as possible. On this point, the Chancellor warned against any unduly high hopes: 'it would be unfair to expect these Commissioners to perform miracles. We do not expect spectacular results'.

The government's supporters from the North East were dissatisfied: Mr. Headlam (Con., Durham, Barnard Castle), for example, regretted that 'the more far-reaching recommendations (of the Investigator) have not been accepted by government', and he pleaded for new industries in the distressed areas. Sir Robert Aske (Con., Newcastle upon Tyne East) remarked that 'the depressed areas constitute a separate problem, and that problem has to be attacked by special and distinct measures which are different from those applied to the rest of the country'.

The Opposition produced no new ideas which would have affected the situation in the short term, either; its themes were the revival of the traditional industries of the depressed areas and the need for changing the economic system. Its conclusions may be summed up in a comment from Mr. Batey (Lab., Durham, Spennymoor), who said there was nothing in the government's proposals worth looking at.

Although the government was at pains to stress that there would be no financial limits if means were found to spend the money with good effect, there was much criticism of the smallness of the initial sum allocated to the Commissioners. Mr. Greenwood (Lab.,Wakefield) was dismissive: 'two Commissioners and £2 million do not touch the root of the problem' [32].

The alternative policies open to the government were spelled out by Oliver Stanley, the Minister of Labour: taking people to industry (transference) and taking industry to the people (work to the workers). He claimed that the second alternative presented serious problems: 'how is one going to attract new industries to the depressed areas'?, he asked, 'by force (or) by closing the London Area henceforth against the setting up of new industries' [33]? In parliamentary terms, this was a clever opening gambit, because he knew of the concern of Opposition Members representing London Boroughs with relatively high levels of local unemployment. He answered his own questions: 'the general view is ... that this problem should be dealt with by way of inducements', but, 'if you offer something, it must be substantial'. By stretching this line of argument ad absurdum , he showed that this would lead to the ruin of industries outside the depressed areas. Inducements could not, therefore, be considered.

Stanley was a progressive Conservative and co-author of a book [34] which had argued that opportunities for State intervention in the economy could safely be examined within Conservative traditions. His speech on this occasion indicated the degree of orthodoxy still being adhered to even by this section of the Conservative party. The only positive suggestion he made was for the government to finance the clearance of sites, because 'you cannot expect the birth of new industries in the graveyards of the old' [35]. But this, in itself, showed the way thinking was developing: the Inter-departmental Committee had turned down this suggestion because it could see only two - equally unacceptable - procedures for clearing sites at public expense.

One of the principal recommendations of the Investigator for Tyneside and Durham had been concerned with the organisation of local government on Tyneside. He claimed that 'a strong prima facie case for some measure of unification of the local authorities on Tyneside appears to be undeniable; and it is equally clear that the prospects of voluntary amalgamation are so remote as to be outside the realm of practical politics' [36]. But since the logic of this led to the consideration of compulsory amalgamation, the Investigator felt that this would raise so many problems that a Committee of experts or a Royal Commission would be required 'to provide an opinion sufficiently authoritative upon which to base the special legislation which would apparently be required'.

The government, accordingly, gave an undertaking that an inquiry would be made into the system of local government on Tyneside. A Royal Commission under the chairmanship of Sir Angus Scott was appointed on 1 May 1935. The Commission reported in February 1937 [37], with four of the five members in favour of amalgamation for the purpose of those services which could be administered over an area larger than that of any local authority then existing on Tyneside, services which it termed 'regional'. One member of the Commission (Mr. Charles Roberts) produced a Minority Report which was in favour of some amalgamation, but proposed that it should be based on enlarged County Boroughs rather than on an extensive area incorporating agricultural parts of Northumberland and Durham. In the event, unification had to await yet another report on local government reorganisation in 1969 - the Redcliffe-Maud Report [38] -, but something on the lines of the recommendations of the Scott Committee was, in fact, put on the statute book by the Local Government Act 1972 and implemented on 1 April 1974. It was partly undone again in July 1985 [39].

The depressed areas took up a good deal of the Debate on the Address on 20 November 1934, which contained a reference to the proposed legislation. Members of Parliament did not have the Bill in their hands until the last day of the Debate. Much of their comment and criticism was based, therefore, on no more than the government had divulged when the Reports of the Investigators were being considered on 14 and 15 November 1934.

The Bill was introduced on 26 November by Ramsay MacDonald, the Prime Minister, and the Second Reading took place on 3 December 1934; but as the debates on the Reports of the Investigators and the Address had already revealed most of what the government had in mind, he had little more to say that was new.

The speech was not well received by the Labour Opposition. Mr. Greenwood (Lab., Wakefield) called the Bill 'the meanest proposal ever made by government'. Almost without exception, Members from the depressed areas - of all parties - criticised the Bill in principle or in detail, and often for what it omitted.

Mr. Lawson (Lab., Durham, Chester le Street) felt that 'this was not a matter which could be dealt with by private persons, even if you call them Commissioners', and he added: 'it is a question of deep State policy and for direct responsibility as far as Ministers are concerned'. But that was exactly what Chamberlain had hoped to avoid. Lawson condemned the Bill because it would do no more than make a 'trifling amelioration of the conditions existing in the depressed areas' and pleaded for a system of national planning, i.e. a location of industry policy.

The attitude of Conservative Members may be summed up in the remarks by Mr.McKeag (Con., Darlington): 'half a slice is better than no bread at all'.

For the Liberals, Mr. Lloyd George (Caernarvon) particularly supported the section of the Report of the Investigator dealing with experiments in agriculture and forestry. This was also supported by Mr.Lansbury, (Lab., Poplar), the leader of the Labour Opposition, and by a number of other members from all parties.

The discussions on the Committee stage of the Bill on 6 and 7 December 1934 underlined the attitudes to inducements to private industry: according to clause 1.5 (a), the Commissioners' functions were not to include 'the carrying on of any undertaking for the purpose of gain, or the provision of financial assistance to any undertaking carried on for gain'.

This restriction was supported - for different reasons - both by Labour and Conservative Members. When Mr. Harcourt Johnstone (Lib., South Shields) proposed an amendment which would enable the Commissioners to assist Societies registered under the Industrial and Provident Societies Act or Public Utility Societies, Mr. Lawson (Lab., Durham Chester le Street) opposed it:-

No one who has to examine the use of public money for purposes of trade ... can lightly accept a proposal of this kind unless he can be quite sure that it does not work in the interests of private gain, and one thing I was pleased to notice in the Bill was the very definite reference to the exclusion of undertakings run for private gain.

The Conservatives would not countenance any assistance by the Commissioners to private firms for a different reason: because it would create unfair competition for firms outside the depressed areas [40].

This attitude was to change over the next two and a half years when it became clear that, without inducements, there was little prospect of attracting new industries to the Areas. This change will be traced in III/3.

The localities within the areas selected for Special Area status were scheduled in the Bill. They included all those 'which have been specially affected by industrial depression' [41]. Against the advice of the Investigator, they excluded the major towns, except Newcastle, but the provisions of the Act were never used there [42]. The Prime Minister anticipated criticism from areas omitted in the Bill: 'we begin with (some) areas for the purpose of discovering from the experiment cures, methods of handling, ways of spending public and private money ... When we have learned, we are going to extend the results' [43]. In the meantime, there was no provision in the Bill which would enable the Minister of Labour to alter the schedule. This would be changed in the 1937 Amendment Act, but it may be noted that, in a wider context, the discussion on what should be the extent of assisted areas has been going on almost continuously ever since: should support be concentrated on those sub-areas where it was plainly needed, or would development there be enhanced by treating regions as a whole? The policy in the last 50 years has often been influenced by economic and political trends. During periods of economic difficulty, there has been a tendency to reduce the number and the extent of designated or scheduled areas.

The Bill was sent to the Lords on 13 December 1934 as the Depressed Areas (Development and Improvement) Bill.

The Debate on the Second Reading in the Lords was short [44]. A Labour Peer, the Earl of Listowel, regretted that there was nothing in the Bill to encourage local industries, nor any reference to the public development company the Investigator for Durham and Tyneside had proposed. He also observed that 'the root causes of the grave malady of unemployment and poverty ... are not to be found in the areas themselves'. In this he echoed the observations of the Investigator and others. Lord Eustace Percy, (Con., Hastings), for example, had remarked in the Commons a few days earlier that 'nothing you can do in the depressed areas themselves can solve the problems of the depressed areas. That is the real charge against the government' [45]. Two speakers struck prophetic notes: Lord Elton believed that the 'measure contained within it very great possibilities' and Lord Hutchinson saw the Bill as 'the beginning of a movement by government to deal with the vast problem of our depressed areas', adding, somewhat surprisingly in the context, 'and also with smallholding development'.

The main contribution by the Lords was to ask for the word 'Depressed' in the Bill to be deleted and the word 'Special' substituted. This was accepted by the government. Harold Macmillan was to remark later that changing the epithet would not help the people who lived in the Areas [46]. The amended Bill was sent back to the Commons on 19 December and received the Royal Assent on 21 December 1934.

The Economist of 1 December 1934 probably expressed the views of informed opinion on the first Special Areas Act when it wrote:-

> Altogether, the impression left by the measure is that the government is once more trying to appease public opinion by a policy of makeshifts and a dispensing of ad hoc assistance ... A sweeping plan for dealing with the depressed areas as a whole is plainly beyond its scope.

The Commissioner found it necessary in his First Report to correct 'much misunderstanding as to the extent of my powers, perhaps partly due to the statements made by members of the government during the passage of the Bill' [47], and to draw attention to nine limitations - intended and unforeseen - which he had already come up against. At a later date, he pointed out that some of these limitations, at least, seriously limited the scope of his work [48], but it was not until the 1934 Act was amended in May 1937 that several of them were removed.

The financial control over the Commissioners proved to be unexpectedly tight and hampered the 'speedy, direct and less orthodox action' Chamberlain had promised. Booth [49] has pointed out that the Commissioners were obliged to submit every project to the Minister of Labour. The resulting administrative delays were long in relation to the duration of the 1934 Act (two years and three months) and special steps had to be taken to reduce them by means of yet another committee.

The Commissioners soon found that the finance to underpin their work was more limited than they had been led to believe. This was merely a reflection of the limited scale of action the government had in mind, fine words notwithstanding.

The reality of the situation was brought home to the Commissioner for England and Wales within a month after the passing of the Act, when he proposed to issue a press release on his intentions. The Treasury thought the draft 'by no means a bad statement', which contained 'much that is virtuous and reasonable', but, 'Mr. Stewart, impressed by the length of time which his wiser proposals will need before they get going, and stung by press criticism to which he is unaccustomed, is putting his faith in public works as an immediate escape from his difficulties' [50].

The Commissioner was, in fact, putting forward a policy which should have recommended itself to the Treasury: 'to assist only such works as could definitely be shown to have value in facilitating the economic development or social improvement of the Areas'. While the provision of employment would in itself have some social value in counteracting the effects of long-term unemployment 'it has not been treated as the controlling factor' [51]. But the Treasury not only ruled out of court any public works undertaken as unemployment relief schemes, it now placed a limit on works of economic benefit. It recommended that the Chancellor had a word with the Commissioner 'and tell him in confidence of the general Budget situation so that he may see ... that there are not countless millions available out of cash revenue' [52]. The Treasury proposed that the Commissioner should be given permission 'to go ahead with grants on small schemes, say, up to £50,000, or, in exceptional cases rather more'. As for financing larger schemes outside the Budget, i.e. by borrowing, that was a matter for deep State policy which had not yet been decided.

The 1934 Act has been the subject of much critical examination in the last 50 years. For example, Dennison [53] - writing before access to the papers was possible - claimed that the Commissioners were not given any clear aims. Pitfield [54] considers the Act 'a product of the government's need to do something dramatic for the Areas and that a multi-faceted approach to the problem of regional unemployment was more acceptable than one relying on the much criticised, politically sensitive solution of transfer'. Booth [55] sees the Commissioners as a device to take the problems of the depressed areas out of the political debate and that, in this respect, the government's thinking on the 1934 Act was the same as that underlying the Unemployment Assistance Act which had recently been put on the statute book.

This view appears to need some qualification: far from removing the problems of the depressed areas from political debate, the government was evidently prepared for a continuing discussion. This was the unavoidable consequence of the appointment of Commissioners from outside the government machine and of the experimental approach.

The Commissioner for England and Wales made sure that the problems of the depressed areas became widely understood. Apart fom his monthly report to the Minister of Labour, he produced three comprehensive reports in 16 months, and two more at intervals of one year. It is not clear whether the government had asked for half-yearly reports to start with, and there is some evidence that it was unprepared for some of their contents. The Commissioner not only reported the situation in the Areas and the actions he had taken; he used the reports to discuss the needs of the Areas, to make veiled criticisms of government policy and to launch his ideas for further initiatives. The reports embarrassed the government, and there was some doubt among Ministers whether the First Report should be published at all [56].

The Commissioner's reports provided opportunities for debate in Parliament. These debates - and the press coverage they received - helped to swing public opinion so strongly in favour of the further stages of intervention the Commissioner had proposed that the Cabinet was obliged to take notice.

The Commissioner's influence was further enhanced by the political support from the Special Areas, which became more focused with the emergence of the local and regional development organisations. The fact that the Commissioner was in a position to apply political pressure was recognised at the time [57].

A realistic critique of the 1934 Act would have to accept that the options open to the government were limited. So far as public works were concerned, there was normally a considerable time lag before they could be translated even into temporary employment. A location of industry policy and financial inducements to private industry - the twin pillars of regional policy in the last 40 years - were politically impossible at the time. Furthermore, a location policy would have required complex legislation and a relatively long time before it would have affected the situation.

The implications of a location policy appear to have been only marginally less unacceptable to the Labour Opposition in Parliament than to the Conservatives. There were two reasons for this: even in the boom conditions in London and the South East in 1934, increases in employment could barely match the rapid growth in the insured population. A ban on new industries would have concerned Labour Members - including Lansbury (Poplar), the Labour leader - who represented London boroughs with high unemployment rates, where the transference policy had caused sharp protests. The second reason was that the Labour Party, like the Conservatives, was opposed to inducements to private industry. An example of this view from a Member representing a depressed Durham constituency was cited above. But a location policy without inducements would not have been effective. Indeed, even the statutory powers introduced in 1948 have always been accompanied by some form of inducements up to the present day. Acceptance by the Labour Party of this essential component of a location policy matured only slowly. When Hugh Dalton made a powerful plea for such a policy in the Debate on the Second Report of the Commissioner on 2 March 1936, he had to explain that he personally was not opposed to inducements, an indication that this was not yet fully accepted by the Party.

An appraisal of the outcome of the early depressed areas policy in relation to the government's intentions must lead to the conclusion that every step taken to avoid intervention made it more inevitable: the appointment of the Investigator for Durham and Tyneside led to a report which pointed to the need for intervention within the Areas, and for a curb on the indiscriminate growth of industry outside . By encouraging the Commissioners implementing the Act arising out of the Investigators' reports to experiment, the government opened the door to further intervention; and by choosing a widely-respected industrialist as the Commissioner for England and Wales, it was likely that any intervention proposed by him would enjoy widespread support in the country. The government's support for local development organisations created local constituencies for the Commissioners and so enhanced extra-governmental power.

Lord Eustace Percy (Cons., Hastings) drew attention to the potential political disadvantage of the Special Areas policy [58]: the government would bear the responsibility for the Commissioners' failures, but would be given little credit for their successful activities, which would be seen as having largely resulted from the ideas put forward by the Commissioner for England and Wales and the pressure he exerted on a reluctant government.

The government cannot have foreseen this outcome, nor that it would become involved in increasing levels of intervention by the activities of a determined individual from outside the government machine.

Although the first mention of most of the ideas put forward by the Commissioner had already been made by Capt. Wallace, the Commissioner would argue them powerfully: the case for preferential treatment of the Special Areas; the need for financial inducements to attract new industry and for better finance for small firms in the Areas; the urgency of putting a limit on the growth of Greater London [59]. All of these would eventually be incorporated in legislation and practice. Furthermore, if it is accepted that the report of the Barlow Commission was one of the major political influences which led to the Distribution of Industry Act 1945 and the Town and Country Planning Act 1947 (see IV/2), it should not be forgotten that the establishment of the Commission was proposed by the first Commissioner for the Special Areas of England and Wales in 1936 [60].

Nor should the ameliorative work of the Commissioner for England and Wales be overlooked. The range of his activities was very wide: he assisted in modernising docks and harbours, in providing new water supplies and sewage works, in building hospitals and clearing land for housing. His assistance in the social field covered many and varied activities, from the care of the old to cookery classes for unemployed youths. He helped many hundreds of families to settle on the land and he encouraged and financed the clearing of derelict sites. He devoted much effort and funding to the training and re-training of young and old alike.

Above all, from the point of view of this study, the Commissioner for England and Wales succeeded in establishing - within the confines of the 1934 Act - the first government-financed trading estates and so took one essential step in attracting new industries to the Areas. The fact that this was achieved within 11 months after the passing of the 1934 Act permits the conclusion that the search for solutions produced at least one important result relatively quickly. The events leading to the authorisation by the government of the first publicly-financed factory estate will be discussed in II/3.

2 Government-financed trading estates: origins

Because government-financed trading estates would before long be established in the North East and elsewhere, an outline is given here of the origin of the trading estate concept. At the same time, the circumstances are discussed which convinced the Commissioner for the Special Areas of England and Wales that such estates were essential in the Areas and why he would conclude that the government would have to finance them. The events culminating in the acceptance of the idea by the government will be examined in the next chapter.

It was shown in I/1 that the prosperity of the North East depended on a small number of heavy industries, most of which were in secular decline. Too few of the people of the region were employed in the lighter industries which were expanding in other parts of the country, particularly in Greater London and the Home Counties.

In its presentation to the Barlow Commission in 1938, the Ministry of Labour would identify 23 such industries, i.e. industries which had expanded faster than the general average in the years from 1923 to 1937. While they were present in the North East, the proportion of the employment they provided in 1923 was much less than in London and the Home Counties, and they grew at a much lower rate (see Appendix 3). Fogarty [1] concluded that, to achieve parity in unemployment with London and the South East 'it would have been necessary for the growing industries to expand in the North East more than twice as fast as in the rest of the country'.

Some interest was shown in the North East in the factors which appeared to facilitate the development of growth industries in and around London and the Home Counties. It was noted that a considerable number of these industries were new starts and that the capital available to the founders was usually quite small. Only a few had the resources to buy sites and develop them, to provide the services and to erect their own factories. Most depended on rented premises.

Particular interest was focused on two privately-financed factory estate companies, which had successfully attracted expanding industries, although they had aimed at different markets:

Trafford Park Estates Ltd, Manchester, was formed in 1896, two years after the opening of the Manchester Ship Canal. Its main objective was to bring business to the canal. Although the company had built a number of small factories to let, it was mainly engaged in preparing and leasing sites to firms building their own factories. More than 40 years later, there were 200 firms on the estate, employing over 50,000 people [2].

The Slough trading estate was established on a site originally developed by the government as a motor transport depot during the first world War. It was acquired in 1920 by Slough Estates Ltd, a company which had been formed to purchase from the government and sell the surplus motor transport from that War. The term 'Trading Estate' arose from the activity of the company, trading as it did in war surplus stores.

When the disposal of the surplus material was completed in 1924, the company began to develop the depot as an industrial estate on which factories would be available for rent. In this respect, the policy differed from that adopted at Trafford Park.

For the first few years, factory accommodation was provided by letting existing buildings, after suitable adaptation where necessary. When the company began to erect new buildings, it adopted standard designs of factories which could be constructed quickly and, because of the economies secured in this way, could be let at lower rents than would otherwise have been possible. 'Bijou' factories were made available for persons manufacturing on a small scale. All services, including railway sidings, were provided by the company.

By 1939, there were 210 firms on the Slough trading estate, employing about 28,500 people [3], an average of 135.7 workers per tenant.

It was the success of the Slough estate in particular which attracted the attention of those who urged the government to finance similar estates in the Areas. They argued that government-financed factories could be offered on better terms than those on the commercial estates, since the aim would be to create employment rather than to make profit.

The possibility that private enterprise might construct a trading estate in the North East was explored on at least one occasion: the Inter-departmental Committee reported that Slough Estates Ltd - 'the only firm likely to be interested' - was approached and 'the possibility of opening up a trading estate in one of the depressed areas was discussed ... with the heads of the company in 1931, but nothing came of it' [4]. Some years later, the managing director of Slough Estates confirmed that his company did not contemplate an estate in the Special Areas. In his view, the Areas were too far from the markets for the products of the type of industries which were normally attracted to estates of this kind [5]. But there is much evidence that private enterprise was unwilling to invest in the depressed areas precisely because they were depressed rather than for any other reasons. Richardson [6], for example, thought it possible that firms in the expanding industries wanted to locate factories as far from the depressed areas as possible. The Commissioner for England and Wales suggested that the reason for this was fear: 'fear that their very distress makes them unsuitable for the development of industrial activity, fear of labour unrest, and fear of further increases in already high rates' [7]. At the same time, the Commissioner believed that 'much of the growth of Greater London is not based on strictly economic factors; psychology plays an important part in the matter' [8]. Many others advanced reasons for the attraction exercised by the London area and, by contrast, the failure of the North East in this respect. The views of the Investigator for Durham and Tyneside on this problem are quoted later in this chapter.

Whatever the reason, the Commissioner saw no prospect of trading estates being established in the North East and other depressed areas by private enterprise. The information available to the Board of Trade confirmed this conclusion [9].

There does not appear to have been much interest in the North East in government-financed trading estates in the early stage of the business recession. It was realised that trading estates would not attract large manufacturing units from outside the region. Firms likely to rent factories on such estates would be relatively small or new and would not, in the short term at least, make a significant impression on the unemployment problem. Trading estates would not, therefore, provide solutions to the problems of the North East on an appropriate scale and within an acceptable time span. In disregard of the changed pattern of world trade, some local opinion - including the Trade Unions - seems to have concentrated on ideas for reviving the traditional industries of the North East and showed little interest in new light industries.

For these and other reasons, the concept of government-financed factories received little political backing in the early years of the recession.

By 1934, the situation appears to have changed: Wallace, the Investigator for Durham and Tyneside, received a number of representations on government-financed trading estates in the summer of that year, but it is not known from whom. The matter was touched upon in his report: 'there are possibilities that one or more sites could be acquired for development along the lines of the trading estates at Slough or Trafford Park, and there is no doubt that the provision of these facilities makes a special appeal to the promoter of a new business' [10].

Given the anti-interventionist stance of the government of which he was a member, the Investigator felt it necessary to qualify the idea that such trading estates should be financed by the government: 'this proposal is made with considerable reserve, since it is recognised that the whole problem of the most effective use of our national credit, and the largely increased savings of our people, for the provision of employment ... requires for its solution the most detailed knowledge and prolonged study' [11].

The idea that the government should finance trading estates in the North East was strongly pressed by the newly-formed development organisations. In October 1935, the North East Development Board made a series of recommendations to the government for the industrial development of the region. These included the following [12]:-

We feel that Industrial Estates should be created in various parts of the area on the lines of the Slough trading estate, Welwyn, Trafford Park, Park Royal etc. ... The finance for this undertaking would have to be provided either by the government or by government guarantee, and there is no reason why such an undertaking should not in time be self-supporting.

At a meeting of its council on 28 October 1935, the Tyneside Industrial Development Board, too, urged the government to finance factories to let, but, as will be seen in II/3, the decision to authorise the Commissioner to build trading estates at the expense of the Special Areas Fund had already been taken by the Cabinet a few days earlier. Nevertheless, the Tyneside Industrial Development Board claimed in its first annual report that its representations, and those of the North East Development Board, 'helped the Commissioner eventually to establish the first trading estate in the North' [13]. The claim was repeated by the president of the Tyneside Board at the second annual meeting, on 27 May 1937: 'they helped largely in creating the atmosphere which resulted in the government agreeing to build trading estates' [14].

At the same meeting, Herbert Shaw, a Vice-President of the Board and former secretary of the Newcastle and Gateshead Chamber of Commerce (1902 - 1932), threw an interesting light on the origin of the idea of trading estates in the North East:-

Some of you may remember that I was chairman of the first Board (The Tyneside Industrial Development Conference) and you can imagine that when I see the success of the Trading Estate (which was then under construction at Team Valley, Gateshead), I am very pleased. You may be astonished to know that 10 years ago or more, that was one of the first recommendations my committee made.

It has proved impossible to find the minutes of the Tyneside Industrial Development Conference for the period referred to by Herbert Shaw and it cannot be confirmed, therefore, that government-financed trading estates were proposed rather than commercial ones. If the Conference did indeed suggest the former as a means of bringing new light industries to the North East as early as 1927, it was almost certainly the first time that the idea had been put forward.

The most persistent individual promoter of the idea was S.A. (later Sir Sadler) Forster, a young Middlesbrough accountant and, from 1933, secretary of the Tees District Development Board (see Appendix 9). He would play a key role later. Writing in 1966 as chairman of the Corporation which succeeded the Company, he recalled that

36 years ago, I started to besiege the top brass of the civil service. Every month I journeyed to Whitehall, confident that this time the idea of government-financed factories in the

depressed areas would be accepted. Month after month I returned empty-handed. I was treated with much kindness, but the government was not ready for what appeared to them a 'novel and unorthodox proposal', which involved government participation in what is normally private commercial enterprise [15].

The major role which government-financed factories on trading estates and smaller sites would play one day in the restructuring of the North East was not foreseen by many. As late as February 1938, when government-financed trading estates in the main Special Areas of Britain were expanding, Noel Mobbs, the chairman of Slough Estates Ltd, told the Barlow Commission: 'the trading estate is a valuable aid to light industry. It is not, and is unlikely to become, a major influence in the commercial world' [16]. Although some financial inducements had become available in the Special Areas before he gave his evidence, Noel Mobbs could not have foreseen the introduction of a location of industry policy - with its restrictions on factory construction outside the Areas -, nor the massive demand for and investment in government-financed factories in the period immediately after the last War.

With the passing of the Special Areas Act 1934, a new phase began in the battle for government-financed factories. The speeches made by members of the government during the debate on the Bill had led some to believe that the Commissioners would be able to build such factories under the Act. Their hopes were initially to be disappointed. The coincidence of a series of events in the summer of 1935, however, enabled the Commissioner for England and Wales to ask for and be given authority to build factories at the expense of the Special Areas Fund (see next chapter).

But it had yet to be demonstrated by the initial experience of the Commissioner that the 1934 Act was unlikely to make more than a marginal impact on the problems of the Areas.

Almost from the start of his work, the Commissioner had tried to attract firms from other parts of Britain to one of the Special Areas, or, at least, to persuade them to open branch factories there [17]:-

> It is natural ... that wherever one goes in the Areas, one should be met by the demand that something should be done to attract fresh industries to the Areas ... I regard it as at once the most important and the most difficult of my duties to try and satisfy it. I have given more time and personal attention to this side of my work than to any other, but it must be frankly admitted that up to the present, the results have been negligible.

One of the means by which the Commissioner had hoped to obtain new industries is of interest: even before the passage of the Special Areas Bill, he had attempted to harness his anticipated powers for clearing sites to existing local potential. An internal note from the Commissioner's office of 7 December 1934 records that

> the Commissioner envisages a scheme under which the Tyne Development Board (then in formation) in conjunction with Forbes Adams (the District Commissioner in Newcastle) may select a site

and get it cleared so as to make it possible for new industry to come. It would then be for Northern Industries Development Ltd (a small local venture capital company) to get the actual industries established on the new site [18].

The idea appears not to have been taken any further, probably because the Commissioner soon realised that the organisations he had hoped to involve would be too small to deliver significant results.

With the help of the Federation of British Industries, the Commissioner for England and Wales addressed a carefully drafted questionnaire to 5,829 firms in May and June 1935, asking them whether they would consider opening factories in one of the Special Areas. 4,066 firms did not reply at all and of those who did, all but 12 gave qualified or unqualified negative answers to the questions put to them in the circular. Of the 12 who replied positively, eight were willing to consider the North East or West Cumberland. The Commissioner reluctantly concluded that 'it had to be assumed that there was little prospect of the Special Areas being assisted by the spontaneous action of industrialists located outside the Areas' [19].

More constructively, he also concluded that their lack of interest required measures to make the Areas more attractive and to provide inducements, such as finance on easier terms than available elsewhere in the country.

The Investigator for Durham and Tyneside had already summarised some of the apparent reasons for the failure of the North East to attract new industries: firstly, there were the high rates which were a feature of all the poorer areas of the country. The de-rating of industrial buildings had reduced the burden, but a competitive handicap was widely believed to remain. Next, there was the impression that the Trade Unions were inflexible and difficult to deal with. Capt. Wallace pointed out that, on the contrary, the days lost by disputes in Northumberland and Durham in the years 1930 to 1932 averaged only 6.1 per worker per annum, compared with 15.1 days in the country as a whole. On the other hand, the fact that the administration of County Durham was generally regarded as a stronghold of Socialism was unlikely to prejudice industrialists in its favour.

Then there was the unfortunate reputation the Areas had acquired as a result of five years of depression. The sight of abandoned pits, closed shipyards, derelict buildings and unemployed men was a great handicap when compared with localities where trade was seen to be expanding. But the Investigator saw the most formidable difficulty in the remoteness of the North East from what was regarded as the largest market for the sale of those goods which the new light industries were mainly engaged in producing [20], a view he shared with the directors of Slough Estates Ltd. A later survey by the Board of Trade actually indicated that manufacturers were willing to set up wherever modern factories were readily available for rent [21], but since there were hardly any such factories in the North East, there was no basis for any hopes that new industries would establish themselves there even _if_ the location had been acceptable.

Heim [22] has attempted to show that, prejudice in favour of the South East apart, such hopes ignored the industrial situation at the time:

large-scale firms in appropriate industries had not yet developed in the inter-War years to the point where they could be expected to set up significant numbers of branch factories in the depressed areas, as they were to do after the second world War. She further claims that, at the industry level, there were barriers to new entrants and restrictive practices, which accounted for the small number of significant new ventures being established in the Areas. Even if her thesis is not fully accepted - it does not, for example, explain the growth of new firms in the London Area in the inter-War period -, the factors she elucidates may well have contributed to the difficulties in obtaining inward investment in the North East.

The number of factories opened and closed every year were recorded, by region, in the Board of Trade Surveys of Industrial Development. Those for the years 1932 - 1934 showed that the net gain of factories for the country as a whole - after deducting closures from openings - was 280. In sharp contrast, there was a net loss of one factory in the North East in the same period [23].

The picture was gloomy, and the Commissioner for the Special Areas of England and Wales knew that a significant new initiative would have to be taken, if only to raise the morale of the people of the North East.

3 The crucial months

The opportunity for a new initiative presented itself in the summer of 1935. The Commissioner for England and Wales had been convinced from the beginning that means would have to be found to stimulate new industrial activity in the Areas and he had been considering what he might be able to do within the limits of his powers on the one hand, and his remit to experiment on the other. The following account traces the political developments which persuaded the Commissioner that the time was ripe to test the scope available to him. Further developments later in the summer and early autumn - including a General Election in November 1935 - increased the likelihood that the government would agree to some unorthodox measure.

Interest in the problems of the distressed areas did not abate with the passing of the 1934 Act. The Areas and unemployment occupied Parliament on a number of occasions in 1935. In a Censure Debate in the House of Commons on 9 July 1935, speeches by two Conservative members showed how rapidly new ideas were developing. Mr. Macmillan (Stockton) [1] pressed for the clearing of sites and equipping them with light, power and railways. Because of delays inherent in the completion of land purchases, little had been done in the North East to clear sites in the first six months of the operation of the Act. It is to be noted, however, that Macmillan's suggestion went a good deal further than mere land clearance and his proposals might well have posed questions of interpretation of the 1934 Act.

Mr. Scrymgeour Wedderburn (West Renfrew) went even further: after making obeisance to the tenet - accepted even by progressive Conservatives - that any form of financial assistance to firms in the Special Areas would be unfair to industry in other parts of the country, he proposed a broadening of the scope of what government might do within accepted economic orthodoxy. Indeed he came close - he may have been the first Member of Parliament to make the suggestion - to proposing government-financed industrial estates: '(the government) can possibly acquire in the Special Areas estates which may be suitable for industrial developments and which might very quickly attract new industries if they were prepared with that end in view' [2].

The clearance of sites for local authorities was authorised by the 1934 Act. The acquisition of sites by the government was a different matter. Wedderburn did not elaborate on site preparation, but it is evident that the political gap between the kind of preparation Macmillan had in mind and putting factories on sites owned by the government was becoming very narrow indeed.

The First Report of the Commissioner for England and Wales was published in early July 1935 - six months after the passing of the 1934 Act. It brought the Special Areas back to the centre of public attention.

Ministers were embarrassed by the Report. 'It was difficult for a government to bat on a wicket of the kind Mr. Stewart had prepared for them', the Minister of Labour would say a few months later [3]. Chamberlain described the Commissioner's own conception of his functions as 'extravagant' and called the treatment in the Report of the directions in which the Commissioner's powers were limited 'a bad point' [4]. The Minister of Health thought that 'the impression might get around that the efficiency of the Commissioners was handicapped by the limitations imposed by the government' [5]. The Cabinet Committee agreed, nevertheless, that publication of the Commissioner's report was unavoidable.

The Economist of 20 July 1935 wrote of the 'atmosphere of gloomy frustration which hangs over the Report'. As for any hope 'still cherished by the government's supporters that the appointment of Commissioners would advance more than an inch or two the solution of the problem of the Special Areas, the publication of this Report will effectively kill it'.

The Report was debated in the House of Commons on 23 July 1935 [6]. The Debate was long but not very profitable. It would have been unrealistic to expect any real signs of improvement in the Areas after so short an operation of the Act but - as the Cabinet Committee had feared - Members attacked the government on the limitations of the Commissioners' powers and the practical consequences which were preventing them from taking any direct action to relieve unemployment. While the Opposition had few new ideas which might have helped to bring about the 'immediate and essential relief' demanded by its Motion, it proposed a policy for the location of industry with more conviction than in 1934, but otherwise the occasion was largely a re-run of the debates which had preceded the 1934 Act. What was surprising was that no speaker referred to government-financed factories, or even to the acquisition and preparation of industrial sites in the sense in which Macmillan and Wedderburn had done two weeks before. Considering the representations which had been made for several years, it must be concluded that such factories were not seen to make more than a marginal contribution to the solution of the problem.

On 26 July 1935 - three days after the debate in the Commons,- The Times printed a letter from Sadler Forster, the secretary of the Tees District Development Board. This set out - probably for the first time in the press - the arguments in favour of trading estates in the older industrial areas and the need for government finance or guarantees. It also anticipated by more than four years the recommendation of the Barlow Commission for a National Planning Board to control the location of industry. The letter is reproduced in Appendix 10.

On 29 July, The Times devoted a leading article to the problems of the depressed areas:-

> Of the first importance is the fact that fundamental remedies have not yet been applied ... That is not the fault of the Commissioners. It ought not to have been an unforeseen cause of disappointment to anyone who understood the task remitted to the Commissioners. They were not endowed with powers to do more than ameliorative and reconditioning work.

The fundamental remedies The Times supported included those put forward by Sadler Forster: government-financed trading estates and a location of industry policy.

The reports of the Commissioners were debated in the House of Lords on 31 July 1935 [7]. According to the Economist of 3 August 1935, there was a 'note of censure in the speeches of noble Lords drawn from all parties and shades of opinion', which it took to be 'cogent proof of public discontent with the government's attitude over the Special Areas'. But, again, no new ideas were put forward, except, perhaps, two suggestions by Lord Portal (who had been the Investigator for South Wales and Monmouthshire the year before), one of which would be all but adopted the following year: that foreigners wishing to come to this country to establish factories should be made to go to areas of high unemployment. Lord Portal also drew attention to the limited powers of the Commissioners and suggested the appointment of a Minister responsible for the Special Areas. This idea, in various forms, would be put forward on a number of occasions from now on. Lord Ridley, the chairman of the North East Development Board, referred to the need for new industries in the Special Areas: 'we must ... do everything possible to encourage manufacturers from abroad and people at home to start new industries'. He made no references, however, to government-financed trading estates. Prof. G.H.J. Daysh feels sure that this omission did not signify any lack of support for such estates [8]. This view is supported by the proposal from the North East Development Board for trading estates a few months later, which was quoted in the last chapter. Indeed, Daysh believes that when the papers of the late Lord Ridley become available, they may well show that he was among those who made representations on the need for government-financed trading estates to the Investigator in the summer of 1934.

In the meantime, the Commissioner had written to Forbes Adam, the District Commissioner in Newcastle (who had been the personal assistant of the Investigator for Durham and Tyneside), on 29 July 1935 [9]: 'it is likely that we shall be pressed to do more in the way of clearing sites for industrial development', an indication that the suggestions made in Parliament by Macmillan and Wedderburn a few weeks earlier had been noted.

The letter asked the views of the District Commissioner on a number of related questions: was site clearance to be left mainly to local authorities, at least to those which had the necessary powers ('Boroughs, but not, apparently Urban or County Councils')? So far as Tyneside was concerned, would it be possible to work through certain Boroughs and the Tyneside Improvement Commission - as was the case already in connection with other activities of the Commissioner -, or would a further organisation be required? If existing bodies were to be used, should they be encouraged to undertake the work themselves, or should there be established a Public Utility Society (see Appendix 11)? Was it enough to clear sites and equip them with roads, railways and quay facilities, or was it desirable to go further and build factories? Should cleared sites be let to new industries at less than economic rents? Subsidies were disallowed by the 1934 Act and it is not clear why the Commissioner asked the question, nor why his concern should have been that 'it would be strongly resented in other areas' rather than that it was barred by statute. Finally, the Commissioner asked Forbes Adam whether he really believed that

industrial development in your area is hindered by lack of sites or of factories. Are there not already many empty sites and factories and would the owners ... have a legitimate grievance if we prepared alternative sites and factories and sold or let them at an uneconomic figure'?

The reply from Forbes Adam of 6 August is missing from the files, but from the Commissioner's note quoted below - and from subsequent evidence -, it may be concluded that he strongly advocated both the need to clear sites and to build factories, as well as a new organisation to carry out this task. 'I fully concur', wrote the Commissioner on 8 August 1935,

with the views expressed by Forbes Adam in his letter of 6th inst. It will be an uphill fight to establish industries and the most favourable conditions should be procured. A trading company with a capable organiser has an infinitely better chance of successs than any local authority, or even a Development Council. A great advantage would be that there would be more direct control and management.

The Commissioner's note ended with this instruction to Tribe, his executive secretary: 'therefore, please see what steps can be taken to proceed at Gateshead on these lines' [10].

The Commissioner referred here to the site of a defunct chemical works at East Gateshead which he was negotiating to have cleared. Further reference to this will be made later. It was not, in the event, the site on which the first government-financed trading estate would be built.

By 12 August 1935, the Commissioner had completed a draft memorandum for submission to the Minister of Labour. Before sending it, he circulated it internally for comment. In a letter of the same day to the District Commissioner in Newcastle, Tribe confirmed that the Commissioner had agreed in principle to support trading estates, but that the approval of the government was needed under clause 1(3) of the Special Areas Act. Tribe asked Forbes Adam to comment on the memorandum by return and - in a clear reference to Adam's contribution to the ideas contained in it - Tribe hoped that 'he would not object to certain plagiarisms' he would recognise [11].

The final version of the memorandum is dated 16 August 1935 [12]. It differed from the draft in some important details and, while leaving out certain matters which might have given rise to political debate, it put the case for government-financed factories in the depressed areas more succinctly: it stated that it was part of the Commissioner's policy to stimulate the development of production for local consumption; it made a strong case for providing facilities for small firms to obtain factories without large capital outlay; it explained why there was no prospect of private enterprise establishing trading estates in the Areas and why such a project was unlikely to be economic, at least initially; it rehearsed the limited powers of the local authorities to do more than acquire sites and it examined whether existing public or private organisations could be entrusted with the task.

As the Commissioner had proposed to the Inter-departmental Committee on 26 July 1935 that he might be empowered to put considerable sums at the disposal of the Development Councils for the encouragement of new industries [13], it is clear that a change of view had occurred in the intervening three weeks: 'there are considerable difficulties in associating trading estates too closely with the work of the Development Councils'. The change may have been suggested by Forbes Adam; it was certainly prompted by a realisation that, in the North East at least, the divergence of the interests of the local authorities represented on the Development Councils would make it difficult to reach agreement even on the siting of a trading estate. This interpretation of the change is borne out by an abandoned passage from the draft memorandum: after explaining why none of the available bodies and organisations were suitable to construct and manage publicly-funded trading estates, the Commissioner had suggested that the trading companies to be established 'might be associated in South Wales with the Development Council, but in the North East ... it would be advisable that there should be no organic connection between the two bodies' [14].

The Commissioner was reassuring about subsidies: the factories would not be let at rents below those normally charged in the vicinity; as to finance, 'it would probably be simplest for the whole of the capital to be supplied from the Special Areas Fund'; the trading companies would not be run for profit and 'the element of risk in this venture must be shouldered by the Commissioner'; the trading companies would be managed 'by a small directorate of local persons of standing and it would probably be desirable to have a government representative on the Board'.

In the final paragraph of the memorandum, the Commissioner conceded that the proposal involved the use of Exchequer funds in 'a straightforward commercial enterprise which should normally be financed by private capital and is open to all the objections that such a course calls forth'. He believed, however, that the circumstances were exceptional:-

> Some practical measures have to be taken to offer a definite inducement to industry to establish itself in these (Special) areas ... The proposal ... should be regarded as an experiment. Moreover it is an experiment which will show the faith of the

government in the future of the Special Areas and would be a practical step in carrying out the Commissioner's policy of helping the areas to help themselves.

It was within the Commissioner's remit to experiment, but, although the government itself had frequently referred to the concept of the first Special Areas legislation as experimental, it remained to be seen whether the Commissioner's proposal would strike a responsive chord.

The memorandum was sent to the Minister of Labour on 16 August 1935. In the accompanying letter [15], the Commissioner made reference to the fact that an Inter-departmental Committee had discussed 'once or twice the question of getting trading estates something like those at Slough and Trafford Park established in the Special Areas'. But the concept was apparently considered daring enough to require considerable justification:-

I quite realise that this proposal is novel and in some ways unorthodox. It entails the government entering into trade in land and buildings in competition with other companies. It seems hopeless, however, to expect private enterprise to take the initiative in the way of establishing such estates in these areas and it seems necessary, therefore, for us to tackle the question in as unobjectionable a way as possible.

From the second part of the quotation, it is clear that the Commissioner did not mean to suggest that the government would enter into competition with private commerce in the depressed areas, but rather that it would engage in activities which elsewhere were carried out by private firms. The point is of some importance, because the Treasury had always insisted that unemployment relief schemes - in so far as it had authorised them at all - should not compete with private business [16]. Even if the Treasury would not look upon government-financed trading estates as unemployment relief schemes, the criterion would almost certainly be applied. It was the Commissioner's objective to reassure the Minister on this point.

The letter and memorandum of 16 August were acknowledged by the Ministry of Labour on 25 September 1935. The response was positive: 'we agree, in general and in principle, to the proposals in your memorandum, if a method can be devised of carrying them out within the framework of the Special Areas Act' [17].

The next few weeks were spent in discussions between the Commissioner, the Ministry of Labour, the Board of Trade and the Treasury on the legal implications of the Special Areas Act 1934 for the proposed trading companies. The Act had expressly barred the Commissioner from carrying on any undertaking for the purpose of gain and from providing financial assistance to any undertaking carried on for that purpose, and while clause 1.5. b (i) of the Act allowed for some exceptions, these did not include the circumstances of the trading companies the Commissioner had decided to establish. It would go too far to recite the complicated discussions and the elaborate arguments for or against the view that the proposed trading companies could be fitted into the constricting requirements of the 1934 Act, but some references are given in the footnote [18].

The Commissioner argued that 'although the making of a profit (or a loss) might be incidental to the establishment of the company, it could not be said that the company was established "for the purpose of gain", but rather for the purpose of assisting in the industrial development of the area' [19]. Stuart King, the Solicitor of the Ministry of Labour, was unwilling to give an instant legal opinion on such an apparently unexceptional view of the matter.

The Commissioner appreciated the difficulties but hoped they could be overcome. If not, 'he indicated clearly that he would strongly recommend to the government to alter the Special Areas Act so as to give him the necessary powers' [20].

But that was precisely what the government was not prepared to do. At a meeting at the Board of Trade on 12 October 1935, it was made clear that, while the government would agree to the establishment of industrial estates in the Special Areas on the lines proposed by the Commissioner, it wished to avoid any legislation either to amend the Special Areas Act or to deal with the particular question of the trading companies. Every possible avenue was to be explored to see whether such companies could be framed within the terms of existing statute [21].

The government may well have been concerned that further legislation would have introduced delay; it is much more likely that the government was anxious about the reaction of some of its supporters in and outside Parliament who remained opposed to State trading under any circumstances. There was an implication at the meeting on 12 October that the government would rather abandon the scheme and lose the electoral advantage - which, it will be shown later, was the main object of the exercise - than to have the matter raised in the House. The trading estate scheme was evidently an acceptable political risk only on that condition.

By 14 October 1935, Stuart King had produced a proposal which, in his opinion, would circumvent the difficulties presented by clause 1.5 of the 1934 Act. It involved a two-company structure: a development company - which would receive financial assistance from the Commissioner - and which, in turn, would promote a management company to which it would channel part of the loan from the Commissioner [22]. The question whether there should be a single development company for all the Special Areas of England and Wales was to be settled by the Commissioner. The establishment of such a company would not preclude the formation of subsidiary estate companies in the Areas.

The question was put to the District Commissioners a few days later. From a letter of 24 October it is evident that they were in favour of 'a separate development company as well as a separate estate management company for each area in which an estate is to be established' [23].

In the event, these legal complexities were found to be unnecessary, but the episode showed how unfamiliar the territory was when the government began to intervene in a local industrial context.

The Cabinet did not discuss the proposal - nor the form which government involvement might take - until the middle of October 1935. Because of the General Election on 14 November 1935, a decision could not be delayed any longer.

The matter had been considered, however, by the Inter-departmental Committee. Its report dealt with the First Report of the Commissioner and with his proposals since then, of which the government-financed trading estates was the most important.

The report examined these proposals under three headings [24]:-

a) those which could be accepted in whole or part under existing policy or departmental authority.

b) those open to considerable objections.

c) those open to serious objections.

The Committee placed the Commissioner's trading estates proposal under heading a).

While the Committee found that 'no evidence was adduced that development in the Special Areas is impeded by lack of facilities such as it is proposed should be supplied' - beyond the Commissioner's statement that he was advised to that effect -, it agreed that

the presence of such facilities does attract industry: among the reasons given in the Survey of Industrial Development 1934 for the location of new factories, 'convenience of premises' was the chief consideration of 55 per cent of the cases in which these reasons were ascertained. It is therefore probable that the adoption of the Commissioner's proposals would offer a definite inducement to new industries to settle in the Special Areas.

Since there were very few modern factories to let in the North East, no evidence could have been gathered there on the 'convenience of premises' as a cause for location. The attitude of industry in the event of factories becoming available for rent in the North East could not, therefore, be foreseen. The Committee was aware of this: 'doubt has been expressed whether this inducement would be sufficient to overcome objections on other grounds which might present themselves in the minds of industrialists'. Nevertheless, the Board of Trade representative on the Committee 'was impressed by the necessity for an experiment in inducing industry to settle in the Special Areas', although he agreed rather readily with the Commissioner that 'the operation is unlikely to prove economic'.

The Cabinet Committee discussed the report of the Inter-departmental Committee on 17 October 1935. It spent little time on the trading estates. Chamberlain had evidently made up his mind to agree: 'he was inclined to think that Mr. Stewart had produced a constructive suggestion in his proposal to develop sites in the Special Areas on the lines of Slough and Trafford Park'. He was prepared to accept the Inter-departmental Committee's conclusion that 'a scheme for grant-aiding the formation of trading estates can be worked out [25].

Accordingly, the Cabinet Committee recommended to the Cabinet meeting on 23 October 1935 that most of the report of the Inter-Departmental Committee - which included only an indirect approval of the Commissioner's proposal to finance trading estates out of the Special Areas Fund - should be accepted and the Cabinet agreed [26].

Although it recommended approval, the Cabinet Committee was pessimistic about the prospects for trading estates in the Special Areas. Indeed, it was even more forthright in its doubts than the Inter-departmental Committee [27]:-

We do not believe that the introduction of new industries into the depressed areas is going to play any very large part in the near future in solving the problem of those areas. Speaking generally, we doubt the feasibility of trying to persuade ordinary industry to go into the Special Areas. The influences telling in the other direction seem to be too strong.

Given this judgment, it is not surprising that neither new industries nor trading estates figured in the Special Areas policies advocated by the Cabinet Committee. The policy priorities were as follows:-

In the first place, we think that as many as possible of these people (who cannot find work in the Special Areas) should be settled on the land. Secondly, transference. The necessary extensions to training schemes to be put in hand. Thirdly, those for whom there is no employment and who cannot be moved out of the region should have their lives made more tolerable. We would keep them as contented and happy as circumstances permit.

The policies and the priorities allocated to them prompt several reflections: Pitfield [28] has examined the development of a regional policy between 1934 and 1937 and whether a 'work to the workers' policy began with the decision to authorise the first government-financed trading estates. While his conclusions are tentative, it will be shown here that bringing work to the workers in the North East and other depressed areas was incidental, initially at least, to other considerations, mainly electoral ones; and since - at this stage - the government saw little hope of obtaining new industries, a later date for the beginning of such a policy seems appropriate.

The importance attached to land settlement at the time the 1934 Act was passed has already been noted. It is certainly surprising that 10 months later - and on the day it had authorised government-financed Trading Estates - the Cabinet considered land settlement to be the most promising policy option. This is the more inexplicable because the Commissioner had warned a few months earlier that the high hopes placed in land settlement were quite unrealistic [29]. The policy priority, however, explains the pressures exerted on the Commissioner and why he eventually spent a quite disproportionate amount - in relation to the results achieved - on land settlement schemes (see Appendix 12).

Given the lack of conviction that government-financed trading estates would contribute very much to the solution of the problems of the Special Areas, and the aversion of the government to any intervention of this kind, why did the Cabinet agree to go ahead, nevertheless?

There is no doubt that it was for electoral reasons. Direct evidence for this conclusion quite apart (see [34] below), there is no other explanation for the abrupt change in the government's stance in the run-up to the 1935 General Election. The change is highlighted by an examination of the government's views on intervention at the beginning of 1935.

In January of that year, Lloyd George had made one more bid to lead a reform movement by proposing an expansionary policy based on the New Deal in the USA. His proposals aroused much interest and the government was forced to take notice [30]; it was argued that, while the USA had increased its public debt by $ 17 Billion , Britain had achieved more without increasing debt at all [31]. Chamberlain insisted that there would be no experiments in the direction proposed by Lloyd George. He repeated once more, that the quickest and most effective contribution which the government could make toward an increase in employment was to create conditions which would 'encourage and facilitate improvements in ordinary trade' [32].

But morale in the Special Areas was deteriorating because neither the government's general policies nor the 1934 Act had noticeably improved the situation and pressure for further action was growing, as the reaction in Parliament and outside to the Commissioner's First Report had shown. Furthermore, the newly established development organisations in the Special Areas were becoming increasingly active. The electoral implications of the local pressure was spelled out by Lord Eustace Percy - a prominent politician from the North East and Minister without Portfolio - who was a member of the Cabinet Committee and attended the Cabinet Meeting of 24 October 1935. The weight attached to his views may be inferred from the fact that his contribution to the discussion was the only one minuted in the Cabinet Conclusions [33]:-

Any statement of policy which did not show that the government was doing everything possible to revive the existing industries of the Special Areas, to attract new industries to them and to promote public works in them to meet the immediate needs, would have a disastrous effect on the government's reputation in the Special Areas and in other industrial districts.

The government had become aware that it could not enter a General Election without at least some new initiatives on unemployment.

Direct evidence for the conclusion that the government agreed to finance trading estates for electoral reasons is contained in a confidential document from the Ministry of Labour written in 1937: 'when the government came to draw up their election programme for the 1935 Election, they wanted some novel proposal in regard to the Special Areas; official opposition to Sir Malcolm's (the Commissioner's) proposal (for trading estates) was withdrawn. [34].

This explains the volte-face by the government between February and October 1935. The Commissioner's trading estate proposal was the only practical one on the table and, while the government was aware that it represented an interventionist step, it would be 'respectably cloaked as loans to private enterprise' [35]; in any event, it was likely to be a relatively low-cost exercise.

In the meantime, the discussions on the form of the companies to develop and manage trading estates continued. The two-company structure referred to earlier was put to the Treasury for comment by the Ministry of Labour on 1 November 1935 [36]. A few days later, however, Stuart King reconsidered the constitution of the proposed company, as is evident from a letter from the Ministry of Labour to the Treasury of 7 November 1935 [37]. The reference to 'the proposed company' indicates that this simpler structure was adopted by the legal advisers sometime in the first week of November 1935.

The letter contained a draft modus operandi for the company to be established, including its powers, accounting principles, the rate of interest on the government loan, the rents to be charged, how to deal with the eventuality of a profit or loss, the means of securing the monies to be advanced to the company, etc.

Finally, the letter asked the consent of the Treasury to 'our informing the Commissioner that, subject to the production of the Memorandum and Articles of Association on the lines set out above, we agree to the formation of the Company for the purpose of administering trading estates in Special Areas'.

A draft letter to that effect was included. It contained some spare space, into which the financial requirements were to be inserted. A copy was sent to the Commissioner, with the request to provide them. The reply was inevitably somewhat vague [38]:-

> It is really quite impossible at this stage to give any estimate of cost; we do not know how many companies there will be or how many estates or what will be the size of the estates ... If, however, you must have some figure for the Treasury, I suggest you say that it may be as much as £750,000. My own opinion is that this will prove on the high side, but one never knows .

At the end of October 1935, the National Government issued its election manifesto [39]. Under the heading 'Special Areas', it contained the following reference to the government's intentions:-

> The introduction of new industries into the Special Areas is extremely desirable. As a result of the efforts which have already been made by the Special Commissioners, and of other plans which are under consideration, it is hoped to enter upon new industrial developments including the preparation of a trading estate in which industrialists can find ready-made factories provided with all necessary services.

Following the publication of the manifesto, the Commissioner 'was bombarded by the press with requests for further information on this subject', although no definite scheme was yet ready for presentation to Ministers. The Commissioner felt it necessary 'to be very discreet', and he was embarrassed, if not angered, by the fact that 'the Conservative Central Office and the Board of Trade have been more expansive'. He further believed that an article in the Daily Telegraph of 31 October 1935 on the subject 'must have been inspired to some extent from official sources'. In a letter to the Ministry of Labour of 1 November 1935 - from which the above extracts were taken - the Commissioner felt, therefore, that he was entitled to know 'whether the general outline of the scheme proposed in the memorandum acccompanying my letter of 16 August, as modified by our discussions with Stuart King, is approved in principle and whether we may now consider the selection of sites' [40].

The Ministry of Labour was not able to inform the Commissioner until 21 November 1935 that 'the Treasury agree to the Commissioner and ourselves now going ahead with the consideration of definite schemes for trading estates' [41]. In the same letter, the Commissioner was asked again what he had in mind 'as regards the number, size and cost of the estates which it is proposed to establish'.

The Commissioner replied on 25 November. He was not in a position to give any indication of size or cost, but he did confirm that 'only one trading estate was intended' [42]. The government's election manifesto, too, had referred to a single estate only. This may have been no more than the immediate objective; in his memorandum of 16 August 1935, the Commissioner had proposed another estate in Wales, and in September the Parliamentary Secretary to the Ministry of Labour had expressed the hope that it would be brought into existence soon [43].

Also on the 25 November 1935, the Commissioner informed Lord Ridley, the chairman of the North East Development Board, that 'although many details remain to be settled, I have now been authorised to proceed with the establishment of a trading estate. It is my intention that the first estate should be in or near Tyneside' [44].

The agreement by the Treasury came only just in time to enable the new Prime Minister to make an announcement in Parliament. Baldwin had taken over from Ramsay MacDonald on 7 June 1935 as head of the National Government, but now he was coming to the House after an election victory in his own right. During the Debate on the Address on 3 December 1935, Baldwin replied to a speech by Attlee, the Leader of the Opposition [45]:

> The Rt. Hon. Gentleman said there was nothing in the King's Speech about the Special Areas ... among the major schemes to which I think reference should be made, is the establishment of one or more trading companies charged with the duty of establishing and equipping estates in the Special Areas. The difficult legal preliminaries in this matter are being actively cleared away and there is every intention of proceeding at an early date to a practical issue which will result in factories being built ... to let at economic rents to industrialists who are prepared to establish new industries.

The legal difficulties to which Baldwin referred were related, from then on, to the Memorandum and Articles of Association of the Company to be formed and to the Agreement between the Commissioner and the Company. The discussions would go on for another five months.

One factor which had to be considered was that the Special Areas Act - and with it, the machinery of the Commissioner - was intended to operate for a limited period in the first place, while the administration of trading estates was, clearly, a continuing task. The Public Utility Society status of the trading entity to be established made it necessary to incorporate a Company without shares and limited by guarantee.

In the absence of any policy on the location of industry, the outcome of this first interventionist step was unpredictable, particularly after the almost wholly negative result of the Commissioner's appeal to British industry in the summer of 1935 referred to in II/2. The News Chronicle of 4 October 1935 referred to this and other appeals and noted that 'new factories continue to be put up in the South, largely in the London area'. In the same piece, the Federation of British Industries was quoted as stating that 'the government's appeal had no result', although the point was made that, up to then, rentable factories were available mainly in the London area. There was no evidence yet, however, that the availability of such factories would increase interest in the Special Areas of the North East.

In spite of its pessimistic views of the prospects for attracting industry to the North East and its wish to distance itself from the failure of any of the Commissioner's activities, the government was concerned that the first publicly-financed trading estate should succeed. How concerned may be inferred from a speech by the Prime Minister on 29 November 1935 in Dundee, in which he seemed to raise the creation of new industries in the Special Areas almost to the level of a patriotic duty: 'from every point of view, from the point of view of our very civilisation, I regard the introduction of new industries in some of these Special Areas as being the most important work to which a British citizen can devote his capital and his brains for the benefit of his fellow men' [46].

The battle was won: political pressure in the face of continuing depression in the Areas, che electoral needs of the government, the determination of the Commissioner for the Special Areas of England and Wales to use his remit in a wider sense than the government had foreseen and the persistence of people like Sadler Forster had combined to achieve a small opening towards intervention.

The Commissioner's summary of his reasons for asking the government to permit him to build factories to let in the Special Areas shows that an apologia for departing from economic orthodoxy was evidently still required [47]:-

> Private enterprise has hitherto refrained from establishing trading estates in the Special Areas, presumably because the risk involved is considered too great. The needs of the Areas are such, however, that I came to the conclusion that it was justifiable in the cirumstances to recommend the adoption of the novel and unorthodox proposal of establishing trading estates financed out of Exchequer funds. Practical measures have to be taken to provide inducements, if new industries are to establish themselves in these areas ... While the creation of government-aided trading estates is open to the same objections often advanced with regard to government participation in what is normally private commercial enterprise, it seems less objectionable than other suggestions which have been made for attracting industries to the Areas by some form of government subsidy.

It was probably the first time that any British government had to accept that 'the relatively passive measures that nurtured the early growth of advanced industrial nations were no longer adequate and must be supplemented by more institutional approaches' [48]. While this observation referred to the promotion of industrial activity in under-developed countries, it might well have been made about the Special Areas which, in a sense, had to make a new beginning.

4 The foundation of the company

It was shown in the last chapter that the first government-financed trading estate was to be developed and managed by a special kind of company. The foundation of the Company, the selection of the chairman and directors and the drafting of the terms under which the Company would operate, presented the next tasks for the Commissioner and the government.

It seems to have been assumed in the North East, that the choice of several - if not the majority - of the directors of the Trading Estate Company should be left to the North East Development Board. Lord Ridley had written to the Commissioner on 31 October, suggesting that the Board should set up a sub-committee to nominate its representatives for appointment to the Board [1]. In his reply of 25 November - in which he announced his authorisation to proceed with the Estate -, the Commissioner reverted to this suggestion and agreed to it [2].

On 13 December 1935, the Commissioner suggested to the Ministry of Labour that a Board of seven members should be aimed for, whose composition would be as follows [3]:-

- the chairman (a North East industrialist to be appointed by the Commissioner)
- one government-appointed director
- one industrialist not associated with the North East area to be appointed by the Commissioner
- four directors to be selected by the Commissioner from names suggested by the North East Development Board.

The Commissioner decided that, of the last four, one should be drawn from representatives of Labour interests, and one should be associated with the London and North Eastern Railway Company, if possible.

Given the local and inter-regional differences of interests displayed in the past, it must be considered noteworthy that the Commissioner should have left the choice of four out of seven members of the Board of Directors to the North East Development Board.

In Newcastle, Forbes Adam did not think this would create insuperable problems: 'we shall take steps to see that those recommended by the Development Board are people without local prejudices as far as possible', but he conceded that 'there is bound to be a good deal of local jealousy in regard to the selection of the site, and it would certainly strengthen the hands of the local members to have some colleagues who were entirely impartial and had no local interests' [4].

The selection of the chairman was immediately the most urgent matter. The Commissioner was undecided whether 'it would be better to have some leading industrialist or appoint someone quite independent', he wrote on 7 December 1935 [5]. On this point, the Commissioner considered whether he should ask the managing directors both of the Slough and Trafford Park estates for advice.

Less than a week later, the Commissioner had made up his mind: on 13 December he reported that he had authorised Forbes Adam 'to approach Col. K. C. Appleyard, of the Birtley Iron and Engineering Works, to sound him out as to his willingness to accept the chairmanship' [6].

On 17 December 1935, Lord Ridley, on behalf of the North East Development Board, sent the Commissioner a list of 17 possible candidates for the Board of the Estates Company. The names were chosen from those 'who either live in or represent Special Areas and are members of our Executive Committee', rather than as a result of selection by a sub-Commmittee, which was never formed. There were added four further names of members of the North East Development Board who had been asked to join the executive committee, but who had not yet agreed. Among them was the name of Col. K.C. Appleyard [7].

In a separate hand-written letter of the same day, Lord Ridley gave the names of seven people from the 'offical' list which, 'after discussion with Forbes Adam', he considered 'as the most suitable' in order of naming: C.A. Nelson, Cmdr. E.R. Micklem, W.L. Runciman, W. Westwood, Col. S. Monkhouse, S. Smith and Sir Frank Simpson [8].

In the same letter, Lord Ridley informed the Commissioner that 'Forbes Adam has seen Appleyard and is very hopeful that he will take on the chairmanship'. He suggested that, if the Commissioner agreed to his preferred list, 'Forbes Adam and I discuss these suggestions with Appleyard, who should, after all, be consulted as he is to be chairman, and then approach these individuals'.

It is evident that the selection of Appleyard was decided sometime between 7 and 13 December 1935, and by 17 December it seemed likely that he would accept.

According to anecdotal information, one or more emissaries, possibly from the Commissioner's Office, descended upon Appleyard one evening while he was dining at a Newcastle hotel and asked him to accompany them back to London. Appleyard was to note a few years later 'that he was thrilled at the sudden invitation' [9].

He was certainly well-equipped for the task: he was the managing director of a local engineering firm related to the coal industry and of its West European subsidiaries and associated companies; he had travelled widely in connection with his business interests; he was the chairman of the North East Employers' Association and a member of the Management Board of the Engineering Employers' National Federation, where he had acquired a high reputation as a conciliator between employers and trade unions. He was a member of the North East Development Board and a former member of Durham County Council. Above all, he was a man of exceptional imagination and drive, and he was almost passionately concerned with the well-being of the North East (see also Appendix 9).

On 19 December, the Commissioner expressed his delight that Appleyard had agreed to accept the chairmanship. At the same time, he put forward his own list of candidates for the Board of the Company - which corresponded exactly to Lord Ridley's short list, except that the Commissioner had added the name of Lord Ridley himself [10].

Since the director to be appointed by the government was not included and as there were nine nominations - including the chairman - for seven Board members, it is clear that the names were intended for consideration only.

The list did not find much favour with Appleyard, who displayed an independence of mind from the very beginning: apart from Lord Ridley and W. Westwood, he felt unable to accept any of the other names proposed. On the other hand, he had some suggestions of his own: his nominees were Col. G.H. Walton, a director of Thomas Hedley & Co. Ltd, H.A. Sisson, a partner in a prominent Newcastle firm of chartered accountants, and G.M. Carter, a local businessman who had started a number of small firms in the region [11]. None of these candidates appear to have been members of the North East Development Board. It was almost certainly Appleyard's aim to make the Board of the Estates Company more independent from that organisation.

The Commissioner, on his part, proposed a surprising name for the government nominee: Israel Sieff, a director of Marks and Spencer Ltd, a tribute, perhaps, to the reputation enjoyed by that company already 50 years ago. Lord Ridley wanted time to consider this suggestion and to test reaction in the North East, which was negative. On 23 December 1935, Forbes Adam informed the Commissioner that Lord Ridley was satisfied 'that Mr. Sieff was objected to merely because of the unlikelihood of him being counted upon for practical help' [12]. This may be interpreted to mean that Lord Ridley was anxious for the Commissioner to know that it was Sieff's residence in London, rather than his origins, which made him unacceptable.

The Commissioner persisted: replying to Forbes Adam on 30 December 1935, he wrote [13]:-

While he (the Commissioner) agrees that there should be a predominance of local representation, he still feels that it would be desirable to have somebody from outside the area, and he still favours approaching Sieff both because of the help he might give through Marks and Spencer and because of his interest in government planning through P.E.P. (Political and Economic Planning, see Appendix 11) ... he would not, of course, approach Sieff unless Appleyard was willing.

A note of 3 January 1936 in the Commissioner's files records a telephone call from Forbes Adam to the effect that Appleyard 'welcomed the appointment of Mr. Sieff, provided that it did not exclude Walton and Carter, whom he was particularly anxious to have on the Board', because they would give immediate attention to the work, which Appleyard feared Sieff could not [14].

So keen was the Commissioner to have Sieff that he was willing to increase the number of directors to eight [15]. He wrote to Sieff, and, in a draft list of directors of 9 January 1936, his name actually appeared as the government nominee [16].

Sieff replied on 10 January: he appreciated 'the compliment', but deeply regretted that 'my plate is so full that it is impossible for me to take on any more work ...'. He did offer, however, to help the Board 'in every way possible', particularly, 'when an expanding business (he might came into contact with) looking for a district in which to put up a new factory ... might be directed towards your trading estate' [17].

Sir Eric Bain, a Yorkshire businessman resident at Harrogate was approached next. He agreed to serve subject to Board meetings not conflicting with his regular weekly commitments in London. The records do not indicate how his services were politely declined.

Nor do the records indicate the reasons for the selection of Col. R. Chapman as the Commissioner's representative on the Board of the Company. His name had not appeared in any previous short lists of candidates. His background, however, was not only impeccable (see Appendix 9), he was also connected with South Shields, a part of the area which had not so far contributed a nominee to the short lists.

By the end of 1935, the drafting of the Memorandum and Articles had apparently made good progress. The Commissioner raised no major points at this stage. The Treasury asked that the Articles should make provision to enable the government to acquire the business of the Company [18], a right which would be exercised in 1948. On the same occasion, it was made clear that the director representing the government would be appointed by the Treasury and that his tenure would be at the discretion of the government. The remit of the government appointee was clarified at a meeting at the Treasury on 23 March 1936: he was not to be merely the mouthpiece of the government; he was to be appointed on the same footing as the other directors and to take his full share in the administration of the Estate without any special restrictions or instructions [19]. The records show that Sir George Martin (see Appendix 9), the government's representative, acted at all times with independence. On a number of occasions, indeed, he would be particularly critical of government policies.

Although it had been the Commissioner's intention to ask the directors 'to give their services' [20], the question of their remuneration was, in fact, discussed at some length. In a letter to the Commissioner of 3 January 1936, Stuart King, the solicitor of the Ministry of Labour, conceded that there was nothing against such payments. Nevertheless, he still felt that 'it would be a pity to depart from the simple proposition that financial assistance will be given by the Commissioner to companies if members of the company are entirely precluded from getting any financial benefit out of the company's activity, whether under the guise of a salary or by way of benefit' [21].

The public service aspect of Board membership was evidently considered politically important. This raises the possibility that the Treasury considered the Team Valley Estate, if not as an unemployment relief scheme, at least like one in a political sense. According to Peden [22], the Treasury assumed implicitly that such schemes should be different from 'normal trade' and should not compete with private enterprise. If the directors acted without remuneration, the Company would not be looked upon as a 'normal' business.

In the event, the directors not only acted without payment, they did not even claim their travelling expenses. [23].

So far as the name of the Company was concerned, the Commissioner evidently suggested one which included the term 'Industrial Estate'. Appleyard did not agree: he told the Commissioner that he definitely preferred the description 'Trading' to 'Industrial' Estate [24]. The Commissioner concurred - possibly with some reluctance - 'to abide by the term "Trading Estate"' [25], and the draft Memorandum and Articles were altered accordingly.

It is difficult to understand Appleyard's preference for the term 'Trading Estate'. While Slough Estates Ltd had commenced life as a trading organisation, the North East estate was intended to be of interest mainly to industrial firms. Did Appleyard believe that, from the point of view of attracting tenants, the more accurate description was of lesser importance than an analogous one with the Slough trading estate? Whatever the reason, it is a curious fact that the Company was to resist the change of its name to 'Industrial Estates' once more - and resist successfully - when the government felt in 1946 that this was a more appropriate description, a change, moreover, which was accepted by the other government-financed factory estate companies at the time.

Appleyard, further, wanted the Company to be known as 'North Eastern Trading Estates', because 'although at present only one estate is contemplated, there may be more and he thought the title should envisage the possibility' [26]. This prescient suggestion, too, was accepted by the Commissioner.

By mid-February 1936, the incorporation of the Company had become a pressing matter. The consideration of the Memorandum and Articles of Association and, to an immediately lesser extent, the Finance Agreement between the Commissioner and the Company, required much attention from Appleyard who, as chairman designate, was obliged to act on behalf of a yet non-existing Company and without the benefit of formal advice from a Board.

One significant event in February 1936 was the appointment of Ronald M. Percival as secretary of the Company. A chartered accountant with Price Waterhouse in London, he was born in the North East and wanted to return there. Although only 30 years old and with no company executive experience, he was soon to render distinguished service to the Company. He was one of the small team which Appleyard gathered around him and which he appeared to select with such a sure touch.

The Company's solicitors were (and remain to this day) the Newcastle firm of Wilkinson and Marshall. Their preliminary comments to the Ministry of Labour on the draft Memorandum and Articles were sent on 3 February 1936. These comments were almost entirely of a legal nature. Among the more general ones may be cited their opinion that the principal powers of the Company were too restricted. Given that the Commissioner and the Treasury were going to have such extensive control over the Company, it appeared to them 'that there is no reason for restricting unduly the powers ... which may turn out to be an inconvenience in the future'. They also questioned whether it was desirable to set out precisely what information the Commissioner may ask for before an advance was made, because this would have the effect of 'making the Board think that they are going to be closely supervised' [27].

Appleyard insisted on several additions to the Memorandum: the first concerned the power of the Company to build executive houses. The considerable construction programme in the North East in the late 1920s and early 1930s had provided almost exclusively the smaller type of dwelling and Appleyard feared that the shortage of larger houses might impede the movement of managerial personnel into the region. The Treasury was reluctant to accept this and the Commissioner eventually wrote to the Minister of Labour on 20 March 1936 on the lack of accommodation for 'superior staff, general managers etc.' [28]. The department had taken the view that it was 'contrary to all experience for it to be necessary in a developed area like Tyneside to provide accommodation for higher staff' and that 'powers should not be taken in the Memorandum to provide it' [29]. But finally, the Treasury gave way: 'as (the Commissioner) attaches importance to the Company having powers to provide such houses, we are willing reluctantly to agree' [30]. The permissive clause was subject to such stringent conditions, however, that Appleyard 'was afraid of arguments in each case whether or not an individual house is essential', and he assured the Commissioner that 'the Board desire to have nothing to do with housing if it can avoid it, unless absolutely essential' [31].

There is no evidence that the Company used this power in the early years. At the end of the War, however, the building of executive housing was seriously considered, because a greatly increased factory construction programme would bring many more managers into the region than before the War.

Other requests by Appleyard included powers to utilise land not immediately required for development for the purpose of agricultural schemes for the unemployed - including the construction of greenhouses for intensive cultivation -, and to build a hotel and canteens. Canteens would be included in the first development scheme.

The discussions on the amendments to the Memorandum and Articles carried on for some more weeks; the Company was finally incorporated on 18 May 1936. Just before, Appleyard had contracted Diptheria and had to negotiate from his bedside.

In a lecture to the Royal Society of Arts in the summer of 1939 , Appleyard was able to show that the powers granted to the Trading Estates Company were wide: 'it was ... the intention of the government ... to enable (the Company) to provide any and every service which could be of value to industry and would, therefore, draw new firms to the North East Coast' [32].

The appointment of Appleyard was widely approved locally. The 'Looking Around' column in the North Mail , Newcastle upon Tyne, of 25 February 1936, for example, commented on the man and the task:-

> Colonel K.C. Appleyard, one of Tyneside's best known and most successful industrialists, by accepting the chairmanship of the first Trading Estate Company to be set up under government auspices, goes some distance towards making history and assumes an office which may prove to be one of the most important in all the present endeavours to help on industrial developments in the North East.

The composition of the Board of the Company was announced on 13 March 1936 [33]. The members were Col. K.C. Appleyard, chairman, Col. R. Chapman, representing the Commissioner, Sir George Martin, representing the government, Cmdr. E.R. Micklem, Lord Ridley, H.A.Sisson, Col. G.H. Walton and W. Westwood. The announcement did not end the local representations; on the same day, Mr. Storey (Con., Sunderland), for example, complained in the House of Commons that Wearside was not represented on a Board 'which will choose the site of the proposed estate' [34].

Although the Company had not yet been incorporated, The Daily Telegraph of 13 March 1936 wrote under the heading 'New Industries for the Special Areas': 'yet another form has been given to the Public Utility Society, the compromise devised by this country between private enterprise and Socialism'. Was there a note of alarm in this formulation by the Conservative newspaper, or even a hidden reproof to the government?

The outstanding problems in connection with the Finance Agreement are apparent from a letter Appleyard addressed to the Commissioner on 24 February 1936 [35]. Appleyard reminded him of 'the hesitation of industrial people to come to the North East Coast', and stressed that the conditions to be offered by the Trading Estate Company would have to be very attractive; indeed, 'more attractive than could be offered by an estate company setting up in the ordinary way as a private enterprise on the lines of Slough and Trafford Park'.

Because only a substantial amount of land and the necessary services would make the exercise worth while, it would take many years before any revenue would be earned on the initial expenditure on land and site development. The Company would find it impossible to pay interest on this non-revenue-earning expenditure for a very long time. Appleyard had made enquiries from a private estate company and found that it made no attempt to earn revenue for this part of their enterprise. He believed, therefore, that the expenditure up to what he called 'factory foundation level' should be met by a free grant from the Special Areas Fund, or else, it should be accepted that no interest would be payable until the Board of the Company were of the opinion that the development of the Estate had reached a point where it was in a position to pay. An arrangement on these lines would permit the Company to offer attractive terms in the first few years.

Appleyard asked that monies advanced for the purpose of building factories should be made available at the lowest possible rate, given that the Company was bound to lose money on the provision of some services until a sufficient number of factories were built and tenanted. As the government was able to borrow at 2% interest, Appleyard suggested that the interest rate should not be higher than 3%, and, if at all possible, lower than that.

If effective steps were to be taken to promote the Estate, a significant expenditure on advertising would have to be accepted. Appleyard proposed that this expenditure should be met by a free grant for a period of three years.

In order to distinguish readily between those activities which should bear interest and those which should not, Appleyard suggested that any expenditure which was not bringing in revenue from tenants should be 'on the free list'. Once the Estate was growing satisfactorily, it might be possible to increase rents slightly, but this matter should be left to the Board, 'who have in their minds ... the serious responsibility ... to spend public money'. In the first three years, the important thing was 'to bring people into the Estate'.

The Commissioner sought the advice of the Treasury on the ideas put forward by Appleyard, which implied inducements to the initial tenants, i.e., subsidies [36]. The reply by the Treasury of 27 February 1936 [37] was predictable: 'the short answer to Col. Appleyard is that the grant of special terms as regards rent to tenants would be in conflict with statute'. The letter continued with a piece of curious reasoning: 'I agree, however', wrote the Treasury official, 'that the rents are not to be fixed as such sums as in aggregate produce 4% on the capital outlay. They are to be fair rentals, though we hope that will come to the same thing as 4% on capital'.

Since rents would be the only income of the Company, it is difficult to understand what the Treasury had in mind.

The political constraints of the times did not allow the government to appear to own the Company. There was no alternative, therefore, but to treat it as an ordinary commercial creditor. Hence the requirement, in clause 4 of the Draft Agreement [38], that the Company 'shall forthwith execute in favour of the ... Treasury solicitor a debenture containing a charge by way of a legal mortgage of all the freehold and leasehold property of the Company and a floating charge of its undertaking and of its property and assets both present and future'.

Two clauses in the Agreement dealt with the eventuality of the Company being unable to pay interest and the circumstances in which the Treasury could demand repayment of the advance. Both these were logical requirements in an agreement with a creditor, but since the Company was limited by guarantee, the fiction would have been shown up for what it was if the eventuality envisaged by these clauses had ever arisen.

Before letting any factories, the Company would have to submit the principles of its rent policies for approval; it was also to obtain approval before engaging any officers or staff with an initial salary in excess of £500 and before establishing any superannuation or other benevolent funds or schemes for its employees.

Finally, the rather academic question of what to do with any excess funds was settled: their application was to be a matter of agreement between the Company and the Commissioner. Such funds were defined as those 'in excess of the amounts required to defray expenses, including interest charges, and to provide reasonable reserves to meet upkeep, maintenance, equipment and other contingencies' [39]. It is to be noted, however, that a writing-down of the Company's assets was not included in the definition. The Company considered such a provision a normal and prudent commercial practice and it would even claim later that its auditors might qualify the accounts because of the absence of such a provision [40]. The Treasury, on the other hand, was adamant that it did not want the Company to accumulate funds for this purpose. It seems to have been important for the Treasury to show interest receipts in its accounts, even if in future it would have to re-lend the monies which in a 'normal' business would be found from a sinking fund.

The Commissioner summed up the remit: 'the success of the Company will not be judged by the state of its balance sheet so much as by its success in filling the Estate with new industries at fair rentals. The government do not want a sinking fund on the capital advanced' [41].

The directors never seem to have understood or accepted the needs behind the Treasury's insistence. This may have been connected with the requirements of statute, but it is more likely that there was a political reason. When the Company began to show a surplus in its accounts during the War, the question of depreciation was to cause much argument with the Commissioner and the Treasury.

Appleyard did not succeed in having the interest reduced to below 4%, but the Treasury was moved to accept that the period before interest payments were to start should be increased from three to five years.

The final draft of the Finance Agreement between the Commissioner and the Company was tabled at the first formal meeting of the directors - on 25 May 1936 - and approved, subject to a few minor changes of text. It was not ready for signature, however, because the amount of the advance required could not be known until the scheme for the development of the Estate had been agreed and costed. The matter was eventually disposed of at the meeting of the Board on 7 December 1936.

Reference has already been made to the Commissioner's reluctant guess in November 1935 that £ 750,000 would be required for the Team Valley Estate, a figure he considered to be on the high side at the time. In a radio broadcast on the occasion of the 21st anniversary of the Company in 1957, Appleyard shed an interesting light on the question of the capital required to launch the Estate:-

I was asked for an estimate of the money which would be required for the first two or three years. My guess, which was pure guess work of course, was £1.5 million, and the figure the Treasury had in mind was £300,000 (less than half the rough estimate provided by the Commissioner). So after some considerable discussion, I was asked to revise my estimate, which I did to £3 million, and finally the Chancellor compromised on a figure of £1.5 million to start with, but with the understanding that if the thing went well and showed the results the government hoped it would ... then I had the assurance that money would not be a limiting factor in future development [42].

It is not clear whether Appleyard's 'pure guess' was arrived at before or after the receipt - in March 1936 - of the report of the consultants retained to advise on the scheme. The cost estimate by the consultants proved to be remarkably close to the amount inserted in the Finance Agreement. But before long, the very success of the Team Valley Estate would lead to the need for more money.

The sentiments expressed in [41] above highlighted the ambivalence in the mind of the government: the Company was to have a social purpose - the creation of new employment - but, at the same time, it was to act as a commercial undertaking.

Within these two aspects of the remit - which would be difficult to reconcile -, the directors of the Company saw their first duty to make the undertaking financially viable. Since all but one member of the Board were industrialists or accountants, the emphasis on a commercial approach would, in any event, have recommended itself to them. As a result, the aim of obtaining tenants of any kind became overriding. This was implied already in Appleyard's letter to the Commissioner of 24 February. Table 3 shows that a proportion of the early tenants were not manufacturers, but tradesmen, wholesalers, depots of national companies and transport contractors. Given the reluctance of firms to move in from outside and the limited amount of new enterprise available within the region, the Company had little choice in the selection of tenants, even if the floor area occupied by non-manufacturing firms produced less than optimum employment figures.

But commercial virtue became so ingrained that the Board found it difficult to adapt to political needs as they arose. The first such example occurred within a year, when the government empowered the Commissioner to build factories outside the confines of the Team Valley Estate. The circumstances will be examined in III/5.

5 The choice of the site

The next task for the Company was the choice of the site for the Estate. Reference has already been made to a site at East Gateshead which the Commissioner had considered a possible one. He had authorised a clearance scheme of 120 acres in the spring of 1935 [1], but outstanding difficulties in the acquisition of the land had prevented the start of work. The Commissioner, nevertheless, considered it 'desirable to proceed with the clearance of the site, whether or not it is eventually chosen for the trading estate'. He had, in fact, authorised a further scheme at East Gateshead, which was geographically related to the first [2].

In the meantime, a committee of the North East Development Board had prepared an interim report on possible sites [3]. Four sites were examined in some detail and the committee listed them in the following order of preference:-

- an area south of Jarrow Slake
- the area at East Gateshead where clearance had already been authorised
- an area behind the Northumberland and Albert Edward Docks on the north bank of the Tyne (known as the Wallsend sites)
- Newburn Haugh, west of Newcastle, near the River Tyne.

These sites were surveyed in 1935 by Prof. G.H.J. Daysh, of the Department of Geography at Armstrong College [4] (now the University of Newcastle upon Tyne), at the request of the North East Development Board.

The committee set out 'fully and fairly the advantages of each site', but insisted 'that it was for others to assess and judge' [5]. Like the committee, Prof. Daysh had favoured Jarrow because of its central position in relation to South Shields and Sunderland, two boroughs suffering from severe unemployment [6].

The Commissioner concluded that it was not possible for him to select a site. That was to be a matter for the Trading Estate Company. In order to enable the Company to reach an early decision after its formation, the Commissioner proposed that a firm of consultants should carry out 'an independent and expert examination of the four sites', and he hoped that their report would be available, together with the interim report of the North East Development Board, for consideration by the directors at their first meeting [7]. The appointment of the consultants would be deferred, however, until after a planned visit by the Commissioner to the North East.

On 8 January 1936, the Commissioner met Appleyard in London and 'was most impressed' [8]. The mutual respect of these two men was to prove of great importance for the success of the enterprise.

It was on this occasion that Appleyard persuaded the Commissioner 'to include the Team Valley south west of Gateshead (in his planned site visits), which he (Appleyard) was inclined to select'.

At this stage, Appleyard appears to have shared the view, widely-held locally at the time, that the Estate would have to be provided with sea access, and since the Commissioner was reported to 'have indicated his willingness to consider building a canal from the Tyne up to the Estate if (the Team Valley) site was selected' [9], it may be concluded not only that his mind was still quite open, but also that Appleyard's early advocacy of the Team Valley site - which was not included in the interim report of the North East Development Board - had impressed the Commissioner.

Prof. Daysh had pointed out that the sites he was asked to examine did not exhaust the possibilities and, by way of example, he had cited the Team Valley 'which may well offer particular advantages for development along trading estate lines' [10]. The idea of developing the northern part of this valley and joining it by means of a canal to the River Tyne had been considered in 1926 [11], and a Town Planning Report of 1928 had designated some parts of the valley for industrial use.

The Commissioner came to Tyneside at the beginning of February. According to the Evening Chronicle , Newcastle upon Tyne, of 4 February 1936, he visited sites at Salt Meadows (East Gateshead), Jarrow (Tyne Dock), Whitburn (Sunderland), Willington and Wallsend in the company of of Lord Ridley, Appleyard, Forbes Adam, Prof. Daysh and an official from his office. The local newspapers seem to have convinced themselves that the Salt Meadows site was the favourite. Thus, the Evening Chronicle reported, under the headline 'Trading Estate Site Search' that 'a party visited Gateshead and spent some considerable time at the Salt Meadows site, which is regarded in many quarters as the probable position of the trading estate', and the North Mail , Newcastle upon Tyne, wrote on 5 February, under the heading 'Tyneside Trading City Move': 'the Saltmeadows site at Gateshead is expected to be chosen for the experimental trading estate on Tyneside'. The Manchester Guardian of the same day was less definite, but gave some additional information on the same site:-

> Newcastle Corporation has already decided to sell its portion of the Saltmeadows Estate to Gateshead Corporation for £14,000 if the site is chosen. Permission to build a riverside quay is included in the deal provided that the quay is not used in competition with the Newcastle Corporation's quays on the north bank of the river.

Again, the assumption that a trading estate would require river and sea access˜ seems to have been made as a matter of course, even if Prof. Daysh does not recall that this was ever particularly stressed in discussions [12].

None of the newspapers quoted mentioned the Team Valley. It is likely, therefore, that the Commissioner visited this site in the company of Appleyard only and in private.

The expert firm appointed to advise on the site was Sir Alexander Gibb and Partners. They were well qualified for the assignment: they had been associated with some of the privately-financed trading estates which were constructed after the first world War in and around London and they had a close knowledge of the Park Royal estate in West London.

According to their report of 13 March 1936 [13], only two sites had been specifically referred to them at this stage: one at Jarrow and one at Gateshead.

The site at Jarrow was that at the top of the list of the report by the North East Development Board. The site at Gateshead, however, was not the second one on this list, but a site at the 'Team River Valley'. The consultants were instructed by Appleyard at a meeting on 5 February 1936, but the decision to leave aside three of the four sites recommended by the North East Development Board - in the first instance at any rate - and to include the Team Valley, is likely to have been agreed by the Commissioner. The consultants were instructed to make a preliminary report

> on the feasibility, from an engineering point of view, of constructing trading estates on these sites ..., to provide an approximate estimate of the amount of money involved in preparing the estates ready for building purposes ..., and ... to indicate generally the lines on which the estates could be efficiently and economically laid out .

Their report on the Jarrow and Team Valley sites stated at the outset that, 'from an engineering point of view there are no unsurmountable difficulties in the way of ordinary development, but if we are to advise on the <u>feasibility</u> of the site, it is, we feel, necessary to consider other aspects than that of purely engineering'.

This was exactly what Appleyard had encouraged them to do: 'he would welcome (their) views and experience in such matters'. As a result, the consultants described, first of all, 'what a trading estate is intended to achieve', before reporting on the feasibility of any particular site.

The justification for quoting at length from the reports of the consultants is twofold: they led to the abandonment of the sites previously considered locally and to the choice of Team Valley on the one hand, and much of the advice they contained was to determine the policies and practices of the Trading Estate Company, on the other.

The report of 13 March 1936 began by examining the circumstances which led to the extensive factory development in the South East of Britain in the period after the first world War, and, in particular, after 1926. The consultants presumed that Appleyard had in mind 'to reproduce this development on the North East Coast'.

One of the first matters discussed in the report was the question of sea access for the proposed estate, which was looked upon 'not only by the Tyne Improvement Commission, to whom this view naturally presents itself, but also to others as almost a sine qua non '. The consultants gave it as their considered opinion that 'for the particular objects that you have in mind, it is largely, if not entirely unnecessary'.

In this connection, the report referred to the intention to introduce light industries into the Special Areas, even if Appleyard had spoken of 'flour mills and soap factories', which the consultants considered 'light heavy'. They quoted the experience of those private trading estates which were the most successful in attracting light industries, i.e. Slough, Welwyn, Letchworth and Park Royal: none of these had any deep water access, and although Slough was served by the Grand Union Canal, this was of such negligible importance that no reference was made to it in the publications of the estate company.

The consultants advised, therefore, that sea transport should be disregarded, and that at least half the likely tenants on the Estate would not require rail connections either. They pointed out that the Park Royal Estate had no rail connections at all.

From the point of view of market access, these arguments were perhaps less relevant - all the estates mentioned were in London or had easy road access to the London market - than the fact that, on the home market at least, the products of the light industries were no longer transported by sea and increasingly less by rail.

Regarding other important considerations, the report underlined the following:

The best location for a trading estate was on a main road. Sites on such a location would be worth at least twice as much for many industries as sites on by-roads. Really noxious and offensive trades had to be excluded, because 'many businesses set considerable store, from the advertising point of view, on amenities and the country-like nature of their surroundings'. On the other hand, 'there would have to be a reasonable freedom with regard to smoke and effluent, subject always to their not being a nuisance'.

As for selling or leasing land - and in the latter case, whether for short or longer terms -, the consultants 'found most satisfactory a lease of, say 21 years (with optional breaks at seven and fourteen years), with option to buy; it is not essential, but the absence of such options certainly restricts the number of enquiries for sites'.

With regard to the method to be adopted in offering factory buildings, experience in and around London was drawn upon once more: 'on the whole, it is, of course, much more satisfactory to build specially for each tenant than to build speculatively. The type of business that looks for a new, specially designed factory is obviously likely to be more stable and more desirable as a tenant'.

The report noted that the availability in advance of requirement of factories of standard design ('stock factories') had proved effective in attracting tenants but that such factories should not exceed 25,000 sq.ft. in floor area. 'Anything larger is very difficult to get rid of and requires, generally, extensive alterations'. On the question of permitting suitable tenants to build their own factories, the report was in favour.

The report pointed out that some estates - notably Slough - insisted on controlling all public services. While this was not satisfactory to every tenant, it was advisable, provided the terms and conditions were flexible. The object should be to ensure as much control as was necessary to preserve amenities, but no more.

So far as the Jarrow site was concerned, the report found that the proposed areas were too different in character for development as a single estate; the report described the area south and above the Newcastle to South Shields Road as High Jarrow. This area, if all of it had been available, extended to about 285 acres. Apart from the fact that the land sloped rather steeply towards the main road and there were some problems with rail access and trade effluent disposal, the site was considered to be 'fairly good', but

it is not immediately close to populous areas, has little positional value from the point of view of advertising, and no special attraction. We would class it only as second rate, unless there were a much greater shortage of available space than is the case.

The report described the areas of land north and below the Newcastle to South Shields Road as Low Jarrow. The main attraction of this site was that it provided ready access to the River Tyne. It formed the hinterland of developments proposed at that time by the Tyne Improvement Commission at Jarrow Slake. The consultants suggested that the area should be earmarked for use by larger and heavier industries requiring deep-water access, rather than for a trading estate intended to attract light industries.

In contrast with High Jarrow, the section of the report dealing with the Team Valley site opened with a wholly positive view: 'in our opinion, and from the point of view from which we have approached the question, there is no doubt that the Team Valley site is very well suited for the development of a trading estate'. The report made it clear, however, that if a large canal to the Tyne and a private wharf were essential, there would be considerable engineering difficulties, although such a scheme was possible. So far as private rail connections were concerned, the cooperation of the Railway Company would be necessary, although it was reiterated that 'the necessity and advantages of a private rail seem somewhat unsubstantial'.

Apart from the problems of the canal and rail access, the site was considered admirable:-

> It offers a real opportunity for an attempt to develop in attractive surroundings - an object that has been too often ignored in the past. There is a large area, reasonably flat, which lies close to the populous areas and can be well served by roads. It has positional value, being conspicuous from the main railway line, and can be seen from the Great North Road. From the engineering point of view, there are really no serious difficulties. We have assured ourselves on such matters as drainage, foundations etc.

The consultants discussed the questions of subsidence and were satisfied that this was not likely to be a problem; there had been very little mining under the site and the upper coal seam was absent. The consultants ignored, however, the complicated question of mineral rights, which would lead to protracted negotiations with the owners (see next chapter).

Among the more detailed proposals which were later to be adopted, an arterial road through the proposed estate may be noted, as also the suggestion that the River Team should be straightened and deepened to afford better drainage, 'but not so as to make it navigable'. Nevertheless, the suggestion involved, in the event, one of the largest river diversion schemes ever undertaken in Britain up to then [14].

The consultants presumed that 'the leases would, of course, be full repairing leases', a recommendation which was later adopted by the Company and which was to become the cause of more disagreement with its tenants than any other, particularly when the factories aged and, at the same time, cost-inflation created financial problems for some smaller firms which had failed to make adequate provisions.

The question of amenities was not ignored in the report, particularly the provision of green spaces to serve both the estate and the wider area. So far as the large existing playground known as 'The Lido' was concerned, however, the report expressed the hope that it would not be considered essential to preserve it, as this would 'prevent the most satisfactory development'.

Excluding the extreme western strip of the site - which was not considered suitable for industrial purposes -, there would be available 625 acres for development. Some later land purchases increased the site to about 700 acres.

The report estimated that the costs of developing the site and the construction of factories on 60 acres in the first place would be about £1.5 million. This was a great deal more than the upper limit estimated by the Commissioner a few months earlier. Although the outline development plan by the consultants was considerably revised in the event, their recommendation regarding the extent of the first stage of factory building was adopted.

On 30 March 1936, the directors held a preliminary meeting, although the Company had not yet been incorporated. The main item on the agenda was the site. The Board decided to ask the consultants to prepare reports on two additional sites. The minutes of the meeting do not give any reasons, but it is clear from the record of the next Board meeting that one of the directors had favoured a site at Wallsend, and another director one at Whitburn. The latter site was also pressed by some Members of Parliament for Durham constituencies [14]. It should be added that an offer of a site was also received from the County Borough of West Hartlepool [15]. The choice of the site was evidently a highly political matter.

The first site to be investigated under the latest remit was in the Wallsend area (the third site reported by the North East Development Board). It was really a collection of sites with a total area of 1,730 acres, which the consultants divided, for practical purposes, into six separate sections. Each was reported on, but it would go too far to discuss the findings in detail here. The general impression given in the report of the consultants of 17 April 1936 [16] was one of problems, and for some sections of the site, of unsuitability.

The second site was at Whitburn, between South Shields and Sunderland and slightly inland (it was also referred to as the East Boldon site). The conclusion of the consultants was that the site - which was considered in four separate sections - had possibilities, and that 'the provision of all the necessary services would certainly offer less difficulty than at Wallsend'.

Nevertheless, the verdict on the Wallsend and Whitburn sites was less than favourable: 'while from the engineering and physical aspects ... both sites are capable of development as small trading centres, ... neither is ideal for that purpose'.

The consultants then tested the general suitability of the sites against the following criteria - as they had done in the case of the Jarrow and Team Valley sites: positional value, nearness to market, availability of labour, convenience of road, rail and sea transport and amenities. They concluded that 'under none of these heads would we rank either estate as high as the Team Valley site'. A further argument in favour of Team Valley was that it was situated 'immediately adjacent to far the most continuous populated area on the North East coast'.

In its final pages, the report of 17 April 1936 went well beyond an appraisal of the sites:-

> It would, ... in our opinion, be an entirely incorrect policy to decide on the location of an industrial estate according to the number of unemployed in the vicinity. As we understand it, the ultimate objective of the Trading Estate is to assist the unemployment problem in the Special Areas by the general increase of industry and prosperity in the whole area ... No trading estate could, we feel, be successfully run if it were looked at in any way as a kind of unemployment relief work. The tenants of the estate will come to it if and because they feel that they will then be able, not only to manufacture, but to dispose of their products with special advantage ... It is primarily to sell products and not to secure labour that they will come North. It. is, therefore essential, in our opinion, that the site chosen should be central psychologically rather than geographically.

The consultants' views on the beneficial effects of a major trading estate on the wider area coincided with those of the Commissioner and of Appleyard. Similar views appear to have been held at least by some members of the North East Development Board: according to a newspaper report of 8 January 1936 - some weeks before the consultants were appointed -, Lord Ridley, the chairman of the Board, commented on the attempts by representatives of both Newcastle and Gateshead to secure the trading estate for their respective towns: 'while I welcome this enthusiasm for the establishment of a trading estate, I feel ... that it would be a pity if the proposal gave rise to local jealousy and rivalry ... The establishment of such a trading estate ... would benefit the whole area and not only the immediate vicinity' [17].

Newcastle and Gateshead apart, the main local authorities in the North East were soon to take a different view, in which they would be supported less than a year later by the Labour Party Commission of Enquiry into the Distressed Areas. The Commission argued strongly against the notion that a single large trading estate would improve the prosperity of the whole area. Indeed, it claimed that such a focus of attraction might seriously impair the interests of other parts of the region [18].

The consultants had anticipated this view - and the reaction of the local authorities which shared it - in their report of 17 April 1936:-

> Although it is not specifically included in your reference to us, we would venture to add here a warning against allowing the inevitable conflict of local interests to result in an attempt at the establishment of more than one trading estate. We feel that if two or more trading estates were now to be established on the North East Coast, the success of the whole scheme would be seriously jeopardised.

This was practical advice, intended for the near future. As for the longer term, the consultants showed remarkable prescience: 'ultimately, when the idea of a trading estate is no longer novel and when the scheme has proved successful in the one case, other trading estates will almost automatically follow'.

But in the meantime, 'your main difficulty will be to secure a satisfactory initial nucleus of factories. Industries have to be induced to come from outside into this area. It must be a difficult matter, and efforts should not be dissipated over rival estates'.

As to the cause of this difficulty, the consultants reflected the contemporary view about the region when they wrote: 'many financial interests in the City (of London) are convinced that the North is dead or moribund. The business and trading view is that although there are millions living in the North, they have no money to spend'. But this view might change: 'once ... this mass pessimism with regard to the North is dissipated, and once it is realised that there are very large markets in the North ..., then, other things being equal, a flow to the North may be expected'.

The context in which this was written must be taken into account: apart from the attractions of the Team Valley Estate itself, there were no financial inducements to industry, and a location of industry policy would not be introduced for more than another nine years.

The consultants were not unmindful of the employment interests of other main centres of population at some distance from the Team Valley:-

> The position of Sunderland and South Shields requires special consideration. We feel that their interests should be safeguarded in the matter of the Trading Estate by the provision of special inducements to tenants of the Estate to employ a percentage of labour from these areas, and at the same time by the provision of special facilities to enable labour from Sunderland and South Shields to take full advantage of the opportunity offered by the Trading Estate .

The question whether it was realistic to include places up to 17 miles away in the assumed labour catchment area of the Team Valley Estate will be discussed briefly in III/6. As to the fare subsidies implied in the last quotation, the Commissioner would later rule them out [19].

The minutes of the second preliminary meeting of the Board of the Company on 20 April 1936 do not record any discussion of the relative merits of the sites, let alone a consideration of any wider regional issues which might have affected the choice. They merely reveal that six of the eight directors, i.e. all but Mr. W. Westwood and Col. R. Chapman - who represented strong local interests - voted for the Team Valley site in the first ballot. Mr. Westwood, who had been in favour of the Wallsend sites, stated before the second ballot that, 'in view of the report of Sir Alexander Gibb and Partners, he was prepared to alter his opinion and vote for the Teams site'. After some discussion, the Board resolved to buy the Team Valley site. Col. Chapman, however, voted against this site in the second ballot. In his opinion, 'the Whitburn site was the best'. There was some irony in his position as the appointee of the Commissioner, who wrote on the following day: 'my own feeling, after inspecting various sites under contemplation, is that the Team Valley site is on the whole the most favourable. It certainly affords wonderful opportunities for expansion should the Trading Estates Company meet with success. I, therefore, unhesitatingly approve of its choice'. 'It is gratifying', he added, 'that Colonel Appleyard's first choice should receive such substantial support from his Board' [20]. Prof. Daysh recalls that the Commissioner was particularly impressed by the fact that an Estate at Team Valley would be highly visible from the main London railway line [21].

The directors were pledged to secrecy, and it was decided that 'as a matter of prudence it would be well ... to make similar enquiries in one or two alternative Areas'. Col. Turnbull of Chester le Street was asked to act as land agent.

The need for secrecy was explained by Percival, the first secretary of the Estates Company, who was present at the Board Meeting of 20 April 1936: 'the site was owned by a few large and many small landowners, including allotment holders. The buying of the site had to proceed with some discretion if we were to obtain it at a reasonable price' [22]. The same discretion might limit the rise of land values in the neighbourhood of the site. Such rises had occurred in the vicinity of some of the private trading estates and had increased the cost of acquiring land for housing and amenities.

The feasibility of acquiring an additional site with direct sea access for the heavier industries was discussed by the Board on the same occasion. In this connection, a portion of the Jarrow site and a 30 acre site cleared by the local authority at South Shields were mentioned. One of the directors - Cmdr. Micklem - was 'strongly of the opinion that it would be a mistake for the Company to dissipate its energies'. It was decided, nevertheless, to ask the land agent to make enquiries, and the possibility was mooted of acquiring an option on one of the sites.

Given the diverse ownership, the purchase of the site took time: one or two of the small allotment holders were unwilling to sell, and compulsory purchase was considered at one stage [23]. The negotiations with a coal mining concern regarding mineral rights were complicated, and the possibility that large parts of the site might have to be sterilised for many years had to be faced. This and related matters will be discussed further in the next chapter. It will suffice here to note that the problems encountered were such that the abandonment of the Team Valley site had to be contemplated at one stage [24]. Indeed, enquiries were made about every available piece of land on either side of the North Road between Newcastle and Darlington, in case it came to the worst [25]. Nothing suitable was found, but mineral rights would have been a problem almost everywhere in the North East.

The Company had informed the Commissioner on 18 July 1936 that 'the site for this Company's first Estate has been chosen' [26]. The delay in announcing the site not only caused public uncertainty, it provided local interests with further opportunities to press the claims of their localities. By early August 1936, the negotiations about mineral rights appeared to make reasonable progress and it was decided, therefore, that the announcement of the decision to build the Estate at Team Valley could no longer be held up. With the Commissioner's authority, the decision was communicated to the press on 10 August 1936. According to the North Mail , Newcastle upon Tyne, of 11 August 1936, the official announcement by the Estates Company contained the following:-

> Subject to the satisfactory completion of outstanding points of negotiation, the Team Valley has been selected by the directors of North Eastern Trading Estates Ltd for the creation of the first estate under the scheme initiated by the Commissioner for the Special Areas ... The most meticulous care has been exercised in the selection of the site, and several possible locations in widely different parts of the North East area have been examined.

> The Team Valley was finally selected out of a large number of suggested sites on account of its size, attractive surroundings, suitability for development, its location as a centre for distribution - both local and national -, its ease of communication by road, rail, river and sea, and for the opportunity it affords for future possible needs of housing development for workers employed there. The central location of the Team Valley, coupled with the present-day mobility of labour will, as the estate develops, ensure that workers residing on both Tyneside and Wearside will share in the opportunities for employment which the estate will offer. In any case, special facilities for easy access to the estate will not be difficult to arrange.

The announcement gave details of the boundaries of the Estate; it reiterated the beautiful surroundings and the immediate reach of a large dormitory area and it stressed the suitability of the site for rapid economic development.

The North Mail , Newcastle upon Tyne, of 11 August 1936 considered the choice of the Team Valley site a wise one. The published comments by civic dignitaries and Members of Parliament in the the Newcastle and Gateshead areas were, naturally, equally favourable.

Yet there were losers, and a feature writer in the North Mail on the following day took account of their disappointment: 'the official announcement to locate the first State-guaranteed trading estate on Tyneside is causing other hard-hit areas to ask, "why not in Sunderland", and "why not in South West Durham"'? But the writer offered some hope to these areas: 'whatever its constitution may permit, North Eastern Trading Estates Ltd does by its title suggest the possibility of more to follow once the Tyneside venture has been established' [27].

The Times of 12 August 1936 was not concerned with the local implications of the choice. After reminding its readers that 10 months had passed since the project had been mentioned in the government's election manifesto, its impatience at the delay had now given place to a sense of relief that 'the most promising of all experiments designed to help the Special Areas has been actively begun'.

REFERENCES AND NOTES

II/1. The 1934 Special Areas Act

[1]   HC Deb 287, 1402.
[2]   "   , 1510.
[3]   Wrench, Sir Evelyn, 1955.
[4]   Times Newspapers Ltd., 1952, p.884.
[5]   Booth, Alan E., 1978, p.141.
[6]   For example, HC Deb 292, 1801: Mr. Curry, (Lib., Durham, Bishop Auckland), 'the Nation is indebted to The Times ... The Minister will agree that (the articles) were the chief cause of the Investigators which have been sent to the depressed areas'. Also HC Deb 295, 227,228: Mr. Macmillan (Cons., Stockton on Tees), 'it would not be an exaggeration to say that the decision of the government to make these appointments was brought about ... largely as a result of the articles which appeared in The Times ... which revealed for the first time to many southern readers the full amount of distress'.
[7]   CAB 23/78, Agenda (26.3.1934) and CC 13 (34), 28.3.1934, minute 14.
[8]   T 172/1827, Chamberlain to Betterton, 16.4.1934.
[9]   CAB 23/78, CC 14 (34), 11.4.1934, minute 1.
[10] RIDT, 1934, section 1, A.1, p.69.
[11] Op.cit.5, p.144.
[12] Op.cit.10, para.92, p.108.
[13] T 172/1827, Betterton to Chamberlain, 20.4.1934.
[14] Op.cit.10.
[15] CAB 27/578, DA, Minutes, 1st meeting, 11.10.1934, p.2.

[16]   Op.cit.10, para.30, p.82.
[17]   Op.cit.10, para.90, p.106.
[18]   Quoted in Forster, Sadler S.A., ca. 1965.
[19]   CAB 58/12, ECA, (H) 138, memorandum by C.R. Attlee, 9.2.1931, point 9.
[20]   Op.cit.10, para.91, p.107.
[21]   Op.cit.10, para.38 (3), p.85.
[22]   Op.cit.5, p.144.
[23]   CAB 27/577, DA [ID], CP 220 (34), Memorandum, 2.10.34.
[24]   Op.cit.10, para.38 (3), pp.85,85.
[25]   CAB 27/577, DA, CP 227 (34), Report.
[26]   CAB 27/577, DA, CP 246 (34), Report, 6.11.1934.
[27]   RIDT, 1934, para.1, p.69: 'remedies of a long-term nature cannot by any possibility be contained within narrow limits, but must of necessity be considered in their relation to a wider area', and para.93, p.109: 'to schedule particular spots in the area for special treatment is not ... a practical proposal'.
[28]   Op.cit.25, point 2.
[29]   HC Deb 293, 1987.
[30]   "   , 1998.
[31]   "   , 1994.
[32]   "   , 2080.
[33]   "   , 2091.
[34]   Boothby, R. et al., 1927.
[35]   HC Deb 293, 2093.
[36]   Op.cit.27, para.48, p.89.
[37]   Royal Commission on Local Government in the Tyneside Area, 1937, chapter IX, Summary, p.73.
[38]   Royal Commission on Local Government in England, 1969.
[39]   Local Government Act 1985, 16.7.1985.
[40]   For example, HC Deb 304, 242, Mr. Scrymgeour Wedderburn, (Cons. W. Renfrew).
[41]   Preamble to the Special Areas Act, 21.12.1934.
[42]   CAB 27/577, DA [ID] (34) 10, Report, 11.1.1937.
[43]   HC Deb 295, 29.
[44]   HL Deb 95, 617 - 648.
[45]   HC Deb 296, 608.
[46]   HC Deb 304, 227.
[47]   CSAEW, 1935, 1st Report, para. 6, p. 5.
[48]   CSAEW, 1936, 3rd Report, para.95, p.31.
[49]   Op.cit.5, pp.148,149.
[50]   T 172/1828, unsigned note to Chancellor of the Exchequer, 25.1.1935.
[51]   CSAEW, 1935, 1st Report, para.47, p.23.
[52]   Op.cit.50.
[53]   Dennison, S.R., 1939, p.101 & p.169.
[54]   Pitfield, D.W., 1978, p.436.
[55]   Op.cit.5, pp.143,144.
[56]   CAB 27/578, DA, Minutes, 6th meeting, 15.7.1935.
[57]   For example, LAB 223/176, District Commissioner (Forbes Adam) to Commissioner, 17.4.1936.
[58]   CAB 27/578, DA, Minutes, 7th Meeting, 8.10.1935, p.6.
[59]   CSAEW, 1936, 3rd Report, paras.17-39, pp.5-14.
[60]   CSAEW, 1937, 4th Report, para.42, p.12.

II/2. Government-financed Trading Estates: Origins

[1]   Fogarty, M.P., 1945, p.178.
[2]   RCDIP, 1940, p.283.
[3]   Ibid, p.285.
[4]   CAB 27/577, DA [ID] (34) 4, Report, 27.9.1935, para.84, p.21.
[5]   Ibid.
[6]   Richardson, Harry W., 1967, p.277.
[7]   CSAEW, 1936, 3rd Report, para.28, p.10.
[8]   Ibid., para.21, p.7.
[9]   Op.cit.4.
[10] RIDT, 1934, para.38 (3), p.85.
[11] Ibid.
[12] North East Development Board, 1936, pp.17,18.
[13] Tyneside Industrial Development Board, 1936, p.25.
[14] Tyneside Industrial Development Board, 1937, p.21.
[15] The Journal , Newcastle upon Tyne, 31.05.1966, Trading Estates
      Review, on the 30th anniversary of the Company.
[16] RCDME, 1937 - 1938, minute 5, 3.2.1938.
[17] CSAEW, 1935, 1st Report, para.25, p.14.
[18] BT 104/1, Commissioner, internal memorandum, Tribe to Ryan,
      7.12.1934.
[19] CSAEW, 1936, 2nd Report, para.17, p.6.
[20] RIDT, 1934, paras.32-35, p.83.
[21] Board of Trade, 1936.
[22] Heim, Carol E., 1983.
[23] Op.cit.21.

II/3. The Crucial Months

[1]   HC Deb, 304, 279.
[2]   " , " , 242.
[3]   CAB 27/578, DA, Minutes, 7th meeting, 8.10.1935, p.9.
[4]   CAB 27/578, DA, Minutes, 6th meeting, 15.7.1935, pp. 4,5.
[5]   Ibid, p.4.
[6]   HC Deb 304, 1669.
[7]   HL Deb 95, 617 - 648.
[8]   Personal interview with Prof. Daysh.
[9]   BT 104/23, Commissioner (Tribe) to District Commissioner (Forbes
      Adam), 29.7.1935.
[10] BT 104/23, Commissioner to Tribe, 8.8.1935.
[11] BT 104/23, Commissioner (Tribe) to Forbes Adam, 12.8.1935.
[12] BT 104/23, memorandum headed 'Trading Companies', 16.8.1935.
[13] BT 104/23, Commissioner (Tribe) to Inter-departmental Committee,
      paper S.A.1, 26.7.1935, referred to in op.cit.12, para 6, (iii).
[14] BT 104/23, memorandum headed 'Trading Companies', 12.8.1935.
[15] BT 104/23, Commissioner (Tribe) to Min. of Labour (Buxton),
      16.8.1935.
[16] Peden, G.C. 1984, p.171.
[17] BT 104/23, Min. of Labour (Allen) to Commissioner (Tribe),
      25.9.1935.
[18] For example, BT 104/23, undated memorandum by Allen, Min. of
      Labour, BT 104/23, Min. of Labour, internal memorandum King to
      Allen, 7.10.1935, BT 104/23, Commissioner, internal minute from
      Tribe to W.F.T. Dalton and Ryan, 27.9.1935, BT 104/23,
      Commissioner, internal memorandum from Dalton, 2.10.1935.

[19]   BT 104/23, Commissioner, internal memorandum from Tribe to Dalton
       and Ryan, 3.10.1935.
[20]   BT 104/23, Commissioner (Tribe) to Min.of Labour (Allen),
       3.10.1935.
[21]   BT 104/23, Commissioner, internal memorandum from Tribe,
       12.10.1935.
[22]   BT 104/23, Scheme XY attached to a note from King (Min. of Labour
       to Lionel Cohen KC, 15.10.1935.
[23]   BT 104/ 23, Commissioner (Tribe) to Min. of Labour (Allen),
       24.10.1935.
[24]   CAB 27/577, DA [ID], Report, DA (34) 4, 27.9.1935.
[25]   CAB 27/578, DA, Minutes, 9th meeting, 17.10.1935, point 4.
[26]   CAB 23/ 82, CC 48 (35), 23.10.1935, para.13.
[27]   CAB 27/577, DA, CP 197 (35), Report, 18.10.1935, para.9.
[28]   Pitfield, D.W., 1978, p.431.
[29]   CSAEW, 1935, 1st Report, para.83, p.37.
[30]   Winch, Donald, 1972, p.222.
[31]   T 172/1828, unsigned note by Treasury official to Chancellor,
       10.3.1937, probably a brief for a speech.
[32]   HC Deb 297, 2209.
[33]   Op.cit.26.
[34]   BT 104/27, 'Confidential Note on the Team Valley Trading Estate',
       for Parliamentary Secretary, Min. of Labour, undated, but ca.
       September 1937, quoted by Heim, Carol E., 1984, footnote 31,
       p.540. A Board of Trade Note of 12.3.19327, quoted in Booth, Alan
       E., 1978, footnote 63, p.156, is phrased in almost identical
       words. The author is indebted to Heim and Booth for drawing
       attention to this information.
[35]   BT 104/27, 'Confidential Note on Team Valley Trading Estate',
       12.3.1937, quoted in the paper by Booth referred to in op.cit.34,
       p.151.
[36]   This is implied in BT 104/23, Min. of Labour to Treasury
       (Gilbert), 7.11.1935.
[37]   Ibid.
[38]   BT 104/23, Commissioner (Tribe) to Min. of Labour (Allen),
       9.11.1935.
[39]   Joint Election Manifesto, 1935.
[40]   BT 104/23, Commissioner (Tribe) to Min. of Labour (Allen),
       1.11.1935.
[41]   BT 104/23, Min. of Labour (Allen) to Commissioner (Tribe),
       21.11.1935.
[42]   BT 104/23, Commissioner (Tribe) to Min of Labour (Allen),
       25.11.1935.
[43]   Op.cit.17.
[44]   BT 104/30, Commissioner to Lord Ridley, 25.11.1935.
[45]   HC Deb 307, 73,74.
[46]   Quoted in CSAEW, 1936, 2nd Report, para.30, p.10.
[47]   Ibid, para.42, p.13.
[48]   Bredo, W., 1960, quoted in Sadler Forster S.A., ca. 1960, p.5.

II/4.   The Foundation of the Company

[1]   BT 104/30, Ridley to Commissioner, 31.10.1935.
[2]   BT 104/30, Commissioner to Ridley, 25.11.1935.
[3]   BT 104/23, Commissioner to Allen, 13.12.1935.
[4]   BT 104/30, Forbes Adam to Commissioner (Tribe), 4.12.1935.

[5]   BT 104/30, Commissioner (Tribe) to Forbes Adam, 7.12.1935.
[6]   Op.cit.3.
[7]   BT 104/30, Ridley to Commissioner, 17.12.1935.
[8]   BT 104/30, Ridley to Commissioner (Tribe), 17.12.1935.
[9]   TWA,1762/4, ca.1938, notes for a speech.
[10]   BT 104/30, Commissioner (Tribe) to Forbes Adam, 19.12.1935.
[11]   BT 104/30, Forbes Adam to Commissioner (Tribe), 23.12.1935.
[12]   Ibid.
[13]   BT 104/30, Commissioner to Forbes Adam, 30.122.1935. Sieff was
        chairman of PEP from 1933-1939. See Appendix 11 and Pinder, John,
        (Ed.), 1981.
[14]   BT 104/30, minute of a telephone call from Forbes Adam to
        Commissioner, 3.1.1936.
[15]   BT 104/30, Commissioner to Forbes Adam, 4.1.1936.
[16]   BT 104/30, Forbes Adam to Commissioner (Tribe), 9.1.1936.
[17]   BT 104/30, Sieff to Commissioner, 10.1.1937.
[18]   BT 104/23, minutes of a meeting at the Treasury, 20.12.1935.
[19]   BT 104/23, minutes of a meeting, probably at the Treasury,
        23.3.1936.
[20]   Op.cit.3.
[21]   BT 104/23, Min. of Labour (King) to Commissioner (Tribe),
        3.1.1936.
[22]   Peden, G.C., 1984, p.171.
[23]   This was confirmed in an interview with Col. Percival.
[24]   BT 104/23, Commissioner (Tribe) to Forbes Adam, reporting a
        telephone call from Appleyard, 1.2.1936.
[25]   Ibid.
[26]   Ibid.
[27]   BT 104/23, Wilkinson & Marshall to Solicitor of Min. of Labour,
        3.2.1936.
[28]   BT 104/23, Commissioner to E.Brown, Minister of Labour,
        20.3.1936.
[29]   Referred to in ibid.
[30]   BT 104/24, Treasury (Barlow) to Min. of Labour (Sir T.W. Philips),
        30.3.1936.
[31]   BT 104/24, Appleyard to Commissioner (Ryan), 3.4.1936.
[32]   Appleyard, K.C., 1939, p.849.
[33]   BT 104/30, undated press release, date known from publication.
[34]   HC Deb 310, 586. Mr. Storey quoted the following unemployment
        figures: Sunderland 39.4%, South Shields 43.9%, Jarrow 47.4% and
        Boldon 40.6%. The idea that the trading estate should be located
        at the geographical centre of this depressed area attracted
        considerable support.
[35]   BT 104/23, Appleyard to Commissioner, 24.2.1936.
[36]   BT 104/23, Commissioner (Dalton) to Treasury (Gilbert),
        26.2.1936.
[37]   BT 104/23, Treasury (Gilbert) to Commissioner (Dalton),
        27.2.1936.
[38]   BT 104/23, Draft Agreement attached to internal memorandum, Tribe
        to Commissioner, 13.3.1936.
[39]   ibid.
[40]   EIEB, minute 1123, 17.4.1942.
[41]   BT 103/23, Commissioner (Tribe) to Appleyard, 27.2.1936.
[42]   BBC Radio Broadcast, 14.5.1957, on the forthcoming 21st
        anniversary of Company: 'Eggs in many Baskets'. The BBC has
        confirmed that the tape of broadcast has been destroyed.

II/5.   The Choice of the Site

[1]   CSAEW, 1936, 2nd Report, para. 70, p.21.
[2]   CSAEW, 1936, 3rd Report, para.150, p.46.
[3]   BT 104/23, Commissioner to Min. of Labour (Allen) 13.12.1935.
[4]   Daysh, G.D.H. et al., 1936.
[5]   Quoted in op.cit.3.
[6]   Confirmed by Prof. Daysh in a personal interview.
[7]   Op.cit.3.
[8]   BT 104/30, Commissioner (Tribe) to Forbes Adam, 8.1.1936.
[9]   Ibid.
[10]   Op.cit.4.
[11]   At the end of 1925, Sir Robert Renwick, a Newcastle shipowner, had
       suggested that the Team gut should be excavated and widened so as
       to provide docks and quays in the northern part of the valley. He
       believed that the future development of industry and shipping on
       Tyneside lay above the bridges. He considered the scheme rather
       more promising than that which led to the construction of the
       Manchester Ship Canal. The idea was widely discussed at the time,
       a plan was prepared and a delegation from the Newcastle and
       Gateshead Chamber of Commerce visited the Manchester Ship Canal
       on 14.1.1926. The scheme did not, however, attract the £2.5
       million estimated to be required (see North Mail , Newcastle
       upon Tyne, 11.8.1936, 'Scheme of 10 years ago recalled').
[12]   Personal interview with Prof. Daysh.
[13]   TWA,1762/2, Sir Alexander Gibb & Partners, Report, 13.3.1936.
[14]   EIEB, preliminary minute 7, 30.3.1936. Since the Company had not
       yet been incorporated, no formal Board meetings could be held.
       The numbering of the minutes started again at 1 at the first
       meeting of the Board after the incorporation of the Company.
[15]   Ibid.
[16]   TWA,1762/2, Sir Alexander Gibb & Partners, Report, 17.4 1936.
[17]   Oxberry, J.
[18]   Labour Party, January 1937, p.8, see quotation in III/2.
[19]   TWA,1762/2, minutes of a meeting at Commissioner's office,
       18.11.1936, item 10.
[20]   BT 104/24, Commissioner to Chief Secretary (Tribe), 21.4.1936.
[21]   Personal interview with Prof. Daysh.
[22]   Personal interview with Col. Percival. The existence of this
       problem was confirmed by Noel Mobbs, chairman of Slough Estates
       Ltd, in his evidence to the Barlow Commission, RCDME, 1937 -
       1938, para.7, 3.2.1938.
[23]   BT 104/24, minute of a meeting between Commissioner and Appleyard,
       2.6.1936.
[24]   Ibid.
[25]   BT 104/24, Commissioner, internal memorandum, Ryan to Tribe,
       26.5.1936, and op.cit.23.
[26]   TWA,1762/2, 'Scheme for the Acquisition of a Site for the proposed
       Trading Estate', attached to letter, Company Secretary to
       Commissioner, 18.7.1936.
[27]   North Mail , Newcastle upon Tyne, 12.8.1936, 'Looking Around'
       column by 'Spectator'. This column and its author is referred to
       at some length in III/2.

PART III: PRE-WAR DEVELOPMENTS

1 Beginnings

The main topics discussed in this chapter are the acquisition of the site, the planning of the Estate and the start of construction. Since this was the first government-financed trading estate, the Company, and, indeed, the Commissioner and his civil service staff, were faced with the need to make decisions which could not be based on any past experience or practice. The Commissioner, in effect, acted as the interface between the Company and the government. Up to then, the Commissioner had been concerned with policy. Now he would be judged by his effectiveness in translating policy into reality.

The first meeting of the Board after the incorporation of the Company took place on 25 May 1936. It formally approved the decision to buy the Team Valley site and the Finance Agreement with the Commissioner, subject to the insertion of the amount of money needed when the information on costs was available. Other decisions included the appointment of Sir Alexander Gibb and Partners as consulting engineers. They were instructed to prepare the Scheme of Development, as required by the Finance Agreement.

The applications for the posts of general manager and chief engineer were discussed. Candidates were interviewed on 8 June 1936 and a short list was prepared from which the Board made the selection at its meeting on 15 June 1936.

Col. M.D. Methven was appointed general manager and Mr.R.H. Blake chief engineer. Methven was to take up his duties on 1 July, and Blake on 22 July 1936. Blake was not to stay for very long, but Methven spent the next 19 years with the Company and played the key role in its activities. He was a man of great ability who had found the owning and running of a succesful small business an inadequate challenge after having commanded a large military establishment at the end of the first world War. His background is outlined in Appendix 9.

The purchase of the site was complicated particularly by the problem of mineral rights, of which the major owner was Pelaw Main Collieries Ltd. During a meeting with the Commissioner on 29 May 1936, Appleyard pointed out that it would be difficult to find a site as large as 500 acres anywhere in the Special Areas of Durham without any coal seams. He thought that by negotiating with the colliery company it would be possible to obtain an area - he evidently meant to indicate the extent of the development - of some 350 acres at Team Valley. The negotiations would take a month or two and compensation for some four million tons of coal would have to be paid, 'something in the neigbourhood of £30,000' [1]. In another document, however, the amount of coal under the site of the Estate was quoted as 12 million tons, including the quantities leased to Pelaw Main Collieries under land not in their possession [2].

The minutes of the Board meeting of 15 June 1936 provide only the briefest details on the negotiations with the colliery company, but they recorded the two principal facts which were to form the basis of an agreement: some parts of the site would not be available for development for a long time, and in return for abandoning its rights to extract coal from under some other parts, the colliery company would have to be compensated.

The problem of the mineral rights was still not resolved by July 1936. Appleyard telephoned the Commissioner on 6 July to say 'that the negotiations were very complicated' [3]. Austin Kirkup, the consulting mining engineer appointed to deal with the matter, reported the following tentative offer by the coal company: a strip of land 1,200 feet wide would have to be sterilised for 20 years, i.e. the Company would have to undertake not to develop land over these coal workings. At the end of that period, the coal company would ensure that no subsidence would occur by supporting the old workings. The coal company would sell the land it owned at Team Valley for £10,000 and the Estates Company would have to pay £10,000 in compensation for the sterilisation of 740,000 tons of coal, a much smaller amount than had been mentioned before. The directors approved this offer at the Board meeting on 30 July 1936.

The progress made in the negotiations seemed to indicate that outstanding details could be settled [4]. This conclusion proved to be premature; one and a half years later Methven would write: 'the situation with this Company (Pelaw Main Collieries Ltd) has become almost impossible. Repeated attempts to meet and settle the many points outstanding have failed, and it is greatly feared it may be necessary to ask the Commissioner's assistance to reach a solution by bringing pressure to bear' [5].

The next problem was how to pay for the site: the draft Finance Agreement required the Company to submit a formal Scheme of Acquisition before applying for the funds to buy the site. Until a site was acquired, however, it would be impossible to prepare such a scheme. The Company found a way out of this dilemma by preparing a preliminary scheme, which was sent to the Commissioner on 18 July 1936 [6].

108

The site to be acquired was described as 'approximately 706.5 acres'. The land was held by 22 different owners, the three largest of which were Gateshead Corporation (253 acres), the London and North Eastern Railway Company (61 acres), and Pelaw Main Collieries Ltd (186 acres), the smaller owners holding approximately 207 acres [7].

Gateshead Corporation was prepared to sell its land at cost, i.e. for £11,500, and to forego the whole of the expenditure it had incurred (£40,000) on improvements, such as levelling, footpaths and the construction of the Lido, as well as any capital appreciation.

The dealings with some of the small owners were difficult. Compulsory purchase was certainly considered in one or two cases. But in the end, the problems were resolved. Apart from the tenants in Tileshed Woods (believed to have been an area marked T on the map in Appendix 13), their 37 subtenants and one or two tenants elsewhere, no compensation was required [8], so that the total amount was limited to £106.25. One disabled sub-tenant, in addition, was to be treated generously, and was later satisfied with a payment of £75. A fireworks factory left gracefully.

At this stage, the site acquisition cost was made up as follows [9], the Company having assumed a figure for the land owned by the London and North Eastern Railway Company:-

253 acres owned by Gateshead Corporation		£ 11,500
61 " " " London & N.E. Railway Company		6,000
207 " " " small owners		32,055
186 " Pelaw Main Collieries Ltd		10,000
Compensation, Pelaw Main Collieries Ltd		10,000
Legal charges and stamp duties, say		3,495
		£ 73,040

In order to cover any likely contingencies, the Company considered that £80,000 would be required. Subject to the individual parcel prices being agreed by the District Valuer within one week, the Commissioner was asked to make this sum available in advance of the submission of the formal Scheme of Acquisition [10].

The Commissioner, in turn, asked the Minister of Labour on 21 July 1935 for permission to make the funds available. While the Minister would have preferred an option on the land at this stage, he agreed [11]. The Commissioner authorised the acquisition of the site on 29 July 1936 [12], on the understanding that the prices for the separate parcels of land would be approved by the District Valuer. The Minister of Labour had asked that, for the time being, nothing should be said in public about any particular site [13].

A more comprehensive scheme for the acquisition and development of the site was sent to the Commissioner on 18 August 1936 [14], a week after the choice of the site had been officially announced.

The scheme was drawn up in accordance with the headings in the draft Finance Agreement. Under the heading 'Proposed Method of Management of the Estate', the document merely reiterated the remit of the Company and the Board. Of more interest is the heading 'Facilities which the Company may offer to tenants on the Estate'; these included 'all necessary services which can reasonably be required by its tenants ... and which are within the powers conferred by the Memorandum of Association'. Apart from adequate lighting on all Estate roads, the list included the following: 'services for the disposal of rubbish and the protection of property; recreational facilities and space for expansion; transport services both for goods and employees; cold storage, weigh-bridge, crane, central goods depot and marshalling yard etc. etc.' Further details included 'sewerage disposal, boiler plant, shunting locomotive and playing fields'.

The cost of the development of the site and the provision of facilities was estimated to be £702,300, and the cost of building factories on 60 - 70 acres about £1 million. For the first two years, £15,000 was provided for management expenses, £5,000 for maintenance of services and £ 20,000 for advertising, propaganda and publicity, making a total projected cost of £1,742,300. It may be noted that this amount was not much higher than the rough estimate produced by Sir Alexander Gibb and Partners in their first report of 13 March 1936 (£1,500,000) and more than twice as much as estimated by the Commissioner in November 1935 'as ... on the high side'.

Appleyard wrote a lengthy covering letter on 18 August 1936 in which he amplified several aspects of the scheme and discussed some matters not dealt with in it [15].

He pointed out that the scheme had been considered by each director individually and by the Board as a whole, particularly as to the features 'which will attract people in setting up factories in the North East Coast' and that the Board was unanimous in its conclusions.

The quality of the development was a matter of special concern to Appleyard (see also III/6): 'if the scheme was to succeed', he wrote, 'it is necessary to create our Estate in pleasant surroundings which will give people the feeling that they are going into a rural atmosphere rather than into the depressing atmosphere always associated with the iron and steel and heavy engineering industries'.

He feared that the establishment of the Estate would encourage indiscriminate building at its fringes and destroy its rural character. There is evidence that at least one neighbouring landowner - Lord Ravensworth - had received a proposition to this effect [16]. The Company made strenuous efforts to aquire the land - on the south western corner of the Estate - but failed. Ravensworth also owned land at Harlow Green - south of the Estate and adjoining the Great North Road. In this case, the Company succeeded [17].

The Commissioner agreed with Appleyard that developments on adjoining land might pose problems, but there were statutory limits to the purchase of land outside the Estate proper. The Commissioner considered 'that it should be possible to preserve the amenities by a suitable town planning', a matter he would take up with the Ministry of Health [18].

The faith he placed in the - then - weak town planning protection was tested at least on one occasion, when a proposal to build a factory just outside the south-east boundary of the Estate was referred to him for urgent counter action [19]: Chester le Street Council was reported to have given a licence for the erection of a factory in an area close to the Team Valley Estate, an area moreover, which had been zoned under the North Durham Joint Town Planning Scheme for residential purposes. The Commissioner wrote to the Town Planning Committee and pointed out that 'any extensive development of areas adjacent to the Team Valley Trading Estate cannot fail to have unfavourable reactions on the development of the estate' [20].

Appleyard's letter of 18 August 1936 reiterated that the Company would be run 'as if it were a normal commercial business', although the Company 'would spend a good deal more on propaganda than a commercial concern could afford, but this, in our opinion, is vital to the success of our work' [21]. A brief account of the Company's public relations activities is given in III/6.

The Commissioner replied on 22 September 1936. He agreed with the general outline of the Scheme for Acquisition and Development of the site and accepted that the cost for the full development of the Estate might well be £2 million, as the Company had estimated. He did not feel able at this stage, however, to commit the Special Areas Fund to this amount regardless of the rate at which sites were taken up by tenants, particularly as it was accepted by all concerned that the Estate should reach a self-supporting basis at the earliest practical moment. He proposed, therefore, to provide sufficient funds to meet the estimated cost of the engineering development for the first two phases referred to in the report by Sir Alexander Gibb and Partners, together with a sum required to construct factories on 30 acres of the Estate. On this basis he was prepared to sanction immediately a sum of £900,000 [22].

In paragraph 6 of the Scheme of 18 August 1936, the Company had stated that 'it is intended that economic rents shall be charged sufficient to provide, when the whole estate is occupied, the interest under the terms of the Finance Agreement and to cover operating and management revenue, depreciation and such reserves as the directors may consider advisable'.

The Commissioner, for his part, considered that the Company should aim to reach a self-supporting position before the Estate was fully developed. He drew attention to the report by Sir Alexander Gibb and Partners, which had estimated that 'in taking 60 acres as the basis of our calculation, we have assumed that it might be necessary to find the capital to develop one tenth of the available area (600 acres) before the Estate could be said to be standing on its own feet' [23].

Somewhat confusingly, the report had added: 'once 60 acres were developed, and, indeed, in all probability long before that , the Estate would be financing future developments on the security of existing factories'. It was this sentence on which the Commissioner appeared to rely.

The Company sent a detailed reply to the Commissioner on 15 October 1936 [24], attached to which was yet another personal letter from Appleyard, dated 13 October 1936 [25]. These documents contained a great deal of new information, reflecting the conclusions which had emerged from the work of the consultants and architects, and from the policy decisions of the Company which had resulted from a growing understanding of the problems and opportunities.

The latest development programme was substantially different from that outlined in the consultants' report of 13 March 1936, which had presented no more than some first, tentative ideas. It had not taken into account any sales considerations nor the consequences of any agreement with Pelaw Main Collieries Ltd.

According to the original plan, development was to begin at the northern end of the site and extend towards the south. As a result of many discussions, however, it had become clear 'that the proper method of development was to start from the centre of the Estate and work outwards in all directions, since this gave much more adequate possibilities of offering a choice of sites to likely tenants'.

The revised proposals of the consultants required the recasting of the whole scheme: while the main north/south highway through the Estate (later called Kingsway) - a feature of the early proposal - remained, the east/west road was to be brought into the Estate at any early stage and at a point where it would face the proposed central administration building (see map in Appendix 13). This would involve the bridging of the main railway line near Low Fell railway station. The requirements of Pelaw Main Collieries Ltd made it necessary to build a viaduct across the main north/south highway at the southern end of the Estate to carry its railway across the valley. These changes in the plan would involve substantially increased costs in the first two years of development.

But the most serious increase in cost - from £15,000 to £100,000 - was to be caused by a change in the original rectification scheme of the River Team after it became known that Durham County Council was planning a drainage scheme for the Team Valley. A very large increase in the flow of the River Team would have to be allowed for in order to take care of the volume of water which might be delivered to the river under cloudburst conditions.

The 60 acres to be developed would be laid out for three groups of factories. Each group would afford somewhat different facilities. The Company considered this absolutely essential, even if it meant laying down roads and providing drainage and sewers for group sites which would not be fully used in the near future.

The Company was able to support its proposals with some preliminary market information. The enquiries for factory space had been larger in number and better in quality than had been anticipated: of the 80 enquiries received, 50 had stated their requirements, which had added up to some two million square feet. The floor area involved would have necessitated the development of 80 acres of the site rather than of the 60 acres planned; furthermore, there were one or two enquiries for larger factories. Even if only a proportion of these were to materialise, the Company could justify the development of 40 to 50 acres on the basis of existing enquiries alone.

Instead of developing 30 acres - an arbitrary figure proposed by the Commissioner in his letter of 22 September -, the Company, therefore, put forward a 10 year plan with a minimum of 60 acres of factory development, with authority to expend money up to 31 March 1938 in the first place.

This was a shrewd proposal: it would ensure the availability of funds for clearance, roads and services for 60 acres; until the end of March 1938 it would not cost much more than the sum the Commissioner had been ready to authorise, and the funds for factories - apart from a basic number - would be asked for as the demand required. In other words, the Company proposed to spend proportionately rather more on engineering development of the site immediately and rather less on factories than the Commissioner had in mind. This meant that his concern about building factories unrelated to the rate at which tenancies were obtained would be mitigated; on the other hand, the proposal to fund the engineering development of 60 rather than 30 acres depended on the belief that tenants would be found, at least in the longer run. This belief was strengthened by the enquiries the Company had already received. In any event, the Commissioner could not act on the most pessimistic assumptions, and he would be in control of expenditure after 31 March 1938.

There may also have been another reason why the Board wanted to develop as much of the site as possible at an early stage: the concern that - with an improving employment situation in the region - the government was not fully committed to the Estate, and that the development of a significant part of the site would make it more difficult for the government to terminate the scheme.

Regarding some of the other points made by the Commissioner in his letter of 22 September 1936, the Company replied as follows: sufficient revenue to cover expenses would accrue after about 40 acres of factories had been completed. This stage would be reached by the end of 1939, i.e. three years after the start of construction. The Company further believed that it would be in a position to pay 4% interest once some 35% of the site had been developed and that this would be the case by 31 March 1947, ignoring any depreciation allowance, on which the Board had not yet formulated its policy. The Company evidently felt able to put some tentative dates on the stages foreseen in the Finance Agreement, dates which the Board had asked to be more conservative than Methven had suggested in his draft [26].

Concerning the sale of land - a matter on which the Commissioner had an open mind -, the Company was anxious 'as far as possible to retain control both of the land and buildings, but if a particularly desirable tenant could only be secured by selling land to him, the Board would be willing to do so'.

The Commissioner replied on 16 November 1936 [27], effectively approving the scheme proposed by the Company. The total amount agreed was £1,432,000. Unless the demand for factories exceeded the forecast, this amount was expected to last the Company up to 31 March 1946.

In the meantime, the District Valuer had put a price of £16,500 on the land to be transferred from Gateshead Corporation, to take account of its appreciation during the many years since it was bought. He added £3,000 to represent the improvement value arising out of the expenditure of £40,000 by the Corporation. The additions, together with some small items of compensation, increased the price from £ 11,500 to £20,000 [28]. In response to the Company's request for instructions, the Commissioner replied on 16 November 1936 that he saw no alternative but to agree [29]. The increases brought the cost of acquiring the site close to £80,000, or about £114 an acre.

For convenience, the events leading to the agreed Scheme of Acquisition and Development and related matters have been dealt with in chronological order, leaving out other matters of interest or importance since the summer of 1936, which will be taken up now.

At the Board meeting on 30 July 1936, the question of the architectural layout of the Estate was discussed and the chairman was authorised to obtain from the President of the Royal Institute of British Architects the names of architects from whom an advisory architect to the Company might be selected. The actual factory design would be placed with local architects and the usual fee of 6% of the contract price would be split between them (4%) and the advisory architect (2%).

In his letter to the Commissioner of 18 August 1936, Appleyard had written - without reference to any particular consultant architect: 'we propose to give this gentleman the task of imagining the Estate in its completely developed form, and we shall instruct him to see that it is made an attractive and pleasant place' [30].

At the next meeting of the Board, on 2 October 1936, Appleyard recommended the appointment of W.G. Holford ARIBA, who had spent a few days before the meeting looking round the site. During this time he had prepared a preliminary layout, which was submitted to the Board and on the strength of which he was appointed, at an annual fee of £200 plus travelling and out-of-pocket expenses.

Holford proved to be an excellent choice. While a basic plan had been provisionally agreed before he came on the scene, the preliminary detailed layout he produced was later to serve as a model for industrial estate builders in Britain and overseas. He was 29 years old at the time and the Estate was one of his early major assignments. He was to have a distinguished career as a town planner (see Appendix 9) and he was considered to have been the principal author of the Town and Country Planning Act 1947, which was to have a major effect on regional development in Britain (see IV/2).

It was surprising that on his death in 1975 neither the main obituary notice nor the several later tributes in The Times referred to his work at Team Valley. This omission prompted W.H. Bevan, then chief executive of the Estates Corporation, to write to The Times [31]. He referred to Holford's contribution to the layout of the Estate and the design of factories:-

> The Estate Master Plan was based on a grid system, the factories being built with sufficient land to allow for ultimate expansion. Considerable attention was given to the reservation of open spaces, with flower beds and trees as additional amenities. Playing fields were also provided ... One of the interesting developments at the outset of the enterprise was the design of a standard type of factory. This was the work of Holford and proved conclusively that a variety of industrial processes could be carried on in such buildings.

It should not have been necessary to prove this again, because standard factories were pioneered by Slough Estates Ltd. in the middle of the 1920s (see II/2). But there were certainly some doubters in the

North East at the time. Miss Wilkinson (Lab., Jarrow) was one of them. In a speech in the House of Commons on 2 March 1936, she remarked: 'I know from my own experience ... as a Trade Union official dealing with many trades ... that to suggest that a man can take over a ready-made factory shell and put in machinery to fit it is fantastic' [32].

Among other matters discussed by the Board at an early stage was the question of local rates. The problem of high rates in the poorer areas of Britain has already been referred to. In spite of the 75% de-rating of industrial buildings, rates in the North East were widely believed to act as a disincentive to industrialists considering new or additional locations for their factories. In order to reduce the burden on tenants still further, the Company offered to accept responsibility for the roads and sewers on the Estate [33]. The offer was accepted by Gateshead Corporation: on 5 August 1936 it was agreed that the gross assessment should be on the basis of 2.5% of contractors' costs of factories together with 2.5% of the value of that proportion of the land of the Estate occupied by any tenant [34].

No attempt is being made here to estimate the resulting abatement, bearing in mind that the Company's costs in providing these services had to be recovered from rents. The net benefit is likely to have been small, but the scheme would reassure industrialists considering a location at Team Valley that any rises in rates would have a minimal effect on their costs. Among businessmen and local authorities elsewhere in the area, however, the further rate abatement at Team Valley seems to have aroused some resentment (see next chapter).

The speed with which the development of the site proceeded was remarkable. The survey commenced on 27 July 1936. The survey party worked seven days a week for eight weeks. On more than one occasion, work continued throughout the night. Specifications and tenders for the first contract to be let were completed in record time, although the chief engineer, who had prepared them, worked almost without assistance and often late into the night. It is not clear why these documents were not prepared by the consulting engineers.

The first contract (for road works) was advertised early in September 1936 and let to George Wimpey Ltd for £56,776 after a report by the consulting engineers on the tenders received had been approved by the Board on 2 October 1936. The Board insisted on the use of local materials. Exceptions would have to be reported and authorised by the consulting engineers.

Contract followed upon contract. The first contracts for factory construction were placed early in February 1937. By this time the weather had turned unusually difficult. At the end of March 1937, Methven reported that 'owing to the shocking state of the ground, building has been carried on under almost impossible conditions. Serious delays have resulted and more or less continuous overtime has had to be worked' [35].

These circumstances forced the builders to ask for a change in the contractual arrangements. For a period of some weeks, the Company was obliged to agree to cost-plus terms for factory construction.

The steel shortage caused by the rearmament programme presented a serious problem: 'the situation with regard to supplies has gone from bad to worse', Methven reported in February 1937, 'and we have asked our consulting engineers ... to advise us as to the possibility of building some of the factories more speedily using reinforced concrete' [36]. This was no short term problem; seven months later Methven would write: 'the steel situation has continued to be acute' [37]. At one stage, the Commissioner was asked to obtain a priority certificate from the Board of Trade. The Company ordered steel from any source promising deliveries regardless of price, with the result that the value of these orders soon exceeded that authorised by the Board.

Delay also resulted from the Company's inadequate organisation to handle the mass of detail inherent in a project of this scale. Methven proposed that three departments should be created and staffed to deal with architectural work, engineering, and quantity surveying, including purchasing. The Board, however, decided against such in-house facilities at this stage and instructed Methven to make more extensive use of local architects and specialist heating and electrical installation consultants [38].

By the end of April 1937, the delay in the completion of roads and factory buildings was causing increasing concern. 24 factories were required to satisfy the firms which had signed leases, and four 'speculatively-built' units to support the Company's efforts to attract tenants. The programme also included two canteens, the central administration building and the central garage. Four further factories were required, for reasons not stated. Work on 25 of these 36 buildings had not yet been started [39].

The information on the progress of construction from the beginning of 1938 is given in Appendix 14, which also contains progressively more complete details on lettings and employment. The data in Appendix 14 is preceded by an extended discussion of various aspects of the early progress records.

The incomplete progress information up to the end of 1937 is given in Table 1. It was found in the Commissioner's monthly reports to the Minister of Labour, but the figures could have been provided only by the Company.

It was expected at least by some people at the time that the initial phases of the project would take several years to complete: in a debate in the House of Commons on 2 March 1936, for example, Miss Wilkinson (Lab., Jarrow) predicted that 'even on the most optimistic basis, it is going to take three or four years even to get the site cleared, the roads made, the power installed' [40].

In the event, the first 20 factories were occupied within 11 months after the contractors had started work - on 6 November 1936. Even if the site had been dry (most factories required piled foundations), the weather perfect and steel had been freely available, the completion of the extensive engineering works - including a major river diversion - and of the first factories in so short a time would nowadays be judged a great achievement. To illustrate the scale of the project, the salient civil engineering data are given in Appendix 15.

116

Table 1
Early Progress at Team Valley

1937	27.3.	01.5.	31.07.	28.08.	13.11.	15.12.
Number of Factories:						
Let	27	31	47	54	58	
Under Construction		11		)	35	32
Completed	0	0	13	20)		28
Occupied					23	26

Source: T 161/1399.

Construction appears to have been generally much faster before the last War than it is now. There is documented evidence of the following example on the Estate: a manufacturer ordered a 24,000 sq.ft. factory of conventional steel frame and brick construction on Saturday, 4 March 1939. Construction began on Monday, 6 March and the tenant started to install machinery on Monday 3 April 1939 [41]. While in this case the construction time was the subject of a wager - and work continued throughout the night -, the rate of construction does not seem to have been untypical.

Not all the original ideas for amenities were adopted. The establishment of service and retail shops on the Estate, for example, was agreed by the Board on 2 October 1936. Indeed, some early sketches - possibly by Holford - show such shops, apparently in an extended central administration building. These facilities would have been a great convenience, particularly to women workers. There were two reasons why they were not provided in the event: doubts whether the 1934 Act would have allowed them to be funded by the Commissioner and protests from traders in Gateshead [42].

Another idea which was not implemented was a physical training and recreational centre on the Estate, although a good deal of preparatory work was done [43].

Such a facility and other more essential ones would have added greatly to the attraction and convenience of the Estate, particularly for small manufacturers. But even with its limitations, the Team Valley Estate Estate created an industrial environment in the North East which was not only far in advance of local experience or expectations but which would serve as a model for publicly-funded industrial estates in Britain and elsewhere.

2 National and local reaction

During the months following the start of construction at Team Valley, the concept of government-financed trading estates received much attention in the press, particularly after the Commissioner for England and Wales had authorised another estate at Treforest in South Wales, and the Scottish Commissioner one at Hillington near Glasgow.

The Times , for example, featured the Team Valley experiment in its Annual Financial and Commercial Review of 9 February 1937. The Economist of 29 May 1937 carried an article entitled 'What is a Trading Estate?', and the June 1937 issue of Business helpfully entitled a piece 'The North for Opportunity'.

While the experience of private factory estates like Slough was carefully noted by the planners of the government-financed trading estates, the fundamental differences in their origins and objectives was not overlooked. Thus the Architectural Journal of 20 May 1937 - an issue devoted to the Team Valley Estate - in an article headed 'The Facts':-

> Slough has few points of resemblance with Team Valley or Treforest; the one came into existence to develop a derelict State industrial area, the others as a contribution to the geographical alignment of industry. The latter conform to public policy in the same sense as they represent good social as well as economic activity.

The writer had understood the significance of what was being brought into existence, even if the hope for a 'geographical alignment' was premature. It should be noted, however, that the potential of government-financed trading estates appears to have been appreciated even before the first factory at Team Valley was ready for occupation.

It was also understood that government-financed trading estates should be established only in places with serious structural problems: when Prof. Abercrombie asked at a hearing of the Barlow Commission 'whether the provision of trading estates represented a new means of town planning' [1], the spokesman of the Ministry of Labour replied: 'if every town in the country had its trading estate, then you might as well give up having trading estates at all'.

This reply might have been made more clearly as follows: if the government were to finance trading estates in too many places - and there were no means of preventing private developments -, it would be difficult, if not impossible, to persuade industry to set up where the need for new employment was particularly pressing.

The same point was also made by Dennison [2]: 'there can be only a limited number of estates, if they are to be effective in attracting new firms to the depressed areas'.

While the reaction in the country to the establishment of the Team Valley Trading Estate was positive - even enthusiastic -, the anxieties of the local authorities and the differences between them - so evident when the site was being chosen - began to reassert themselves and found an echo in the local press. The publicity officer of the Estates Company felt obliged to draw the attention of Appleyard to three critical pieces in the <u>North Mail</u> , Newcastle upon Tyne, in the month of July 1937 alone. These throw a revealing light on local attitudes at the time. All these pieces appeared in the 'Looking Around' column and were written by 'Spectator'.

There was, first of all, dissatisfaction on the part of local authorities which had hoped but failed to obtain a government-financed trading estate for their localities. Thus 'Spectator' on 2 July 1937: 'Sunderland has a grievance. There is probably foundation for Sunderland's belief that Tyneside has received more State aid than the Wear in countering unemployment', and, again on 10 July 1937: 'Jarrow demands a trading estate. So does South West Durham. Similar propositions have been discussed at Sunderland, at South Shields and on Teesside'.

Neither 'Spectator', nor the local authorities concerned seem to have been aware that, by this time, the Commissioner had already decided to build small estates in South West Durham and at Pallion, Sunderland (see III/5).

On 28 July 1937, 'Spectator' noted that 'most of the centres outside Tyneside have protested against the location of the government-fostered trading estate at Team Valley'. As this decision had been taken a year before, what was the purpose of recalling these protests at this time? It is likely that the timing was connected with the Special Areas Amendment Act (see next chapter), which had been passed some two months earlier: the local authorities were giving notice to the Commissioner that they were expecting him to use his new powers to build and let factories in their localities. The piece by 'Spectator' on 2 July 1937 points to such an interpretation: 'Sunderland feels that if it cannot have a government-fostered trading estate on the ambitious lines of what is now taking shape at Team Valley, it should at least have the Commissioner's assistance in the acquisition and leasing at easy rents of premises suitable for the new industries the town is anxious to attract'.

The news that the Estates Company was signing up tenants rather faster than expected led some local authorities to believe that they were missing out on something important. On 10 July 1937, 'Spectator' wrote that 'the bright prospects of the Team Valley venture have encouraged other areas to attach a high value to this form of subsidised enterprise'.

Some local authorities feared that the Team Valley Estate would not only attract firms which might have settled within their boundaries, but that some of their established industries would move there. These fears were reflected, perhaps even played upon, by 'Spectator' in his piece of 2 July 1937:-

> Sunderland probably cannot complain that Team Valley is attracting industries from Wearside and so bringing to Gateshead employment which might reasonably be expected in its area, but the rest of Tyneside might, with justice, complain that established businesses are being taken away from other Tyneside towns and concentrated in the Team Valley.

This same concern is found in the interim Report of the Labour Party Commission on the Distressed Areas of 27 January 1937: while praising the concept of trading estates, it warned that

> there is ... a danger which should be guarded against, namely that such an estate in a Special Area may attract industries not so much from outside, as from other parts of the Area. Further, if new industries are concentrated in one part of the Special Area, the industrial and social position of other parts may become worse than before [3].

In the absence of a location of industry policy, and following the failure of his efforts in the summer of 1935 to interest British industry in establishing factories in the North East, the Commissioner was bound to depend on small or new local firms to fill a proportion of the factories at Team Valley. But the fear that industries already established in the North East would move to Team Valley proved to be largely groundless. This is the conclusion which may be drawn from the origins of the first tenants of the Company in Appendix 22. Some figures given by Methven and quoted below support this conclusion.

The possibility that the Team Valley Estate might attract established firms from within the Tyne & Wear area had been discussed by the Board of the Company as early as 2 October 1936. On that occasion, Methven was instructed 'not to go out of his way to encourage these as tenants, save where expansion in their present situation was difficult'. The matter was raised by the Commissioner in the course of Methven's visit to his office on 18 November 1936, i.e. at the time when the contractors had just moved on to the Team Valley site. It was suggested to Methven that the Company might, at a later stage, 'obtain stiffer rents from people who wanted to transfer from one part of the area to another' [4]. In a note to the Commissioner of 25 January 1937, Methven reported that, of the 166 enquiries for factories received up to that time, 'only 17 were in respect of pure transfer' [5]. The Times of 22 April 1938 claimed that 25% of the first 1,000 jobs at Team Valley were in businesses which had transferred from other parts of the region. Methven had this claim checked and found 'that only 109 jobs were brought over from Newcastle' [6]. This was due mainly to two firms, but as a result of these moves, their employment had increased to 201, indicating that they could not have expanded in their Newcastle premises.

Writing in 1939, Dennison did not see the transfer of firms from other parts of the region to Team Valley as very significant: 'some of the firms ... are of local origin (meaning new firms,), some are simply expansion schemes of existing firms, and a few are removals of local firms' [7].

Unrealistic expectations about rentals and other terms at Team Valley certainly stimulated some enquiries from established firms: 'there are a number of people in the region who appear to believe that they can get extraordinarily cheap rentals and facilities on the Estate' [8]. But other factors also played a part: some of the local firms showing interest in the Estate 'are being forced to move by unsuitable premises or for other reasons' [9].

Since no comparable factories for rent were available in the Special Areas of the North East, the effect of rent levels on the decisions of some local firms to move to Team Valley cannot be known. It is likely, however, that rents were of lesser importance than other considerations.

Contrary to the assumptions made by some local authorities and others, the Company had no intention to subsidise rents except in a few special cases and for an initial period only [10]. Indeed, it would have acted beyond its powers if it had subsidised rents in a general way, the financial constraints quite apart. Rents were set at 6% of the cost of building factories, with the aim of yielding 4% interest on the total borrowing from the Special Areas Fund [11]. The concessionary rents for the 1,500 sq.ft. nursery factories, (£1 per week, representing a concession of about £0.50) - which were occupied, in the main, by new starts - were the only general exceptions the Commissioner had authorised. But even then, the Company reserved the right to raise the rents once tenants began to make profits. A list of the rent concessions - other than for nursery factories - offered by the Company in the years from 1937 to 1939 is given in Appendix 17. The Commissioner's general policy on rent subsidies after the 1937 Amendment Act will be briefly discussed in III/5.

The rate abatement, too, seems to have contributed to the fears by local authorities of losing established firms to Team Valley. 'Spectator' reflected these fears in his piece of 10 July 1937, hinting, at the same time, at abuses of the Special Areas legislation:-

Team Valley has admittedly secured a number of genuinely new industries; but it has also accepted a number of removals from existing businesses. No doubt there is a gain in the higher output and expansion of business which may be anticipated from modern industries, but removal from competitively rated to subsidised premises was no part of the government's scheme.

The rates issue has been discussed in the last chapter. The abatement of rates at Team Valley - resulting from the Company taking over some of the responsibilities of the local authority on the Estate - was not only small but had to be paid for out of rents. Nevertheless, even a small competitive advantage offered to firms on the Estate aroused anxiety and even anger elsewhere in the area.

Finally, there were two other lines of comment or criticism found in the press at the time. Both were taken up by 'Spectator' in his column of 10 July 1937. The first one has already been referred to in connection with some evidence to the Barlow Commission: 'a multiplication of trading estates will inevitably engender cut-throat competition among them'.

The second one may be called the 'sour grapes' argument: 'it may be that the potential value of trading estates is exaggerated ... Ultimate success in the attraction of an adequate number of industries remains in doubt ... Jarrow and others would do well to ponder this aspect of the position'.

There is a good reason for quoting extensively from 'Spectator': the writer of the column was a journalist by the name of Fletcher, who acted as publicity officer for the North East Development Board, and, for a time, at least, was also connected with the Tyneside Industrial Development Board. It can be assumed that the views he printed reflected the different attitudes within these Boards at the time.

Fletcher left the North East at the end of 1937 to become publicity officer for Grimsby. In that capacity, he returned to the question of the contribution made by the Team Valley Estate to the reduction in unemployment in a letter to The Times of 17 September 1938, a year after the first factories began to be occupied: 'much good has resulted from the work of the Commissioners for the Special Areas, but, as represented by the trading estates, it does appear that considerable expenditure is being involved to do little more than attack the edges of the (unemployment) problem'. Fletcher claimed that the average employment of the firms at Team Valley was only 26. Given the general unwillingness or inability of large firms from outside the region to move or establish branches there, it was inevitable that the employment of the mainly small or new firms would, initially, at least, be modest. There was, in fact, a steady and continuous increase up to the War: by December 1939, the average had risen to almost 50 employees per firm [12].

The argument that the Estate would make little or no impact on unemployment was advanced by others. The Commissioner recognised the problem of unduly high expectations: in his Third Report of November 1936 - written before construction at Team Valley had begun -, he quoted an observation by the chairman of the private Trafford Park Estate Company [13]: 'those who were responsible for trading estate companies should not be unduly depressed if progress was slow. The Trafford Park estate ... had been nearly 40 years in reaching its present satisfactory position', to which the Commissioner added his own words of caution: 'it would be foolish to expect immediate and spectacular results'.

Local jealousies apart, the run-up to the Special Areas Amendment Act also resulted in pressure from other quarters. The need for financial inducements as a means of attracting industry to the depressed areas had become recognised and was widely discussed. This caused some national trade organisations to lobby Parliament in order to ensure that no commercial harm would be caused to their members outside the Special Areas. Early in March 1937, the Board of Trade was obliged to explain the policy: the Commissioner and his advisers would consider carefully any existing productive capacity in Britain and the size of the market before giving financial assistance under the proposed Amendment Act to any firm intending to set up a new factory in the Areas [14]. This reassurance was issued a few days before a debate in the Grand Council of the Federation of British Industries on a resolution expressing the hope that 'the interests of industry as a whole will not be overlooked'.

The anxieties of the local authorities in the North East were understandable. They found it difficult to look beyond their own pressing problems. Even 35 years later, Manners, Keeble et al. were to note that 'North Eastern influence (on the decision-making processes of central government) is still unfortunately lessened by local authority internecine wrangling' [15].

Behind the local arguments, however, there loomed a serious question, of which the protagonists appear to have been only dimly aware: the choice between concentration and dispersion of efforts to regenerate the region. In a sense, it was the argument about Transference all over again, but this time within a regional context.

The concept of a single, powerful centre of industrial growth - 20 years before Perroux [16] would outline the theory of growth poles - was unfamiliar to people and authorities alike. Those who saw it as the way forward for the North East assumed - from the experience of the South East but without local evidence - that workers would be willing to travel reasonable distances to places where jobs were being created. The local authorities, on the other hand, and perhaps the majority of the workers, wanted work to be brought to them and to maintain old patterns of industrial settlement.

The announcement of the selection of the Team Valley site had referred to the 'present-day mobility of labour', but this merely implied that the transport facilities available would enable workers to be mobile, rather than described their attitude to mobility. It was in this sense that workers residing on Wearside were expected to share in the opportunities being created at Team Valley. On a later occasion, the relatively high mobility of labour in the South East of the country was cited by the future sales manager of the Estates Company as one of the factors the region had to compete with.

Some of the assumptions made at the time were unrealistic for another reason: peak-load road transport from places up to 17 miles away from Team Valley (e.g. Wearside) was relatively uneconomic. It was expensive in relation to the wages available to young workers, who formed about half the workforce on the Estate at the outbreak of the War. Indeed, even the cost of travelling from Newcastle was to cause problems for tenants later [17].

While pronouncements were made by various authorities regarding the intended catchment area of the Trading Estate, there appears to have been little serious examination of the relative economic merits of concentration or dispersion of public investment in the regional context. The North East Development Board had proposed trading estates 'in various parts of the region' [18], but this apparent endorsement of a policy of dispersion was probably due more to the pressure from its constituent local authority members than the result of informed debate.

Appleyard certainly had foreseen the possibility of further government-financed trading estates in the region; the name of the Company reflected this. The consultants who advised on the site had suggested an initial concentration on the Team Valley Estate merely as a practical matter, but there is no evidence that these views were based on any wider economic considerations.

Both the interim Report of the Labour Party Commission on the Distressed Areas already referred to and the final Report on Durham and the North East Coast had proposed a policy of dispersion[19]:-

> There should be a number of trading estates, distributed over the North East, to give the best results in well-dispersed employment and social amenities. Individual factories and sites should also be provided as required. The estates would vary in size, according to local conditions, but there should certainly be one in South West Durham.

But - South West Durham apart, which clearly required special help - the report did not argue the case for a policy of dispersion, which was made on social and even political grounds. The economic consequences for the region were not examined.

The government underwrote the concept of concentration. The agreement by the Commissioner to buy the large site at Team Valley must be considered the first evidence for this. The later establishment of sites outside the Team Valley Estate did not fundamentally alter the policy, it merely added another component. Methven recorded many years later that 'the first Commissioner, Sir Malcolm Stewart ... had agreed that it was essential to concentrate the Company's effort'. Sir Malcolm retired in November 1936. According to Methven, 'the second Commissioner (Sir George Gillett) somewhat altered the emphasis ... and was to call for "outside sites"' [20]. The origin of these sites will be examined in III/5.

The only evidence for a deliberate policy of concentration from the first Commissioner himself is found in the Third (and his last) Report, of November 1936, where he wrote that the Team Valley 'is well placed to benefit the whole of the unemployed on Tyneside and surrounding districts ' [21], although no definition was given as to what constituted 'surrounding districts'. Elsewhere in the report, the 'growth pole' idea was being mooted, if in a somewhat rudimentary form: 'it is hoped that trading estates will become centres from which increased activities will radiate' [22].

Further evidence of a policy of concentration is contained in the Address given by Appleyard at the third annual general meeting of the Estates Company on 19 July 1938 [23]:-

From time to time there has been some faint criticism of the scale on which this enterprise is being developed, and it may be as well for me to say that the Board set out, with the full approval of the Commissioner and the Government, to attract light industries in numbers commensurate with the North East Coast and the size of the unemployment which exists in bad times.

The second Commissioner, at the end of the reporting year in which he had authorised the first 'outside sites', appeared to confirm the policy in his Fourth Report of September 1937: 'this site (the Team Valley) was selected, ·... after the most careful consideration and after taking the best advice obtainable, as the site the development of which would be likely to conduce most successfully to the industrial rehabilitation of the whole of the North Eastern Special Area' [24].

The most conclusive evidence for a deliberate policy of concentration, however, may be found in a memorandum to the Cabinet Committee by the Minister of Labour in June 1938 [25]: commenting on a proposal by Lord Portal to restrict Special Areas status but to provide small numbers of government-financed factories in the places scheduled, the Minister wrote:-

When the Commissioner was first authorised to proceed with the establishment of trading estates he had to consider two alternatives:
  (i) the establishment of one large, fully equipped estate in each Special Area, situated where it was most likely to attract new industries; or
  (ii) a number of small estates situated near the areas of heaviest unemployment.
  The Commissioner deliberately and in the face of considerable opposition from some of the areas chose (i).

The memorandum cited the reasons for this decision, although it is not clear whether the arguments adduced were provided by the Commissioner at the time or whether they were post hoc : the ability to provide technical and commercial services on an estate of the size of Team Valley which would be impossible on a small one; the lower costs of construction, because several contractors would be employed and would tender more competitive prices; the lower overhead management expenses; the excellent transport facilities available which would enable the Team Valley Estate to draw labour from a wide area so that no rehousing of any working population had to be contemplated. Perhaps the most interesting argument was a hard-headed one, an argument, moreover, which had been advanced by the consultants of the Company: 'the main purpose of the estate is to attract new industries and the main attraction is not the sentimental desire to relieve unemployment but the business desire to make profits. The more economically situated the site, the more likely is it to attract new industries'.

Later experience would confirm this view: in spite of inducements available after the 1937 Amendment Act, it proved initially to be very difficult to attract industries to South West Durham, for example, an area in the North East particularly hard-hit by unemployment but relatively less accessible' [26].

The Minister of Labour added that Lord Portal's proposal for a change in assistance policy was 'exhaustively examined before drafting the Special Areas Amendment Act and was unanimously rejected on administrative as well as political grounds'.

Insofar as Lord Portal's proposals would have resulted in a number of small trading estates in places of special need, they appear to have come close to the ideas of the Labour Party Commission, the chairman of which was Hugh (later Lord) Dalton, Member of Parliament for Bishop Auckland in South West Durham.

The issue of concentration versus dispersion was settled soon after Dalton became President of the Board of Trade in the wartime Coalition in 1942: the decision was in favour of dispersion ('work to the workers' within the region), as the Labour Party Commission had proposed. The policy was written into the Distribution of Industry Act 1945 - piloted and all but seen through Parliament by Dalton - and implemented by the post-War Labour Government. The events leading to the Act are examined in IV/2.

The policy was one of the reasons why the Team Valley Estate - which was expected to create 40,000 jobs within 30 years [27] - would never achieve more than half the aim of its founders.

3 The 1937 Amendment Act

The near-boom conditions in 1936 in the country as a whole created a widespread public unease about the continuing depression in parts of the North East and other Areas. While the government claimed it was 'doing all it could to induce industry to move to the Special Areas', it relied on 'example and influence' [1].

But in the face of the realities in the Areas, established ideas and attitudes towards State intervention were changing in the country and in Parliament, particularly in regard to two forms of intervention: financial inducements to attract industry to the Special Areas and a location of industry policy which would prevent a continuation of the uneven development of industry in the country. Moreover, attitudes were changing on both sides of the political spectrum, and the developing consensus would soon lead a reluctant government more deeply into intervention.

Before discussing the next stage in the evolution of regional policy, - indeed, to understand this evolution - it is necessary to examine the changing political climate.

The Commissioner for the Special Areas of England and Wales played no little part in bringing about. the change. He had come to the conclusion that government intervention would have to be intensified and he argued this powerfully in his Third Report. The government could not ignore the Commissioner's views, because they had gained considerable influence. The District Commissioner in Newcastle had earlier confirmed this in a letter to the Commissioner: 'public opinion of almost any political complexion is remarkably unanimous in support of the policy you advocate' [2].

The problems of the Special Areas received much attention in Parliament in the first half of 1936. Debates on the Second Report of the Commissioner, on unemployment and on the location of industry took place in March. The first measure providing finance for new and expanding industry in the Areas was enacted in May 1936 (see next chapter).

The debate in the Commons on the Commissioner's Second Report took place on 2 March 1936 [3]. Mr. Dalton (Lab., Durham, Bishop Auckland), who opened the Debate, argued for positive State action to induce new industries to set up in the Special Areas and advocated a system of government licensing of sites for new factories.

Some Members on the government benches seemed to agree with him on the need for such a policy. The Rt. Hon. Viscount Wolmer (Con., Hants., Aldershot), for example, was distressed that the special nature of the problem was not dealt with by special measures and new ideas. In his view, the reports of the Commissioners contained 'some very important new ideas' which he wanted the government to implement. It was soon clear that a curb on the growth of industries in and around London was one of the ideas he favoured: 'the Conservative Party is not afraid of planning', he asserted, ' laissez faire has been abandoned by all the parties, even the Liberal Party, and the adoption of a tariff system commits us to the principle of the location of industry'.

The object of tariffs - introduced by the National Government -, he claimed, was so to plan industry that factories come into the country rather than remain abroad. These factories should be built in places where the national interest required it. He suggested the setting up of an advisory committee and that anyone from abroad wanting to put up a factory should be required to satisfy this Committee that it would be placed in the locality best suited to the national interest, or, at least, to show reasons why it should not be sited in one of the Special Areas. He believed that this was no more than an extension of the principle of town planning: 'but we are having the whole country town-planned in little sections. We must follow a logical and consistent policy in this matter. Once you start to plan, you must plan completely'. More than three years later, the Barlow Report would make a similar point.

If Viscount Wolmer advocated a location of industry policy for foreigners in the first place, he may have judged this to be the most that was politically possible in the short term. Such a policy had already been mooted by Lord Portal in his maiden speech in the House of Lords on 31 July 1935: 'would it be possible', he asked, 'not only to suggest to foreign firms coming to this country but to make them put down their factories in some of these areas where people are out of work' [4].

Wolmer's proposal was followed up within a few days by the Ministry of Labour in connection with the terms of admission to Britain of refugee industrialists from Hitler's Europe [5].

It is evident that a consensus was emerging between some Conservatives and the Labour Party on a policy of locating industry, although this did not necessarily extend to the degree or the means of control.

Conservative Members were not, however, of one mind in this matter. Some made the case against such a policy on a premise which, as a generalisation, was no longer tenable, whatever classical location theories may have held: that location decisions by industry were made always on purely economic grounds. A speech by Lord Dunglass (Con., Lanark) is a good example of this view [6]:-

> The promotion of industrial enterprise is a risk, and the final choice of an industrial site must always depend on one or more economic factors ... If the government then come along and forbid (the industrialist) putting his factory in the place which he has decided is best ... what is the position? ... Either the industrialist will give up the enterprise, in which case there is a real risk of the factory being taken to another country; or the industrialist will agree to go to the depressed area and probably, for some reason, his enterprise will fail. Then he will go to his shareholders and say, the government insisted that I should take my industry into a depressed area; they are, therefore, responsible for the mess we are in, and it is up to them to get us out.

Another controversial topic was raised in the debate: financial inducements to attract private industry to the Special Areas. Dalton approvingly quoted the town planner Thomas Sharp, who had proposed that

> the government should offer special inducements to new industrial concerns to establish themselves in the derelict areas ... if inducements and encouragement fail, then it should enforce an industrial planning scheme that will direct us out of the muddle and misery of present unplanned and uncontrolled 'enterprise'.

Since the Labour Opposition had resisted subsidies for private firms before the 1934 Act, Dalton seemed to signal a change in attitude, although he made it clear that this was a personal view: 'speaking for myself, I have no objection to a government guarantee (to firms moving into the Special Areas) provided the community gets value for it' [7]. In response to an interjecting question by Sir Patrick Hannon (Cons., Birmingham, Moseley), Dalton confirmed that he was in favour of such guarantees even under the existing capitalist system, provided the government met his proposals on a policy for locating industry and for the equalisation of the public assistance rate burden, which he had advocated.

The Supply Day Debate on 3rd March 1936 [8] was devoted to Unemployment. So far as the Special Areas were concerned, it was a continuation of the debate of the previous day. Further support emerged from the government benches for some form of location of industry and State planning. For example, Sir Robert Aske Bt. (Con., Newcastle upon Tyne East), supported one of the conclusions of a report by the North East Development Board that 'the location of industry is one of the most important aspects of any attempt to improve the balance of industrial activity in the Special Areas'.

Mr. Boothby (Con., Aberdeen & Kincardine East) left the government in no doubt that some of its supporters were dissatisfied with the outcome of the debate of the previous day, because no effective action to deal with the problem of unemployment in the distressed areas had been proposed. He, too, supported a location of industry policy: 'we lay down a lot of conditions of every kind before we allow a manufacturer to set up a factory in any particular district. I cannot see why the government should not lay down some direction in regard to the location of new industries which are proposed to be set up. It is absolutely within the prerogative of the State'.

It is evident that Aske and Boothby, like Wolmer in the debate on the previous day, were speaking for a growing number of Conservative Members for whom a policy of industrial location - with all the problems and dangers this might involve - was no longer a bogey.

Boothby, furthermore, put forward some new ideas which would be carried into effect many years later in one form or another: regional planning and regional economic advisory councils.

The emerging consensus was confirmed from the Opposition benches by Mr. Jenkins (Lab., Monmouth, Pontypool) when he said that he was able to agree with much of Boothby's speech.

In a Ballot Debate on the location of industry in the House of Commons on 11 March 1936 [9], Mr. Edwards (Lab., Middlesbrough) proposed that no new industries should be allowed to be established within a radius of 40 miles of London. Dr. Burgin (Con., Bedford, Luton), the Parliamentary Secretary to the Board of Trade, agonised over the political problems involved: 'as between an authoritarian state ... and a western country or republic, there is all the difference between complete control on the one hand and the complete absence of control, on the other. The question raised in the Debate today is really whether it is possible to have a half-way house'.

While Burgin agreed with the analysis of the problems of the depressed areas presented by Edwards, he was unable to accept the proposed remedy: 'if the Hon. Member means that the government should take powers by statute to prohibit an individual from starting a factory where he wishes to go in order to compel him to go to some place where he does not wish to go, I fear that this is not a proposition which I could recommend to the House' [10].

Burgin spelled out the political difficulty he perceived in preferential policies for the Special Areas: 'I believe the government's duty to foster industry is an equal duty to the older and to the newer industrial areas. I do not think that it is for the government to select the industrial area they wish particularly to sponsor', a view that was shared by many Conservative Members and probably by the majority of industrialists in the country [11]. Burgin did not believe that 'the House as a whole is prepared to sponsor complete government control with the power of veto'. It was a sign of the times that, less than nine months later, the government would be forced by the defection of many of its supporters in Parliament to consider the policies Burgin had found so unpalatable (see [27] below).

Edwards was unwise to promote the concept of a location of industry policy by such a specific and simplistic Motion. Boothby and his friends were unable to support it, even if Boothby 'was unhappy about the distress in the Special Areas, the strategic risks resulting from the concentration of industry around London and the duplication of social capital inherent in a policy of transference'. Accordingly, he proposed the following amendment to the Motion:-

H.M. Government should endeavour to discourage the undue concentration of modern industries in the Southern Counties and to encourage new industries, where practicable, to establish themselves in the older centres'.

This may, at first sight, appear like back-pedalling by Boothby, who, a week before, had come out positively for a location of industry policy. But a closer reading indicates that such a policy was implied, even if the means were not spelled out.

Opinions in favour of some form of statutory action to achieve a more desirable location of industry were not lacking. Sir John Withers (Con., Cambridge University), for example, believed that 'the government should exercise powers of prohibition in certain circumstances', and Mr. Tinker (Lab., Leith) asked 'what value is there in the Prime Minister's suggestion that industrialists should go into the derelict areas? There must be some form of pressure, because otherwise they would not go there'.

The government was prepared to accept the Boothby amendment, which was carried. It was to be the resolution most nearly proposing a location of industry policy to be passed by the House of Commons before the beginning of the last War.

The debate had shown the quandary into which the government had manoeuvered itself: on the one hand, it made frequent appeals to industry to locate in the Special Areas; on the other, it refused to contemplate any step which would go beyond persuasion, a policy which, according to Mr. Greenwood (Lab., Halifax), the Deputy Leader of the Opposition, had failed.

Although Members of the Opposition sitting for constituencies which would have been affected by the Edwards proposals seemed to be lukewarm in their support, the Opposition generally seemed to support them.

No Member mentioned the change in the technological situation: because of the electricity grid, power was now available almost anywhere in the country, and a good transport system enabled materials and goods to be moved cheaply. Some of the past desiderata for locating industry no longer applied.

The factor which caused the greatest interest in the Special Areas was the approaching end of the 1934 legislation, on 31 March 1937. The problems the 1934 Act was intended to alleviate, if not to solve, had not gone away. While employment in some parts, for example on Tyneside, had improved considerably (see Appendix 19), the reduction in unemployment which had occurred in the North East as a whole since the Act came into force was almost matched by the number of people transferred to other parts of the country under official schemes. Even more worrying, the unemployment situation in the country had improved at a greater rate up to 1936 than in the Special Areas [12], so that the Areas were evidently falling ever further behind. While this situation would reverse in 1937/38, the abandonment of the Special Areas legislation in 1936 was unthinkable. Indeed, a growing body of opinion, pressed for the replacement of the 1934 Act by a more effective measure.

The government decided in the summer of 1936 to continue the 1934 Act without amendment [13]. This decision would prove to be an error, in that it misjudged the temper of the country and of the House of Commons.

As summer turned into autumn, the government received much advice and criticism. In a report by the North East Development Board, for example, Lord Ridley wrote about the existing legislation: 'there is no coherent effort to treat the problem as a whole. It is nibbling at little pieces of it'.

In his last report before his resignation of 27 October 1936, the Commissioner recalled that the 1934 Act had provided no direct means to reduce unemployment. He believed that 'the time was now ripe for a second experiment which ... would make an attempt to deal more directly with the problem of unemployment' [14]. On the assumption that this would come about, he examined the options open to the government. These were: persuasion of firms to locate in the Special Areas, compulsion to make them locate there - or the prevention of factory construction in certain parts of the country [15] - and inducements [16]. The Commissioner had placed parts of his report in the hands of the government in July 1936 [17], and it is likely that the sections in which he urged more direct steps to reduce unemployment and the examination of the choices available formed part of the earlier document.

On persuasion, the Commissioner agreed with the Deputy Leader of the Opposition: it had failed almost completely [18]. The Commissioner was not in favour of compulsory location, but argued strongly for a curb on industrial expansion in the Greater London Area [19], although he knew that the effect of this on the Special Areas would be slow and uncertain. For more immediate effect, this left only the last option: financial inducements. These were to be of two kinds: exemption from income tax on undistributed profits not exceeding £500 and relief from local rates, and long-term loans at a low rate of interest 'to procure the introduction to the Special Areas of technical processes new to this country' [20].

The relief from income tax would save industry only some trifling amounts of money. The relief of local rates - already reduced by 75% - was more important, if only because it would remove the fear of industrialists that they might be raised. Government loans for new processes would have a direct effect on employment, even if they would be applied to relatively few projects.

As for the readier access to finance by small firms which the Commissioner had considered essential, the passing of the Special Areas Reconstruction (Agreement) Act in May 1936 (see next chapter) was a first step in this direction. Although the government would act only as a guarantor for a part of the loans which would be made available to new or expanding industry, it was, in fact, a first recognition that inducements to industry were necessary, if the situation in the Areas was to be dealt with more effectively than hitherto. To that extent, the Act may be seen to have been a political watershed, even if Mr. Shinwell (Lab., Durham, Seaham) described it as 'of all the pettyfogging, miserable, piffling and futile proposals that have ever come before this House, this is the least effective both in its intentions and its substance' [21]. Nevertheless, the fact that a significant change in government thinking had taken place was recognised at the time: Mr. Magnay, (Lib.Nat., Gateshead West), in whose constituency the Team Valley Trading Estate would be established, exclaimed in the House of Commons: 'to be frank, I never expected the Chancellor of the Exchequer would do this' [22].

The Times of 27 October 1936 carried a second leader entitled 'Urgent and Menacing', a quotation from a letter concerning the economic and social problems of parts of Durham which the Bishop of Durham had addressed to Parliament. In its comments on Bishop Henson's letter, The Times fired a shot across the bows of the draughtsmen of the King's Speech: 'forecasts of the business in Parliament in the new Session give no indication of any additional immediate action for the benefit of the Areas in which industrial depression lingers'.

The plight of the depressed areas was not to be forgotten and The Times believed that the march of the unemployed men of Jarrow - which was then approaching London - may be 'a wholesome if poignant reminder of the responsibility of the flourishing communities to those that have fallen into such an evil case'.

The Times also supported Dr. Henson's entreaty to the government 'to remember that the distressed areas propound a question which must be answered effectively if order and liberty are to be secure'. The leader ended by giving the government its marching orders:-

> The government's benevolence to the distressed areas has been shown ... Benevolence, however, is not enough; it must be reinforced by energetic efforts to provide not merely palliatives but the remedy of employment ... It is not to be admitted that the machinery and the resources of the modern State are incapable of removing the reproach of the distressed areas. Concerted action by the government could not fail.

In the event, the government ignored this advice and the King's Speech on 3 November 1936 offered no more than an extension of the 1934 Act [23].

There were early signs that this would not satisfy Parliament. In the Debate on the Address, Sir Archibald Sinclair (Lib., Caithness and Sutherland) voiced a widespread feeling - as subsequent events were to show - when he said 'it will be useless to extend this legislation unless we have an opportunity of amending it and making it a better Act' [24].

The government sensed the depth of feeling of the House of Commons too late. The attempt to avoid a debate by including the 1934 Act in an Expiring Laws Continuance Bill caused widespread resentment.

The usual procedure was to include in such Bills any Acts which were to be prolonged for some time. When it was intended to continue an Act for only a few months, a short Bill would normally be introduced, giving the House an opportunity to debate the Act which was to be prolonged.

The procedure adopted by the government on this occasion was widely criticised. Members feared that if the 1934 Act were included in the Continuance Bill, the government might never proceed with any amending legislation, because the government had many other pressing preoccupations, of which the rapidly deteriorating international situation was the most worrying. Although Chamberlain had claimed that the government did not have enough time to consider what to do about the Special Areas - in spite of the fact that the substance of the Commissioner's Third Report had been in its hands for three months -, there was a suspicion that, but for the strength of feeling displayed in the House, the government might not make a statement on its intentions.

The suspicion was largely justified. Chamberlain had never considered the Commissioners as part of the permanent machinery, but rather as filling a gap until the Unemployment Assistance Board could take over from them [25]. For Chamberlain, the Special Areas continued to present a problem of unemployment rather than a restructuring task.

The result was that the Debate, although technically on an Amendment to remove the 1934 Act from the Continuance Bill, turned into a full-scale debate on the problems of the Special Areas and the Third Report of the Commissioner [26].

During the Second Reading of the Continuance Bill on 17 November 1936, Chamberlain made a wide-ranging statement. He reviewed the problems of the Areas in the light of the reports by the Commissioner, whose recommendations the government was accused by many speakers on both the government and the opposition benches to have consistently ignored. In response to pressure from all sides of the House, Chamberlain pleaded for more time to consider the next step, but he teased the House with the possibility that he might have 'something to say later on about any further proposals which the government may have to make'. It never came to a formal statement on this occasion, but the Chancellor, nevertheless, revealed a good deal of what the government had in mind.

Referring to the Commissioner's recommendation that the Special Areas required preferential treatment involving unconventional principles, the Chancellor said that this was one proposal to which 'I can whole-heartedly subscribe'. He claimed that the 'whole theory of the setting-up of the Special Commissioners was to give preferential treatment to the Special Areas'.

On the location of industry, Chamberlain did not see 'anything revolutionary in that proposal, because really it is only an extension of the common practice of town planning schemes ... where we lay down that in a part of (a built-up area) no new factory shall be erected'. Why, then, was the government not prepared to contemplate any restrictions on the further expansion of industry in the London Area? Because, Chamberlain remarked, 'it is not difficult to see that even if new factories are excluded from the Greater London Area, it does not follow that an industry ... will ... at once go off to South Wales. I should think it would be much more likely to go to Birmingham'.

The government concluded, therefore, that it would not be sufficient to consider Greater London, and it would be necessary to carry this sort of planning well beyond London. But that was 'a biggish proposition and one that wants examination and, therefore, that examination it shall have' [27].

In other words, the government was prepared at least to study a location of industry policy. This willingness contrasted sharply with its attitude in the debate on 11 March 1936. But the change may not have been solely due to the pressure exerted from all sides of the Commons: in response to the Commissioner's plea for a limit to the further expansion of industry in and around London, the Treasury had commented that

> the government, in other connections, have had in mind the difficulties which arise from the continued growth ... of Greater London. In normal times, the provision of public services ... are presenting increasing difficulties. In times of emergency these problems would cause acute concern, and there is also the question of vulnerability. In these circumstances, the government are considering how the question can most profitably be further investigated [28].

While the preparation of a location of industry policy was likely to take a considerable time, inducements to attract industry to the Areas would have a more rapid effect. Surprisingly, 'State inducements' - as the Commissioner called them in his reports -, however 'unconventional', were apparently acceptable to the government, as the Chancellor indicated [29]:-

> If these proposals were to be applied to the country as a whole, I think I should still be inclined to offer firm resistance to them, but if they are put to me as an experiment in the Special Areas, to see how far they are likely to act, as the Commissioner says, as an attraction to industry to go there, ... I am perfectly prepared to say that I will accept in principle the suggestion of the Commissioner.

Among other ideas the Chancellor admitted to be considering was how best to implement the Commissioner's suggestion for certain reliefs of income tax and rates for new industries which 'will be one of the extended powers to be given to him (the Commissioner)', and he intimated that there would be other new powers. He also indicated assent when a Member asked whether the government was considering rate equalisation [30].

As for the rest of the long debate, the government was criticised from all sides, particularly by its own supporters, both for the procedure adopted with the 1934 Act and for its failure to act more effectively in the Special Areas. This led Mr. Ede (Lab., South Shields) to say at the half-way stage of the debate: 'I have not heard ... a single word in support of the government. That, I think, is unique, at least in my experience of the House of Commons'.

On 19 November 1936 the Chancellor made a speech in the Town Hall at Leeds in which he touched upon the problems of the Special Areas. He confirmed that it was intended to bring in fresh legislation, before 31 March 1937, if possible, and he hinted that the government might go even beyond the recommendations made by the Commissioner.

The second leader in The Times of 20 November 1936, entitled 'To Save The Areas', was critical of the Chancellor's speech the night before:-

There will have to be some hard and quick thinking in the meantime ... The government cannot fail to be aware, after recent discussions in the House of Commons and in the country, of the volume of opinion which calls for the saving of the areas. Only prompt and adequate measures will satisfy the conscience of a people that has been roused to a fresh sense of the necessity of rescuing the areas from decay.

The leader noted with satisfaction that Chamberlain had accepted the principle of 'State inducements to attract new industries into the Areas', but it was critical that no such acceptance in principle had yet occurred in regard to the control of the industrial expansion of Greater London, although the Chancellor was apparently prepared to examine the matter 'without preliminary prejudice'.

The Committee stage of the Continuance Bill was taken on 8 December 1936. An Amendment by Mr. Batey (Lab., Durham,Spennymoor) was withdrawn after Viscount Wolmer had persuaded the government to accept his own Amendment, which effectively increased the life of the 1934 Act by only two months.

There is no doubt that the government was made to change course, as Macmillan pointed out [31]:-

When the Special Areas Act was first put into the Expiring Laws Continuance Bill, it was to be continued ... until March 1938; that is to say, three weeks ago it was the policy of the government, as announced in the King's Speech, to take no further steps with regard to the Special Areas ... In that short time, owing to the interest and pressure exerted by the House of Commons, there has been this tremendous change.

Macmillan recalled that the Second Reading of the Bill had been blocked by a member of the government benches (Viscount Wolmer) 'helped by hon. Members on all sides of the House', and that, gradually, 'there was built up a determination ... that this matter should be dealt with on much more comprehensive lines'. For good measure, Macmillan warned the government that ... 'the revolt is spreading behind the government Front Bench very powerfully'.

The government had learned a lesson: so far as the Special Areas were concerned, a large body of its own supporters had become committed to policies directly opposed to those the government would have liked to pursue. This lesson would be remembered when the future of the Special Areas legislation was being decided two years later.

A few days before the Second Reading of the Continuance Bill, the Treasury had declared its opposition to the 'second experiment'. In a note to the Chancellor, in which he examined ways of attracting new industries to the Special Areas, Sir Warren Fisher wrote [32]: 'there is no satisfactory solution to be found in a government attempt to lure all and sundry to the places to which, above all, they desire not to go'. Furthermore, the Treasury was concerned not to upset established policies: 'any scheme which sets up hopes of the early installation of new works would kill transference'. On the particular proposals of the Commissioner, Fisher conceded that income tax rebates and rate relief might be discussed, but he was afraid that any substantial subsidies -

the Commissioner's proposals hardly amounted to that - 'would probably alarm employers' federations'. On loans, Fisher feared that 'the government was likely to be sold a pup', but sensing that some inducements were now politically unavoidable, he did not want the Treasury to be involved: 'if it were decided to try some specious-looking experiments, it would be better to leave them to the Commissioner for the Special Areas of England and Wales alone'.

Chamberlain was not pleased with the note from his Permanent Secretary and he added the following to Sir Warren Fisher's paper: 'I think it is possible to destroy very effectively any proposals for attracting new industries, but politically speaking, this is not a wholly satisfactory matter as it leaves things as before'. At the same time, Chamberlain again displayed his cynical attitude to the Special Areas: what he wanted from the Treasury was an examination of a policy of inducements 'not for its effectiveness, but whether this can do some harm'.

Whatever the government had in mind, it clearly had made a mistake in attempting to include the 1934 Act in the Continuance Bill and it was now obliged to produce something substantial in order to fulfil the expectations of the Areas and of the country. A leading article in The Times of 19 January 1937 reminded the government of this situation:-

> It would be fatal if the government's Bill were to embody a compromise between the general view that new and drastic action is necessary and the particular view, which lingers on in some quarters, that these areas should be considered as economic cemeteries, the character of which may be made more pleasant by planting a few flowers, straightening up a few tombstones and employing a new sexton or two, but cannot be radically changed. The condition of the Special Areas is a challenge to the efficiency of the government and of the democratic system.

In preparation of the Amendment Bill, the Inter-departmental Committee met on 11 January 1937. Two related topics predominated in its report [33]: the extension of the Special Areas and inducements to industry. The Committee believed that the number of firms which could be persuaded to establish themselves in the Areas by any inducements which were within the possibilities of practical politics would be limited; that the wider the areas were drawn, therefore, the smaller would be the results in any particular place; that the greater the range of attractions of some areas, the more difficult it would be to ensure that the worst spots would benefit from inducements. The scope for extension was also believed to be limited by political constraints: even if one could count on public sympathy with the plight of a few places, 'the wider the area the greater the probability of opposition being raised to the policy of inducements from other parts of the country'.

On inducements, the Committee evidently still shared the views exemplified by Lord Dunglass (ref.[6] above); according to these, inducements represented 'the use of taxpayers' money to bribe industry to go ... where it is uneconomic'.

In some other respects, the Committee was more positive and flexible, for example, it considered the tax and rate reliefs proposed by the Commissioner to be rather 'exiguous' (meaning meagre, slender), and agreed with him 'that there should be linked with these inducements ...

the provision of free or cheap sites'. This would have a double purpose:
it would enable the Commissioner to attract industries to places within
the Special Areas where they were most needed, and it would help to
clear derelict sites which were often the main contributors to the
repellent character of these places. The Committee was not only in
favour of variations in inducements depending on the needs of particular
localities, it proposed to leave the decisions on the appropriate level
of inducement to the Commissioners.

The Committee did not agree with the Commissioner's suggestion that
his functions should be taken over by a Cabinet Minister, even though
the idea had been supported - not for the first time - in the Lords a
few weeks before [34]. The reason given by the Committee for rejecting
the idea was that

> the whole field of expenditure in the Special Areas lies within
> the purview of one or other of the Departments and for each
> sphere there is already a Minister responsible to Parliament. To
> have a Cabinet Minister responsible for the Special Areas and
> the Special Areas Fund and to leave the other aspects of the
> same service under the present Ministers might very well lead to
> difficulties.

But these were no more than important details. The significant fact
was that, by the end of 1936 - and in spite of its doubts about
obtaining new industries on a scale which would make an impact on the
problems of the Areas - the government was inclined to accept the views
of the Commissioner, of Parliament and of The Times that the attempt
had to be made.

In anticipation of the publication of the Amendment Bill, the first
leader in The Times of 26 February 1937 examined the options open to
the government. The choice was 'between active intervention to revive
the Areas by replacing dead undertakings with new industries, and
acquiescence in their decay, removing out of them all the young and
energetic inhabitants for whom employment could be found elsewhere, but
regarding the areas themselves as almshouses for the irremovables'.

To underline the message, the leader writer challenged the tenets of
the Conservative Party: 'the direction and force of government policy
(are) subject to the belief or disbelief in the efficacy of
State-directed movement to restore economic vitality'.

The Times made it quite clear where it stood: 'as the years have
passed, the need for directing and controlling action by the government
has become more plain. There is no other authority capable of taking and
applying the necessary decisions and treating each area appropriately'.
The question of intervention had been removed from the realm of economic
management. It had become a political necessity.

The government announced on 1 March 1937 that the First Reading of the
Amendment Bill would be on 19 March. At the same time, it published a
White Paper, which was in the form of an account of its Special Areas
policy, followed by a Memorandum on the Financial Resolution which would
provide the necessary authority for introducing the Bill [35]. The White
Paper revealed little that has not already been - or will be - covered
in this work, except the fact that only £2.8 million of the £9 million

committed by the Commissioner had actually been spent up to 31 January 1937, indicating how difficult it was to make an impact on the situation in the short term.

The White Paper recited what had been done to provide work in the Special Areas through government contracts and the location of munitions factories. These matters will be referred to again in IV/3.

The government explained why it had decided to introduce inducements: 'the time has now come when, with the aid of some financial assistance directly applied, it will be possible to introduce into the Areas new industrial undertakings of the "light" type and thus provide more stable, because more diversified, employment' [36]. The Commissioner had argued the case in almost the same words.

In addition to various technical matters, the Financial Resolution proposed the creation of certified areas. It was a response to the pressure from areas with high unemployment - for example, South Lancashire -, which were not scheduled under the 1934 Act. The device of certification would enable the government to give some assistance to such areas without being committed to extend the Special Areas.

The Amendment Bill provided two kinds of inducements: the Commissioners would make contributions towards rent, rates and income tax (and later, towards the National Defence Contribution), while the Treasury would make loans, subject to the recommendations of an advisory committee, up to a total of £2 million in the first place. The amounts of Commissioners' contributions would be at their discretion, so that they could 'vary the inducements according to the necessities of the particular places to which they desire to attract industry' [37].

The Bill also empowered the Commissioners to finance and let factories anywhere in the scheduled Areas. The objectives of this new power and the manner in which it was implemented will be discussed in III/5.

The government's proposals were approved in the first leader in The Times of 2 March 1937:-

> There is no hesitation, and no hampering limitation in the new measures anounced by the government to attract industries to the distressed areas. The White Paper issued yesterday offers financial inducements surpassing those which the first Commissioner for the Special Areas of England and Wales recommended in his final Report ... The proposals abolish the restriction that the Commissioner's help must not be given to undertakings carried on for the purpose of gain. That by itself is a notable departure from the rule, which still has validity in normal circumstances, that the State shall maintain strict impartiality in its relations with industrial undertakings. The justification for the departure is in the abnormal circumstances of the Special Areas and the social and economic and national importance of reviving industrial life in largely populated areas, from which it is ebbing away and leaving desolation.

The Times noted that, by these measures, 'the government will bring the pressure of financial inducements, but not compulsion, to bear on the location of industry'. The Commissioner himself would have the most profound effect on location, because he was required to approve the place in which an undertaking wishing to qualify for the exceptional financial benefits had to establish itself.

The Times was not, however, completely satisfied: 'the government have not exhausted all the suggestions that have been under consideration. In particular ... a limit should be put on the industrial development of London'. Nevertheless, the conclusion of the leader writer was positive: 'if the government's programme for the Areas is not complete, it is advanced a long way by the policy expounded in the White Paper'.

On the next day, 3 March 1936, The Times summarised reports from correspondents in the Special Areas:-

> On Tyneside and the North East Coast, the general impression on the government's plans are favourable ... Lord Ridley, chairman of the North East Development Board and Sir Arthur Lambert, Northern chairman of the Special Areas Reconstruction Association Ltd, believe that a beginning has been made with a policy calculated to bring real and lasting progress to the districts most in need of national help ... The only criticism so far is that, in spite of repeated representations by civic leaders, no Minister has been made definitely responsible for giving effect to the proposals.

In yet another first leader, on 8 March 1937, The Times strongly supported such an arrangement: 'the control of policy for the Special Areas and the still wider depressed areas should be directed by a Cabinet Minister possessing high administrative ability and unwearying resource'.

This demand had been made before, most recently in the interim Report of the Labour Party Commission on the Distressed Areas, and it was to be made again in one of the Minority Reports of the Barlow Commission (see IV/2).

The government responded to the widespread demand for a location of industry policy by an announcement on 9 March 1937 of its intention to appoint a Royal Commission. After recalling the Commissioner's plea for control of the further expansion of industry in the Greater London area, the Minister of Labour remarked [38]:-

> This extension is occurring, not merely in London, but in other great cities, and it gives rise to grave problems, not merely of industry, but of health, communications, vulnerability from the air, and other problems that go far beyond the issue raised by Sir Malcolm Stewart. The government feel that these wider issues deserve authoritative and comprehensive study.

The debates on the Amendment Bill did not reveal any new ideas or matters which would be of interest in the evolution of regional policy. The essential changes in attitudes had already taken place. The Act received the Royal Assent on 6 May 1937.

Daysh and Symonds noted the change in the political climate which had made the Amendment Act possible: 'in 1937, Parliament accepted by a large majority a doctrine which had been unanimously opposed three years before - the financing of private enterprise from public funds' [39]. Sir George Gillett (the new Commissioner), too, commented on this change [40]:-

It is surprising and most significant that within the short period of two and a half years, public opinion both inside and outside Parliament should have undergone such a remarkable change that, when the Amendment Bill came up for discussion ..., there was practically no opposition to the proposal ... to give the Commissioners powers to offer inducements designed to persuade industrialists to establish undertakings in the Special Areas ... the force of his arguments, based on the practical necessities of the situation, was such that they commanded the ready acceptance of the nation.

So far as the location of industry was concerned, the new Commissioner clearly foresaw the future involvement of the State and paid tribute to the work of his predecessor [41]:-

If, as is not improbable, the State comes in the years to come to assume an increasing responsibility for the location of industry, whether on strategic or economic or social grounds, will not historians point to Sir Malcolm Stewart's Third Report and the Special Areas (Amendment) Act 1937 as marking the first definite step in this direction.

In the event, the new powers of the Commissioner made little impact. Only a small number of factories were built in the particularly hard-hit sub-areas of the region (see III/5), and by the end of September 1938, the total of rent, rate and tax inducements had amounted to no more than £100,000 (see Appendix 12). The Treasury loans - together with the funds provided by two other financial sources - were more widely effective (see next chapter). But the fears of industrialists outside the Areas of unfair competition from subsidised firms in the Areas - expressed quite forcefully at the time of the Amendment Act - proved to have been absurdly exaggerated.

The significance of the pre-War Special Areas legislation rested more in the fact that it prepared the next stage of regional policy than in its short-term achievements. The influence of the pre-War experience on the formulation of a much more interventionist post-War regional policy will be examined in IV/2.

For the sake of completeness, it should be added that the 1937 Act was to expire on 31 March 1939. The question of what to do after that date exercised the government and the civil service from the end of 1937, when the Inter-departmental Committee reported in favour of allowing the Special Areas legislation to lapse [42]. The Committee was afraid that if the Acts were continued, they would not only become a permanent feature of government administration, but pressure would be exerted by the existing Areas for more assistance and for other parts of the country with equally or even more severe problems to be included in the schedule of assisted areas.

But since the Commissioners' activities could not simply be discontinued - the trading estates quite apart -, they would have to be taken over by other government departments and by the Unemployment Assistance Board, and because the provision of capital had proved to be so effective in stimulating new economic activities in the Areas (see next chapter), special arrangements would have to be made to continue and extend these facilities.

The Treasury, too, urged that the legislation should lapse. It pointed out that the Acts were intended 'to be of a temporary nature to deal with an acute problem in a special way' [43]; the machinery established for this purpose was considered unsuitable for absorption in the permanent system of administration 'since it overlapped the functions of many government departments'. Sir John Simon, the Chancellor, put his objection to the permanence of the Commissioners in a similar way: 'the normal administration in this country is on a functional basis, through the medium of different government departments and not on a geographical basis' [44], and he, like most of the rest of the Cabinet, was opposed to intervention in principle, save in exceptional circumstances. Because of the improvement in the situation of the Areas, he - and other members of the government - considered that such circumstances no longer existed.

But the Special Areas had many champions who would be dismayed by the ending of the legislation and the government had to tread warily; it was anxious to avoid a repetition of the situation on 17 November 1936, when its own supporters deserted over its intention not to amend the 1934 Act.

The importance the government, individual Ministers and the civil service attached to this question may be gauged from the fact that of the 24 reports and memoranda submitted to the Cabinet Committee on the Reports of the Investigators and Commissioners for the Special Areas between 10 October 1934 and 28 June 1939, 11 were concerned with the expiry of the 1937 Act.

The Cabinet Committee decided on 29 June 1938, to allow the Special Areas' legislation to lapse, subject to recommendations by the Inter-departmental Committee on how to deal with the continuation of the activities initiated by the Commissioners [45].

At the next meeting of the Cabinet Committee on 10 November 1938, however, a number of Ministers - including the Minister of Labour - appear to have changed their minds, partly because the economic situation had deteriorated since the Inter-departmental Committee had first reported almost a year earlier. Chamberlain, now the Prime Minister - who remained chairman of the Cabinet Committee - , sensed that he would not obtain majority support for a policy of discontinuation. Accordingly, it was decided to extend the legislation for a year, i.e. to 31 March 1940, and, furthermore, to take powers to extend the facilities of the Treasury Fund by a short Loan Facilities Bill.

The Minister of Labour announced the government's intentions in the Commons on 14 November 1938 [46]. The Bill was introduced on 1 August 1939 [47], a few days before the summer recess. When Parliament was recalled on 24 August 1939, it was concerned with a much weightier issue: the imminence of the War. The Loan Facilities Bill never received a Second Reading and was withdrawn on 27 September 1939 [48].

On the face of it, the Bill was a technical measure to top up the Treasury Fund and to enable it to be used in places outside as well as within the Special Areas. But the government may have had an additional motive: the loan facilities under the Bill would have outlasted the extended 1937 Act. The continuation of loan assistance would have made it politically less difficult to let the Special Areas legislation finally lapse in 1940.

The government appears to have discussed the termination of the Special Areas legislation on one or two occasions during the War (see IV/1) - when it proved to be unnecessary and was inactive -, but in the event, the legislation was extended until it was replaced by a far more interventionist measure, the Distribution of Industry Act 1945 (see IV/2).

4 Finance for industry

The purpose of the Team Valley Trading Estate was to facilitate the
introduction of new industries to the North East. But there were many
who thought that factories alone would not achieve this aim: new firms
and expanding industries would require ready access to capital.

Although this proposition was widely accepted, it had been taken for
granted in the civil service that worthwhile ventures would have no
difficulties in obtaining support from the banks. There was no need,
therefore, for any government-backed loans. Indeed, the
Inter-departmental Committee had suggested in 1934 that such facilities
would attract unsound ventures [1]. Two years later, the Treasury had
warned the government - in connection with the proposed Treasury loans -
that 'it might be sold a pup' [2]. The gradual change in outlook on the
role of financial assistance as an inducement to new and expanding
enterprises represented an important aspect of the evolution of regional
policy.

For the purpose of this study, a distinction must be made between the
roles played by finance in facilitating the expansion of manufacturing
activities in the depressed areas of the North East in general, and in
attracting new or expanding industries to the pre-War
government-financed factories in particular. Before drawing a conclusion
on the relative importance of these roles, an account is given here of
the situation in 1934, and of the steps taken in 1936 and 1937 to
improve it.

The availability of finance for small and medium-sized firms in the
country as a whole was examined by the Macmillan Committee on Finance
and Industry, which had reported in June 1931. The Committee concluded

that, even where security was perfectly sound, great difficulty was experienced to raise sums ranging from small amounts to £200,000 [3].

In the North East there was an additional problem: the lack of locally-based financial institutions. The Investigator for Durham and Tyneside had reported that representative opinion considered this situation a real handicap to the promotion of new enterprises. The problem was seen to be due to the rationalisation of the banking system, which had resulted in the extinction of the small local banks. Accommodation for anything but very modest funds had to be sought in London. When Attlee had asked the Economic Advisory Council in 1931 whether this concentration of banking and financial institutions was one of the reasons for the growth of new industry in and around London, Sir Alfred Lewis of the National Provincial Bank had claimed that the big banks 'were doing all in their power to decentralise' and that 'never before had local managers been given such wide powers of responsibility' [4]. But the experience in the North East was otherwise. A report to the Tyneside Industrial Development Conference in 1930 had confirmed the existence of a major problem [5]. The Investigator for Tyneside had raised it again, yet in spite of the evidence he produced, the 1934 Act had made no provision to overcome it.

Wallace had drawn attention to the fact that even the more specialised finance houses did not meet the need. While organisations such as Credit for Industry Ltd had been established - probably as a result of the Macmillan Report - with the express purpose of promoting more investment within the country, their activities were limited to financing the expansion of existing businesses [6]. Jarvie, the managing director, specifically cautioned against 'the provision of any sum of money to be handed over to a large number of small people whose only asset is hope - and that a doubtful one' [7].

Given that the Cabinet Committee examining the Commissioner's trading estate proposal had considered it unlikely that industry would move into the Special Areas on any significsant scale, it would have been logical to encourage new local enterprise by any means. But it was precisely this kind of activity for which it was difficult to raise capital.

This recognition had caused a group of Tyneside businessmen - again led by Col. S. Monkhouse - to set up a small industrial finance company in 1933, Northern Industries Development Ltd. Its object was to to help to create new manufacturing ventures rather than secure an adequate return on its capital. Wallace felt that this approach might point the way: 'within the limitations imposed by its financial resources, it has proved of real value, and I believe that some such organisation on a much larger scale would be worthy of government support' [8]. The Commissioner referred to this brave venture in his First Report, but concluded 'that the capital they were able to raise on Tyneside was not sufficient to ... give the experiment a fair chance' [9].

As a result of the frequent representations he continued to receive from all the Areas, the Commissioner proposed to the government on 26 July 1935 that a fund be set up for the specific purpose of stimulating the establishment of new and the expansion of existing industries in the Areas [10]. The timing of this initiative is of interest: within less than three weeks, the Commissioner would propose government-financed factories. If and when these became available, it would become more important than ever that capital was readily available.

The Commissioner had become convinced that neither the banking system nor any other institutions would provide what was necessary, and the relatively small amounts involved would rule out public subscription. On the other hand, he did not believe that private enterprise should be financed with government funds. He hoped that the necessary money would be found by financial interests in the City of London. If it were to prove impossible to obtain such funds without some form of government guarantee, however, he 'should regard the giving of such a guarantee as one of the unorthodox measures essential to the Special Areas if they are to be given the opportunities for effective recovery' [11].

In a series of recommendations to the government in October 1935, the North East Development Board claimed that all efforts to attract new industries to the Area had brought to light the necessity for having a special financial organisation in the Area, the function of which would be to finance start-up industries as well as the development of existing ones [12].

The recommendations were made a few weeks before the government formally agreed to finance a trading estate in the North East. The North East Development Board was almost certainly aware of the discussions which were going on. Indeed, since it also pleaded for government-financed trading estates, it is likely that both recommendations were intended to strengthen the Commissioner's negotiating position with the government.

The Commissioner's representations were discussed by the Cabinet Committee on 16 October 1935 [13] - the day before the Committee approved the first government-financed trading estate. One Minister suggested low-interest loans, to be provided through the local authorities. The Chancellor had an alternative proposal, incorporating the Commissioner's suggestion for government guarantees: applications for loans should be received and sifted by the local Development Boards. If they were in favour of an application, it would be passed to the Commissioner. If he approved it, 'he would ask the banks to go beyond their usual practice in extending credit'. The Commissioner would have authority in such cases 'to guarantee the first 25% of any loss which might ensue'. Chamberlain's proposal involved three organisations, a rather cumbersome procedure. In the event, the idea was dropped in favour of leaving the task to a finance house which would be established for the purpose.

A confirmation that the government was preparing some action came from Lord Eustace Percy, Minister without Portfolio, in a speech to the North East Development Board on 28 November 1935 [14]:-

There is a factor of credit for these new industries ... I can go so far as to say that the government realises the full force of the recommendations which Mr. Stewart (the Commissioner for England and Wales) has placed before them and that in one way or another, credit grants will not be lacking for new industries with sound prospects.

By this time, the Bank of England had concluded that 'criticisms of the financial machinery available for developing business, and particularly small business in the Special Areas, can no longer be ignored' [15]. The Treasury, too, realised that some form of government backing for additional finance was now politically inevitable. It doubted, however, whether it was really needed - doubts which were shared by the financial community. If that supposition proved to be correct, any government action would be embarrassing, because loans would not be taken up. It was anxious, therefore, to limit the amounts available to £1 million [16]. A later Inter-departmental Committee took a negative view for the opposite reason: if loans were to prove effective, the government would find it hard to resist pressures to extend the scheme [17].

Because of the conflicting advice, - and in spite of the political pressure - the government found it difficult to proceed with a first small measure of financial intervention, which, in any event, ran counter to its basic beliefs. The Commissioner was kept waiting for six months before the government was ready.

On 21 April 1936, the Chancellor announced that the government was willing to experiment [18]: 'accordingly, arrangements are being made for the formation of a company called the Special Areas Reconstruction Association Ltd (SARA) with a nominal capital of £1 million and with the special function of financing small businesses, either existing or to be formed hereafter, in the Special Areas'. No capital would be subscribed by the State, but assistance would be given in the form of a guarantee against losses amounting to about 25% and a contribution to management expenses. There would be in each Area a local Board and an office for the purpose of collecting applications and assisting in their examination. As a general rule, advances would be limited to £10,000 for any one loan. The funds would be subscribed by banks, insurance companies, other financial institutions and industry. This arrangement was exactly on the lines proposed by the Commissioner.

Heim [19] sees the willingness of the financial community to subscribe the funds to have been motivated 'by the desire to ward off demands for more far-reaching government intervention to deal with the politically pressing issue of severe unemployment in the depressed areas'.

The justification for this measure as an experiment recalls the government's attitude to the 1934 Act: when political pressure made unorthodox action unavoidable, it was presented as an experiment. And just as Chamberlain was pessimistic about the chances of success of the first government-financed trading estate, he was 'not sanguine of success' regarding this measure. 'I would not be surprised' a note believed to be by him records, 'if a good part of any money lent is lost' [20]. In the event, this forecast proved to be wrong: in its report for 1943, SARA showed that, of the 145 firms assisted, only 20 had failed and a further four were in the hands of the receiver. The total loss suffered by SARA was only 4.1% of the money lent [21].

The participation by the government required a short Bill, and this was enacted on 6 May 1936. It was a beginning, but not an adequate one. Within a year, the Special Areas Amendment Act 1937 would make provision for government loans.

In December 1936, help came from another, unexpected quarter: Lord Nuffield donated £2 million to the Treasury for the particular purpose of providing financial support to new or expanding enterprises in the Special Areas [22]. Again, the loans were to be limited, in principle, to £10,000. This source was to prove particularly useful because it made available approximately half of its funds against preference shares [23]. This not only overcame the lending limit, it enabled such funds to be used to attract further money either from SARA or the Treasury, or, indeed, from the banks.

The Special Areas Amendment Act was discussed in the last chapter. Under section 6 of the Act, the Treasury was empowered, subject to the advice of a Special Areas Loan Advisory Committee (SALAC), to advance monies to persons carrying on any industrial undertaking established in the Special Areas subsequent to 6 May 1937, provided that the undertaking was likely to employ at least 10 people. The initial amount of money available was £2 million, but, in contrast with the rules of SARA and the Nuffield Fund, there was no limit to the size of any one loan. While the other funds were restricted by their lending limits to the smaller firms - although this did not apply, in practice, in the case of the Nuffield Fund -, Treasury assistance was evidently mainly intended for larger projects. The Commissioner had proposed that Treasury loans should be used particularly to finance industrial processes new in Britain [24].

In total, £5 million had become available by May 1937 for supporting the growth of industry in the Special Areas of England, Wales and Scotland: £1 million from the financial sector - supported by a partial government guarantee -, £2 million from a charity, and £2 million from the Treasury. Adjusted for the value of money, these amounts were considerable - even by the standards of later policies - and they played a significant part in priming new activities in the Areas.

Heim [25] has investigated the role assigned to these funds and the political background. It will be shown in the next chapter that early steps were taken to ensure the cooperation of the three Funds with each other and with the Commissioner, who coordinated the loans provided by them with the inducements he was able to offer under the Amendment Act, particularly to firms willing to move to the more 'difficult' parts of the Special Areas.

In his Fifth Report, the Commissioner reported that capital assistance from the three sources had been granted to 88 undertakings in Durham and Tyneside up to 30 September 1938 [26]. The contributions from the funds were not stated separately for the North East, but in respect of all the Special Areas, the Nuffield Fund had provided £1.61 million, SARA £0.57 million and the Treasury £0.95 million, a total of £3.13 millions. Loans were not restricted to firms in government-financed factories. Indeed, it will be seen that such recipients were very much in the minority in the North East of England.

Even if the figures provided by the Commissioner were not quite consistent with those given in a report by Lord Portal earlier in 1938 [27], they do permit some conclusions on the operations of the Funds: the fact that the Nuffield Fund was closest to being exhausted indicates that it was the most accessible. It was certainly 'the easiest to administer and the most flexible and helpful, owing to the greater freedom with which it can be used' [28]. Neither the Treasury nor the SARA funds could be deployed as readily, because public money or money partially guaranteed by the government was involved.

It is not the object here to examine in detail the operation of the three Funds or to list all the firms which obtained accommodation up to the beginning of the War. The information appears to be available, though not all of it is easily accessible [29].

A record is readily available, however, of the commitments of the Funds in the North East up to 1 February 1938 (in the report by Lord Portal referred to above). The information is reproduced in Appendix 16. Because more than 60% of the £5 million available from the three funds had been committed by this time (in all the Special Areas of the country), the information permits a number of further conclusions.

The list shows that the Nuffield and Treasury Funds cooperated in financing relatively large projects (Group 2), with most of the money going to two firms proposing to set up in Jarrow. The high ratio of capital to estimated jobs shows that they were capital-intensive industries. The Treasury Fund alone financed two other capital-intensive projects, the larger one again in Jarrow (Group 5). This type of financial support was in line with the aim to implant manufacturing processes new to this country in the Special Areas, although the financing of relatively large projects - as distinct from small firms - caused political difficulties with industry outside the region [30].

The Nuffield Fund and SARA cooperated in financing firms in Group 3. The Nuffield Fund alone financed firms in Group 4. It will be noticed that the firms in this group, in aggregate, made the smallest capital contribution of any Group, apart from the single firm in Group 1, which obtained support from all three Funds without providing any capital of its own. Finally - and in view of the criticism voiced in Parliament a year earlier this is of interest -, the largest number of firms (41 out of 75 in the list) was assisted by SARA alone (Group 6). The fact that the loans were relatively small or very small - with an average of £3,737 per firm - was in line with the remit of SARA, as Heim has shown [31]. While the average contribution to the total capital by the firms in this group was 32%, 25 of the 41 firms contributed none.

The total committed by the three Funds in the North East up to February 1938 was £1,408,790, and the capital contributed by the firms themselves was £856,670, making a total of £2,265,460. The average contribution by the firms was 37.8% of the total capital, although the percent contributions differed greatly between and within the groups.

The investments were expected to result in employment for 6,384 people, but the time estimated to achieve this was not specified, nor has it been investigated whether all the projects materialised. A relatively large one, a china manufacturing plant, (E.Rosenthal, Group 2) certainly did not. If all the jobs had materialised, the contribution by the Funds would have been £221 per job on average.

It can be seen from Appendix 16, that, so far as they can be identified, only 14 of the 75 firms on the list were located or intending to locate on the government-financed trading estates in the area. Included in the 14 were all those firms which had by then agreed to come to St. Helen's Auckland in South West Durham (2), Pallion (1) and Tynemouth (1), i.e. to the 'outside sites' (see next chapter). It would appear that only 10 actual or intending tenants at Team Valley had obtained financial support up to that time, including some of the more significant ventures. Since the Team Valley Estate had secured between 50 and 60 tenants at the time of the Portal Report, it seems that lack of support from the Funds did not prejudice the start or expansion of the large majority of firms there. This must have surprised the Commissioner and others.

What emerges is that there were evidently a considerable number of new or expanding firms in the region as a whole, and that the importance of the Funds at Team Valley was not decisive, at least in terms of numbers of firms assisted.

The conclusion must be that - except on the 'outside sites' - Funds and government-financed factories played mainly a parallel rather than a complementary role in obtaining new economic activity in the region.

Lord Portal claimed that 'finding capital for industry is far more economical and in keeping with the industrial situation than any other form of inducement' [32]. Since the first factories at Team Valley had been occupied for less than six months before Lord Portal reported, this cannot have been a well-considered view. Indeed, the Minister of Labour, in a memorandum to the Cabinet Committee on 13 June 1938 did not agree with it: 'no doubt the provision of capital has been of great assistance, but so also has the provision of factories, which is capital assistance in another form' [33]. While it remained to be seen which was the more economic form of assistance, 'it seems quite possible that the government will get a better return on the money they have lent for the development of the Team Valley than on the capital they have put into new industries through the Treasury Fund'.

Return on money apart, the government must have been interested in the relative effectiveness of the Funds and the government-financed trading estates in creating employment. From the figures available, it is possible to make a very rough comparison between the cost per <u>forecast</u> job resulting from the involvement of the three Funds, and the cost per <u>actual</u> job resulting from the public investment at Team Valley (ignoring the fact that, up to February 1938, at least 10 firms at Team Valley had obtained offers of loans from one or more of the three Funds).

At the end of 1937, the revised estimates of the Company to 31 March 1941 foresaw a total expenditure at Team Valley of £2,336,500 [34]. Of this amount, £1,287,500 was allocated to the development of the site and amenities and £1,049,000 to factory construction. For the purpose of the argument it is assumed that the money was, in fact, fully spent and that the factories built occupied one quarter of the developed site. The site and amenity cost of the factories constructed can then be assumed to have been £321,875. The total investment in the factories and sites in use was, therefore £1,370,875. At £221 per job, this investment would have had to result in 6,203 jobs to equal the <u>forecast</u> performance of the Funds.

By 1 September 1939, 4,000 jobs had been created at Team Valley (see Appendix 14). During the War employment reached almost 7,000 [35], although only a few more - admittedly large - factories had been constructed, probably all but one financed by the Company [36]. While the employment is overstated by the number of jobs in the factory not financed by the Company, it may, neverthless, be seen that Lord Portal's assertion proved to be incorrect.

The importance for the Special Areas of ready access to capital - and the fact that the banks were not functioning adequately in this respect - was not lost on the government. When the discontinuation of the Special Areas legislation was discussed by the Cabinet Committee in the summer of 1938, the continuation and expansion of the Treasury Fund, at least, was well supported.

5   The outside sites

The next stage in the evolution of government-financed factories in the North East began with the Special Areas (Amendment Act) 1937. Section 2 of the Act empowered the Commissioner to clear sites and build factories anywhere in the Special Areas. This - and other new powers - would enable him to assist those parts of the Areas which had not benefited very much from the improvement in the labour market and remained in special need.

The pressures exerted by local authorities and politicians may well have influenced the Commissioner to request the powers under Section 2 of the Act, but there is much evidence that he had independently come to the conclusion that trading estates on the Team Valley pattern would not meet the needs of more than a few of the larger localities. They were designed for a working population within a limited radius, however defined in practical terms. The Commissioner saw a need for single or small groups of factories in a number of the smaller places, particularly where the main source of employment had ceased to exist: 'large districts ... could not be served by only one estate and ... attempts must be made to induce industry to go to other places in the Areas' [1].

The new powers offered new opportunities for the Commissioner, but they also raised new policy questions and problems of administration. They had to be exercised within the enlarged Special Areas machinery, which now included not only the trading estates companies in the North East of England, South Wales and South West Scotland, but also SARA, the Nuffield Trust and the Treasury Fund.

The Commissioner for England and Wales had formed some.preliminary conclusions, which he wished to discuss with the executives of the organisations concerned and in the presence of his District Commissioners and industrial advisers (and their Scottish colleagues). Accordingly, he convened a conference in London on 3 March 1937, a few days after the publication of the Amendment Bill. The general theme of the conference was 'The Attraction of Industries to the Special Areas'. The meeting was to consider particularly a policy of variable inducements to attract firms to the more 'difficult' places, a modus operandi which would avoid competition for tenants between the trading estates companies, and the procedure for clearing sites and erecting factories in places outside the trading estates.

The response to the Commissioner's circular in the summer of 1935 had shown that British industry was not interested in establishing works in the Special Areas. Now that factories to rent were becoming available, the position began to change, as the early experience at Team Valley had already demonstrated. Under the new circumstances, there was a danger that the three trading estates companies might compete for tenants. The problem would assume an added dimension once the Amendment Act was passed, because the Commissioner would become yet another provider of factories to rent.

The competing interests of the Areas were recognised before any of the government trading estates companies had been incorporated. The matter was voiced in Parliament by Major Herbert (Con., Monmouth) on 2 March 1936: 'I feel the time will shortly come when the Special Areas will have to compete one against the other for the entry of trade and industry into their areas' [2].

It was evident that a procedure would have to be established to prevent the companies outbidding each other in terms of rent concessions. Some industrialists might seek information from all three estates companies. It was necessary 'to prevent overlapping and to minimise the danger of unscrupulous applicants playing off one part of the organisation against another' [3]. The Commissioner was concerned that the estates companies should not themselves offer any rent concessions but should refer such requests to him. He would act as a confidential clearing house. This would ensure uniformity in regard to policy.

Appleyard expressed the opinion that the Team Valley Estate would become such an attractive location that 'in the normal way, the Company did not wish to give any inducements at all, and if a tenant asked for special concessions, they would refuse' [4]. There might be special cases, however, where rent concessions for a period of up to two years might be considered. Appleyard's statement was probably intended as an invitation to his colleagues from the Welsh and Scottish trading estates companies to take the same view.

Competition between the companies apart, the Commissioner would now be able to decide that one Area was in greater need than another and use his new powers accordingly. This led Appleyard to voice the fear that 'the Commissioner might favour South Wales against the North East' [5]. But Sir George Gillett assured the meeting that

there would ... be no question of utilising the new concessions
under the Bill to the advantage of one area and the disadvantage
of another, but there would undoubtedly be isolated places of
the type of Bishop Auckland (in South West Durham) and Dowlais
(in South Wales) which would require exceptional treatment
within the area [6].

The Commissioner would exercise overall influence on all inducements,
including loans. Lord Portal, the chief industrial adviser of the
Commissioner for England and Wales, informed the meeting that the
Nuffield Trust and SARA were in close contact and coordinated their
activities; he presumed that the Treasury Fund would establish a similar
connection with them.

The Commissioner then explained to the conference how he proposed to
have sites cleared and factories erected in places where he decided that
this was necessary: the trading estates companies would act as his
agents.

There appears to have been little discussion on this suggestion and
the meeting agreed, perhaps a little too readily in the light of later
developments, 'that the trading estate companies would be willing and
able to act as agents for the Commissioners' [7].

Following the passing of the Act on 6 May 1937, the Commissioner took
steps to implement his new powers. Since he had already briefed the
companies, most of the contents of his letter of 27 May 1937 [8] were
already known to the Company:-

> (The Commissioner) had reached the conclusion that the sites
> will be cleared and factories provided most expeditiously and
> conveniently if he can enlist the cooperation of the trading
> estates companies for the purpose of clearance and the actual
> erection and letting of factories on his behalf ... Generally
> speaking, (he) contemplates that the provision of factories
> under this section will be carried out on a number of scattered
> sites, some, however, of which may be adequate to accommodate
> more than one factory, but on each of which actual development
> will be restricted to the provision of factories for which the
> Commissioner is satisfied that an actual demand exists on the
> part of an industrial concern about to be established in the
> district.

The last part of the above quotation contained an aspect of the policy
of which the Company may not yet have been aware: while clearance and
site preparation were to be carried out as soon as the Commissioner had
selected a site, no factory would be built until a tenant had been found
and a lease signed [9].

Although the powers of the Company were not limited specifically to
operations at Team Valley, the existing arrangements between the
Commissioner and the Company were not suitable for the new task. The
Commissioner recognised this: 'it is clearly not feasible to treat such
sites on the same lines as the Team Valley Trading Estate; moreover, the
financial arrangement with your Company is strictly limited to
activities on the Trading Estate and its form is inappropriate for such
cases'. He therefore proposed the following procedure:-

Any sites required for the provision of factories in the circumstances described above should be acquired by (the Commissioner) and handed over to your Company under a separate agreement in each case, the basis of which would be that the site is leased to your Company for 99 years for development ... the cost of the development being borne by monies to be advanced from the Special Areas Fund, and the rent reserved for the site under the lease being the annual excess of income from factory lettings over expenditure on maintenance, management, reserves for depreciation and the like.

The letter informed the Estates Company that the Commissioner's approval would be required in advance of any site development. Factory construction as well as rents would equally be subject to his approval. On the assumption that the Company would accept these proposals, a general procedure was appended.

Considering that the chief officers of the trading estates companies had agreed at the meeting of 3 March 1937 to act as the Commissioner's agents - both in the clearing of sites and the construction of factories -, the Commissioner may have been surprised by the ensuing events.

The Board of the Estates Company considered the Commissioner's letter at its meeting on 7 June 1937. The Board minute recorded that

after considerable discussion, in which Commander Micklem expressed the view that the Company should concentrate solely on the development of the Team Valley Trading Estate for the time being, the Board approved the suggestions put forward (by the Commissioner) in principle, subject to drawing up an agreement satisfactory to the Company. The chairman undertook to deal with the Commissioner on any points in the draft agreement which he considered in any way inimical to the present activities of the Company.

The possible effect of the 'outside sites' - as they came to be called - on the development of the Team Valley Estate caused a great deal of anxiety to the Company. This is evident both from the correspondence with the Commissioner and from internal memoranda and Board minutes.

Some concern was hardly surprising: the development of the Team Valley Estate was still in an early stage. The first factories were not yet ready for occupation, and while the number of enquiries - and, indeed, the number of tenancies obtained - was greater than had been anticipated, this large venture needed many more tenants before it would become viable.

The Company also sensed an implication that the Team Valley Estate was not sufficiently well sited to serve, if not the whole of the North East, at least a large part of it [10].

Methven asked the opinions of his colleagues: Whitehouse, the sales representative and future sales manager, expressed surprise that labour was not willing to travel reasonable distances to work and suggested that, if the North East wished to compete with the South East, it would have to display an equal degree of mobility [11]. He also raised practical objections: small groups of factories would cause problems both for the industrialist - who would find too small a pool of labour in the locality - and, indeed, for the workers - who might suffer inordinately if one of these factories were ever to close down. At the same time, such isolated small sites would cost more to develop and the cost of factory construction would be higher.

Percival, the Company secretary, was concerned by the political implications [12]:-

The Commissioner's funds are not unlimited, and it would be tragic if capital which ordinarily would have been devoted to the development of Team Valley should be diverted to other sites ... The more the Commissioner does in this direction, the more difficult will it be for him to stop: if he agrees to Sunderland, how can he possibly refuse West Hartlepool, South Shields and even Tynemouth.

He also drew attention to a possible conflict of interests: 'our Board is composed almost exclusively of men interested in Tyneside, and for this reason (they) give their services to the Company ... But if the success of Team Valley was to be prejudiced by these outside sites, how could the Board possibly fail to be biased'?

The Inter-departmental Committee had foreseen the problem: after examining how the 'Commissioner's' factories were to be built, the Committee had reported that the choice lay between using the government trading estate companies - in areas where they existed -, or to create ad hoc organisations. The only argument against the former solution was 'the possibility of a clash of interest between their concern for their main estate and their interest in other parts of the area' [13]. The Committee felt that if the assistance offered to different places were graduated and if the decision on this point rested with someone other than the companies, the difficulty could be overcome, provided the goodwill and cooperation of the companies were obtained.

Appleyard objected strongly to a particular aspect of the draft procedure for the Commissioner's sites: the need to submit plans for each factory. Without wishing to cast any reflections on the Commissioner's office, Appleyard wrote 'most of us know very well what happens when details of this kind have to be submitted for approval to a government department' [14]. A recent experience had strengthened his fears: the Company had been kept waiting for six months for a decision on the lighting of a factory being built for a government department.

There was little further development during the summer months of 1937, the draft agreement having been turned over to the lawyers. At the Board meeting on 12 July 1937, a specific request by the Commissioner that the Company undertake the clearance and development of a site at East Gateshead was noted and approved, subject to a satisfactory agreement.

The outside sites and the proposed extensions of the Company's activities were discussed again at the Board meeting on 4 October 1937. It was reported that the Commissioner had agreed to the establishment of a factory at Tynemouth. The site for this factory was a small portion of an area described on the plan as a trading estate. This led Sir George Martin - the government representative on the Board - to say that 'he viewed with considerable alarm the opening up of many areas in the North East for industrial purposes ... the Team Valley was a national undertaking, and if other trading estates were started in the Areas, thus causing the Team Valley Estate to serve Gateshead alone, the expenditure on which they had embarked could not possibly be justified' [15]. Commander Micklem remarked 'that there would be no end to these extensions if they were given way to. It was clear that any industries setting up in these other places were a direct potential loss to the Team Valley Estate'.

The Board put down the proposed outside sites to 'political expediency' and agreed that, from the national standpoint, the success of the Team Valley Estate was paramount. It resolved, therefore, 'that the Board view with much disquiet the tendency on the part of the Commissioner for the Special Areas to multiply industrial sites in different parts of the area which are locally called "trading estates"' and that

> the chairman be instructed to make strong representations to the Commissioner in this sense, and to indicate that the Board will have to reconsider its decision to act as the Commissioner's agent if its activities are to be dissipated over a large number of schemes to the disadvantage of its main task, which is the creation of the Team Valley Trading Estate as a North East enterprise.

The Board resolved, further, 'to enter a strong protest against the selection of Tynemouth as the centre for an industrial area'.

The Tynemouth site illustrated the Commissioner's dilemma: a prospective tenant was obtained by the publicity efforts of the Tyneside Industrial Development Board (as a result of its participation in an exhibition at Charing Cross Underground Station, London, in 1937). Since the area in which the Development Board wanted the factory to be sited had a high unemployment rate and there were unfavourable structural factors, the Commissioner acted well within his remit and powers when he agreed to build a factory there and to offer inducements to the prospective tenant. But he was obliged to take into account another matter: the funding of the Development Board was almost continuously being questioned - in the Newcastle Council at least - and the Board had to show some results if it was to survive. Its precarious position may also have been the reason for its negative attitude to the Team Valley Estate [16].

Appleyard and Sir George Martin visited the Commissioner at the end of October 1937. They reported to a Board meeting on 1 November 1937 that the Commissioner had confirmed the central role of the Team Valley Estate. The Commissioner had felt strongly, however, that in cases where local authorities or development boards had succeeded by their own efforts to attract industries to their districts, they should be entitled to retain them, if only as a reward for their efforts! Sir George Martin observed that this would enable every local authority to act, in effect, in competition with the Team Valley Estate.

Regarding single sites, the Commissioner appeared to agree with the Company's views, at least so far as light industries were concerned, but he had insisted that such sites should be opened to heavy industries.

Sir George Martin feared that this might result in precisely the sort of situation which they were trying to cure: the dependence of a locality on a single industry. So far as Tynemouth was concerned, the Commissioner was committed to the single factory. He assured the visiting directors, however, that he would not agree to the development of a trading estate there and, indeed, 'would do all he could to discourage such an idea'.

But in spite of its reservations, the Board agreed on 1 November 1937 to cooperate with the Commissioner at Tynemouth and in South West Durham, while cooperation at Pallion (Sunderland) seems to have been tacitly agreed before.

So far as South West Durham was concerned, the Commissioner had pointed out in his Third Report that this area presented one of the most difficult problems of all the Special Areas [17]. While the employment situation on Tyneside and in East Durham had markedly improved, it did not appear to have changed significantly for the better in South West Durham (see Appendix 19). In a letter of 30 October 1937 [18], the Commissioner rehearsed once again the arguments for special treatment, and it became clear to the Board of the Company that 'all the government's forces were to be concentrated to attract industry to that area' [19]. Indeed, following a report by Sir Alexander Gibb and Partners, a special organisation was set up in September 1937, the South West Durham Improvement Association Ltd, with powers and funds to make the area more attractive to industry [20].

South West Durham apart, there were sound arguments in favour of outside sites, and not just 'political expediency', as the Company had claimed. Nevertheless, the Commissioner admitted that he was under political pressure [21]:-

Local criticism (of the concentration of effort on the Team Valley Estate) need disturb you far less than us, because of your remoteness from the rarefied political atmosphere ... I am sure that a great deal more interest will be taken in the individual sites, and I anticipate closer interest in our activities amongst the politically minded. It is for this reason that we shall be driven to take a rather more active interest in the detailed affairs on individual sites than we have thought to take in connection with the trading estates proper.

The Company confirmed the recent discussions with the Commissioner in a letter of 3 November 1937 [22]. It noted that the Company's views on single sites had been accepted. Concerning the role of the Team Valley Estate and the scale of operation which followed from this, the letter recorded the Company's understanding of the situation as follows:-

(the Board) viewed with special satisfaction the opinion expressed by the Commissioner that the Team Valley Estate is regarded by him as the only Trading Estate in the North Eastern Area in the full sense of that term and the main focal point for the attraction of light industry to that area. This statement relieves from the minds of my Board the apprehension that they had embarked upon too large a scheme in view of the others for which their cooperation is now being enlisted.

At the same time, the Company could not forbear to advise the Commissioner of its view that limits should be set to the opening up of new factory sites: 'my Board feel ... that with East Gateshead, Pallion and South West Durham, the North East area is well served with alternative locations for industry and they desire to convey to the Commissioner their feeling that no further extension of the movement to set up these small industrial areas should take place'.

Finally, the Company offered to ensure that 'a proportion of the light industries coming to the area would be diverted to the new sites'. It is not known whether the Company was ever in a position to implement this offer. The Inter-departmental Committee, in any event, had assumed that 'the initiative in attracting undertakings to sites other than the trading estates proper would rest with the Commissioner'.

Although some reasons for the concern of the Company about the outside sites have already been advanced, the continuing anxiety poses a problem of interpretation: the proposed site at Pallion covered 17 acres, and that in South West Durham 15 acres. The site at Tynemouth was small and, until after the War, supported only a single factory, as the Commissioner had promised. The Team Valley Estate, by comparison, extended to 700 acres, even if part of the site would not be available for many years. As for East Gateshead - once a candidate site for the first trading estate in the North East -, there was no immediate intention to do more than clear the sites, as much for aesthetic reasons as for providing industrial land. In any event, there were serious acquisition and clearance problems and work was not to start until the middle of 1939, only to be terminated again for the duration of the War.

The development of the three small sites would hardly pose a serious threat to the future of the Team Valley Estate. It is likely, therefore, that it was the <u>principle</u> of the outside sites rather than any other considerations which caused the Estates Company such apprehension. As Percival had observed earlier, once the principle was accepted, there were many places in the North East with good claims for government-financed factories, and if, in the end, Team Valley was to serve only the Gateshead area, Sir George Martin's concern about the viability of the venture would be justified.

The Company's concern also caused it to magnify the financial implications of the outside sites for the Team Valley Estate. In his letter of 30 October 1937 [23], the Commissioner had accepted that the policy of creating industrial areas where factories would be financed by him 'may retard, to some small extent, the development of Team Valley and may postpone for a short time the date at which the Company can be expected to pay full interest on the capital advanced'.

The Company was unwilling to accept a forecast of such minimal consequences. In its letter of 3 November 1937 it had claimed that 'at the present time there is being diverted to Pallion and to South West Durham a number of factories equal to that which the Board had anticipated they might get into Team Valley in its first year and, in rent roll and importance, a little beyond that'.

At first sight, this claim is difficult to accept: there was room for a total of about 15 factories on the outside sites. At the time, there were four being 'diverted' to South West Durham, five to Pallion, and one to Tynemouth. Was it likely that the Company had aimed for no more than 10 tenants at Team Valley in the first year? In any event, the Company had done much better than this [24], although many of the tenants were very small firms.

Furthermore, the Company's reference to 'factories being diverted' was misleading: with one or two exceptions, the projects on the outside sites had not progressed beyond the enquiry or negotiation stages. A few days earlier, the Commissioner had confirmed that no tenants had yet been obtained in South West Durham (see [25] below).

From the reference to the rent roll, it is clear that the Company was troubled by the relatively large floor area being negotiated at St. Helen's Auckland and Pallion, rather than by the number of prospects. It will be shown later that the factories on the outside sites were almost twice as large - on average - as those at Team Valley.

The Company's stance involved a certain contradiction: on the one hand it feared the competition from the outside sites, on the other it claimed that it would be difficult to find tenants for them. The Company's letter of 3 November 1937 rehearsed both arguments:-

> The diversion of the energy (required to turn the Team Valley Estate into a viable venture) to other places is bound to have a very serious effect upon the Team Valley Estate, not only because of the factories diverted but also on account of the fact that the selling effort necessary to get people into these other areas is a good deal greater than is necessary in Team Valley.

Although the Company overstated its responsibility for obtaining tenants for the outside sites - if it had any at all -, it realistically appraised the efforts necessary. This was confirmed by the Commissioner in his letter of 30 October 1937 [25]:-

> The industrial development of the district (South West Durham) is dependent very largely upon the introduction of light or semi-light industries, but although the Commissioner and those associated with him have made many efforts to secure the establishment of such industries in the district, it has to be admitted that up to the present these efforts have had little or no effect.

Even with the available inducements, the Commissioner succeeded in obtaining the first tenants for the outside sites only six months after the passing of the Amendment Act, and even then, the circumstances were unusual, as will be explained later (see [31] below).

Since the Special Areas Fund had such a large stake in the Team Valley Estate, the Commissioner would certainly have wished to avoid any real difficulties for the Company to arise out of the exercise of his powers under the 1937 Act. For this reason, it is possible that the Company's representations did have some effect on the Commissioner's policy. This may be inferred from the Commissioner's letter of 13 December 1936 [26], in which he spelled out how far he was able to accept the opinion of the Board regarding further industrial sites in the North East:-

He fully sympathises with the view that, so far as possible concerns desirous of establishing light industries in the Durham and Tyneside area should be encouraged to utilise the Team Valley Estate or one or other of the group sites available; and unless exceptional circumstances arise, he anticipates that this will in fact be the result of the policy he has already adopted. At the same time, your Board will appreciate that the Commissioner's powers under the Special Areas Amendment Act 1937 are not limited to the provision of factories or inducements to persons establishing themselves on any specified site. While therefore the general policy ... will be as indicated above, he feels ·that he would be unjustified in leading your Board to assume that in no conceivable circumstances would he lend assistance by way of the provision of site or factory to an industry desirous of establishing itself within the North East Special Area in a district other than those covered by the foregoing arrangements.

The Commissioner, in the event, added only a single site to the list - at Crook in County Durham. The commitment of funds for the purchase of a site at Jarrow was mentioned by the Minister of Labour [27], but no other details have been found. Because it proved to be impossible to complete the clearing of the site at East Gateshead before the War or to proceed at Crook, St. Helen's Auckland in South West Durham, Pallion and Tynemouth were to remain the only pre-War outside sites.

Given the new circumstances, the Company now asked to be relieved from the more arduous terms of the Finance Agreement. In its letter of 3 November 1937, the Company had enquired

whether it is not possible to waive entirely the provisions of the Agreement for the payment of interest after the initial five year period. My directors feel that if this is done they will no longer be in a position where under one agreement they are expected to make a financial success of the Team Valley Estate, whilst at the same time they are, at the request of the Commissioner and acting as his agents, definitely preventing themselves from achieving this, particularly as they will not be the final arbiters as to where people shall go, since clearly the financial attractions that the Commissioner can offer together with those of SARA and the Nuffield Trust are exercised to the disadvantage of the Team Valley Estate, although they are, of course, to the advantage of the Commissioner's general policy.

The Commissioner believed that the Company was 'overestimating the effects of this partial diversion of their energies from the Team Valley Estate' [28]. As for waiving the obligation of the Company to pay interest altogether, the Commissioner considered this

to be quite impossible ... unless the whole conception of the financial relations between the Commissioner and your Board were radically revised. The removal of the obligation to pay interest would ... involve ... a much closer financial control over the activities of your Company in relation to Team Valley than either he or your Board would consider practicable or desirable.

In other words, the Company would have to accept the constraints of a commercial business as the price of freedom from control of all aspects of its operations by the civil service.

The Commissioner asked the Company to leave the matter open for consideration at a later date, and this was agreed at a Board meeting on 10 January 1938, on the understanding that the Company was entitled to raise the matter at some convenient time 'when they have a clearer conception of the effect of developments in other parts of the Area'.

While the early establishment by the directors of an alibi for a possible inability to pay interest in due time can be understood, their assumption that the Commissioner would exercise his financial discretion under the 1937 Act to the disadvantage of the Team Valley Estate needs some further comment.

The Commissioner certainly had intended to reserve the inducements he was able to offer for those parts of the Special Areas with the most serious problems, but the policy was not immutable. On one occasion in 1938, the Company asked the Commissioner to use his powers in favour of three firms which were considering to rent factories at Team Valley. The Company believed that inducements 'would turn the scale' in these cases [29]. The request gave the Commissioner the opportunity to set out his policy in a letter of 25 October 1938 [30]:-

> The question of the application of the Commissioner's powers granting contributions towards rent, rates and income tax to undertakings on the Team Valley Estate was very fully discussed when the 1937 Act was on the stocks, and we understood that Col. Appleyard concurred in the opinion that, in view of the attractions already offered by the Team Valley Estate, the general extension of the contributions to firms going there was unnecessary. Accordingly, as you know, the Commissioner does not, as a rule, offer inducements to firms proposing to set up on the Team Valley Estate.

After referring to two exceptions to the rule which had already been made at Team Valley, the Commissioner explained the circumstances in which he would make further exceptions:-

> We are reluctant to add to these unless a case arises in which the Team Valley is the only place in the North Eastern Special Area which the applicant will consider or which is in any way suitable for their undertaking, and where without some inducement the persons concerned will almost certainly set up their undertaking outside the Special Areas.

It is clear from the exceptions that the Commissioner's practice had become more flexible since he had first outlined his policy to the estate companies on 3 March 1937. The probable reason for this was that the number of firms willing to go to the outside sites was limited, and he certainly did not wish to turn away potential tenants from the North East altogether. His dilemma strengthened the negotiating position of firms who would not consider any other location in the North East than the Team Valley Estate.

Up to the War, the Company had offered rent concessions to 10 tenant firms, amounting to £2,600 in total (Appendix 17). In the light of the Commissioner's instruction to the trading estates companies to refer requests for rent concessions to him, he had almost certainly authorised them. The inducements the Commissioner had in mind in his letter of 25 October 1938 included rent concessions, but went beyond them. It is the additional inducements - although small in cash value - which he particularly wished to limit at Team Valley in order to improve the balance of advantage in favour of the the outside sites. But every firm coming to these sites would have obtained financial accommodation from one of the loan funds, and this would have been the most decisive inducement.

The need of a large number of manufacturers to escape from Hitler's Europe provided new opportunities for the Special Areas, and the Commissioner cooperated with the Home Office in steering suitable projects into the Areas. The Commissioner had at his disposal a potential sanction in such cases which could not be applied to British persons or firms: he was in a position to decline his support. For some applicants and their families, this would have literally amounted to a sentence of death. It does not surprise, therefore, that two of the first refugee firms in the North East agreed to settle in South West Durham [31]. They (and a later arrival) would eventually occupy over 75% of the factory space built at St. Helen's Auckland before the last War (see Appendix 21).

Although the Commissioner may well have exerted some pressure, the needs of the outside sites and of these firms (and of one which agreed to go to Tynemouth) were, in fact, particularly well matched: the refugee ventures promised to be somewhat larger than average on the one hand, and they needed all the financial help the Commissioner and the loan funds could offer, on the other.

A brief account of refugee industries in the North East will be given in the next chapter.

The negotiations between the Commissioner and the Company on the outside sites continued into 1938 and the separate agreements for the sites were eventually signed. These agreements will not be discussed here in detail, but there were some specific differences compared with the practice at Team Valley, beyond those of principle already mentioned: for example, the responsibility for roads was placed in the hands of the local authorities and tenants would be encouraged to buy their sites and factories.

In the event, the competition from the outside sites proved to be less serious than the Company had feared - or, at least, made out to the Commissioner. In June 1938 the Company was able to inform HM The King, the Prime Minister, the Minister of Labour and the Commissioner, that they had secured their 100th tenant [32]. Although this was strictly true, a number of service and professional tenants were included who would occupy no more than one or two offices in the central administration building at Team Valley. Furthermore, it is believed that a number of those who had signed undertakings to rent factories failed to complete. But as a public relations exercise, the announcement made an impact.

By contrast, only 10 tenants had been secured for the outside sites a year later.

It is possible to quantify the relative importance of the outside sites. In a letter to the Commissioner of 13 June 1939 [33], the Company reported as follows:-

Floor area completed   at Team Valley: 843,466 sq.ft.

"   "   "   " Outside Sites: 138,440 sq.ft.

By mid-1939, therefore, the floor area of the factories on the outside sites amounted to 14.1% of the total in government-financed factories in the North East.

The figure given for Team Valley appears to have anticipated the achievement by the end of June 1939 (see Appendix 14). But while further factories were completed at Team Valley (Appendix 14 shows 890,805 sq.ft. occupied and completed by the end of 1939), it is believed that no further factories were built at the outside sites up to that time. If that assumption is right, the share of the floor area on the outside sites was reduced to 13.5%.

The monthly schedules supplied by the Company to the Commissioner enable at least a crude calculation to be made of the average amount of space occupied by tenants, subject to the proviso regarding the definition of 'factory' at Team Valley in Appendix 14. This proviso is unnecessary for the outside sites, because each factory was occupied by a single tenant.

According to the information for May and June 1939, the position was as follows (see Appendix 14 and [33] above):-

at Team Valley: 98 factories, total area occupied 740,142 sq.ft.
                 = 7,552 sq.ft. per factory (average)

on Outside Sites: 10 factories, total area occupied 138,440 sq.ft.
                 = 13,844 sq.ft. per factory (average)

Realising that he would succeed in attracting only a limited number of firms to the outside sites, the Commissioner evidently aimed to obtain larger projects than the average at Team Valley in order to make an impact on the local unemployment situations.

The establishment of the outside sites under the Special Areas Amendment Act 1937 (and the Treasury Fund created by the same Act) marked the beginning of the direct involvement of central government in regional development in Britain. The relative independence of the Estates Company had lasted exactly one year: from the incorporation of the Company in May 1936 to the passing of the Amendment Act in May 1937.

The term 'outside sites' - coined at a time when the Company saw the Team Valley Trading Estate as the centre of industrial development in the North East - ceased to have any meaning when government-financed factories spread across the region after the last War, but the term continued to be used by the Company for some years. The post-War sites up to the end of 1948 will be discussed in V/1 and V/2.

6 The early years of the company

The two years between the occupation of the first factories at Team Valley in the late summer of 1937 and the onset of the War were eventful ones for the Company. A highlight of this period was the visit of HM The King and Queen to the North East on 22 February 1939. The Royal couple spent some three hours at Team Valley and formally opened the Estate in the presence of 500 people. The King and Queen later lunched at Team Valley with men and women from all walks of life in the North East. The King unveiled a commemorative tablet in the north hall of the administration building. In the afternoon, the Royal party travelled to St. Helen's Auckland for a brief visit to the small estate there, while Sir Malcolm Stewart, the former Commissioner, unveiled another tablet in the south hall of the administration building.

From the large amount of material covering this period, it is evident that some topics predominated:

The quality of the development continued to be of great importance to Appleyard. Within the resources available, everything would be done to achieve high standards.

Because of the negative attitude of British industry towards the North East - shown up so glaringly in the response to the Commissioner's circular in the summer of 1935 -, the demand for factory space was initially quite unforeseeable. The anxiety on this score was reflected in an intensive public relations effort.

Refugees from Hitler's Europe began to play a significant role just at the time when the rate of letting factories to nationals began to decline. But the introduction of these industries did not proceed entirely smoothly.

Most of the tenants were engaged in industries new to the region. They employed mainly women and juveniles. The Trade Unions were unfamiliar with this type of labour and the relatively low wages it commanded at the time, while the Company found itself under pressure to include fair wages clauses in its leases.

There was some concern - both on the part of the Commissioner and the Company - that the improvement in the employment situation on Tyneside might result in the government losing interest in the rapid development of the Team Valley Estate. There is some evidence that this concern influenced the development policy of the Company.

In the following, these topics will be briefly examined.

But the most interesting questions of the early years arise in regard to the tenants on the Estate: how readily did the Company find them?, who were they?, where did they come from?, what industries were they engaged in and what impact did they make on employment in the two years before the War?

An attempt will be made to answer these questions. Detailed information on tenants will be found in Appendixes 20, 21 and 22.

THE QUALITY OF THE DEVELOPMENT

The site was magnificent: located within the Tyneside conurbation, it had a definite rural character. The wide valley of the River Team was contained between wooded slopes. To the West, Ravensworth Castle could be discerned, to the East was Low Fell, the residential suburb of Gateshead. To the North, Newcastle could be seen at a distance across the river. To the South the view was open towards Birtley.

There was something of a visionary in Appleyard. This was evident already in his early correspondence with the Commissioner. He was determined to show 'what could be done by industrial planning ... in the most modern fashion' [1]. The Estate was not only to become an efficient industrial site, but it would also be 'as beautiful as it can be made within the limits of industrial requirements and a moderate expenditure of money'.

Aesthetic aspects of the layout and of the detailed architectural design remained a constant preoccupation of Appleyard. For example, there were to be no pitched roofs which might recall traditional factory buildings. In spite of the experience that flat roofs caused condensation problems, they were used throughout, with parapets hiding any sight of them. An attempt was made to maintain this requirement even during the darkest days of the War [2]. The Post Office was persuaded to install the entire telephone network underground, although this added to the cost. To reduce it, the Company arranged to have contractors on site who would open the trenches and cover them up again after the telephone cables had been inserted. It was one of the first schemes of its kind undertaken in Britain. The lighting standards, too, received special attention and were designed by Holford himself. Flood lighting was installed at a number of the early factories, visible from the main railway line and from the Great North Road. This was considered a great success.

Amenities played a large part in the Company's planning. They included small green spaces in front of most factories, large flower beds in prominent public places and grassy verges on the main highway. In order to ensure a plentiful and cheap supply of plants and flowers, the Company started its own nurseries almost before any factories were completed. Sports grounds and public gardens were included in the earliest plans.

Judging by the results, more imagination and will appear to have been applied at Team Valley than at the conception of the next two government-financed trading estates being developed. It must be said, however, that these sites did not present the same opportunities as the Team Valley [3].

From the moment the first factories were rising above ground, visitors to the Estate seemed to agree that Appleyard's aims were being achieved.

The quality of the development being created did not go unnoticed by the first workers on the Estate, and their home environment was compared unfavourably with it. In an undated note for a speech - probably in late 1937 or early 1938 -, Appleyard recorded that three young girls in an unnamed firm, offered an afternoon off, begged their employer to let them stay 'because the works were so much nicer than home'. Girl workers in another Team Valley factory asked for the club room to be opened on Sundays, 'so that they could entertain their friends in decent surroundings'.

PUBLIC RELATIONS

Public Relations were taken seriously by the Company from the beginning. An advertising agency - the London Press Exchange Ltd - was appointed at the second Board meeting, on 15 June 1936. The agency obtained a good deal of press coverage on the activities of the Company. Visits to Team Valley by groups of journalists and industrialists were encouraged as soon as there was something to see. On 26 May 1937, for example, some 50 journalists were shown over the Estate, although no factories had yet been completed. The visit produced good notices and was expected to lead to closer cooperation with the press. A visit from the trade press took place on 1 December 1937. On this occasion, a speech by Sir Frederick Marquis (later Lord Woolton), one of the industrial advisers of the Commissioner, received wide publicity in the national and the trade press. An overseas Press visit on 9 December 1937 was attended by some 60 people and led to at least four specific enquiries from abroad.

Visits by organised groups of the Press and trade organisations - for example, toy and leather goods manufacturers - were not by any means the only ones. The visitors' book recorded an almost continuous stream of representatives from government departments, Members of Parliament, academic institutions, local authorities, individual industrialists and private persons, indicating the great interest which the Estate had aroused at home and abroad.

An excellent prospectus of the Team Valley Estate entitled 'Today's City of Tomorrow' was published in 1937 and later, a film was produced entitled 'New Fields for Industry', apparently for the New York World Fair in 1939.

Other publicity activities included the appointment of an exhibition officer and the preparation of a scale model of the Estate, which was displayed in a shop rented by the Company at 130 Grainger Street, Newcastle upon Tyne, from 26 May to 5 June 1937. While intended mainly to inform the public about the Estate, it did, in fact, result in a number of enquiries for factories. The model was later exhibited in other places, including the head offices of the London & North Eastern Railway Company at Marylebone, British Industries House, Oxford Street, Charing Cross Underground station - all in London - and elsewhere. The Company also exhibited at British Industries Fairs, and although the number of enquiries received there was not large, they were of good quality.

In addition to advertising the Estate, efforts were seen to be necessary to publicise the attractions of the region itself. For many years, reports of industrial difficulties and social distress had created a one-sided image. The success of the Estate was seen to depend to a large extent on the attitude of industrialists making location decisions, on managers who might be asked to move to the North East, and on their wives and families. Accordingly, the Board considered the preparation of a book on the amenities of the region. A draft for such a book, written by a Mr. F.A. Willis, was not accepted and other authors were asked [4]: Prof. G.M. Trevelyan - of an old Northumberland family -, Dean Alington of Durham, H.V. Morton the travel writer, and Sir William Beach Thomas. None of these were able to help. The task was eventually undertaken by Douglas Goldring, on behalf both of the Company and the North East Development Board, which had also felt the need for such a work. The book, entitled A Tour of Northumbria , was published at the end of 1937 [5] . It was well received by the Board and was sent to all enquirers from outside the region. Methven was able to report that 'its reception by the Press and public has been extraordinarily good' [6].

Appleyard did much travelling and speaking all over the country, mainly to Chambers of Commerce. His reference in Leeds to the availability of nursery units at Team Valley at a rent of £1 per week resulted in a number of enquiries being received from outside the North East. Few, if any of these came to anything, but they did indicate a need for small, low-rental factory space in other parts of the country, too.

More formal opportunities were not overlooked. Appleyard lectured to the Royal Society of Arts in May 1939 [7]. Boyd, of the Commissioner's office, gave a lecture to the Society of Chemical Engineers in London in November 1937 [8], which included a brief progress report on the Team Valley Estate. His aim on that occasion appears to have been to solicit ideas for new products or processes based on raw materials indigenous to the depressed areas.

In December 1938 - nine months before the War - Appleyard travelled to Germany to address the Anglo-German Society on government-financed trading estates at Essen on 15 December, no doubt in pursuit of tenants. On the same day, he broadcast from Cologne. He went on to speak in Copenhagen on 16 December [9]. He carried with him a collection of slides and a photograph of the scale model of the Estate. The model did not represent the actual layout of the factories, but the fact that the photograph was left in Germany was to cause some anxieties at the outbreak of the War. A Board minute records that the government was asked about the wisdom or otherwise of the visit to Nazi Germany after the appalling pogroms a few weeks earlier. The government, apparently, 'approved strongly' [10]. According to the minute, Appleyard was to go again in January 1939 to speak in Berlin and Copenhagen.

The publicity effort attracted some unusual proposals. To give one example: in March 1937, the establishment was contemplated of a large pea cannery, subject to the satisfactory outcome of a cropping experiment at Team Valley [11]. The experiment was very successful, but the canning company decided against the project.

A wide range of ideas was tried out to obtain tenants, and to help establish new firms which might become tenants. The visit of journalists on 26 May 1937 was used to announce a scheme for overseas firms, which was initiated and given wide publicity by the Evening Chronicle , Newcastle upon Tyne: the Company would offer free warehousing accommodation for a short period, while an experimental sales campaign on behalf of the overseas firms would be run by the newspaper. In the event of the campaign leading any such firms to establish themselves in this country, they were expected to rent a depot or factory at Team Valley [12]. The Unemployment Assistance Board was asked to identify men who might possibly go into business in a very small way [13]. Leading local industrialists were approached and 'showed the greatest readiness to cooperate in advising or assisting in any way in their power to suggest new lines (products) to be established' [14].

A scheme for improving the performance of existing tenants by some form of 'after-care' service was suggested by a member of the Commissioner's staff. A meeting to discuss this idea was to be held in October 1938 at the Commissioner's office, but no follow-up has been found.

Public Relations were evidently developing strongly and must have taken up a good deal of Appleyard's and Methven's time. Table 2 would indicate, however, that these efforts - supported by the national press and specialised publications - did not achieve very much: enquiries leading to tenancies began to fall off soon after the public relations effort should have become more effective, i.e. after the first buildings began to rise above ground in May 1937. Some reasons for this disappointing outcome will be examined later in this chapter.

REFUGEES

In his report for the year to 30 September 1938, Methven noted that 'the initial rush of enquiries ... has been overcome'. While he claimed that the flow of new enquiries had not yet shown any sign of abating, 'more sales effort is required, but any slackening in the rate of letting to nationals is being largely made good by foreigners encouraged by the Ministry of Labour to establish their industries in the Special Areas' [15].

Refugees have already been mentioned in the last chapter. The history of refugee industries in the North has been recorded by the present author in another work [16], but because of their relative importance in the early years of the Company, the background will be repeated here.

The first reference to the potential of refugee industries for the Special Areas was made by the Commissioner in February 1936 [17]:-

Owing to ... unsettled conditions in certain countries abroad, it came to my notice that a number of foreign firms were considering the establishment of industries in this country. I have ... been in touch with representatives of some of these firms with a view to exercising persuasion on behalf of the Special Areas, and ... I am hopeful of success in more than one instance.

Reference has been made in III/3 to speakers in the Commons and the Lords who had advocated a location of industry policy for foreigners, in the first place at least, and to the amendment tabled by Boothby in the debate on the Location of Industry in the Commons on 11 March 1936, which the House had approved.

Relying on this resolution, the Ministry of Labour initiated a correspondence with the Board of Trade and the Home Office, the gist of which was that the admission of refugees intending to set up factories in Britain should be made conditional on their willingness to go to one of the Special Areas - or, at least to an area with high unemployment - rather than to the London area or the Home Counties [18], for which they had shown a strong preference. While the Board of Trade would have liked refugee manufacturers to settle in the Special Areas, it reminded the Ministry of Labour and the Home Office of the statement by the government on 11 March 1936 that it would not compel manufacturers to put up factories in areas to which they did not wish to go [19].

This correspondence indicates that refugees were beginning to be seen to present opportunities as well as problems. While up to then the Home Office merely responded to applications for admission by refugee manufacturers, applications of potential benefit to the Special Areas would now be encouraged.

The working practices of the Home Office, however, were unsuitable for this novel approach and a new aliens' admission procedure was introduced in May 1937. This included, for the first time, the Commissioners for the Special Areas. From then on, they received copies of the questionnaire which had to be completed by intending refugee manufacturers. The Commissioners would discuss each application with the Ministry of Labour. The Board of Trade would be consulted on the general merit of each case and to ensure that the proposed project did not create unreasonable competition for British industry - which would have caused political difficulties. The Commissioner would be able to offer assistance to refugees and help to procure capital from SARA, the Nuffield Trust and the Treasury Fund, if he was anxious to attract a particular project.

The Home Office had no powers under any of the Aliens Orders to make the admission of aliens dependent on settlement in any particular area. In its replies to applicants, the Home Office went no further than to point out that 'the question of the locality in which it is proposed to establish the enterprise will be considered, among other matters' [20]. But at a time when people were becoming increasingly desperate to get out of Germany, Austria and Czechoslovakia, the Home Office had a powerful weapon for steering refugees into the Special Areas: it let it be known that admission to Britain would be granted more quickly to anyone proposing a project in the Special Areas than in the Greater London Area [21]. By means of this procedure, the Home Office, in effect, implemented a location of industry policy some nine years before it was generally adopted in Britain (see IV/2).

It may be noted that the new procedure was established at a time when the 1937 Amendment Act would enable the Commissioner to offer inducements to attract industries to those places in the Areas where they were particularly needed. The new procedure also coincided with the expected completion of the first factories at Team Valley.

By February 1939, the Home Secretary was able to announce that some 200 of the 300 factories established by refugees were located in the Special Areas [22]. The number is likely to have increased sharply after February 1939, because the majority of refugees arrived during the eight months before the outbreak of the War.

In response to representations by the Commissioner about the delays in processing applications from refugee manufacturers, a further change in the admittance procedure was effected early in 1939 by the establishment at the Home Office of a separate branch to deal with industrial enquiries from aliens [23].

The enquiries from refugees did show up one of the problems in the relationship between the Commissioner and the companies: insofar as he did not particularly wish to attract refugee applicants to places in which he had a special interest under the 1937 Act, he would pass them to the most appropriate estates company. The Company seems to have been concerned that it might not receive its share of such enquiries. Like the other government estates companies, the Company actively sought to obtain refugee manufacturers by its own efforts. Whitehouse, the sales manager, was sent to the continent of Europe on a number of occasions to make contacts. He appears to have been less than pleased that, under the procedure, any enquiries he received on his journeys had to be passed to the Commissioner [24].

The share of the Commissioner's enquiries apart, the Company was uneasy about the methods adopted by the other estates companies to obtain tenants. For example, in his report for February 1937, Methven implied that the maintenance of a London office by the Welsh company put it at an advantage, and he considered the single case known of that company offering a potential tenant a rent-free period of one year as unfair practice [25]. This incident would imply that the Company did not go quite as far in its concession policy, although it had certainly offered rent rebates to some early tenants (see Appendixes 17 and 20). Although the Commissioner had instituted a procedure for avoiding competition between the companies in March 1937, some rivalry was never entirely absent.

By the end of 1939, 25 refugee firms (of which one had already gone out of business) had rented government-financed factories in the North East. Of these, 21 were at Team Valley, three at St.Helen's Auckland in South West Durham and one at Tynemouth (see Appendixes 18 and 21).

Their number in relation to the total number of manufacturing tenants at Team Valley is of interest. Table 3 shows that there were 76 manufacturing tenants at Team Valley. The 21 refugee manufacturers, therefore, comprised 27% of manufacturing tenants, although they occupied initially only 14% of the floor area - more than half of the total being occupied by a single firm.

About 15 other refugees had reserved factories (see Appendix 14, Notes on Progress Information, 2.f) but did not arrive. Some failed to get out of Europe before the outbreak of the War, others may have failed to obtain the capital they had counted on (the Nazis did not allow them to bring any with them). In one or two cases, they appear to have gone to the government trading estate in Wales. In another case, however, a change of plan in the opposite direction is also known.

Not all refugees coming to the North East before the War settled in government-financed factories; there were at least four which were attracted to the area by the Tyneside Industrial Development Board. Three started in older buildings in the Tyneside area [26], and one at a sand quarry some miles away.

The employment figures of refugee firms at Team Valley and the outside sites for 1940, 1963 and 1974 are known (see Appendix 18). Although by 1974 the number of firms was reduced to 17 by closure, acquisition or removal, the surviving firms had quadrupled their employment compared with that in 1940 (from 1,253 to 4,817). As several firms employing about 100 people in all in 1940 had moved away from Team Valley to other locations on Tyneside before 1963 - mainly because female labour was becoming very scarce -, the growth in employment in the firms remaining at Team Valley is slightly understated. The movement away from Team Valley continued, and with the establishment of post-War refugee firms in other parts of Tyneside and elsewhere in the North East, the importance of such firms on the Team Valley Estate declined further. By 1974, less than half the employment in refugee firms in the region was at Team Valley.

It would have been surprising if the establishment of refugee industries had not been accompanied by some jarring notes. British manufacturers seem to have been inordinately sensitive to possible competition. A rather offensive question relating to the refugee firm at Tynemouth was asked in the House of Commons in March 1939 [27]. The question was discussed in the Evening News , North Shields and effectively answered in a leading article on 28 March 1939. The Trade Unions, too, made a number of unjustified claims, which will be discussed under 'Industrial Relations' below.

The Company evidently felt it necessary to explain the role of refugees. In a lecture to the Tyneside Geographical Society, Methven was reported to have said [28]:-

> Regarding aliens and foreigners, we have been told that we are creating a new Jerusalem and that we need an Esperanto office on the Estate. Well, I consider these statements a compliment. We have been grumbling in this country long enough about unemployment. We have as good workmen as anywhere in the world, but we tend to be a bit conservative. If any alien can come here, start a new industry, reduce unemployment, reduce our imports and increase our exports, and then adopts our nationality, then I say 'good luck' to them.

'If you could appreciate what these people are doing', he added, 'you would take your hats off to them'.

INDUSTRIAL RELATIONS

The type of labour employed at Team Valley attracted unfavourable comment. Again, Methven had to explain (in the lecture referred to above): 'in view of the comments often made that we are particularly employing girls and juveniles, let me say that ... we are out to attract light industries and light industries use girls and juveniles'.

The Trade Unions in the area were not yet well represented in the light industries employing women and juveniles, but they reacted vigorously to what they held to be low wages in these industries. Some of their attacks were directed at the refugee firms. For example, Councillor J. Middleton, the Northern District Secretary of the National Union of General and Municipal Workers, was reported to have included the following remarks in a speech on 17 September 1938: 'a large proportion of those now occupying factories built at the expense of the British public and employing British subjects at wages which can only be described as "sweated" are foreigners' [29].

These remarks drew the following reply in a letter to the North Mail Newcastle upon Tyne, on 26 September 1938:-

> Councillor Middleton makes a sweeping allegation to the effect that Team Valley firms owned by foreign refugees are exploiting labour. I desire to protest in the strongest possible terms against such an accusation, not in the least, because Cllr. Middleton has made no examination of the wages paid in my factory nor that of many foreign-owned factories. I pay a little more than the wages advised by the Labour Authorities ... my traveller was refused business in Darlington, although the customer had no idea what wages we pay. He took his line from Mr. Middleton's statement. If the North East requires new industries, this is not the way to get them.

The Manchester Guardian of 1 October 1938 reported that the Company had agreed to a trade union request for an impartial enquiry into wages. This was untrue, but the Commissioner could not ignore the announcement. In response to an enquiry from him, the Company pointed out that it drew the attention of any prospective tenant - particularly a foreign one - to the current wage rates in the district and that it tried to find out whether an enquirer intended to be a good employer; whatever the initial position might have been, the Company believed that fair wages were now being paid by all its tenants and that, if it were to insist on particular wage rates, it would incur a future responsibility to see that they were being paid. The Company concluded that it could not and should not interfere. The Commissioner agreed with this view [30]. In so far as these remarks referred to refugees, neither the Company nor the Unions seemed to have been aware that the permission granted to any foreigner by the Home Office to settle in Britain with the intention of establishing a manufacturing concern included the following standard condition: 'permission to conduct business in the United Kingdom is subject to the payment of not less than the minimum rates of wages set out in the Notices issued by the appropriate Trade Board, if any' [31].

Related to wages, concern was caused by the cost of transport. Two important tenants complained about bus fares; they absorbed too large a proportion of juvenile wages. Methven felt that this problem had a bearing on the agitation for higher wages [32].

At his lecture to the Royal Society of Arts in May 1939, Appleyard agreed that the fares from Newcastle - a mere one and a half miles away - 'are ... very much on the high side', and for boys and girls under 18 - who formed approximately half the labour force at Team Valley at the time - the cost of travel from outside the Newcastle area was 'almost prohibitive' [33]. The Company proposed to bring pressure to bear on the Transport Commissioner and to consider alternatives such as running its own transport.

The problem rumbled on: one of the largest employers on the Estate claimed that an extension to his factory was put in jeopardy because 'of the question of transport, which causes difficulties in getting labour on the present fares' [34]. The tenant considered buying tickets in bulk and reselling them more cheaply to his workers, if the Company were willing to provide a small subsidy. This was refused.

The labour situation as a whole appears to have been more satisfactory. Methven was gratified by 'the enthusiastic terms in which employers strange to the region spoke of the quality of the labour available to them. Many similar statements have been made during the past 12 months' [35]. He claimed that satisfaction with labour was the main factor in the decisions of six tenants to order extensions to their factories after less than one year on the Estate.

GOVERNMENT CONTRACTS AND THE IMPROVING EMPLOYMENT SITUATION

Even before the start of the rearmament programme in 1936, the Commissioner had appealed to the heads of the three Service departments to place contracts in the Special Areas [36]. Further opportunities for preferential treatment of the Areas were presented by the railway electrification programme, which was partly financed by the government. In the event, the enabling legislation included a clause requiring preference for the Areas. The Commissioner, further, asked that such preference should be extended to all expenditure controlled by the government. He also pleaded for the establishment of munitions factories in the Areas, when the opportunity arose [37]. This matter will be dealt with more fully in IV/3.

The rearmament programme resulted in substantial contracts being placed in the Special Areas: between 1 April 1936 and the end of August 1938, they amounted to £47,260,700 [38]. No separate figures have been found for the North East, but it is known that the shipyards in the region and the Armstrong Whitworth works at Scotswood - re-equipped by the government for defence work - benefited considerably.

There were conflicting views, however, about the effect of defence contracts on the employment situation in the Areas. Chamberlain 'had little doubt that the new defence programme would do much to wipe parts of the Special Areas off the map' [39]. The table in Appendix 19 certainly shows a sharp drop in unemployment during the relevant period. But the Commissioner not only believed that the recovery in the Areas 'had been independent of armament work', he did not consider such work an unmixed blessing: 'the defence programme has retarded development in the Areas by creating such a demand for constructional materials that the erection of new factories has been delayed and their tenants have found difficulty in getting delivery of machinery and materials' [40].

Given the government's lukewarm interest in government-financed factories, the first Commissioner had warned - almost two years earlier - that the expansion of the trading estates 'should not be diminished on account of the prospective improvement (in the employent market) arising from the defence programme. Otherwise, history will repeat itself when the programme is completed' [41]. He reminded the government that the object of the publicly-financed trading estates was not only to create employment, but 'to procure a better balanced industrial production'.

The same concern may have influenced the Company's development policy of the Team Valley Estate in 1936. In a personal interview in January 1985, Dr. Raymond K. Appleyard, the son of the late first chairman of the Company, confirmed that his father had some doubts about the commitment of the government to the expansion of the Team Valley Estate.

There is some evidence that the Company's development policy included a pre-emptive component: when the Company submitted a revised estimate on 25 November 1937, it transpired that it had built fewer factories than foreseen in the agreed scheme of 1936, but that it had levelled 200 acres of the site instead of the agreed 60 acres [42]. The Company had not exceeded its total budget, but it now needed more money for the factories which it was letting as fast as they were being built. In a note of 30 November 1937, Dalton, of the Commissioner's office, observed: 'we suspected that work on the development of the Estate was proceeding at a greater pace than was indicated in the original scheme ... it is surprising that the Board should have taken the decision to proceed along these lines without first indicating to us that they were exceeding our approval' [43].

In the 12 months to September 1937, unemployment on Tyneside had fallen by a further 11,700, i.e. by 19% (see Appendix 19). The possibility cannot be excluded that in preparing a much larger area of land than authorised or immediately needed, the Company had acted deliberately to forestall any attempt by the government to limit the Team Valley experiment.

TENANTS 1937 - 1939

The announcement of the site for the Trading Estate in the summer of 1936 and the start of construction at Team Valley in November 1936 aroused much interest and lettings of factories started well. The dates on which the tenants occupying factories up to the end of 1939 made their first enquiries are given in Appendix 20 and are analysed in Table 2, showing separately manufacturing tenants from inside and outside the region, and non-manufacturing tenants irrespective of origin. The enquiries from future refugee tenants are not analysed, as the dates on which they made their first contacts with the Company were due to special circumstances and unconnected with any interest in the Team Valley Estate as such. Office tenants in the central administration building are also omitted, although the Company treated them for record purposes in the same way as factory tenants, a procedure which inflated the numbers. The two government tenants have also been omitted from the analysis.

Table 2

Number and Dates of Enquiries leading to Tenancies at Team Valley

| | 1936 | | | 1937 | | | 1938 | | | 1939 | | |
	A	B	C	A	B	C	A	B	C	A	B	C	
January	-	-	-	0	3	-	2	-	-	1	-	1	
February	-	-	-	1	-	-	-	-	3	-	-	-	
March	-	-	-	3	2	1	-	-	-	-	-	1	
April	-	-	-	-	-	4	2	1	-	-	-	-	
May	-	-	-	1	-	-	-	-	1	-	2	1	
June	-	-	-	3	-	-	1	-	1	1	-	-	
July	-	1	-	1	2	1	-	1	-	-	-	-	
August	1	1	1	-	-	2	1	1	1	-	-	-	
September	-	-	2	1	1	2	-	-	1	-	-	-	
October	1	-	1	1	-	-	-	1	1	2	-	-	
November	2	-	-	2	-	-	-	2	-	-	-	-	
December	3	1	-	1	-	-	1	-	-	-	-	-	
A	7			14			7			4			32
B		3			8			6			2		19
C			4			10			8			3	25
													--
Totals	14			32			21			9			76

Pre-1936 enquiry   1
Unknown date   1
Government tenants   2
Refugees firms   21

101

A = enquiries from manufacturers within the region.
B =   "   "   "   outside "   "   .
C =   "   "   non-manufacturing firms irrespective of origin.

The highest rate of enquiries from local manufacturers resulting in lettings was achieved in the last quarter of 1936, i.e. the quarter marking the start of construction at Team Valley. The overall rate of enquiries leading to lettings was highest in the first quarter of 1937. It may be noted that the peak occurred before any factories were available and before press and trade visits were encouraged in support of the public relations effort. The figures show, further, that more future tenants made their first enquiries in 1937 than in 1938 and 1939 put together.

It may be assumed that the first manufacturing tenants were either particularly in need of factory space or especially enterprising. Their positive experience at Team Valley could have been expected to encourage others. Why did this not happen and why did enquiries leading to tenancies decline just when the first factories were approaching completion?

Three groups of possible causes require examination: the business recession in 1937/38; the War scare in the second half of 1938 and the general uncertainty in the period before the War in 1939; and finally, the limited extent of local enterprise and the reluctance of firms outside the region to consider a location in the North East.

The effect of the business recession in 1937/38 was almost certainly one of the factors in the decline in the number of successful enquiries from outside the region. The same factor may have discouraged more enquiries from the region itself, even if this particular recession did not affect the North East as much as the country as a whole.

But the evidence is contradictory: while net employment opportunities in the region between mid-September 1937 and mid-September 1938 declined [44] - in spite of the rearmament programme -, some measure of business confidence may, nevertheless, be inferred from the fact that a substantial number of manufacturing firms in the North East had obtained expansion loans up to the end of January 1938 from the Funds described in III/4 (see Appendix 16). It has already been noted that the large majority of these firms were not located at Team Valley or the outside sites.

The effect of the fear of War cannot be measured, but it almost certainly accounted for the small number of successful enquiries in the last half of 1938 and throughout 1939. It does not explain, however, why the demand, particularly from manufacturers outside the region, began to fall off in the last quarter of 1937, a period which was not yet affected by any immediate concerns.

In seeking to explain why the rate of successful enquiries from new and established local manufacturing firms declined more than a year before the Sudeten crisis of the late summer of 1938, an examination of the activities of the tenants of local origin (see Appendix 21) may provide some insights.

While they were engaged in light manufacturing industries, there were very few firms in those sectors which were growing elsewhere (see Table 4).

On the other hand, only one of the founders of the new firms appears to have come out of the traditional industrial milieu of the region (No. 3 in Appendix 21). With one or two important exceptions, the new manufacturing activities by established local firms were also unrelated to the main activities of the region.

The lack of representation both in growth sectors and in traditional activities must lead to the presumption - and it cannot be more - that the number of local individual new starters and established companies which might have created viable ventures in any sectors was limited. It follows from this that the demand for light industrial space from within the region would have been limited even without the recession and in a calmer political situation.

So far as individuals from outside the region were concerned who set up new businesses, or companies which moved existing works from other locations, the ready availability of new factories and the hope of benefiting from the available inducements seemed to have been the main motives for coming to Team Valley. As for branch plants, labour shortages in the locality of the main plant and the desire to manufacture nearer the market were the reasons for the establishment of a number of firms at Team Valley. But a large proportion of the manufacturing tenants from outside the region were unusual or special cases - as the information in Appendix 22 would indicate -, which may explain to some extent why the demand for space at Team Valley from this source was also limited. British industry needed more time to change the attitudes it had revealed to the Commissioner's questionnaire in the summer of 1935 [45].

The summary analysis in Table 3 permits some conclusions on the tenants at Team Valley according to origin, and on the relative importance of manufacturing and non-manufacturing activities.

Since the employment figures of individual tenants of 50 years ago could not be obtained, except - for special reasons - for the refugee firms, the floor area rented by tenants has been used as an indicator of potential employment, with the proviso that the number of workers per 1,000 sq.ft. will have varied according to the type of product or service. It is likely, however, that the variation between manufacturers was less than between all tenants.

Of the total industrial floor area initially occupied, non-manufacturing activities (I.B+C+D + II.B + III) occupied 190,566 sq.ft. or 26%. This means that approximately one quarter of the space at Team Valley was occupied by activities with a low employment/floor area ratio.

In spite of the considerable public relations effort, only 30 firms were attracted from outside the region (including only one, so far as can be established, from abroad), of which 21 were manufacturers, compared with 55 from within the region, including refugee firms, which were small - with one exception - and are treated in Appendix 21 as new local starts. A number of them had no previous manufacturing experience.

The tenants from outside the region (II + III) occupied 56% of the total initial floor area (412,514 sq.ft. out of 735,674 sq.ft.)

The manufacturers from outside the region occupied 53% of the floor area used for manufacturing (289,538 sq.ft. out of 545,108 sq.ft.). The average area occupied by them was three times greater than that by manufacturers from inside the region. The reason for this was that the latter included new starts by local people and refugees and - with one or two exceptions - small new or expansion schemes by local firms.

Because the firms from outside included established businesses and branch plants, their larger average size does not surprise. For the same reasons, it may be assumed that these firms employed more workers per 1,000 sq.ft. than local firms. If this assumption is correct, the percentage of the employment in manufacturing provided by firms from outside will have beeen larger than the percentage of the floor area they occupied.

Refugees initially occupied less space than the average of all manufacturers from within the region. The later development of employment in refugee firms is given in Appendix 18.

Table 3
Analysis of the Team Valley Tenant Data in Appendix 21

I. FIRMS ORIGINATING FROM WITHIN THE REGION

	No.of Firms	First Area occupied sq.ft.	% of Total Area
A. MANUFACTURERS			
a) New Firms started by Local Individuals	15	46,700	6.35%
b) Refugees	21	79,712	10.84%
c) New Mfg. Activities or Expansion by local firms	19	129,158	17.56%
TOTAL	55	255,570	34.75%
Average Space per Manufacturer		4,647	
B. TRADES	4	7,500	1.02%
C. ROAD TRANSPORT	2	17,875	2.43%
D. DISTRIBUTIVE TRADES	8	42,215	5.74%
TOTAL	14	67,590	9.19%
TOTAL Tenants from within the Region	69	323,160	43.93%

II. FIRMS ORIGINATING FROM OUTSIDE REGION

	No.of Firms	First Area occupied sq.ft.	% of Total Area
A. MANUFACTURERS			
a) Setting up a new Business	8	79,500	10.81%
b) Moving or expanding a Business	5	65,038	8.84%
c) Setting up a Branch Plant	8	145,000	19.71%
TOTAL	21	289,538	39.36%
Average Space per Manufacturer		13,787	
B. DISTRIBUTION & SERVICE DEPOTS	9	72,682	9.88%
TOTAL Tenants from outside Region	30	362,220	49.24%
TOTAL Industrial Tenants	99	685,380	93.17%
III.GOVERNMENT TENANTS (non-mfg.)	2	50,294	6.84%
TOTAL Industrial Floor Area		735,674	
TOTAL Tenants	101		
TOTAL Manufacturing Area occupied		545,108	74.10%
TOTAL Non-Manufacturing Area occupied		190,566	25.90%
		735,674	100.00%

A discussion of the floor area occupied by tenants and the employment they provided <u>after</u> the end of 1939 would not be fruitful for two reasons: firstly because the subsequent rapid growth of some firms was entirely due to War contracts. At the end of the War, these firms reduced their operations again, although some appear to have continued to occupy more than their pre-War space. Secondly, about 15% of the floor space was requisitioned for War production or storage from the middle of 1940 (see IV/1). Several substantial firms were affected as well a number of smaller ones.

There remains to make an attempt to examine the relevance of the manufacturing activities at Team Valley to the structural needs of the North East.

The evidence by the Ministry of Labour to the Barlow Commission on the employment changes in growth industries from 1923 to 1937 has already been mentioned in II/2. A summary of the evidence is given in Appendix 3. The London and Home Counties showed the largest rise (32.1%), Northumberland and Durham the second lowest (4.1%).

The North East started with a great handicap: in 1923, only 22.5% of its insured workers were attached to the growth industries, compared with 55.5% in the London area. If the region was ever to catch up, employment in the growth industries in Northumberland and Durham would have had to increase at a much faster rate than in London (and faster than the average for the country), as Fogarty would point out later [46]. The establishment of the Team Valley Estate may be looked upon as a first attempt to accelerate the necessary adjustment.

The manufacturing and non-manufacturing industries which contributed to a favourable structural change in the London Area and which were also present in Northumberland and Durham before the establishment of the Team Valley Estate are listed in Table 4. The information was obtained from the more detailed presentation by the Ministry of Labour to the Barlow Commission. Shown against each industry is the percentage of floor area taken up by tenants in that industry at Team Valley. 72 of the 99 industrial tenants (72.7%) were involved in the relevant industries (see Appendix 23), occupying about the same percentage of the floor area.

Table 4 shows that the group of tenants occupying the largest percentage of the floor area was engaged in the Distributive Trades (Group 19). While this was satisfactory from a structural point of view, these trades are characterised by a small ratio of employment/floor area occupied. The next largest group was in Bread, Cakes and Biscuits (Group 17), a sector in which employment had actually fallen in the London area and risen in Northumberland and Durham. The significance of the relatively large amount of floor area taken up at Team Valley is difficult to interpret, particularly as one tenant, overshadowing the rest of this group in importance, was highly mechanised, i.e., the ratio employment/floor area he occupied was relatively low.

In terms of percentage of floor area occupied, the next two industrial groups were General Engineering (Group 15) and Motor Vehicles, Aircraft & Cycles (Group 3). These industries - unusual at Team Valley - had a double relevance, in that they were both growth industries and, at the same time, employers mainly of male labour.

Table 4
Percent Increases in Employment in Industry Sectors
with greater than Average Rates of Expansion 1923 - 1937, represented
both in London & the Home Counties and Northumberland & Durham,
and % Floor Area occupied by each Industry at Team Valley

Manufacturing Industries	London & Home Counties	North'land & Durham	% Area at Team Valley
1 Electrical Engineering	+151.6	+128.9	0.76
2 Electric Cable, Lamps, Apprts.	+144.4	- 7.5	2.85
3 Motor Vehcls, Aircraft, Cycles	+113.7	+ 0.5	6.67
4 Miscell. Metal Goods	+125.2	- 27.6	2.72
5 Furniture Making, Upholstery	+ 80.0	+ 0.8	2.24
6 Metal Manuf.(not Iron/Steel)	+ 69.8	- 27.6	0.20
7 Paper & Paper Board	+ 48.4	- 19.6	1.09
8 Miscell. Food Industries	+ 37.8	+120.7	5.07
9 Glass & Glass Bottles	+ 32.5	+ 19.6	1.22
10 Carboard Boxes, Stationery	+ 29.3	+ 0.1	2.24
11 Chemicals, Oil,Paints,Soap Ink	+ 28.1	+123.6	0.61
12 Leather & Leather Goods	+ 27.4	- 12.0	0.41
13 Dressmaking & Millinery	+ 21.4	+ 4.3	1.32
14 Drink Industries	+ 20.7	+ 10.2	1.02
15 General Engineering	+ 20.2	+ 1.4	8.22
16 Printing Publishing, Bk.Bdng	+ 19.8	+ 0.9	0.41
17 Bread, Biscuits, Cakes	- 4.3	+ 16.7	12.40
18 Tailoring	+ 21.6	- 10.2	6.85
Non-Manufacturing Industries			
19 Distributive Trades	+ 74.5	+ 59.6	15.62
20 Road Transport (excl.Buses/Trams)	+ 24.9	+ 56.3	2.43

Sources: Appendix 23.
    RCDME, 1937 - 1938, London & Home Counties, Table VI, p.295,
        Northumberland & Durham, Table X, p.299.

The next largest amount of floor area was taken up by Tailoring (Group 18), an industry in which employment in the region had been falling, against the trend in London. By establishing the suitability of the female labour in the region, the early firms in this group laid the foundation for a substantial industry later. The Miscellaneous Food sector (Group 8) was the only other to take up more than 5% of the floor area at Team Valley. Like Bread, Cakes and Biscuits, the evaluation of the relevance of this sector poses problems of interpretation, which are increased in this case by the large percentage growth in employment - against the trend - in Northumberland and Durham in the previous 15 years.

The other sectors were represented by small percentages of the total floor area. A larger presence would have been desirable particularly in those growth industries in which employment in Northumberland and Durham had fallen against the trend in London and the Home Counties - particularly because some of these industries employed a large proportion of male workers: Electric Cable, Lamps and Apparatus (Group 2), Metal Manufacture (Group 6) and Paper and Board (Group 7).

Another set of figures presented to the Barlow Commision showed the
eight industries with the greatest employment expansion in the country
as a whole. The figures are reproduced in Table 5, which also records
the percentage of the floor area occupied by these industries at Team
Valley, so far as they were represented.

Table 5
Percent Increases in Employment in Industry Sectors in the UK
with the greatest Expansion in Employment 1923 - 1937
and % Floor Area occupied by each industry at Team Valley

Industry Group	Increase since July 1923 in Numbers	% of 1923	% Area at Team Valley
Electrical Wiring & Contracting	29,020	255.0	0
Heating & Ventilating Apparatus *	12,730	249.1	0.20
Artificial Stone & Concrete	18,400	182.9	0
Electrical Cable,Apparatus,Lamps	106,180	148.8	2.85
Silk & Artificial Silk	44,300	122.0	0
Scientific & Photographic Instruments & Apparatus	20,000	117.6	0
Electrical Engineering	54,480	91.2	0.76
Motor Vehicles, Cycles & Aircraft	60,130	65.1	6.67

Sources: RCDME, p.281, * No.67 in Appendix 21.

Four of the eight industries were not represented at Team Valley at
all and three others only in a small way. The sole industry group which
occupied more than 5% of the floor area was Motor Vehicles, Cycles and
Aircraft.

It may be seen that only a few of the industries established at Team
Valley before the War had any structural significance. Furthermore, the
firms in these industries were very small employers. The impact on the
local labour market of the employment created by the Estate at the end
of the pre-War period will be discussed in the Conclusions.

The importance of the Team Valley Trading Estate was neither in the
actual employment provided by the tenant firms nor in the contribution
they made to structural change in the short run. What mattered was that
a practical mechanism had been demonstrated for creating employment by
public investment in factories. This would be carefully noted by those
who would be charged with the development of the post-War policy, the
aim of which would be to prevent a recurrence of serious unemployment in
the Areas. An account of the development of the policy - and of the
influence of the pre-War government-financed trading estates on the
policy for the post-War years - will be discussed in IV/2.

REFERENCES AND NOTES

III/1. Beginnings

[1]   BT 104/24, minute of meeting of Appleyard with Commissioner, 2.6.1936.
[2]   TWA,1762/2, enclosure with letter, 18.7.1936, Company Secretary to Commissioner, headed 'Scheme for Acquisition of the Site'.
[3]   BT 104/24, record of a telephone call to Commissioner, 6.6.1936.
[4]   Op.cit.2.
[5]   TWA,1395/1371, General Manager's report for December 1937.
[6]   TWA,1395, Box 580, File M 1130, 18.7.1936.
[7]   Op.cit.2.
[8]   Ibid.
[9]   Ibid.
[10] Ibid.
[11] BT 104/24, Treasury (Gilbert) to Ministry of Labour (Marlow), 28.7.1936.
[12] TWA,1762/2, Commissioner to Company Secretary, 29.7.1936.
[13] BT 104/24, Min. of Labour (Somervell) to Commissioner (Tribe), 20. or 21.7.1936.
[14] TWA,1762/2, Company Secretary to Commissioner, 18.8.1936 'Scheme, of Acquisition of Site for the proposed Trading Estate', enclosure with letter.
[15] TWA,1762/2, Appleyard to Commissioner, 18.8.1936.
[16] TWA,1762/2, Appleyard to Commissioner, 13.10.1936.
[17] The rationale for acquiring some land from Ravensworth Park is given in 'Report on the Activities of the Company during the Year to 30 September 1937', TWA,1762/3. In spite of the personal interventions by Lord Ridley and Cmdr. Micklem, negotiations with Lord Ravensworth proved to be difficult, particularly because the Company was faced, in any event, with claims for compensation for a variety of rights arising out of Ravensworth's ownership of certain sites: rights of entry, rights of way and coal royalties related to the core land for the Estate. At one stage, these claims threatened to cause embarrassment to the Commissioner. The compensation claims were settled in 1937 for £4,000, (EIEB, minute 152, 2.2.1937), but Ravensworth finally refused to sell any part of Ravensworth Park (EIEB, minute 272, 5.7.1937). In June 1938, he agreed to sell 84 acres at Harlow Green for £6,750 (EIEB, minute 440, 13.6.1938).
[18] TWA,1762/2, typed copy, Commissioner (Tribe) to Company, 22.9.1936, p.3.
[19] It appears from [20] below that Methven appealed to Chester le Street Council not to grant permission for a factory to be erected within sight of the Estate. When the Council ignored the plea, Methven asked the Commissioner to intervene.
[20] TWA,1762/4, Commissioner (Thompson) to Town Clerk, Chester le Street, 18.2.1938.
[21] Op.cit.15.
[22] TWA,1762/2, Commissioner to Company, 22.9.1936, typed copy, inadequately addressed.
[23] TWA,1762/2, Sir Alexander Gibb & Partners, Report, 'Sites for Trading Estate', in the form of a letter to Appleyard, 13.3.,1936, p.17.
[24] TWA,1762/2, Company Secretary to Commissioner, 15.10.1936.
[25] Op.cit.16.
[26] EIEB, minute 64, 2.10.1936.

[27]   TWA,1762/2, Commissioner (Ryan) to Company Secretary, 16.11.1936.
[28]   TWA,1762/2, Company Secretary to Commissioner, 3.11.1936.
[29]   TWA,1762/2, Commissioner (Ryan) to Company Secretary, 16.11.1936.
[30]   Op.cit.15.
[31]   TWA,1762/11, copy of unpublished letter from W.H.Bevan, marked by
        this author 'October 1975'.
[32]   HC Deb 309, 1103.
[33]   The rationale for this is given in TWA,1762/4, Company (Methven)
        to Commissioner (Boyd), 23.3.1938.
[34]   TWA, 1762/2, Methven to District Commissioner (Forbes Adam),
        5.8.1936.
[35]   TWA, 1762/2, General Managers' report for March 1937.
[36]   Ibid, report for February 1937.
[37]   Ibid, report for September 1937.
[38]   EIEB, minute 229, 3.5.1937.
[39]   Op.cit.35, report for April 1937.
[40]   Op.cit.32.
[41]   EIE, Journal of Events, a diary kept intermittently between 1939
        and 1956 by Methven's secretary, Miss Helms, or by Methven
        himself.
[42]   Interview in 1977 with F.J. Donnelly, formerly with the successor
        organisation of the Company.
[43]   The importance of this matter may be judged by the fact that the
        Board of the Company considered it on at least five occasions and
        over a period of almost 18 months, e.g. minute 385, 7.3.1938,
        minute 473, 19.9.1938, minute 497, 7.11.1938, minute 673,
        26.6.1939, and minute 721, 16.8.1939.

III/2. National & Local Reaction: Policy.

[1]   RCDME, 1937 - 1938, Q.2684, cited in Dennison, S.R., 1939, p.167.
[2]   Dennison, S.R., 1939, p.168.
[3]   Labour Party, January 1937, p.8.
[4]   TWA,1762/2, 'Points touched upon at an Interview with Ryan
        et al.', 18.11.1936.
[5]   BT 104/28, Appleyard to Commissioner (Tribe), 25.1.1937.
[6]   BT 104/28, Appleyard to Commissioner (Tribe), 2.5.1938.
[7]   Op.cit.2, p.166.
[8]   Op.cit.6
[9]   Ibid.
[10]   Appleyard stated this to be the Company's policy, see TWA,1762/3,
        'Notes of the Conference on the Attraction of Industries to the
        Special Areas called by the Commissioners for the Special Areas
        of England, Scotland and Wales, held at Broadway Buildings, on
        3rd March 1937, p.5.
[11]   TWA,1762/4, Company to Commissioner (Boyd), 9.2.1938, confirmation
        of the unchanged basis on which the Company calculated rents.
[12]   TWA,1762/5, Report, 'Activities of the Company from September 1938
        to December 1939', 20.2.1940, p.5.
[13]   CSAEW, 1936, 3rd Report, para.122, p.39.
[14]   T 172/1828, Board of Trade (Browett) to Min. of Labour
        (Chegwidden), 8.3.1937; the resolution referred to was to be put
        on 10.3.1937.
[15]   Manners, G. et al., 1972, p.375.
[16]   quoted by McCrone, G., 1971, p.215.
[17]   Appleyard, K.C., 1939, p.862, in reply to Mr. A.W. Todd.

[18]   North East Development Board, 1936, pp. 17,18.
[19]   Labour Party, April 1977, p.22.
[20]   TWA 1762/6, undated memorandum by Methven, intended for
       transmission to the President of the Board of Trade prior to
       the meeting on 29 November 1944, see V/4.
[21]   CSAEW, 1936, 3rd Report, para.126, p.40.
[22]   Ibid, para.3, p.1.
[23]   EIE, Annual Reports.
[24]   CSAEW, 1937, 4th Report, para.276, p.69.
[25]   Cab 27/578, DA (34) 16, memorandum from Minister of Labour (E.
       Brown), 'The Future of the Special Areas Scheme', 13.6.1938,
       Appendix I, 4, p.11, in preparation for meeting of Cabinet
       Committee on 29.6.1938.
[26]   TWA,1762/3, Commissioner to Company Secretary, 30.10.1937.
[27]   Appleyard, K.C., 1939, p.862, in reply to a question: 'when the
       development is complete, it (the Team Valley Estate) should
       provide employment for somewhere between 40,000 and 50,000
       people'. Dennison, S.R., 1939, p.167, wrote that it would take 30
       years to achieve this employment, but he may have obtained this
       estimate from the Company.

III/3. The Special Areas (Amendment) Act 1937

[1]   HC Deb 310, 1388, Mr. E.Brown, Minister of Labour.
[2]   Lab 223/176, Forbes Adam to Commissioner, 17.4.1936.
[3]   HC Deb 309, 1023-1142.
[4]   HL Deb 98, 977.
[5]   Home Office, closed aliens' files, Ministry of Labour,
       ET.1315/1936, Besso to Sir Ernest Holderness, 11.3.1936.
[6]   HC Deb 309, 1094.
[7]   "   " , 1031.
[8]   "   " , 1215 - 1335.
[9]   "   " , 2145 - 2215.
[10]   "   " , 2203.
[11]   The likelihood that financial inducements would become available
       in the Special Areas led to exaggerated fears of unfair
       competition in the rest of the country. See also III/2 [14].
[12]   CSAEW, 1936, 2nd Report, para.95, p.28. (the Report was published
       in February 1936).
[13]   CAB 27/578, DA (34) 9, Memorandum, 9.6.1936, to which was attached
       a short report from the Inter-departmental Committee dated
       27.5.1936 in which three possible courses of action were
       examined. It favoured course III, i.e. 'the (1934) Act to be
       continued after 31.3.1937 by inclusion in the Expiring Laws
       Continuance Bill'. The secretary of the Cabinet Committee
       (Howorth) wrote to all members of the Committee on 9.6.1936: 'the
       Chancellor of the Exchequer (Chamberlain) agrees that course III
       is the one that should be followed; he understands that that view
       is shared generally by members of the Cabinet Committee and in
       the circumstances - unless any member wishes it - it is not
       proposed to ask that Committee to meet to consider the
       Inter-departmental Committee report'.
[14]   CSAEW, 1936, 3rd Report, para 13, p.4.
[15]   Ibid, para.17, p.5, and para 19, p.6.
[16]   Ibid, para.28, p.10.
[17]   Ibid, covering letter to Minister of Labour, 27.10.1938, p. iii.

[18]   Ibid, para 17, p.5.
[19]   Ibid, para.20, p.7.
[20]   Ibid, para.30, pp.10,11.
[21]   HC Deb 311, 818.
[22]   "   " , 1934.
[23]   HC Deb 317, 11.
[24]   "   " , 46.
[25]   CAB 27/578, DA, Minutes, 10th meeting, 26.1.1937, p.6.
[26]   HC Deb 317, 1579-1758, 17.11.1936, Second Reading.
[27]   HC Deb 317, 1596.
[28]   T 172/1828, unsigned note to Chancellor of Exchequer 25.1.1937.
[29]   Op.cit.27.
[30]   HC Deb 317, 1604.
[31]   HC Deb 318, 1910.
[32]   T 172/1828, Warren Fisher to Chancellor, 14.11.1936.
[33]   Cab 27/577, DA [ID] (34) 10, Report, 11.1.1937.
[34]   HL Deb 103, 897 (Lord Bishop of Winchester), 919 (Lord Ridley).
[35]   White Paper, 1937.
[36]   Ibid, para.15, p. 9.
[37]   Ibid, para 17, p.10.
[38]   HC Deb 321, 1026,1027.
[39]   Daysh, G.H.J. & Symonds, J.S., 1952, p.117.
[40]   CSAEW, 1937, 4th Report, para. 58, pp.16,17.
[41]   Ibid, para.59, p.16.
[42]   CAB 27/577, DA [ID] (34) 14, Report, 23.12.1937.
[43]   CAB 27/578, DA, Minutes, 15th meeting, 10.11.1938, Appendix,
        'Draft Statement Prepared in the Treasury'.
[44]   CAB 27/578, DA (34) 21, memorandum by Sir John Simon, 8.11.1938,
        point 5.
[45]   CAB 27/578, DA, Minutes, 14th meeting, 29.6.1938.
[46]   HC Deb 341, 646.
[47]   HC Deb 350, 2181.
[48]   HC Deb 351, 1454.

III/4. Finance for Industry

[1]   CAB 27/577, DA [ID], CP 220 (34), Report, III, 1, 31.
[2]   T 172/1828, Warren Fisher to Chancellor, 14.11.1936.
[3]   Macmillan Committee, 1931, para.404, pp.173,174.
[4]   CAB 58/2, EAC, 12.2.1931, p.6.
[5]   BT 64/11, quoted in Heim, Carol E., 1984.
[6]   RIDT. para.38(3), pp.85,85.
[7]   BOE, SMT 2/16, Jarvie to Norman, 27.9.1935, quoted in
        Heim, Carol E., 1984, p. 547.
[8]   Op.cit.6.
[9]   CSAEW, 1935, 1st Report, para.31, p.17.
[10]   CSAEW, 1936, 2nd Report, para.52, p.15.
[11]   Ibid, para.53, p.16.
[12]   North East Development Board, 1936, pp.17,18.
[13]   CAB 27/578, DA, Minutes, 8th Meeting, 16.10.1935, point 2.
[14]   Op.cit.12, p.28.
[15]   T 175/90, memorandum 'Financing Small Business', by E. Skinner,
        Assistant to the Governor of the Bank of England, undated, quoted
        in Heim Carol, E., 1984, p.537, who dates it ca. October 1935.
[16]   Heim, Carol E., 1984, p.538.

[17]   Lab 9/3, 'Areas of Heavy Unemployment', Inter-departmental,
        Committee report, undated. Heim, Carol, E., 1984, dates it
        ca. October 1938.
[18]   HC Deb 311,   51, 21.4.1936.
[19]   Heim, Carol, E., 1984, p.534.
[20]   T 161/930/1.41848/1, note dated 24.12.1935, quoted in
        Heim, Carol, E., 1984.
[21]   Heim, Carol, E., 1984, p.547.
[22]   CSAEW, 1937, 4th Report, paras. 222-225, p.56.
[23]   CAB 27/577, DA (34) 15, Report 'Financial Assistance to Industry
        in the Special Areas', by Lord Portal to Prime Minister
        (Chamberlain), II, p.3.
[24]   CSAEW, 1936, 3rd Report, para.30 (proposal 4), p.11.
[25]   Heim, Carol, E., 1984.
[26]   CSAEW, 1938, 5th Report, para. 107, pp.30,31.
[27]   The discrepancy is evident from the following figures for Durham
        and Tyneside in both cases

	Date	No. of Firms	Total Sums lent	References
Lord Portal	31.1.1938	77	£3.16 million	op.cit.23.
CSAEW	30.9.1938	88	£3.14 million	op.cit.26.

        It is possible that a number of projects reported by Portal were
        withdrawn in the period between the two reports and were replaced
        by lower offers to more firms.
[28]   Op.cit.23.
[29]   Heim has found the papers of the Nuffield Trust at Deloitte,
        Haskins and Sells, London. Some SARA papers are in T 187/44, and
        the Treasury Fund (Special Areas Loan Advisory Committee, SALAC)
        papers (1937-1941) are in T 187/34.
[30]   Heim, Carol E., 1984, p.542.
[31]   Ibid, pp.540-546.
[32]   Op.cit.23.
[33]   CAB 27/577, DA (34) 16, memorandum from Minister of Labour,
        (E.Brown), 13.6.1938, 'The Future of the Special Areas Scheme',
        Appendix I, (1), p.11.
[34]   TWA,1762/4, CSAEW and North Eastern Trading Estates Ltd,
        Supplementary Finance Agreement, 9.4.1938.
[34]   TWA,1762/4, 'A Supplementary Agreement of 9th April 1938 to the
        Financial Agreement of 6 February 1937' between the CSAEW and the
        Company shows that the Commissioner agreed to a sum of £2,336,500
        (compared with £1,432,500 in the original agreement) The
        negotiations started with the submission by the Company of a
        'Revised Scheme for the Development of the Team Valley Trading
        Estate on 25.11.1937, TWA 1762/3. The correspondence leading to
        the Supplementary Agreement is in TWA, 1762/3 and 1762/4. The
        money actually lasted until 1946, see TWA, 1395/1386, Finance
        Department, Board of Trade (Campling) to Methven, 8.2.1946.
[35]   For reasons given in· Appendix 14, the collection of employment
        information ceased in September 1941. The data nearest to the end
        of the War is given in BT 106/100, 'North East Development Area,
        Numbers on Pay-roll in Government Financed Factories & Trading
        Estates'. For 23.3.1946, the employment at Team Valley was 7,729.
        On the one hand, there will have been a run-down of War
        production in the· previous nine months, and a change-over to
        civilian work on the other, but it is unlikely that more than a

few of the extensions authorised early in 1945 will have been completed and employed any labour. On balance, the employment figure of 7,000 at the end of the War can be justified.

[36] TWA,1395/1386, Finance Dept., Board of Trade (Campling) to Methven, 8.2.1946.

III/5. The Outside Sites

[1] CSAEW, 1938, 5th Report, para.3, p.1.
[2] HC Deb 309, 1960.
[3] TWA,1762/3, 'Notes of the Conference on the Attraction of Industries to the Special Areas Called by the Commissioners for the Special Areas of England, Wales and Scotland, held at Broadway Buildings on 3 March 1937', p.3.
[4] Ibid, 2(c), p.5.
[5] Ibid, 3, p.7.
[6] Ibid, 3, p.8.
[7] Ibid, 2(a), p.3.
[8] TWA 1762/3, Commissioner to Company Secretary, 27.5.1937.
[9] The special wishes of prospective tenants would have had to be taken into account if firms were to be induced to move to the supposedly less attractive places, so that even a single speculative factory on each outside site might not have been appropriate.
[10] EIEB, minute 297, 4.10.1937.
[11] TWA,1762/3, unsigned and undated memorandum, 'Outside Sites', probably by Whitehouse, sales representative (later sales manager of the Company), ca. August 1937.
[12] TWA,1762/3, Percival to Methven, memorandum, 'Sites outside the Team Valley Estate', 16.8.1937.
[13] CAB 27/578, DA [ID] (34) 10, Report, 11.1.1937.
[14] TWA,1762/3, Commissioner to Appleyard, 24.7.1937.
[15] Op.cit.10.
[16] For an example, see EIEB, minute 172, 2.2.1937, according to which the Secretary of the Tyneside Development Board had informed the Company that it was his Board's policy not to pass enquiries for factory sites to the Company unless suitable accommodation could not be found elsewhere.
[17] CSAEW, 1936, 3rd Report, para.145, p.45.
[18] TWA,1762/3, Commissioner to Company Secretary, 30.10.1937.
[19] EIEB minute 314, 1.11.1937.
[20] CSAEW, 1937, 4th Report, paras.329-333, pp.79-80.
[21] TWA,1762/3, Commissioner to Appleyard, 25.8.1937.
[22] TWA,1762/3, Company Secretary to Commissioner, 3.11.1937.
[23] TWA,1762/3, Commissioner to Company Secretary, 30.10.1937.
[24] See [32] in text and below.
[25] Op.cit.18.
[26] TWA,1762/3, Commissioner to Company Secretary, 13.12.1937.
[27] HC Deb 342, 441.
[28] Op.cit.26.
[29] The letter was not found, but the quotation from it was referred to in the Commissioner's reply of 25.10.1938, see [30].
[30] TWA,1762/4, Commissioner to Methven, 25.10.1938. It might be noted that in a letter of 24.10.1938, TWA, 1762/4, Commissioner to Company (Bell), a list was given of the firms with which the Commissioner had inducement agreements. There were two at Team

Valley, seven on the outside sites (i.e. all the firms which had by then had agreed to go there), one firm at South Shields (which did not start operations) and one firm outside the Company's or the Commissioner's sites. The list indicates that the Commissioner did not count rent concessions at Team Valley as 'inducements'.The number of firms with inducement agreements is believed not to have grown by more than a few more. The list confirms the policy of the Commissioner and indicates how little he was able to use his powers under the 1937 Act.

[31] Apart from Sigmund Pumps - a large venture requiring the type of labour probably not available in South West Durham -, Mellolite, was the first refugee firm in a government-financed factory in the North East (No.27 in Appendix 21). It had made contact with the Company in February 1937, i.e. before the Amendment Act and was settled at Team Valley. The next refugee firm agreed to go to the Tynemouth site. The refugee firms at South West Durham West were next, i.e. before any further ones at Team Valley.

[32] TWA,1762/4, copy of a telegram from Company to Prime Minister, Downing Street, London, 11 am, 18.7.1938, announcing the 100th tenant.

[33] TWA,1762/5, Methven to Commissioner (T.W.F. Dalton), 13.6.1939. The Company reported 152,440 sq.ft. built on the outside sites, but one factory (for Norman Kennedy) does not appear, in fact, to have been built, leaving 138,440 sq.ft.

III/6. The Early Years of the Company

[1] TWA,1395/2, Appleyard to Commissioner, 18.8.1936.
[2] TWA,1762/6, Appleyard to Methven, 10.6.1941.
[3] The sites were much smaller: Treforest 250 acres and Hillington 320 acres.
[4] EIEB , minute 87 (a), 2.11.1936.
[5] Goldring, D., 1938.
[6] TWA,1395/1371, General Manager's report for May 1937.
[7] Appleyard, K.C., 1939.
[8] Boyd, C.H., 1937.
[9] EIEB, minute 524, 12.12.1938.
[10] Ibid.
[11] TWA,1395/1371, General Manager's report for March 1937.
[12] TWA,1395/1371, General Manager's report for July-September 1937.
[13] Ibid.
[14] Op.cit.11.
[15] TWA,1762/4, 'Report on the Activities of the Company during the Year to 30 September 1938.
[16] Loebl, H. 1978.
[17] CSAEW, 1936, 2nd Report, para.59, p.17.
[18] Aliens files are normally closed for 100 years. By courtesy of the Records Officer at the Home Office, the author was able to inspect relevant files for the previous work cited. The present reference is Ministry of Labour, ET.1315/1936, Besso to Holderness, 11.3.1936.
[19] Home Office, closed aliens files, Board of Trade, IM 995/36, Fennelly to Cooper, 15.4.1936.
[20] Home Office, closed Aliens files, the standard form of letter and questionnaire is reproduced in op.cit.16, Appendix 15.
[21] Op.cit.16.

[22]   Speech by Home Secretary, Sir Samuel Hoare, to the Society for the
        Protection of Science and Learning, 'Refugees: their contribution
        to English National Life', 6.2.1939, at Universitry College,
        London, Wiener Library, London.
[23]   TWA,1762/5, Commissioner (Emmerson) to Company Secretary,
        27.2.1939.
[24]   TWA,1762/5, unsigned memorandum to Appleyard, probably from
        Methven, 27.2.1939.
[25]   TWA,1395/1371, General Manager's report for February 1937.
[26]   Castlecraft Ltd Newcastle, Tyneside Chemical Co. Ltd, Gateshead,
        and Adpreg Ltd, North Shields. Lime Sand Mortar Ltd set up at
        Greenhead, Ryton. There may have been another refugee firm
        outside the Estate, i.e. Ludwig Mueller Ltd, but no details have
        been found.
[27]   HC Deb 333, 2199,2200.
[28]   Quoted in North Mail , Newcastle upon Tyne, 29.10.1938.
[29]   Quoted in North Mail , Newcastle upon Tyne, 19. 9.1938.
[30]   TWA,1762/4, Commissioner (Emmerson) to Methven, 19.10.1938.
[31]   TWA,1762/4, for example, letter from Home Office (Cooper) to H.
        Howard & Co, 21.9.1938, re founders of Alsco Cardboard Boxes Ltd.
[32]   TWA,1395, Box 347, Private File Appleyard, Methven to Appleyard,
        28.10.1938.
[33]   Appleyard, K.C., 1939, p.862, in reply to Mr. A.W.Todd.
[34]   Op.cit.32.
[35]   Op.cit.15, Employment, pp.5,6.
[36]   CSAEW, 1936, 2nd Report, para.55, p.16.
[37]   Ibid., para.58, p.17.
[38]   CSAEW, 1938, 5th Report, para.77, p.23.
[39]   CAB 27/578, DA, Minutes, 9th meeting, point 32 [ii], 17.10.1935.
[40]   CSAEW, 1937, 4th Report, para.38, p.11.
[41]   CSAEW, 1936, 3rd Report, para. 3, p. 1.
[42]   BT 104/27, Company Secretary to Commissioner, 25.11.1937,
        appending 'Revised Scheme for the Development of the Team Valley
        Estate', in which the revelation was made. Also in TWA, 1762/3.
[43]   BT 104/27, Commissioner, internal memorandum, T.W.Dalton to
        Thompson and Tribe.
[44]   This statement refers to the region as a whole. Between 13.9.1937
        and 12.9.1938, unemployment on Tyneside declined from 53,764 to
        52,995, a drop of 1.4%, while in County Durham it increased from
        47,353 to 58,946, an increase of 24.5%. This overall increase in
        unemployment occurred in the face of continuing transference and
        unassisted migration. It might be added that, for the same
        period, the per cent unemployment in Great Britain as a whole
        increased by about two and a half times as much as in the Special
        Areas of England and Wales. Source: CSAEW, 5th Report, paras.
        49,50, pp.15,16.
[45]   CSAEW, 1936, 2nd Report, para.17, p.6.
[46]   Fogarty, M.P., 1945, p.178.

PART IV: THE WAR: BEGINNING OF DEVELOPMENT AREA POLICY

1 The company in the war years

By the beginning of the War, the Company and the Commissioner had built modern factories at Team Valley and the outside sites with a total floor area of approximately 1.2 million sq.ft. These factories would not only provide additional production facilities for the War effort, they would also enable the region to reap some longer-term benefits from the War: the training of more people in skills uncommon in the region - for example, in precision engineering - , and a more rapid introduction of female labour than might have been possible in peacetime.

For the Company, the War years up to 1944 were relatively passive ones, in the sense that the further development of the Team Valley Estate and the outside sites was halted. The year 1944, however, began a period of intense activity and foreshadowed a fundamental change in the role of the Company.

The following account of the War years aims to highlight three principal topics: the effect of the War on the Company, the early deliberations by the Company on the problems of the post-War world, and - before the end of the War -, the preparations for a high level of State intervention in the Special Areas at the end of the War.

The War - and the period just before - forced many changes on the Company. The second Commissioner, Sir George Gillett, resigned on health grounds soon after the Royal opening and was replaced by Sir James Price (see Appendix 9). As a reserve officer, Appleyard was called up before the actual start of the War. His activities during the War are recorded in Appendix 9. He was to chair only two more meetings of the Board of the Company [1]. Chapman, one of the directors, was elected deputy chairman on 6 September 1939. From November 1939 he acted as chairman of the Board - which met every other month until the last year of the War -, except for a period of illness in the first half of 1944. On 16 July 1945, he was elected chairman, for a year in the first place; he retained this position until the appointment by the Board of Trade of an executive chairman on 1 May 1948.

After the end of October 1939 and for the duration of the War, Appleyard would attend only two more meetings of the Board. He remained a director of the Company until 1948, but played no further part in the management. He continued to receive all Board papers and he corresponded quite frequently with Methven and occasionally with Chapman. He spent most of the War in London, where he met a number of highly-placed people in government and industry. On a number of occasions, these contacts enabled him to provide information on opportunities for the Company and the North East and, on one occasion at least, on the government's post-War plans with regard to the Special Areas.

Although Appleyard had been connected with the Company for less than four years, he had formed its policies and practices and impressed his ideas and style on its officers, particularly on Methven, Percival and Whitehouse, and to a lesser extent, on the Board. He had rendered a service of inestimable value to the North East. By the development of the first government-financed Trading Estate, he had helped to forge a weapon which post-War governments would use as one of the principal means in their efforts to prevent the re-emergence of unemployment in the Special Areas.

Percival, the Company secretary and Whitehouse, the sales manager, as well as several directors, joined the armed forces, as did many members of staff, leaving the Company to operate with a skeleton staff for the duration.

Appleyard's visits to Germany in December 1938 and early in 1939 had inadvertently created a possible security problem: he had left one or more copies of an 'aerial' photograph of a wooden model of the Team Valley Estate. It was feared that this might be used by the Nazi Air Force to attack the Estate. The chief constable of Gateshead suggested camouflaging all factories. The Civil Defence Commissioner was consulted; he discussed the matter in London, but no action was taken.

Air raid precautions had been discussed by the Board as early as 4 April 1938. The publication of the Civil Defence Bill in 1939 led to a meeting at the Commissioner's office, from which it emerged that he had no powers to pay for air raid shelters for the Company's tenants. The tenants urged the Company to bear the capital cost and to recoup it by an increase in rent. The Commissioner agreed to this proposal, but the matter was not straightforward: while factories employing more than 20 people would be compelled under the Civil Defence Bill to provide shelters for their workers, many of firms on the Estate employed less than that number. It was likely that their employees would use the nearest available shelters. To prevent the foreseeable difficulties, the Company decided to provide all the shelters itself, leasing space in them to individual firms, large and small.

While this scheme was being prepared - it was not approved until 21 August 1939 [2] -, the Company arranged for slit trenches to be dug in a number of places on the Estate, floored and supported by timber and covered with corrugated iron sheets. Underground shelters were built later, but a policy to build above ground was adopted in November 1941, possibly because of cost, but easier and speedier access may also have been considerations.

Assistance was given to tenants to comply with other requirements of the Civil Defence Bill - for example, the training of employees in first aid - and a nucleus force was created from the Company's own employees for first aid, fire fighting, anti-gas defence and to form rescue parties.

The Commissioner informed the Company on 3 September 1939 that his office would be closed and that all matters should be referred to the Accountant-General of the Ministry of Labour. In the event, the Commissioner's office was not closed but removed to Southport. As for factory building, the instructions were as follows: 'for the present, the construction of factories in hand and clearance work should be continued subject to the discretion of the Board in the light of local circumstances. No new factories should be started or a commitment of any kind made in regard thereto without the specific sanction of the Ministry of Labour' [3].

The Company replied on 27 September [4], outlining what had been done to adapt to the War situation; because a considerable proportion of the staff and employees had joined the fighting or civil defence forces and had not been replaced, the payroll had been greatly reduced, in spite of a commitment to make up their Services' pay to the amount they received in salary before they joined up; other expenses had been cut and the elimination of street lighting would lead to further savings. As a result, the Company expected that there would be a surplus of income over expenditure of £14,000 for the year starting 1 January 1940, before allowing for depreciation, factories becoming empty or losses of rent on account of war damage or war conditions. Indeed, the financial statement for September 1939 showed a surplus of income over expenditure for the first time [5].

There were under construction, for completion by 30 October 1939, seven factories, with a total floor area of 36,250 sq.ft. and five more with an area of 31,750 sq.ft. to be completed by 1 January 1940. Six tenants had been promised extensions with a total area 68,000 sq.ft., but building contracts had not yet been placed.

Enquiries for factory premises from the civil business sector had almost completely ceased, but there was some interest from firms proposing to manufacture war or civil defence supplies. The Board undertook to examine every enquiry very closely and only to proceed with those which appeared to be of national importance, paying particular attention 'to the potentiality of any undertaking for succeeding in the export markets ... and to carry on a successful civil business at home after the end of the War' [6].

In a personal letter to the Commissioner's office, Appleyard urged 'that the Company should be left alone without any formal control, as it had been up to date'. The Board 'were not foolish people. They realised the necessity not to spend one penny of public money more than can be justified by definite financial results of a lasting character'. He hoped that 'having been trusted so far with the establishment of this large enterprise, the Commissioner and the Treasury will feel that my colleagues can be trusted still further with the carrying out of a carefully considered wartime scheme' [7].

The Commissioner sent further instructions on 1 December 1939 [8]. While the erection of factories for tenants on work of urgent national importance would be justified, each case would have to be submitted for sanction. Before submission, a priority certificate would have to be obtained from the appropriate Supply Department. Factories for non-defence purposes - for example, for export production - would have to be authorised by the Board of Trade. The completion of the factories under construction was approved, but those for which contracts had not yet been placed - of which all but one were extensions to existing factories - could proceed only after priority certificates had been obtained. The building of any factories in advance of requirement was later ruled out altogether. Even the unlicensed construction of factories from materials already in stock was refused.

On 18 December 1939, Appleyard wrote a long letter to Chapman, sparked off by the suggestion - probably by the Commissioner - that the Company should hand over the roads and some services to Gateshead Corporation, in order to reduce its administrative expenditure still further. Appleyard was strongly opposed to this, because it might lessen the attraction of the Team Valley Estate after the War.

The post-War scenario painted by Appleyard was a sombre and, happily in the event, a completely false one. He believed that the North East would be worse off than after the first world War: 'we are likely to live in a desperate - not a special or even a depressed area' -, but the Team Valley Estate

is likely to be one of the brighter spots ... if we as a Board stick close to the ideas we have worked to up till now ... We have laid out a beautiful and well-planned place. We get tenants because of it. We get publicity because of it. And however bad the times, we shall get a proportion of both if we keep it on its present lines. If Gateshead take over roads and lighting and refuse collection, you can picture for yourself what will happen when things get very bad. Naturally, all these services will be cut to a minimum and we shall have our roads filthy, our verges unkempt,... refuse ... and mess round our factories and our street lighting cut ... We ought not to deliver any part of our undertaking into their hands.

'If a time ever came', he added, 'when the most fierce economy will have to be exercised ... I would sooner exercise that ourselves' [9].

Except for the manufacture of uniforms and trailer and stirrup pumps for fire fighting, there was little or no government contract work on the Team Valley Estate at the outbreak of the War. At the end of 1939, 20 small tenants formed a company, chaired by Tom Magnay, MP for Gateshead West, 'to receive government enquiries for national requirements, and by grouping and spreading the work throughout this association, to undertake as much War work as is possible, having regard to the many and varied activities of the light industries represented by tenants on the Estate' [10]. It is not known whether this initiative met with any success. By 1941, however, the large majority of tenants were engaged on work of national importance. Indeed, there would have been little or no material for any other kind of work.

On 1 December 1940, the Commissioner asked the Company to submit immediately its capital estimates to the '4% interest' stage [11]. Given the restrictions on the erection of factories and the uncertainties created by the War, this was a curious demand. It appeared that the Commissioner's requirement was connected with the still impending ending of the Special Areas legislation and the closure of his office. The extension of the Special Area Acts to 31 December 1940 in the first instance reduced the urgency for a reply and the matter was not pursued to a conclusion. The Acts were extended throughout the War.

One of the questions which exercised the Board in the early part of the War was the cost of repairing any possible air raid damage. The Commissioner was unable to give an undertaking regarding special funds for this purpose. The question was settled by the War Damage Act 1941, which obliged tenants to insure their factories and plant.

In the event, there were only two episodes affecting the Estate during the whole of the War: on the night of 28 October 1940, German aircraft dropped a number of incendiary bombs to the east of the Estate, one or two actually landing within the boundary. They burned out without doing any damage. On 8 December 1941 a number of high explosive bombs fell on agricultural land on the Estate and did some damage to adjoining property. The damage sustained by the Company was so slight, however, that 'it is not at all likely that we shall take steps to make it good' [12].

Following a series of air raids on the North East in the summer of 1940, rumours about the Team Valley caused Methven to write a reassuring letter to Sir George Martin on 28 June: 'as for the Trading Estate, it has definitely escaped anything, and I think I can authoritatively say that there has not been a bomb dropped within 10 miles of us' [13]. The letter also gave some information on the Company's response to enemy air raids in the early days of of the War:-

As soon as these nightly raids started, I got the executive staff here and two of Alexander Gibb's fellows to volunteer to take one turn in nine (having got nine fellows) to be on the Trading Estate at night, so that we are manning the hydrants, gas, water mains and electricity, in case anything happens; also a good few of the tenants have given us duplicate keys to their factories so that we can get in should incendiary bombs start fires at night. The executives' turn of duty includes Saturday afternoon and the whole of Sunday.

A Fire Prevention (Business) Order came into operation in the district on 25 January 1941. As a result, group fire watching was arranged for the whole Estate. Permission was granted to approved individuals to sleep in factories or offices.

A number of other defence measures were taken: a detachment of the Local Volunteer Defence Force manned the central administration building every night. Signposts directing drivers to the Estate were painted out. Preparations were made to protect windows against blast by replacing ordinary glass with wired glass. Watchmen were installed on the roof of the central administration building. Later, they were linked with factory premises through the street lighting wiring. This made it possible for workers who were willing to ignore the red alarm to carry on working until the watchmen reported enemy aircraft in the vicinity of the Estate before taking shelter. The army stationed some troops at Team Valley, who were accommodated in hutments on the Estate. A searchlight was set up on a site at the north end of the Estate. Contingency plans were made in case of a German invasion. When the Home Guard was formed, units were recruited from among employees of Team Valley firms.

Refugee tenants with German and Austrian passports were interned on 12 May 1940, some for over a year. The Company took what steps it could to assist the various parties which attempted to keep the businesses going, but there was serious hardship in several cases.

From the beginning of 1940, the Supply Departments began to requisition factories. A big project which had been discussed with the Admiralty was abandoned; instead, the factories of three substantial firms - which had come from outside the region - were requisitioned [14]. A list dated 18 July 1940 [15] shows that 16 businesses, occupying about 130,000 sq.ft. (some 12% of the factory floor area at Team Valley), had closed down or were in the process of doing so because of War conditions, i.e. lack of staff or raw materials, closure of markets, internment or requisitioning.

The rent receipts, however, were actually increasing. This was due not only to the fact that all available factory space was let but also because government departments were obliged to pay the going market rental for requisitioned factories. Given the shortage of manufacturing space, rentals increased. The directors were not unduly worried by the position, although they expected that difficulties would arise when the requisitions came to an end [16].

With the reductions in the Company's staff, more offices became available in the central administration building. There were some unusual tenants among those who occupied this space: for example, the Ministry of Social Security of the Czech Government in Exile, which established a dental surgery there [17].

A large factory was built for Vickers on behalf of the Ministry of Supply. This factory caused considerable arguments both on siting and design. In spite of condensation and other problems, the Company had always insisted on flat rather than pitched roofs. When Appleyard heard that a departure from practice was likely in this case, he wrote on 10 June 1941 [18]: 'I certainly hope that in the event of buildings being put up with pitched roofs, that the effect will be blinded by some high parapet walls'.

In the same letter - it is hard to believe that the country was fighting for survival - Appleyard warned:-

Our nice Trading Estate has been built up on carefully thought-out and agreed lines which have proved very acceptable from the aesthetic point of view. It would be very foolish to be stampeded into doing anything which would detract from the effect which we are trying to get and later on we shall very much regret any backsliding that may be permitted. It is all very well people saying that it can all be put right after the War. Experience shows that these things are never put right because the money is not available and I think we ought to make every possible endeavour, in spite of the War and all its consequences, not to depart from our fixed principles without very good reason.

The siting of what is believed to have been the same factory was an example of the attempts to keep up standards during the War: Appleyard had evidently been asked by someone in the Ministry of Supply why the Company had insisted to build the factory on a site in Block E, i.e. on the north western edge of the Estate, and Methven was asked to explain: 'it was not the sort of factory we would put up; we would prefer not to build it, and we reserve our rights under the Compensation Defence Act to require the building to be removed at the end of the emergency' [19].

Now that the Company made a surplus on its operations, the argument about depreciation was reopened. The Company took the view that, in order to comply with good practice, it should be allowed to provide for the depreciation of its assets before its ability to pay any interest was assessed. It relied, once again, on the clause in the Finance Agreement with the Commissioner, which required it to operate in accordance with the best modern practice. The Treasury took a different view. The Commissioner wrote on 26 March 1942 to say that the Company would not be allowed to depreciate long-term assets, e.g. factory buildings, as such a course 'would have the immediate effect of creating a Depreciation Reserve Fund out of moneys which would otherwise be available to the Exchequer by the payment, out of the Company's profit, of interest ... on the loans made to the Company' [20]. A provision would be allowed, however, for short-term assets and for repairs of roads which could not be undertaken because of shortages of materials or labour during the War.

The Company reiterated that it considered the ruling imprudent. It would continue to prepare annual accounts in accordance with normal practice, if only because the auditors might not give an unqualified report otherwise. If they were forced to pay interest nevertheless, the Company would, in fact, be insolvent.

After a long correspondence, a provision equal to the amount allowed by the Inland Revenue for Wear and Tear was finally agreed [21], but the question continued to arouse arguments with the Commissioner. Whenever interest became due, the Company delayed payments by advancing all kinds of reasons why it could not pay.

Immediately after the outbreak of War, the Company had offered 132 acres of unused land to the Local Agricultural Advisory Committee. Later, it had offered land for allotments. By the end of 1941, the County War Agricultural Committee required the Company to use a large proportion of its arable land to be grown in wheat, and some acres of potatoes and oats. In order to provide the quantity of manure required, it became necessary to embark on mixed farming.

When Regional Production Boards were established in 1942, Lord Ridley was appointed chairman of the Northern Board. One of the objectives of the Boards was to assist the steering of War production into those parts of the country where there was still some unused labour. The removal of such labour - mainly young women - from places in the North East would lower the longer-term industrial capacity of the region. For this reason it was considered desirable to bring industry to the workpeople rather than move them to other centres of war production.

Lord Ridley informed the Board of the Company - of which he remained a member - that the government was considering sites in the area, perhaps even at Team Valley, for new factories which would absorb the residue of available woman labour. He warned, however, that the Company might have to tolerate a temporary lowering of its standards of tidiness, amenities and details of planning for the duration of the War, presumably because such an insistence might militate against building on the Estate under the new policy. The Board agreed to be more flexible, but feared that 'greater latitude was almost certain to result in unrest and dissatisfaction among tenants when a reversal of a complacent policy was necessitated' [22].

A note on the origins and history of the Regional Production Boards is given in Appendix 11. The Northern Board was to play a rather negative role in the events affecting the Company in the immediate post-War period (see V/4).

Lord Ridley returned to the question of special government factories on the Estate at the end of the following year. At a Board meeting on 30 November 1943 - which he chaired -, he asked whether the Company was willing to accept the unusual types of structures which might be erected by government departments. The Board's response was that the Company would do everything possible to help, particularly with buildings which might be suitable for industrial occupation after the War. If the buildings were totally unsuitable for this purpose, however, the Company would require them to be removed when no longer required [23].

The background to these soundings by Lord Ridley is not known; it is unlikely that they were connected with the 1942 policy, because any surplus labour in the Region would have been absorbed in the intervening 18 months; it is possible that Lord Ridley referred to the large reserve factories the government would soon decide to build in the Special Areas at the suggestion of the Ministry of Production, (see IV/3 and V/2). In the event, none of the six factories were built at Team Valley, but two were were built at pre-war outside sites.

An impending Bill giving requisitioning authorities the right to acquire freehold was noted with alarm by the Company, particularly so far as it might affect the core sites on the Team Valley Estate. In this connection, the factories requisitioned by Vickers on behalf of the Ministry of Supply caused the most immediate concern. But the implications of the Bill for the future of the Team Valley Estate were wide, as Chapman pointed out in a letter to Sir Frank Tribe [24]:-

> At Team Valley, we are gradually becoming an Estate for housing government departments and government factories. I think about 50% of our factory capacity is now occupied by or on behalf of the government and shortly a further large factory is to be erected by or for the Ministry of Supply ... You will well appreciate how determined the directors are not to consent to a sale of any of the freehold.

The Company asked the Commissioner to protect its interests. The newly-established Ministry of Town and Country Planning (see next chapter) became interested and proposed to introduce a clause in the Bill to protect good planning from negative effects.

Although development of the Estate had effectively stopped, the Company had financed a number of extensions - some of them large -, the air raid shelter programme and two major War factories. By the middle of 1943, the Company could see a time when the money provided under the Supplemental Finance Agreement of 9 April 1938 [25] would run out. The Commissioner, who considered it unwise to negotiate a new Finance Agreement at this time, reassured the Company that further capital would be forthcoming and that his office should be informed from time to time of the forward requirements [26].

Towards the end of 1943, local interests in the North East began to discuss the policies to be pursued in the Special Areas after the War. The Northern Industrial Group, an informal body of industrialists and trade union officials (see Appendix 11) became active. The future of the pre-War depressed areas also became the subject of questions and debates in Parliament (see the next chapter).

The Company, too, was beginning to think about the post-War needs of the Area (this matter will be disussed in more detail in V/4). The views of the Board may not have been as bleak as those of Appleyard at the beginning of the War, but the directors took it for granted that great efforts would be required to attract industry to the Estate. They failed completely to anticipate the unprecedented post-War demand for factories.

Given the assumptions - and extrapolating from the pre-War experience -, the Board spent much time in discussions on how to achieve low rentals for land and buildings. Rentals would have to based on more favourable interest charges and conditions than before the War, so that 'the Team Valley might form a focal point of great attraction to new industries in the North East after the War' [27].

Accordingly, it was decided that the chairman and Sir George Martin were to seek an interview with the Commissioner, in the hope that he would arrange a meeting for them and Lord Ridley with Bevin, the Minister of Labour. The object of the meeting would be to persuade him to support an appeal to the Treasury to permit the Company to charge the lowest possible rents after the War [28]. The matter of rents was taken up again at the Board meeting on 21 January 1944. In preparation for the meeting with Bevin, detailed calculations were tabled of the effects on rentals of lowering the interest rate from 4% to 3%, of relieving the land of the whole running expense and of the Company being relieved from paying the agreed interest until such time when the Estate would be fully developed.

The Company's concern solely with rents seems curiously irrelevant in retrospect. The government had given several indications in Parliament in the second half of 1943 that it was anxious to prevent the re-emergence of serious unemployment in the former depressed areas and that a much higher level of intervention was contemplated than before the War (see next chapter). Yet the Board minutes do not indicate any discussions on the implications of such a change in direction until well into 1944.

In view of a forthcoming conference of all the government-sponsored trading estates companies in London on 17 February 1944, the approach to Bevin was deferred until the results of the conference were known and analysed [29].

The conference conclusions do not seem to have been discussed by the Board until 12 May 1944. The Board minutes record the following matters arising out of the conference: on rentals, the joint action proposed by the other estates companies did not go as far as the Company would have wished, but there was agreement on other matters; the companies 'felt strongly that they should be freed from competition with other government departments' - a reference to the construction in the Special Areas of standard factories by the Ministry of Works (see IV/3 and V/2) -, and 'that they should be entrusted with the management of the government's wartime and Royal Ordnance Factories'; in the interest of employment, refugee industries should be given the opportunity to continue trading after the War; finally, the companies pledged their loyalty to the Commissioners and their willingness to serve them, particularly in and around their respective Special Areas, (by then called 'Development Areas', see next chapter), but if necessary, in any part of the country.

The conference was evidently aware that a major new policy document was about to be published (the White Paper on Employment Policy, see next chapter) and that it would not be advisable to press for meetings with Ministers at this time. From their professed attachment to the Commissioners, however, it can be inferred that the companies had no prior knowledge of the contents of the White Paper, which would propose that the Special Areas Acts be terminated and the Commissioners' functions in regard to trading estates transferred to the Board of Trade.

The White Paper was published at the end of May 1944, but it is doubtful whether its implications were fully appreciated by the Company, which evidently continued to believe that its record of sound financial management would stand it in good stead with the government. A remark by Sir George Martin at the ninth annual meeting of the Company on 14 July 1944 confirmed this expectation: he expressed much pleasure that it had been possible to commence making interest payments to the Commissioner. He felt that these payments 'would be of material assistance in assuring the future of the Company and its being allowed to play its right and proper part in the period of transition from War to Peace' [30]. In the event, its record of financial management would have little or no bearing on the role assigned to the Company. Other considerations would weigh far more heavily with the government.

The steps taken by the Company in the late summer and autumn of 1944 to bring its record and views to the notice of Ministers are related in some detail in V/4. The administrative changes and the expansion of the Board of Directors just before the end of the War - at the request of the government in November 1944 - are also described in the same chapter.

The White Paper had outlined policies which, if implemented, would result in some redistribution of industry in Britain. Although the details of how the government intended to achieve this aim were still unknown, the Company began to realise that, contrary to its earlier expectations, a fairly large number of new firms would arrive in the region after the end of the War.

The Company was concerned that the shortage of executive housing might make it difficult to accommodate the managers of such firms. This concern was first expressed when the Company was founded. Appleyard had fought hard for powers to build houses (see II/4). These powers proved to be unnecessary before the War, because only a small number of owners and managers moved into the region. Under the White Paper policies, a different situation could be expected.

Accordingly, the Company reserved some six acres of land for housing purposes [31]. Apart from appointing an architect in July 1944 and discussing some outline ideas, however, no further action was taken until June 1945, when the Board appointed a sub-Committee to look at layout plans. At the same time, the Company applied for permission to build executive houses wherever they were needed. [32]. As the permissions did not appear to be forthcoming, the question was discussed with the Board of Trade. The outcome was that the provision of housing for executives and key personnel would be left to the local authorities [33].

The Company continued to attach great importance to housing and it warned that a failure to provide the type of house required 'would result eventually in the loss of prospective tenants' [34]. At one location, the Company actually sponsored a housing development [35].

The organisation for implementing the White Paper proposals, both at the headquarters of the Board of Trade and in the regions, was set up in the autumn of 1944 (see next chapter). Until the White Paper proposals were on the Statute Book - and beyond - the Board of Trade would rely on its control of the building licensing machinery, which would enable its headquarters and the Distribution of Industry Committees in the regions (see next chapter) to exercise effective control over the building programme and the location of factories. The source of finance was still uncertain, because it could not be foreseen whether and when an Act implementing the White Paper proposals would be passed which would empower the Board of Trade to build factories in the Areas. In the meantime, the factories being planned would be financed through the Commissioners, i.e. by the Ministry of Labour.

On 2 February 1945, the Company authorised the construction of factories for the first time since building for private industry was halted at the beginning of 1940 [36]. The term 'authorised' in the Board minutes was used out of habit, but it hardly reflected the new situation; the selection of the type of industry and of sites, the approval of tenants and the financial authority were no longer a matter for the Company alone, and, before long, it would have no voice at all in these decisions (see V/4).

The size and location of factories authorised in the months before and just after the end of the War in Europe is given in Appendix 24. The floor area was considerable in relation to that built before the War. Given the decision by the government in November 1944 to restrict further building at Team Valley [37] (see V/4), it was notable that a high proportion of the floor area authorised involved extensions and new factories for existing tenants at Team Valley. It was not, apparently, the government's policy to limit the expansion of sitting tenants.

In addition to these projects, the planning of two new trading estates in the region began before the end of the War in Europe.

The first was to be built at Hartlepool. The interest of the West Hartlepool Borough Council in an estate at Seaton Carew was of long standing. A deputation from the Borough had been received at the second preliminary meeting of the Board of the Company on 20 April 1936. A further approach to the Company was made by the Town Clerk in a letter of 18 January 1944 [38]. On that occasion, he was advised to take up the matter with the Commissioner, but the Company offered to assist in developing an industrial site, if necessary as the Commissioner's agent [39].

By the beginning of February 1945, two alternative proposals were on the table for the development of 98 acres of land lying between Hartlepool and West Hartlepool: one from the Company and another from Sadler Forster, the Regional Controller of the Board of Trade at Newcastle. Methven was instructed by the Board of the Company to prepare a plan - in conjunction with Prof. Holford, if possible - and to try to reach agreement with Sadler Forster. Holford visited the site in March 1945 and submitted a sketch plan, which was approved by the Board on 9 April 1945. Methven was asked to prepare a Scheme of Development and Administration for submission the Board of Trade, using the Team Valley Scheme as a guide.

At a Board meeting on 11 May 1945, Methven outlined the report which he had sent to Hartlepool on the feasibility of an industrial estate in the Borough. A sub-Committee of the Board considered the scheme in some detail. A general development plan dated 19 May 1945 was forwarded to the Board of Trade in London, followed by the comments of the sub-Committee early in July.

The procedure earned a rebuke from Sadler Forster: on 13 July he wrote and suggested that such reports should be transmitted through him [40]. The Company, unused to an additional channel of communication - and probably wishing to assert its independence - replied that the Board 'was of the opinion that the correct course for them to take in order to obtain speedy consideration of official papers was to forward one copy to the Board of Trade in London and a second copy to the Regional Controller' [41]. The Company could not have foreseen that within less than three weeks Sadler Forster would be the head of the new Directorate for Industrial Estates at the Board of Trade in London and, therefore, their immediate master!

At the end of August 1945, the Board of Trade decided to lease the Hartlepool site to the Company for 99 years, and to ask it to manage the estate for a fee to be decided. [42].

The Hartlepool sub-Committee of the Board was renamed the Southern Sub-Committee [43], reflecting the fact that its remit would now include more major sites in County Durham. On the same occasion, a Northern Sub-Committee was formed. These sub-committees each comprised six or seven directors. The expansion of the Board earlier in the year proved to have been essential, if the new responsibilities of the Company were to be properly supervised.

It was not until 21 September 1945 that the Board of Trade authorised the start of some work at Hartlepool. It was the first major new project in the North East which was handled by the Whitehall machine since the passing of the Distribution of Industry Act 1945 (see next chapter). In the Company's view, the start of the scheme was delayed unnecessarily and it would express this view to the President of the Board of Trade during his visit to the North East on the following day, 22 September 1945 (see V/4). But it was only a foretaste of the delays and problems which would result from the control of the government factory construction programme by the Board of Trade in London. The problems will be discussed in detail in V/1 and V/2.

Another new trading estate was proposed just before the end of the War at one of the sites considered but rejected in 1936. At the Board meeting on 9 April 1945, Methven reported that the Board of Trade had handed him rough plans with suggestions for the development of a site immediately south of the Jarrow - South Shields Road, the 'Bede' site. For reasons not stated in the minutes, 'the Board was not impressed with the selection of the site' but, because the Board of Trade continued to press it, Methven was asked to investigate the possibilities. The Company continued to insist that the site was unsuitable, and while offering to clear it, it urged that development should be concentrated on another site [44]. The matter would be discussed with Sir Stafford Cripps, who, in the event, supported the Bede site. By October 1945 authority was received to proceed with clearance and some roads.

The last six months of the War in Europe were a period of intense activity, but they did not fully prepare the Company for any fundamental changes in its role and functions. So far as trading estates and factories were concerned, The Board of Trade, together with the regional Distribution of Industry Committee, assumed the function of the Commissioner, although more actively and bureaucratically. Administratively, the Company treated the proposed new trading estates and other sites in the same way as the pre-War outside sites, and referred to them as such.

But even if the Company was not fully aware of it, these months were the harbingers of the great changes which would be ushered in by the Distribution of Industry Act 1945. The origins of the Act, which was to have a profound effect on the fortunes of the North East and the future of the Company, will be discussed in the next chapter.

2 The evolution of post-war policy

The account of the wartime history of the Company in the last chapter briefly touched upon the implementation of a post-War policy for the North East and other pre-War depressed areas which would prevent a recurrence of serious unemployment. One of the principal aims of the policy was to broaden the industrial bases of the Areas by controlling the location of industry in the country as a whole.

There is a good reason for examining the origins of location policy and the events leading to its adoption in 1945 in some detail: while the policy had several components, by far the most important form of government action in the Areas was the provision of factories and industrial estates [1].

It must be stressed, however, that the concept of the post-War location policy was a limited one. It differed little from that of the pre-War diversification policy in the Special Areas, which G.D.H. Cole described as 'unplanned, in the sense that it did not rest on any considered judgment about the right location of industries up and down the country', but merely represented 'a desire to attract any sort of industry into areas in which there was an evident shortage of jobs' [2].

The policy, nevertheless, made a considerable impact on the North East in the longer term and, in the period covered by this study at least, it affected the congested parts of the country, as it was intended to do.

The following account of the evolution of the policy is divided into sections which correspond to the sequence of events: the appointment of the Royal Commission and its Report; the political developments during

206

the War, leading to the 1944 White Paper on Employment Policy; and finally, the two Acts of Parliament which implemented a location of industry policy in Britain for the first time.

THE LOCATION OF INDUSTRY 1931 - 1940

The location of industry became a political issue during the depression years. As early as 1931, Attlee had made the case for limiting industrial expansion in the Greater London area: 'it may be true', he wrote to the Economic Advisory Council, 'that London is the biggest market and that industrialists wish to locate there, but the logic of this is absurd. It is impossible to countenance indefinitely the growth of London' [3].

The issue was discussed in Parliament several times before the middle of 1937. These occasions - and the views expressed by The Times - have already been examined in the relevant context. A location of industry policy was also promoted by private bodies, for example, by Political and Economic Planning [4] and The Next Five Years Group [5].

No account of the development of the policy would be complete without touching on the role played by Hugh Dalton (see Appendix 9). Although not a Northerner by birth and from a privileged background - his father was chaplain to a succession of Monarchs -, he represented the Durham Bishop Auckland Division for the Labour Party in Parliament from 1929 to 1931 and, again, from 1935 until his retirement in 1959. The conditions he found in his constituency aroused his anger and compassion and he later claimed that he had devoted more time to the study of the problems of the Areas and had pressed more continuously and firmly for action than any other politician of his day.

At the Labour Party Conference in 1936, Dalton had proposed a Commission on the Distressed Areas. The Commission was appointed on 17 November 1936, with Hugh Dalton as chairman. There were two other Commissioners, who would be joined in each Area visited by two local Labour Members of Parliament. An interim report was published in January 1937, followed by five regional reports [6].

Although Booth [7] has claimed that these reports contained little more than a mixture of fundamentalist dogma, rejected Labour Party policies and suggestions for improvements in the workings of the Special Areas legislation, the interim Report argued strongly in favour of a location of industry policy. This was to be implemented by giving powers to a Minister for the Special Areas 'to require all new industries or factories (or substantial extensions to existing concerns) to establish themselves in some part of the Special Areas, unless they can prove to his satisfaction that there is a conclusive and overwhelming case for their going elsewhere' [8].

This proposal went further than any which had been mooted up to then. It should be noted, however, that the Labour Party Commission made no reference to any general pattern of location. The approach was criticised later by G.D.H. Cole, because it was limited 'to making piecemeal plans for increasing the level of employment in particular areas' [9].

Before long, Hugh Dalton would occupy positions of political power from which he would be well placed to press for and implement a location policy: in February 1942 he joined the War Cabinet - in which he was the only Minister to represent a formerly depressed area - as President of the Board of Trade. In the Labour Government of 1945, he was Chancellor of the Exchequer. In both positions, he provided the political, not to say the emotional, impetus for a location of industry policy.

The intention to appoint a Royal Commission had been announced by the government during a debate on the Special Areas Amendment Bill on 9 March 1937. On 7 July 1937, Chamberlain - by then Prime Minister - gave details of the constitution and terms of reference of the Royal Commission on the Distribution of the Industrial Population, which was to be chaired by Sir Anderson Montague - Barlow (see Appendix 9), a former Minister of Labour. Questioned on the terms of reference, the Prime Minister indicated that, in his view, the location of industry was directly covered by them. When another Member suggested that the Commission would be expected to formulate a policy for the depressed areas, the Prime Minister replied that the Commission would be concerned with much wider questions, although the enquiry certainly had a bearing on the depressed areas.

In so far as the terms of reference implied that solutions of the problems of the depressed areas had to be looked for within the context of a national policy for industrial location, they were in line with the suggestions made both by the Investigator for Durham and Tyneside in 1934 and by the Commissioner in his Third Report in October 1936, as well as by Members of Parliament, for example by Lord Eustace Percy (Con., Hastings) [10].

The appointment of the Royal Commission was the last step before the War in the progress towards a location of industry policy in Britain. Most of the significant events in the development of the policy took place during the War, culminating in an Act of Parliament within a few weeks after the end of the War in Europe. This Act effectively created a location policy for the first time, although the permanent means to implement the policy would not be available until the Town and Country Planning Act 1947.

The report of the Royal Commission was published in January 1940 [11], a few months before the worst moments of the last War. Under the circumstances, the report made little impact at the time outside a narrow circle. The evidence cited later in this chapter, however, shows that the report began to have a profound effect on political attitudes later in the War.

Indeed, the seminal effect of the report on post-War policies has until recently been unquestioned. McCrone [12], for example, believes that the report influenced regional policies in Britain for a generation. Booth [13], on the other hand, has shown more recently that the development of the post-War location policy owed less to the Barlow Report than to factors arising out of the War itself: the expectations of the people on the one hand, and the experience gained from the organisation of War production and the close links between industry and the civil service, on the other. Booth accepts, however, that the Barlow Report was one of the seminal influences in the evolution of the post-War location policy.

Among the conclusions and recommendations accepted unanimously by the Barlow Commission (see Appendix 25) was the establishment of a 'Central Authority, national in scope and character' (recommendation 2), the function of which 'should be distinct from and should extend beyond those within the powers of any existing government department' (3). The Commission recommended the dispersal of industries and industrial populations from congested urban areas (4b), and the encouragement of a reasonable balance of industrial development throughout the various divisions and regions of Great Britain coupled with the appropriate diversification of industry in each division or region (4c). Recommendation (5) demanded immediate action in regard to 'the continued drift of the industrial population to London and the Home Counties, (which) constitutes a social, economic and strategical problem'. The mention of strategic considerations reflected the turbulent times in which the Commission reported.

The Commission's terms of reference did not include the examination of Unemployment, and the problem of the Special or depressed areas was covered only in so far as those areas were disadvantaged by the concentration of industries in large conurbations or particular areas.

While there was agreement that action had to be taken to change the pattern of the geographical concentration of industry and people, there were differences among the members of the Commission on how the policy should be implemented. The main contention arose in connection with the function and powers of the Central Authority: the majority report proposed that the Authority should be a Board with research, advisory and regulatory functions in the location of industry and, particularly, that it should have the power, in London and the Home Counties, to control the establishment of industrial undertakings.

A note of reservation by three Commissioners suggested more emphasis on local action. They proposed that regional bodies related to the Central Authority should be set up; that the regional bodies should prepare measures promoting regional development which would go hand in hand with the negative power of control; that the power of regulating the establishment of new factories should eventually cover the whole country and, finally, that the powers of the Commissioners for the Special Areas should be transferred to the new Central Authority.

Three other Commissioners could not accept that the Central Authority should be a Board. They proposed a new government department, which would prepare a national plan for the distribution of industry. It would take over the powers of the Commissioners for the Special Areas and apply them anywhere in the country where it considered it necessary. It would have powers to promote trading estates, satellite towns and public utilities. It would schedule areas where industrial development would be unrestricted - subject only to local planning regulations - and areas where, with certain exceptions, further development would be prohibited.

It may be noted that the Cabinet Minister proposed by the Labour Party Commission and others would be responsible only for the depressed areas. By contrast, the government department proposed by this Minority of the Barlow Commission would plan the location of industry in the national context. In the event, neither a Central Authority nor even a Minister responsible for the depressed areas was ever accepted. The concept of government by geographical areas rather than by departmental function was - and largely remains - alien to the British system of government.

Finally, one member of the Barlow Commission entered a dissenting memorandum on planning in relation to the location of industry, in which he pointed out some of the practical problems which would be encountered because of the defects of the then existing planning legislation.

Any mention of the Barlow Report is usually intended to refer to the Majority Report, but it is as well to realise that there were, in effect, four reports, as Dalton reminded the House of Commons on 7 June 1944.

McCrone [14] has pointed out that the Barlow Report stressed the economic case for regional development. While he showed that the case was not conclusive, it was and remains stronger than regional policy makers in Britain have ever allowed.

The War delayed the implementation of any part of the Barlow Report. Its first fruit was the Town and Country Planning (Interim Development) Act 1943. Up to 1942, the planning powers of the government which related to the use of land were exercised by the Ministry of Health. During 1942, they were vested in the Minister of Works and Planning.

The 1943 Act transferred the planning functions to a new Ministry of Town and Country Planning, with the duty of 'securing consistency and continuity in the framing and execution of a national policy with respect to the use and development of land throughout England and Wales' [15]. The tradition of entrusting planning control to local authorities was continued, but the Act armed them with wider and more effective powers.

The influence of the recommendations of the Barlow Commission on the concept underlying the remit of the new Minister was recognised at the time: 'the advance towards a new conception of planning under positive central direction crystallised in these recommendations of the Barlow Commission marks a turning point in the evolution of planning in this country' [16]. The new Ministry was not to have much influence, however, on the formation of the post-War location of industry policy.

Dalton welcomed the Barlow Report 'as the voice of an ally'. Surprisingly, he looked upon the Ministry of Town and Country Planning as the 'Central Authority' [17], in spite of the fact that the Royal Commission had intended that all its recommendations should be carried out by this Authority, and not just the national planning of the use of land. The new Ministry did not correspond to the concept even of those who had signed the Majority Report, let alone those of the Minorities. Booth [18], indeed, believes that the establishment of the Ministry of Town and Country Planning made a comprehensive solution on the lines of the Barlow Report impossible.

POLITICS AND POLICY 1941 - 1943

Given the many - immediately much more urgent - preoccupations of the government during the last War, the extent of the preparatory work on post-War policies appears surprising in retrospect. The formulation of policies was studied and discussed by a succession of Reconstruction Committees of the War Cabinet, by the academics in the Economic Section of the War Cabinet and, quite separately, within a number of government departments. Some of this activity started early in 1941, when the outcome of the War was still in doubt.

The strands making up the weft of the post-War policy for the pre-War depressed areas are very complex and it would eventually need a Minister of Reconstruction to pull them together. They are described in detail in a major study by Addison, in the biographies of Ministers in the Coalition Government (most recently, in the Life of Hugh Dalton by Pimlott), in Volumes II and III of Dalton's Memoirs , in the autobiography of Jay, and in the research papers by Booth and others (see Bibliography). Only a partial outline of the events leading to the relevant legislation will be given here.

The origins of the post-War policies for employment - and for social security and education - cannot be understood in terms of governmental activities alone. They reflected the changes brought about by the War in the attitudes of the people of Britain and in their expectations for the post-War world. As early as June 1942, a national opinion survey had revealed that the public accorded top priority to 'work for a living wage for everyone who is capable of doing it' [19].

When Dalton arrived at the Board of Trade in February 1942, 'he began to think and work again on the pre-War distressed Areas' - in spite of the sombre War situation. He felt that he had the chance to 'finish the job (he) had begun in 1936 as chairman of the Labour Party's Commission on the Distressed Areas'. His views had never changed and he was quite sure what was needed: 'the cure for that distress was new and more varied industry in all these areas; "taking the work to the worker". I had known that for a long time. Until now I had not been able to apply this cure. But now I might' [20].

He was displeased to find that the departmental evidence to the Barlow Commission 'had an extreme laissez-faire bias, opposing any serious control of industrial location'. He told his officials that 'he had firm views (on this question), based on long study, and that the policy of the Department, at all levels, must now change' [21].

The location of industry had engaged the attention of Ministers before Dalton came to the Board of Trade. A memorandum of 9 January 1942 [22] summed up the interim conclusions of ministerial meetings and the contents of papers since February 1941. From a reference to 'the proposed National Development Executive', it is evident that the Barlow Report had figured prominently in these discussions. The memorandum concluded 'that the decisions already taken would seem to rule out a policy of allowing any factory to be set up where it likes without attempting to control or influence it in any way'.

Dalton established a Reconstruction Department in the Board of Trade, staffed by civil servants and academics. Post-War regional policy was one of the interests of the department. Since one of the principal functions of the Board of Trade was the regulation of industry - and because the implementation of any post-War policy was likely to involve a much greater control of private industry than before the War -, Dalton considered that the Board of Trade was the proper department to administer the Special Areas policy.

It may be asked, nevertheless, why the Board of Trade under Dalton was able to concern itself with the pre-War Special Areas, given that the - now frozen - policy was still administered by the Ministry of Labour.

The reason was as follows: the wartime production effort required the mobilisation both of manpower _and_ factories. The Ministry of Labour was responsible for the the former and the Board of Trade, through its Control of Factory and Storage Premises Division (see Appendix 11), for the latter. When the War economy had reached the full employment level, there was still some labour available in the pre-War depressed areas - particularly female labour. The task of the Control Division was to find premises in these areas. It was through this Division that the Board of Trade first established a presence in the regions. Booth [23] has found that the post-War use of the Control in the location of industry was foreseen as early as 1942 by its first controller, Sir Cecil Weir.

Dalton claimed that 'Bevin (the Minister of Labour) always gave me good support on location questions' [24], and Jay has recently confirmed this [25]. It appears that this support also extended to Dalton's aim to control the post-War regional policy from the Board of Trade.

In May 1943, the Cabinet Committee on Reconstruction Priorities had a paper before it on 'The Maintenance of Employment and Depressed Areas' [26]. Dalton - who was not a member of the Committee - agreed with some of the contents of the paper, particularly with the need to maintain demand. As for the rest, the paper was concerned with the removal of obstacles to labour mobility. On the location of industry, it had a single reference, which was not pursued: 'it is sometimes suggested that the State should assume powers to direct industry to labour rather than labour to industry'.

Dalton complained that the paper did not 'focus the problems of the depressed areas' and warned that 'unless we deliberately take steps to prevent it, this problem will repeat itself with appalling exactitude'. He went on to state that 'both to secure full employment and for other reasons, I regard some national control of industrial location as essential' [27].

In order to arm himself with more evidence in support of a location policy, Dalton initiated surveys on the post-War employment prospects in the Areas. The preliminary results of these surveys were published in October 1943 [28]. The survey for the North East forecast that, in the absence of any special action, an unemployment rate of 25% would have to be accepted. Dalton had obtained his ammunition.

The Economic Section of the War Cabinet claimed that the surveys presented too gloomy a picture [29], but almost all forecasts of the period foresaw high or very high unemployment in the pre-War depressed areas after the War, although not necessarily for some years. In the context of the War and the expectations of the people, these forecasts explain why the Coalition Government would be prepared to adopt policies bearing a family resemblance to pre-War Labour Party policies.

In September 1943, Dalton persuaded Douglas Jay (see Appendix 9), a young socialist economist, to leave the Ministry of Supply and to join him as his personal assistant and special adviser on post-War industrial reconstruction and employment. Jay had been responsible for securing labour for defence contracts and he was 'one of the first advocates of taking work to available workers, rather than giving contracts to the lowest tenderer and hoping that population mobility would take care of industrialists' labour supply problems'. He was keen 'to use all that he had learned about the location of labour and the mobility of industry during the War in the service of a new full employment policy which would prevent the curse of the depressed areas arising after the War' [30].

This was a fateful appointment for the Areas because, for good or ill, the solutions of their problems would be largely derived from wartime experience. Booth [31] has pointed out that this was scarcely suprising, because wartime planning for the post-War period was inevitably a hurried process - involving major decisions under the pressure of time - which would allow few alternatives to be considered.

Jay claimed that, while Dalton knew _what_ he wanted, he did not know _how_ to achieve it. This left a great deal of scope to Jay, who saw his plans to depend on three stages: firstly, the injection into the projected White Paper on Employment of a passage which would authorise an ambitious programme, secondly, to draft and pass through Parliament a Bill which would give the Board of Trade legal powers to carry out the programme, and thirdly, to set up within the Board of Trade the departments and the regional organisation 'similar in some ways to the wartime machine at the Ministry of Supply' [32].

Jay's plans included the enlargement of the pre-War government-financed trading estates and the construction of new estates; the building of factories in the Areas by the government, to be let or sold to private firms; the conversion of Royal Ordnance Factories into new industrial estates and the disposal of other wartime factories in the Areas for civilian production, and finally, the control of new industrial building in congested areas like the Midlands and London.

Two successful experiments had persuaded Jay that his strategy would work: the wartime location of new industrial capacity wherever labour was available, and 'the rapid growth of the pre-War government-financed trading estates' [33].

Booth [34] has argued - against the accepted view - that the Barlow Report exerted a relatively small influence on post-War regional policy formation. He seems to have come to this conclusion partly because Jay has claimed that he had never read the Report [35]. Ignoring other important formative influences, the position may, perhaps, be summarised somewhat differently: the Barlow Report helped to create the political climate favourable for a location policy and reinforced pre-War Labour Party ideas on physical planning, while Jay and others worked out the implementation of some of the recommendations of the Report by drawing on experience which owed little or nothing to it.

The debates in Parliament during 1943 showed that changes in attitudes were taking place at the centre and on the right of the political spectrum in regard to the responsibility of the State to secure employment for all who wanted to work.

Sir Kingsley Wood (Con., Woolwich West), the Chancellor of the Exchequer, confirmed this in a debate on post-War economic policy on 2 and 3 February 1943: 'the basic objective that we must set ourselves', he said, 'is active employment for the people of this country, ... we must not repeat the tragic story of the years between the Wars'.

These changes were prompted by the need to reassure the people - particularly those in the fighting services - that the bad old days would never return. It was this consideration above all others which influenced the policy discussions and made possible the radical departures from the non-interventionist policies of the pre-War period.

The economic policy debate gave Dalton an opportunity to indicate the two main aims of policy for the Special Areas, which, even if not yet agreed formally, were likely to enjoy support in the Cabinet: the diversification of industry and the modernisation of the staple industries.

By the middle of 1943 - the year Churchill called 'The Hinge of Fate' - the prospects for an allied victory had greatly improved. This circumstance alone would have stimulated more public interest in the post-War world, but there was another reason: the Ministry of Supply was beginning to release labour. While this was easily absorbed in the War economy, anxieties began to emerge about the post-War employment prospects. These anxieties were reflected in Parliament and in the Press, and given voice in the pre-War depressed areas.

The pressure exerted by Dalton and other Labour Ministers in the Coalition for a location of industry policy was now reinforced by the The Times : in the issue of 23 October 1943, a correspondent pleaded for post-War policies which would achieve a spread of industries in order to make the country one economic unit and obliterate the old division between the prosperous and the Special Areas. On the assumption that no decision of principle had yet been taken, the correspondent put forward two alternative policies for consideration: the provision of inducements which would draw industries away from the South East and the Midlands, or the national planning of industry. He felt that the government would probably favour the former approach. Regarding the Board of Trade Surveys which were still in progress, the correspondent surmised that they would show that even the areas most favoured by the War - and the North East was not among them - lacked confidence in their future.

Lord Ridley, the chairman of the Northern Industrial Group (see Appendix 11), referred to this article in a letter to The Times on 4 November 1943. He demanded 'that a positive government policy of planning industry, whether by inducement or direction or both, should begin now'. He claimed that the industrial balance of the North East had been worsened by the War, 'because new, lighter industries had hardly grown and some smaller units had been displaced for temporary wartime production or storage'.

The Times printed further letters on the same subject: Sir Cuthbert Headlam, (Con., Newcastle upon Tyne North), extended Lord Ridley's arguments on 11 November 1943:-

> There is no doubt a genuine feeling of anxiety regarding their future among both employers and employed ... They feel that, unless some policy for the introduction and development of new industries within the area is adopted and put into force before

the cessation of hostilities, they will be faced with a repetition of the unemployment of the years before the War ... It is high time that the government should turn its attention to the many problems connected with the location of industry.

Sir Malcolm Stewart, the first Commissioner, wrote on 15 November 1943, giving some advice to the new Minister for Reconstruction:-

Since the direction of the location of industry is bound to prove a slow process and unlikely to provide with sufficient rapidity a remedy for the needs of Tyneside and similarly affected areas, perhaps Lord Woolton will give consideration to the prior needs of areas most susceptible to unemployment and the desirability of offering government financial aid to established businesses wishing to expand.

These letters prompted a leading article in The Times on 22 November 1943, which was addressed to those who were not personally or directly affected by the problems of the Special Areas and who might be tempted to think that such problems were 'of melancholy importance between the Wars, but not germane to any discussion of the future'.

The appointment of the Minister for Reconstruction just before the start of the 1943/44 Parliamentary Session confirmed that the planning of the post-War period was about to enter a more active and public phase. The Times of 12 November 1943 called it 'the best of introductions to the new Session'.

The King's Speech opening the Session included the following: 'in the months to come, my Ministers will complete their plans for the period of transition through which we must pass before the troubled times of War give place to the settled conditions of peace. It will be the primary aim of my Government that in this period food, homes and employment are provided'.

The Economist of 6 December 1943 pointed out the particular significance of this aim for the Areas and reminded its readers that the term 'Special Area' recalled a dismal and discreditable chapter in British history. '"Food, Work and Homes" was a magnificent slogan for the post-War era', the Economist continued, 'but the Special Areas had a claim to priority in its application'.

A few weeks earlier, Dalton had indicated that the government was considering specific means to achieve this aim: 'the extension of trading estates and the early release of government factories for peace-time production are among the measures now under consideration by H.M. Government' [36].

An Amendment to the King's Speech - signed, significantly, by Conservative Members from Scotland, Wales and the North East Coast - was debated in the House of Commons on 8 December 1943. It regretted that 'there is no mention of any national policy for a better location of industry, designed to prevent so far as possible a recurrence of the unemployment which prevailed in the period between the Wars in areas mainly dependent on heavy industry'.

Dalton welcomed the Amendment and 'the strong feeling which had been expressed on all sides of the House' and claimed that 'our national policy has already been declared. The policy we aim at is full employment in peace, no less than in War'.

The Debate confirmed that the people in the formerly depressed areas were becoming increasingly concerned about post-War employment prospects. One speaker noted the irony that, in providing employment for all, the War had achieved what peace failed to do [37].

The House expected the government to prepare a constructive post-War policy and was willing to accept considerable changes, if these would ensure reasonably full employment. The planning and location of industry featured in most of the speeches, even if the term 'planning' was admitted by one speaker to be often confused with 'regimentation'.

During the Debate on the Amendment, Dalton announced that he had decided to rename the Areas 'Development Areas' [38]. He liked this description much better than 'depressed', 'distressed' or 'special. 'It was positive, and put hopeful emphasis on the fact that these were areas where, more than elsewhere, there must be development'. The term had been suggested by G.L. (later Sir Laurence) Watkinson, 'by far the liveliest, on location questions, of all my permanent civil servants' [39]. The map of the Areas would later be redrawn. The new Development Areas would be more extensive than the Special Areas. In the North East, they would include the whole of Tyneside and County Durham, parts of Northumberland and the North Riding of Yorkshire.

Dalton reported that his Controller of Factory and Storage Premises and his Regional Controllers had already been in touch with a number of industrialists. The building licensing system required them to go to the Board of Trade to discuss their post-War building plans and every effort would be made to steer such enquiries to the regions. Dalton claimed that this line of approach had already produced some results: 'we have found a remarkable degree of willingness, especially on the part of big firms, to consider suggestions by the Board of Trade as to the future location of their factories'.

Dalton also predicted the problems of reconciling the need for houses and factories after the end of the War. He foreshadowed the continuation of the wartime building licence regime and recognised its wider policy potential: 'this will be a most powerful lever for influencing the location of industry in the transitional period'.

Further pressure was being exerted from within the North East: according to The Times of 28 January 1944, the Northern Industrial Group had sent a memorandum to the Minister for Reconstruction in which it had asked for a national policy of industrial location. In the third leader of the same day, headed 'Prospects for the North East', The Times wrote:-

> The War has scarcely altered the lopsided industrial structure of this region, because strategic considerations have prevented the introduction of any important enterprises of new types; the transference of local workpeople has continued and may aggrave the region's economic difficulties after the War ... In this particular case the argument on social grounds that work should

go to the workers seems unanswerable ... The legitimate claims of Northumberland, Durham and the North Riding of Yorkshire require a genuinely national policy, but the success of this, in turn, will depend, as the Northern Industrial Group recognise, on Britain's success in maintaining employment at a high level.

Opinion in favour of a location of industry policy was not, however, quite unanimous. A Note by the Economic Section of the War Cabinet of 20 October 1943 [40] spelled out some of the inconsistencies in the arguments advanced up to then; for example, the likely incompatibility of the aims of diversification with decentralisation, and of diversification with the optimum adaptation of new industry to the existing character of a region.

The Section also saw dangers in a total ban on further industrial development in London and the Home Counties. It proposed a policy which would distinguish between the transition period immediately after the end of the War and subsequent years. For the former period, the Section suggested the use of certain wartime controls in order to prevent the emergence of heavy localised unemployment, but for the longer term, it warned: 'the introduction of discrimination between areas into an economic system, where non-discrimination is an obtainable as well as a desirable goal, is a serious matter meriting some caution'.

But these reservations could no longer affect the course of events, which was set immutably on a path towards a location policy.

THE 1944 WHITE PAPER ON EMPLOYMENT POLICY

The White Paper was published in May 1944 [41] under the signature of the Minister for Reconstruction. It was a document of great significance: for the first time, a British government had pledged itself 'to maintain a high and stable level of employment'. For the Development Areas, the connection between employment and a location of industry policy was spelled out in Chapter III, entitled 'The Balanced Distribution of Industry and Labour'.

The negotiations which preceded the White Paper were complex. It could not have been otherwise, because employment policy involved almost all aspects of economic and financial management, and, therefore, the theories, views and interests associated with them.

The events leading to the White Paper will not be discussed here in any detail. This has been done by others in recent years: Booth [42], for example, has described the discussions on post-War employment policy and the clash of views between the Economic Section - which had put forward broadly Keynesian ideas - and the Treasury, which was deeply pessimistic about Britain's post-War prospects and remained largely wedded to economic orthodoxy. In 1943, Sir John Anderson, the Lord President, found it necessary to set up a steering committee to bridge these conflicting positions. Without compromises, the White Paper might never have been published.

The evolution of the White Paper was traced by Booth in another paper [43]. He concluded that pre-War notions of physical planning, the Barlow Report, Keynesian views on demand management and the political and social evolution during the War all played a part, but that the most formative influence on Chapter III was that of the wartime production establishment.

Jay [44] has described the events from the autumn of 1943, as he saw them from the Board of Trade. His main objective at that time was to persuade the Inter-departmental Committee drafting the White Paper (chaired by Norman Brook) to insert the required paragraphs which would enable him to carry out his plans. In the Board of Trade he 'encountered mercifully little doctrinaire opposition to the idea of some government steering of the location of industry'. The opposition encountered in Cabinet came from from Beaverbrook and Bracken. But 'with the decisive backing from Bevin', the White Paper was passed by the Cabinet in the spring of 1944.

The White Paper recognised the continuing importance of the basic industries to the prosperity of regions like the North East and the need to improve their efficiency, particularly to secure overseas markets. Given that the plants had been working without interruption throughout the War and that there had been little new investment, modernisation would be a major undertaking. As for the necessary finance, the government 'would help these industries to reach the highest pitch of efficiency'.

But even with the high level of domestic demand foreseen in the White Paper, the basic industries alone could not provide employment for all. Unless additional measures were taken, unemployment and an undesirably large outward migration would result.

The government proposed to deal with local unemployment in three ways: by influencing the location of new enterprises, by removing obstacles to mobility and by expanding retraining facilities.

The establishment of new enterprises in Development Areas would be encouraged by the following means:

There would be a statutory requirement to notify plans to build new factories or to transfer factories from one area to another before such plans had reached an advanced stage. This would enable the government to exercise a considerable influence over the location of industrial development.

Complementary policies - 'the stick and the carrot' - would be adopted to affect the location of industry more directly: powers would be taken, on the one hand, to prohibit the establishment of new factories in districts where serious disadvantages would arise from further industrial development. Inducements would be offered to industrialists, on the other, to set up factories in areas where diversification was urgently needed.

The inducements would include opportunities to lease or buy munitions factories in the Areas and priority over other areas in the granting of building licences for new factories or extensions. The government would continue and extend the pre-War policy of building factories in the Areas on individual or collective sites for sale or lease. As for financial assistance, viable enterprises establishing themselves in the Areas, particularly in the more 'difficult' parts, would be given 'adequate facilities for obtaining short-term loans and, where necessary, share capital'.

As a further - if indirect - inducement, the government undertook to 'secure the full development in these areas of the basic services on which industry depends and to stimulate the modernisation of their capital equipment, including housing'.

Finally, the White Paper explained why the government would support a policy of dispersing investment in the Areas: neither the social capital nor the corporate life of existing communities could be sacrificed, except in special circumstances: 'there may be small and isolated villages which offer no hope of sound economic revival ... In these rare cases the population may have to be re-established elsewhere'. There might be other special cases where individual workers would have to seek work elsewhere in the Areas. McCrone [45] considers that this was sound economic reasoning: while some labour movement within the region would be necessary, 'not every depressed hamlet would be assisted'. But where a large population was involved, 'the government was not prepared either to compel its transfer to another area or to leave it to prolonged unemployment and demoralisation'.

Dalton described the policies enunciated in the White Paper 'as a most notable step forward in public policy', and much of the document became his 'official charter', on which he would rely in subsequent arguments [46].

There was no mention in the White Paper, however, of a 'Central Authority'. While the Board of Trade was to become the 'single channel through which government policy on the distribution of industry can be expressed', the responsibility for the implementation of Development Area policy would be shared with a number of other government departments (the Ministries of Labour, Agriculture, Town and Country Planning and the Scottish Office). This departure from the Barlow recommendations was widely criticised at the time [47]. Dalton claimed later that the liaison between the Board of Trade and the other departments worked well, 'but it made a great difference that my department now had the captaincy' [48].

The welcome accorded to the White Paper was reflected in The Times of 30 May 1944: 'from the chorus of approbation with which the White Paper on Employment has been received, it is clear that a great advance has been made towards an agreed national policy on this crucial issue'.

Referring to those who believed that the White Paper did not go far enough, The Times observed that 'it is important that (revolutionary changes) should be effected in the traditional British way, step by step, with all shades of opinions taken into account ... and every endeavour made to secure the widest possible support'.

The Supply Day Debate on 7 June 1944 - the day after the Allied landings in France - was devoted to the Location of Industry. It was an unfortunate choice of topic, because a full debate on the White Paper was scheduled for 21, 22 and 23 June. The rule that impending legislation could not be discussed during Ballot Debates would limit discussion.

Nevertheless, the debate yielded important information at least on the intentions with regard to government-financed factories: in Dalton's view, trading estates 'were never carried as far as they should have been'. It was the government's intention 'that there shall be more trading estates. So far, the tendency had been to have one for each area, but we do not think that this is enough, and we shall aim at a larger number and a wider dispersion of trading estates' [49].

It may be noted that this was exactly what the Labour Party Commission on the Distressed Areas - under the chairmanship of Hugh Dalton - had proposed some seven and a half years earlier. Indeed, one Member of Parliament observed later that the White Paper contained a number of general principles which 'the Labour Party had advocated for many years' [50], and another Member discerned in the White Paper 'distinct traces of having been influenced by a Fabian Society Tract on Full Employment' [51]. This was the result of the tendency - noted, among others, by Booth, Addison and Pimlott - for Labour Ministers in the Coalition to dominate in discussions on post-War planning.

The debates on the White Paper revealed a wide measure of agreement, even if some Members believed that the powers the government proposed to take went too far, while others thought they did not go far enough. The consensus was expressed by a Unionist Member: 'we must recognise that, if stability is to be obtained, there must be some control. It is to a large extent a choice between two evils' [52].

The Times commented in leading articles both before and after the debates on the White Paper: on 20 June 1944, it referred to 'public doubt, whether the government, while sincerely willing the end, are prepared also to will the means with the conviction and determination which alone can make them effective'. On 22 June, it wondered how - given all the unstable factors in the economy - stable employment could be achieved, and on 26 June, it noted with apparent satisfaction that 'on the basic issue - namely that under modern conditions, no reliance can be placed on the automatic working of market forces to ensure full employment, and that general unemployment is a disease no longer to be tolerated - there is well nigh universal agreement'.

It had been argued by some that the aims of the White Paper could not be achieved under private ownership of industry. The Times retorted that 'the responsibility of the State to maintain an adequate level of expenditure at all times will be independent from the question of ownership'.

The ideas expressed in the White Paper on the location of industry - as on other matters - would have appeared rather radical a decade earlier, and the reception of the White Paper showed how far public opinion had moved under the impact of War. Unemployment among returning servicemen and women would not only breed cynicism and discontent in the Areas, it would be unacceptable to the country.

Two steps were now required to give effect to Chapter III of the White Paper: a draft Bill and the establishment of the administrative machinery. Jay expected to be deeply involved in both steps, but his position was still that of Dalton's personal assistant, i.e. he had no executive authority. After much discussion and lobbying inside the Board of Trade, Jay and Sir Philip Warter (see Appendix 9) - the Controller of the Factory and Storage Premises Division - became joint heads in June 1944 of a new section at the Board of Trade, with the ranks of Assistant Secretaries. They set out at once to build the organisation which would implement the aims of the White Paper.

In London, a Regional Distribution of Industry Division was set up at the headquarters of the Board of Trade, which would be assisted by an Inter-departmental Distribution of Industry Committee. Panel A of the committee would be concerned with the disposal or conversion of wartime government factories and Royal Ordnance Factories, while panel B would deal with approvals of new factory location and construction. It is not known whether the Directorate for Industrial Estates, which became operational on 1 August 1945, was part of the initial plan for the headquarter's organisation.

A Location Planning Room was established in the Division. This provided the most comprehensive information - covering the whole country - on sites for the location of new industries. It had already been used at the Ministry of Production - where it was housed before - to assist large firms in the choice of sites for their post-War developments.

The influence of the Barlow Commission could be discerned in the regional organisation: the Majority report had proposed that 'for the purpose of securing the advice and assistance of persons having local knowledge and experience', the 'Central Authority' should have powers 'to establish divisional or regional bodies to study problems of industrial location throughout the country'. One of the Minority reports had insisted that the setting up of divisional or regional bodies should not be optional, but that it should be 'a definite requirement of the scheme of regulation and control'.

This advice appears to have been followed. Regional Inter-departmental Committees on the Distribution of Industry were established in accordance with a memorandum of 21 October 1944 from Sir Philip Warter [53]. These committees were associated with the Regional Production Boards (see Appendix 11), where the relevant government departments and 'some persons having local knowledge and experience' were already represented. When the Act implementing the White Paper had been passed, the committees would assume statutory functions.

The regional offices of the Control of Factory and Storage Premises Division became the regional offices of the Board of Trade. Each regional Distribution of Industry Committee would be chaired by the Regional Controller. The committee based at Newcastle met for the first time on 30 October 1944, and initially, weekly thereafter.

THE DISTRIBUTION OF INDUSTRY ACT 1945

While the organisation to implement Chapter III of the White Paper proposals was rapidly being established, not even a beginning had been made to prepare a Bill which would provide the legal framework. Dalton was to have a hard fight on his hands to persuade the Coalition Government to proceed with the necessary legislation. He has described these events in Volume 2 of his Memoirs.

On 21 November 1944 Dalton wrote to the Prime Minister, expressing once more his concern about the employment prospects in the Development Areas, particularly when the number of those seeking work would be swollen by men and women returning from the Forces. National measures for full employment would have to be supplemented by special steps to stimulate and diversify industry in the Areas. He ended with this plea: 'I hope you will give me your support in pressing on with a Bill for a better-balanced distribution of industry. I am very much troubled by the thought that this next session may pass, and possibly this Parliament come to an end, without any legislation on this subject' [54].

His concern was justified: 'my Distribution of Industry Bill was not in the first draft of the King's Speech for the new session though, as I pointed out to my colleagues, without legislation the pledges given in the White Paper could not be redeemed'.

After more argument, Dalton secured a mention of the Bill in the King's Speech. To obtain it, 'I made a concession to the opponents of my Bill, several of whom were most persistent. I gave up the right, which I was claiming for the Board of Trade, to build factories outside, as well as inside the Development Areas'.

When the Cabinet Office sent for 'his Bill', Dalton was actually unprepared and the first three drafts had to be completed in great haste. Once the outline Bill was ready, it had to be approved by the War Cabinet. There was Tory opposition to the measure, interfering as it did with the rights of firms to put their works where they liked. In a letter to Attlee on 22 November 1944, Bevin reported 'a great struggle on Distribution of Industry', a term Bevin preferred to 'Location of Industry' [55].

On 3 December 1944, Churchill wrote to Bevin and proposed that 'as the discussion on the matter in the Cabinet had shown political issues to be involved, the Distribution of Industry Committee (consisting of three Labour and two Conservative Ministers) should be strengthened by the addition of Beaverbrook, the Lord Privy Seal' [56] - an opponent of the concept enshrined in the Bill, as Jay had found earlier -, a proposal which Bevin, who chaired the committee, turned down firmly.

At this stage, the success of the draft Bill seemed less than certain and Dalton sent 'letters to a number of influential and not unfriendly colleagues, each letter adjusted, to the best of my powers, to the character and outlook of the recipient, canvassing support for my Bill'.

Dalton knew that there was now no more than a chance that the measure would be passed before the government broke up, as everyone knew it would when the War in Europe ended. There were last minute hitches: the absence of the Prime Minister in Yalta and Cairo nearly stopped consideration of the Bill by the War Cabinet on 6 February 1945. This would have upset the timetable. Dalton wrote to Attlee, the Deputy Prime Minister, and to Lyttelton, the Minister of Production, and threatened resignation. The Bill was finally accepted by the Cabinet on 7 February 1945.

The Bill was tabled in the Commons on 21 February 1945. The first leader in The Times of 23 February called it 'a triumph for the principles of the Barlow Report and personally for Sir Malcolm Stewart'.

The Second Reading took place on 21 March 1945. In introducing the Bill, Dalton claimed that its purpose was 'to abolish distressed areas'. He warned the House that, unless the government obtained powers such as those indicated in the Bill, 'it will be quite impossible to prevent a relapse ... within the next few years, into severe and prolonged unemployment in certain localities'. The Bill 'was not the last word in legislation on this subject', but it represented 'the largest common measure of agreement of those of us who are today associated in the (Coalition) Government'.

Clause 1- of the Bill gave powers to the Board of Trade to build factories - as well as houses for key workers - in Development Areas.

Clause 2 enabled the Board of Trade, with the consent of the Treasury, to make loans and grants to non-profit-making trading or industrial estate companies. These powers were not dissimilar to those in the hands of the Commissioners for the Special Areas.

Clause 3 empowered any Minister of the Crown to make special grants or loans, with the consent of the Treasury, towards the cost of improving basic services in Development Areas.

Clause 4 enabled the Treasury, with the advice of a Committee (the Development Areas Treasury Advisory Committee, DATAC), to make loans or grants to firms in the Scheduled Areas. This facility existed under the 1937 Special Areas Amendment Act, but this time there was no overall limit to the total amount of money available.

Clause 5 gave power to the Board of Trade to acquire and improve derelict land, by compulsory purchase if necessary.

Clause 6 provided for changes of the areas scheduled: subject to approval by Parliament, the Board of Trade would be able to add to the schedule any area where a serious unemployment problem appeared to be developing. Provision was made also for the removal of areas from the schedule three years after the passing of the Bill, if the situation had so improved that Development Area status was no longer required.

Clause 7 repealed the Special Areas Acts 1934 and 1937 and wound up the Special Areas Fund. The assets and any outstanding commitments would be transferred to the appropriate government department, i.e. in most cases to the Board of Trade. Except for clauses 3 and 4, the powers under the Bill would be exercised by the President of the Board of Trade.

Up to this clause, the Bill dealt with powers to be exercised within the Development Areas. The next clauses covered the wider aspects.

Clause 8 required anyone outside the Areas proposing to build a factory or extension in excess of 3,000 sq.ft. to notify the Board of Trade. The provision was intended to enable consultations to take place with industrialists before their plans had taken final shape.

At this point in his exposition, Dalton was at pains to point out that there were no powers of compulsion in the Bill. This was an ingenuous argument, because - the building licensing system quite apart - clause 9 would give power to the Board of Trade, subject to an affirmative resolution by Parliament, to prohibit the building of factories in areas where there were serious economic and social objections to the undue congestion of industry.

In fact, Dalton had looked upon clause 9 merely as providing a reserve power 'against the time when the wartime powers of control pass away'. In the meantime, the building licensing system - 'a negative control' - would enable the Board of Trade to achieve most of its policy objectives.

The 'Central Authority' apart, the Bill incorporated some of the major recommendations of the Barlow Commission. Intriguingly, Sir A. Montague-Barlow confided to Dalton on 23 February 1945 that he was no longer a Conservative 'but still had much influence with Conservative Members of Parliament and would use this in favour of my Bill'. Barlow met his promise by writing a letter to The Times on 8 March 1945 in support of the Bill.

The Debate on 21 March 1945 revealed a considerable body of opinion against the Bill as it stood: there were Members from industrial regions outside the Development Areas, who could not accept the kind of control of factory buildings or extensions proposed in the Bill. Although the rebuilding of war-damaged factories was exempt from control provided the floor area of the new buildings did not exceed that of the buildings they replaced by more than 3,000 sq.ft., some Members felt that the limit on expansion would discourage firms in London and other cities from rebuilding. On the other side, there were those who did not think the Bill went far enough and would have preferred a straightforward direction of industry into the Development Areas. Objections of another kind were raised by Members for constituencies which had suffered severe sectoral decline before the War and which were left out of the schedule of Development Areas. Nevertheless, the Bill passed its Second Reading on 23 March 1945 without a division.

The Bill started in Standing Committee on 8 May 1945, the day the War ended in Europe. In spite of the excitement, a quorum was found and the first three clauses and most of clause 4 were agreed. On 10 and 15 May clauses 4 to 8 were agreed and a beginning was made on the contentious clause 9. Dalton hoped 'that another week, after the Whitsun recess, would see the end of it'. But the Prime Minister resigned on 23 May and the Coalition broke up. Churchill resumed office as head of a caretaker government. Lyttelton (Con., Aldershot) became President of the Board of Trade and Capt. Waterhouse (Con., Leicester South) continued as Parliamentary Secretary. Fortunately for Dalton, 'Lyttelton had always been friendly about my Bill and so had Waterhouse. They would both be friendly and accommodating about it now'.

On 28 May, Dalton spoke to Lyttelton and 'offered to propose ... at next day's meeting of the Standing Committee to drop clause 9. Lyttelton accepted gratefully'. The absence on 29 May of several members who had insisted on their constituencies being included in the Schedule of Development Areas - and who had signified their intention to speak at length - enabled the Committee stage to be completed on that day.

Dalton recorded his relief in his Memoirs : 'the following week, the Bill went through Report and Third Reading with hardly any criticism, and received the Royal Assent on 15 June, the day Parliament was dissolved ... it had been "a damned close-run thing"'.

Pimlott [57] has claimed that 'the Distribution of Industry Act had been conceived in the expectation that a Conservative, or at best, a Coalition government would be in power to administer it'. Addison [58] has explained why the social and political changes brought about by the last War should not have made the election of a Labour Government in June 1945 as unexpected as it appeared to many contemporaries and even to Labour Ministers in the Coalition. Nevertheless, the many pressing matters requiring the attention of the new government might have delayed the introduction of a similar measure by many months, if not longer, had Dalton's Bill failed.

THE TOWN AND COUNTRY PLANNING ACT 1947

The government used the building licensing powers with considerable effect in controlling the location of industry in the immediate post-War period. But these powers would have to be phased out eventually and legislation was required to ensure the continuity of location policy.

The legislation was enshrined in the Town and Country Planning Act 1947 [59]. Since the planning of the use of land also applied to land for factories, the Act provided a convenient means of restoring the 'negative control' which would have resulted from clause 9 in the 1945 Bill. Under the Act, anyone wishing to put up or change any building would in future have to obtain planning permission from one of the local planning authorities set up by the Act. In the case of factory buildings or extensions larger than 5,000 sq.ft., however, clause 14 (4) of the Act provided, that this permission would have no effect 'unless it is certified by the Board of Trade that the development in question can be carried out consistently with the proper distribution of industry, and a copy of the certificate is furnished to the local planning authority together with the application'.

These certificates became known as 'IDCs' (Industrial Development Certificates), and they were intended to become effective tools for controlling the location of industry.

The Act received the Royal Assent on 6 August 1947, but in order to allow time to establish the required planning machinery, it came into force in stages. The IDC procedure commenced on 1 June 1948. A comprehensive policy for the location of industry now existed.

From that date, the building licensing procedure ceased to be the means of controlling the location of industry, but it continued to fulfil its other function in a period of continuing shortages of materials: to licence only such buildings for which there was a good social or industrial reason. With the return to normal supply of materials, the licensing machinery was abolished in 1954.

14 years had passed since the Investigator for Durham and Tyneside had first proposed a location of industry policy as a means of dealing with unemployment in the Areas. When the 1947 Act came into force - and for many years afterwards - the North East enjoyed virtually full employment. The location policy pursued with singlemindedness by the Labour Government made only a relatively small contribution to this satisfactory situation in the period covered by this study. The evidence for this will be presented in V/1, V/2 and in the Conclusions.

3   The wartime factories

Apart from two large munitions factories and some extensions, factory construction at Team Valley had ceased a few months after the start of the War. But the needs of the War resulted in a substantial amount of new factory and storage space being built by the government elsewhere in the North East.

The White Paper on Employment Policy had proposed that these wartime factories be leased or sold for civilian production when they were no longer needed. When the War in Europe was drawing to a close, the future of these factories had to be decided and, as soon as they became vacant, their conversion undertaken. The task - and the management of the factories - was transferred progressively to North Eastern Trading Estates Ltd.

As they played a major part in attracting new industries to the North East, an account is given in this chapter of the history of these factories, together with a record of their locations and floor areas, so far as they could be ascertained.

There were, in the first place, the Royal Ordnance Factories at Newton Aycliffe and Spennymoor, both in County Durham. Given their large employment potential, the question arises whether their location was influenced by any longer-term considerations of regional policy.

Lonie and Begg have examined the evidence for any connections between the location of ordnance factories and regional policy before the second world War. They concluded that the War Office - and, to a lesser extent, the Admiralty - tended to locate new factories predominantly in areas believed to be beyond the range of German bombers: 'the happy coincidence that depressed areas were, by and large, in relatively safe areas appears to have added impetus to the government's regional policy at the time' [1]. So far as the North East was concerned, however, this matter was not so straightforward.

The possibilities were considered - probably for the first time - in the summer of 1934, when the Investigator for Durham and Tyneside discussed with the Chief of the Air Staff whether the Air Ministry might insist, if and when a rearmament programme was decided on, 'that the demand should be met from dispersed centres of production'. The Air Ministry advised the Investigator that 'the vulnerability of (the North East) to air attack rules out such a proposal in this case' [2].

A rare opportunity to establish ordnance factories in the Special Areas presented itself in 1935, when the Committee of Imperial Defence recommended the removal of three ordnance factories to safer places (the Royal Filling Factory at Woolwich, the Royal Gun Powder Factory at Waltham and the Royal Gun Factory at Enfield), the first two as early as possible. The Committee recommended sites at Queensferry, Gretna, the Glasgow District and Oswestry. It was at pains to show 'that it had not overlooked the claims of the distressed areas', but 'the recommendations ... were naturally governed by the conditions of security, and considerations such as transport facilities and the proximity of sources of supply of materials and labour' [3].

The Committee - like the Chief of the Air Staff a year earlier - saw difficulties in siting ordnance factories, particularly the filling factory, near built-up areas or conurbations in the North East: 'in the selection of a locality for a new filling factory, we have given special consideration to four depressed areas', but 'for defence reasons ... the areas of Durham, Tyneside and South Wales are unsuitable'. The reserve factory at Birtley, some eight miles south of Newcastle upon Tyne, was being considered for reconditioning only because there were no explosives involved. The Army Council was prepared, therefore, 'to accept the risk of the locality rather than incur the expenditure of erecting buildings elsewhere' [4].

The references in the report to depressed areas indicate that the Committee of Imperial Defence was under some pressure to consider them for locating ordnance factories.

At a Cabinet meeting on 31 July 1935, the report of the Committee was accepted, but emphasis was laid on the psychological importance of giving some help to isolated Special Areas, the population of which was difficult to move to other centres. The Cabinet Resolution, therefore, insisted on a re-examination of possible sites at least in South Wales [5].

In anticipation of the rearmament programme, the Commissioner for England and Wales, too, 'had on several occasions represented to the government the desirability of considering the claims of the Special Areas if they (the government) decide to erect any new munitions works' [6].

It was shown in II/3 that the Cabinet Committee considering the Commissioner's trading estate proposal in October 1935 had doubts about the willingness of industry to move to the North East; at the same time, the government itself might be able to influence attitudes: 'if it were possible to establish one or more government factories in the areas - a matter which is under consideration -, a useful lead would be given and, in time, private employers might also go there' [7].

When the rearmament programme was being launched a few months later, the government confirmed that this was indeed its policy. In a debate in the Commons on 2 March 1936 Ramsay MacDonald remarked that

> the government have been pressing upon employers to found industries in the Special Areas. Now the government themselves propose to adopt the recommendations which they have been pressing upon private employers and to place important orders and plan new industries within those areas in the course of the development and execution of the rearmarment programme [8].

The policy was strongly approved - perhaps even suggested - by the Treasury, which considered it 'a far more natural solution ... for government to establish industries which are naturally fitted to the places they have to fit' than to provide inducements to industry to move to the Areas. The Treasury found it 'maddening ... (that) when an opportunity has unexpectedly come into the government's hands, it has to be sacrificed to the need for swift preparation for War' [9]. There was evidently no time to consider the location of ordnance factories in any depth.

In March 1937, the White Paper on Special Areas policy revealed that explosives and filling factories were, indeed, being removed to places in the Special Areas of Scotland and South Wales [10]. So far as South Wales was concerned, the Cabinet had prevailed over the Services.

The rearmament programme introduced another factor: labour shortages began to appear in some categories of skills in the south of the country. Peden has shown that the Ministry of Labour had become aware of this and suggested that contracts should be taken to the men rather than the other way round [11]. Peden and Pitfield [12] have noted, further, that the Treasury had exhorted the Defence Departments to place contracts in areas of high unemployment.

Keynes had urged the proper use of resources to prevent inflationary pressures resulting from the increasing defence spending. He believed, however, that the Services were only paying lip service to the idea that defence work should assist, so far as possible, the regional aims of the government: 'one feels that the War Departments are inclined to regard Special Area measures as a form of charity, doubtlessly praiseworthy, which interferes, however, with getting on with the job in the most effective way' [13].

To sum up pre-War attitudes: the government - particularly the Treasury - were anxious to link the location of ordnance factories with Special Areas policy. The Service chiefs, for their part, were looking for safe areas with the necessary labour and facilities. Insofar as Special Areas coincided with safe areas, the Services were willing to cooperate. The North East, however, was not considered to be safe and no new ordnance factories were planned there at this stage. Apart from the reopening of the Royal Ordnance Factory at Birtley, the only major preparation made in the region was the re-equipment by the government of the Armstrong Whitworth factories at Newcastle - as agency works - for armament production.

The attitude of the Services towards the North East appears to have changed out of necessity: early in the War, the Ministry of Supply decided to increase the number of Royal Ordnance Factories from nine to 53 [14]. They would be large establishments, each employing between 10,000 and 25,000 people. The choice of places with the required labour yet not too close to built-up areas was limited, particularly when security from air attacks had also to be taken into account. By siting a filling complex at Aycliffe - some five miles from Darlington - the safety doubts had evidently been overcome.

The security aim was achieved: it has been possible to ascertain from someone who worked at Aycliffe throughout the War that the works never suffered any damage from enemy action [15].

But the main objective appears to have been to tap sources of labour in South West Durham. From this point of view, Aycliffe was not the best site, because there was almost no labour in the immediate vicinity [16]:-

> Unfortunately, ... sites in the more populous parts were not available for development at once, owing to difficulties of drainage and subsidence, and for reasons of expediency, the Royal Ordnance Factory was sited off the coalfield at Aycliffe. At the peak period some 15,000 people (largely women) were employed and these had to be drawn from all parts of Durham, some workers travelling over twenty miles each way daily.

The large majority of the workers relied on the railways. The details of the transport operation, which involved the construction of two stations inside the complex and the extension of one outside, are recounted in the wartime history of the London and North Eastern Railway Company [17].

All the evidence leads to the conclusion that the choice of the Aycliffe site was not determined by any longer-term regional policy considerations. This view is supported by the Report of the Select Committee on Estimates in the Spring of 1947, which stated that 'the Royal Ordnance Factories (at Aycliffe and Spennymoor) were sited for security and not for industrial purposes' [18].

But whatever the rationale for their location, it was fortunate that the region found itself at the end of the War with a substantial addition to its stock of light manufacturing space, even if the Select Committee found it necessary to note, in regard to Aycliffe - 18 months after it was taken over for civilian use - that 'extensive work at considerable cost would be required to complete its conversion into an industrial estate, and even then it might be far from satisfactory' [19]. Such doubts had already been voiced during the preparatory stages of the Distribution of Industry Bill 1945 by the Board of Trade, which had considered the complex 'unsuitable for general purposes' [20].

The abandonment of buildings could not be justified, however, at a time when it was believed that the lack of immediately-available factory space might make industrialists hesitate to come to the North East Development Areas.

In the event, the factories at Aycliffe were in great demand in the years after the War, in spite of the problems associated with the buildings.

Pepler and MacFarlane have explained the significance to the region of the ordnance factories at the end of the War [21]:-

> It is perhaps not sufficiently realised that in the last War the North East Coast gained little from the dispersal of industry to safer localities. As a vulnerable area, it received no key industries from the South and few factories were erected capable of easy conversion to peace-time use, nor were new projects of importance started, apart from a few Royal Ordnance Factories.

Pepler and MacFarlane may not have been fully aware of the considerable amount of other government factory construction in the region during the War, which is described later in this chapter.

The transfer of the ordnance factories to civilian industry was initiated immediately after the end of the War in Europe. At a meeting at the Board of Trade in London on 30 May 1945, Methven was informed of the recommendation of the Distribution of Industries Committee of the Board (not to be confused with the eponymous regional bodies) that the Royal Ordnance Factories at Aycliffe and Spennymoor should be managed on permanent trading estate lines by North Eastern Trading Estates Ltd. The factories would be leased to the Company on the same basis as the outside sites belonging to the Commissioner. When the Distribution of Industry Bill became law, the factories would pass from the Ministry of Supply to the Board of Trade, and in the event of the Bill being rejected or modified, to the Commissioner for the Special Areas of England and Wales [22].

Methven appears to have been taken aback by the timetable: Aycliffe was to be taken over on 31 July 1945. Production at the factory would stop on that date. The government was anxious to minimise the period between close-down and the entry of private firms in order to prevent the development of a major local unemployment problem. The decision to close the works was taken at short notice, for Spennymoor there would be a little more time [23].

The Aycliffe complex occupied a large site. The main works covered an area of 419 acres, and there were 245 acres on adjoining land. There were 138 buildings with a floor area of 2.93 million sq.ft. [24]. A large part of this space was unsuitable for industrial use, but it was expected that about one million sq.ft. could be converted. This would provide the Aycliffe estate with about the same floor area as existed at Team Valley at the beginning of the War.

The public services were sufficient for a town of 25,000 people. At peak production, about twice as many people worked at Aycliffe as at Team Valley during the War. The government hoped that employment for 5,000 people could be created at Aycliffe in peacetime.

The task for the Estates Company was enormous: the buildings were not designed for use by industrial firms, let alone in accordance with the standards adopted at Team Valley. Each building would have to be surveyed and a great deal of repair and modification would be required.

A large amount of demolition work would have to done and the semi-sunk bunker space filled-in. To complete even the survey and the conversion specifications within the two months before the works closed would require an exceptional effort.

Under the circumstances, it was a great achievement to have factories available for early occupation, even if their proper conversion would make only slow progress (see Appendix 27). Helped by the immediate post-War demand, the factories let by October 1945 would meet about half the employment target set by the government [25].

The transfer to the Company of the Aycliffe and the Spennymoor complexes did not involve any cash transactions, but the Company insisted that the buildings be valued in order to establish a basis for calculating rents.

Aycliffe was an unusual site for a government trading estate: such estates were normally established in places where significant populations required new employment opportunities. At Aycliffe, there was virtually no population at all. Until the New Town was established, workers had to travel from the surrounding area. When the two wartime railway stations were closed, considerable difficulties resulted.

The possible contribution of New Towns to the solution of urban congestion and sprawl in London, Glasgow and other large conurbations had been discussed well before the last War. It was seriously considered ever since the establishment of the Ministry of Town and Country Planning in 1943. A proposal for a New Town at Aycliffe was examined by a Cabinet Committee on 13 May 1946 [26]. At that time, only one New Town - at Stevenage - had been approved. At Aycliffe, there were initial objections. At a time when coal had become critical to British post-War recovery, some thought the New Town would draw away people from the coal fields. Others feared that the development of Bishop Auckland might be impeded. Nevertheless, the Cabinet approved the project on 23 October 1946, although with an initial population target of only 10,000, considerably less than that originally proposed. It was designated on 19 April 1947. The first sod was cut on 28 June 1948.

Newton Aycliffe was the name of a fairly large area covered by farms. The nearby village of Aycliffe supported a population of less than 500 people, by far the smallest settlement to be designated in Britain up to then. The New Town would be built around a trading estate, a reversal of the usual practice.

At a time when New Towns were thought of as tools for urban redevelopment, Aycliffe was the first to demonstrate that they could fulfil a wider role, but

> it was only in the in the 1960's, after more than a decade of experience, during which the New Towns of Central Scotland and North East England had demonstrated their success as centres for industrial growth, that their role as an important weapon for regional policy came to be properly recognised and their size and siting began to be considered with this end in view [27].

The Aycliffe Estate remained under the control of North Eastern Trading Estates Ltd and its successor organisations for almost 30 years.

Firms on the estate provided work for about 9,000 people at the peak, but employment began to decline in the late 1960s. This appears to have been one of the reasons why the the New Town Corporation was anxious to assume control. The estate was handed over to the Corporation - with some reluctance - in 1973 [28]. New industrial zones were laid out and modern factories constructed, making it possible to demolish most of the wartime buildings over a period of years.

The Royal Ordnance Factory at Spennymoor was a much smaller entity. It was designed for the production of small arms ammunition. There were six main buildings, the largest two of which acommodated a non-ferrous foundry and a rolling mill. The other buildings were suitable for light engineering. Of the 5,700 people who worked there during the War, 3,700 were women. About half the labour force was drawn from Spennymoor. The information on the size of the works is not completely clear, but the space suitable for industry appears to have been 450,380 sq.ft. [29]. It was taken over by the Company in September 1945 and let to one large and a number of smaller firms.

The background to the decision early in 1944 to locate six reserve munitions factories in the North East will be examined in V/2. They were built by the Ministry of Works; their locations and sizes were as follows [30]:-

Hartlepool	74,228	sq.ft.
Middlesbrough	63,080	"
Pallion (Sunderland)	61,164	"
South Shields	65,665	"
Southwick (Sunderland)	74,860	"
St. Helen's Auckland	69,417	"

	408,414	sq.ft.

The take-over of these factories by the Company on behalf of the Board of Trade was complicated by a number of factors, including the need to effect the change in ownership from the Ministry of Works, lack of title to requisitioned land, and lack of detailed information on the contents of the factories and services provided.

The factories at Pallion and St. Helen's (West) Auckland were built on land belonging to the Board of Trade - as the successor to the Commissioner - and the take-over presented few problems. The difficulties arose with the factories built on requisitioned land. The Ministry of Works did not own the land and it took several years to negotiate the freehold. There was the further complication that leases were granted by various government departments to tenants who had moved in as soon as the factories were completed.

The involvement of the Company with the management of these factories proceeded in stages. On 3 June 1946, the Board of Trade asked the Company to collect the rents. The Company had, in fact, been doing this for some months already. It was not until 20 October 1947 that the Board of Trade made a formal request to the Company to 'undertake the full duties of management' [31], and even then, it was to take some further months before the formalities were completed.

On 29 March 1947, the Board of Trade requested the Company to manage the buffer depots of the Ministry of Food which were no longer required. The list included the following [32]:-

Bishop Auckland	25,900 sq.ft.
Newburn 1	26,257 "
Newburn 2	26,257 "
Stanhope	26,344 "

	104,758 sq.ft.

On the Team Valley Estate, there appear to have been only two government-owned modifications to factories which had not yet passed into the ownership of the Board of Trade by August 1947: a small extension to factory D.42 (4,557 sq.ft.), and the internal alterations to factory M. 105. The two large wartime factories, built for the Ministries of Supply (E.106) and Aircraft Production (F.109), were owned by the Company.

The last group of readily-identifiable wartime buildings were those at the Ministry of Supply clothing depot at West Chirton, Tynemouth. This was to be taken over gradually as the Ministry moved out. The original request to the Company to manage this large depot seems to have been made in 1947. The Company considered the buildings suitable for industrial purposes, but considerable modifications would be required to turn them into factory units.

In a letter of 15 June 1948 to the Board of Trade, the Company noted that the experience so far in taking over this depot 'confirms the fears ... that the transfer of the estate is likely to be a lengthy process' [33]. By 1 September 1948, the Ministry of Supply vacated the whole of the depot and the Company took over the management on 1 October 1948.

The floor area of the buildings at Chirton was 506,212 sq.ft. [34]. The depot became an important trading estate, with its own management structure.

Finally, there was a large group of miscellaneous buildings erected or acquired by government departments, most of them during the War. No attempt has been made to arrive at a complete record of these buildings. In principle, it should be possible to construct such a record from the Board of Trade estimates of employment in government-owned factories [35], but as the lists included employment in buildings not yet transferred to the Company or already sold, buildings erected since the end of the War and those included in the identifiable groups discussed in this chapter, it would be no mean task.

Excluding the miscellaneous group of buildings, the floor area which became available in wartime government factories and stores, according to the records in the Company's files, can now be be summarised:-

Aycliffe, approx.	1,000,000 sq.ft.
Spennymoor	450,388 "
Standard Reserve Factories	408,414 "
Food Depots	104,758 "
West Chirton	506,212 "

	2,469,772 sq.ft.

Table 6 shows that the total floor area of government wartime factories available for conversion to civilian use was 3,435,000 sq.ft. Since 2,469,772 sq.ft. have been accounted for in the identifiable groups, the floor area of the miscellaneous buildings was just under one million sq.ft. They included almost certainly some existing factories which the government had acquired during or immediately after the War (probably, for example, part of the former Armstrong-Whitworth agency works at Scotswood, Newcastle upon Tyne).

It was fortunate for the North East that the lack of progress at Team Valley during the War was made up by construction elsewhere in the region. The floor area of factories built or acquired by government departments or agencies amounted to about three times that available at Team Valley and the outside sites at the outbreak of the War.

Even if not all the space would be available immediately, the transfer of the wartime factories greatly extended the process of dispersal of industrial development in the region which had started with the outside sites before the War. This process would gather momentum when the post-War factory construction programme would start to roll. The programme and its implementation will be discussed in the next chapter and in VI.

REFERENCES AND NOTES

IV/1. The Company in the War Years

[1]   In September and October 1939.
[2]   EIEB, minute 721, 21.8.1939.
[3]   TWA,1762/5, Commissioner (Thompson) to Company, 3.9.1939.
[4]   TWA,1762/5, Company Secretary to Commissioner, 29.9.1939.
[5]   EIEB, minute 774, 16.10.1939.
[6]   Op.cit.4, p.6.
[7]   TWA,1762/5, Appleyard to Commissioner (T.W.F. Dalton) 28.9.1939.
[8]   TWA,1762/5, Commissioner (Dalton) to Company (Secretary), 1.12.1939.
[9]   TWA,1762/5, Appleyard to Chapman, 18.12.1939.
[10]   EIEB, minute 800, 21.12.1939.
[11]   TWA,1762/6, Commissioner (Dalton) to Company (Methven), 1.12.1940.
[12]   EIEB, Journal of Events, an irregular diary, entries from 3.1.1939 to 15.2.1956. Initially, Methven may have written it himself, but later it was kept by Miss Helms, Methven's secretary.
[13]   TWA,1762/6, Methven to Martin, 28.6.1940.
[14]   TWA,1395, Box 766, File M 1804, a letter from Methven to the Commissioner (Dalton) on 30.1.1942 lists the factories requisitioned by the Admiralty as E.10, F.24, D.33, A.37, F.31 and F.32.
[15]   TWA,1395, Box 766, File M 1804.
[16]   EIEB, minute 886, 19.7.1940.
[17]   There were many Czechoslovak nationals working at Team Valley. Apart from those employed by Sigmund Pumps Ltd, almost the whole of the inital engineering staff of Bren Manufacturing Company Ltd - which Miroslav Sigmund was largely responsible for setting up - consisted of Czechoslovaks who had reached this country after the outbreak of the War.

[18]   TWA,1762/6, Appleyard to Methven, 10.6.1941.
[19]   TWA,1762/6, record of a telephone conversation between Methven and
        Appleyard, 17.11.1941.
[20]   TWA,1395, Box 766, File M 1804, Commissioner (Dalton) to Company
        Secretary, 26.3.1943.
[21]   TWA,1395, Box 766, File M 1804, Commissioner (Dalton) to Company
        Secretary, 17.5.1943.
[22]   EIEB, minute 1178, 6.11.1942.
[23]   EIEB, minute 1306, 30.11.1943.
[24]   TWA,1395, Box 766, File 1804, Commissioner (Dalton) to Methven,
        29.1.1942, enclosing an undated extract from a letter Chapman to
        Commissioner (Tribe).
[25]   In the event, the money seems to have lasted until 1946. See
        TWA,1395, file 1386, Finance Dept. Board of Trade (Campling) to
        Methven, 8.2.1946.
[26]   EIEB, minute 1257, 21. 6.1943.
[27]   EIEB, minute 1305, 30.11.1943.
[28]   Ibid.
[29]   EIEB, minute 1320, 21. 1.1944.
[30]   EIEB, record of Ninth Ordinary Annual General Meeting.
[31]   EIEB, minute 1414, 14. 7.1944.
[32]   EIEB, minute 1562, 8. 6.1945.
[33]   EIEB, minute 1639, 3.12.1945.
[34]   Ibid.
[35]   At Darlington, in connection with the Aycliffe Trading Estate.
        Communication from Mr. J.D. Crabtree, Principal Planner, Aycliffe
        Development Corporation, 15.5.1985.
[36]   EIEB, minute 1478, 2. 2.1945.
[37]   TWA,1762/6, Methven's minutes (Memorandum) of the meeting with
        the President of the Board of Trade, 30,11.1944.
[38]   EIEB, minute 1334, 21. 1.1944.
[39]   EIEB, minute 1389, 12. 5.1944.
[40]   EIEB, minute 1568, 16. 7.1945.
[41]   Ibid.
[42]   EIEB, minute 1586, 3. 9.1945.
[43]   EIEB, minute 1575, 16. 7.1945.
[44]   EIEB, minute 1585, 3. 9.1945.

IV/2. The Evolution of Post-War Policy

[1]   McCrone, G., 1971, p.114.
[2]   Cole, G.D.H., Introduction to Fogarty, M.P., 1945, p.xxxi.
[3]   CAB 58/12, ECA, (H)138, memorandum by C.R. Attlee, 9.2.1931,
       point.9.
[4]   See Appendix 11 and Pinder, John. (ed.), 1981.
[5]   The Next Five Years Group, 1935.
[6]   Labour Party, January 1937 and April 1937
[7]   Booth, Alan, 1982, p.9.
[8]   Labour Party, January 1937, p.7.
[9]   Op.cit.[2].
[10]   HC Deb 296, 608.
[11]   RCDIP, 1940.
[12]   Op.cit.[1], p.104.
[13]   Op.cit.[7].
[14]   Op.cit.[1], p.30.
[15]   White Paper, 1951, p.1.

[16] Ibid., p.6.
[17] Dalton, Hugh, 1957, p.434.
[18] Op.cit.[7].
[19] Addison, Paul, 1975, pp. 215,216.
[20] Op.cit.[17].
[21] Op.cit.[17], p.435, footnote 1.
[22] BT 106/12, memorandum on 'The Location of Industry'.
[23] Op.cit. [7], pp.11, 12.
[24] Op.cit.[17], p.440.
[25] Jay, Douglas, 1980, p.112.
[26] CAB 87/13, PR (43) 26, War Cabinet, Committee on Reconstruction
      Priorities, under the chairmanship Jowitt, the Lord President of
      the Council, 18.5.1942.
[27] CAB 87/13, PR (43) 29, 'Memorandum by the President of the Board
      of Trade', 27.5.1943. In a later memorandum, Hugh Dalton
      effectively developed all the arguments he was able to marshall
      in favour of a location of industry policy. CAB 87/13, PR (43)
      50, 2.9.1943. There was an appendix on ' Inducements to
      Industrialists to enter difficult Areas', and another on the
      Barlow Report. Nothwithstanding the views of Booth, op.cit.7,
      Dalton seems to have felt that this report carried politcal
      weight in the Coalition.
[28] BT 106/20, memorandum 'Location of Industry', by the Board of
      Trade in consultation with a number of Ministries, which included
      the preliminary results of the surveys undertaken in the Areas,
      undated, but ca. October 1943.
[29] BT 106/21, EC (43) 13, War Cabinet Committee on Post-War
      Employment, note by the Economic Section, 20.10.1943, 'Location
      of Industry'. The Section had already commented on op.cit.[28],
      under cover of a letter of 7.10.1943 by S.R. Dennison.
[30] Op.cit.[25], p.108.
[31] Op.cit.[7], p.19.
[32] Op.cit.[25].
[33] Ibid.
[34] Op.cit.[7], p.16, particularly in criticism of McCrone.
[35] Ibid. Booth has obtained this information from a personal
      interview with Jay.
[36] HC Deb, 392, 1043.
[37] HC Deb, 395, 1053.
[38]   "   , 1073.
[39] Op.cit.[17], p.438.
[40] Op.cit.[29].
[41] White Paper, 1944.
[42] Booth, Alan, 1983, pp.109 - 111. The discussion appears to have
      started with a paper by James Meade of the Economic Section
      entitled 'The Prevention of General Unemployment'. Booth has
      quoted the source as T 230/13, revised version, 30.4.1941.
[43] Op.cit.[7].
[44] Op.cit.[25], pp.112,113.
[45] Op.cit.[1], p.107.
[46] Op.cit.[17], p.443.
[47] For example in the Commons, HC Deb 400, 1399, Mr. Daggar, (Lab.,
      Abertillery): 'there are too many Departments fiddling with this
      problem. It seems to be the business of every Minister and yet
      the business of none ... there should be, as the Barlow Report
      recommends, the formation of a central authority to undertake
      this task'.

[48]   Op.cit.[17], p.440.
[49]   HC Deb 400, 1379.
[50]   HC Deb 401, 255.
[51]   HC Deb 401, 288.
[52]   HC Deb 401, 365.
[53]   BT 208/20, CL (R) 53. 'Regional Committees on the Distribution of
        Industry'.
[54]   Op.cit.[17], p. 446.
[55]   Op.cit.[25], p.113.
[56]   Bullock, Alan, 1967, p.316
[57]   Pimlott, Ben, 1985, p.406.
[58]   Addison, Paul, 1975.
[59]   It received the Royal Assent on 6.8.1947. The Act relating to
        Scotland was passed later.

IV/3.   The Wartime Factories

[1]   Lonie, A.A. & Begg, H.M., 1979, p.498.
[2]   RIDT, 1934, para.30, p.82.
[3]   CAB 24/256, CP 145 (35), Committee on Imperial Defence, sub-
        committee on Defence Policy & Requirements, Air Defence, Interim
        Report of sub-Committee.
[4]   CAB 23/82, CC, 41 (35), p.140.
[5]   Ibid.
[6]   CSAEW, 1936, 2nd Report, para.56 p.16.
[7]   CAB 27/577, DA, CP 197 (35), Report, 18.10.1935, para.9.
[8]   HC Deb 309, 1040.
[9]   T 172/1828, Sir Warren Fisher to Chancellor, memorandum 'How to
        attract new industries', 14.11.1936.
[10]   White Paper, 1937, para.11, p.7.
[11]   Peden, G.C., 1979, p.83, quoted by op.cit.[1], p.497.
[12]   Ibid and Pitfield, D.W., 1978, p.439, quoted by op.cit.[1],
        p.497.
[13]   Keynes, J.M., 'Borrowing for Defence - is it inflation?' A plea
        for an organised policy. The Times , 11.3.1937, pp. 17,18,
        quoted by op.cit.[1].
[14]   Fogarty, M.P., 1945, p.53 quoting HC Deb 382, 1072.
[15]   Interview with Mrs. A. Dewar at Aycliffe Development Corporation
        offices on 8.5.1985. This lady was a draughtswoman who worked on
        the site from the time the Royal Ordnance Factory was being built
        until it closed down.
[16]   Grenfell Baines, 1948, p.7, quoting from a report by J.R.James,
        research officer on the regional staff (presumably at Newcastle
        upon Tyne) of the Ministry of Town and Country Planning.
[17]   Crump, Norman, 1947.
[18]   Select Committee on Estimates, 1947, Second Report, para.58.
[19]   Ibid.
[20]   BT 106/53, Board of Trade (Jay) to Treasury (Proctor), 6.11.1944.
[21]   Pepler, G., & McFarlane, P.W., ca.1949. I am grateful to Dr. F.
        Robinson of the Centre for Urban and Regional Studies, University
        of Newcastle upon Tyne, for drawing my attention to and lending
        me this report.
[22]   TWA,1762/7, minutes of 'A meeting in London on 30.5.1945 to
        consider the questions involved in transferring the R.O.Fs.
        Spennymoor and Aycliffe to the North Eastern Trading Estate
        Company'.

[23]   Ibid.

[24]   TWA,1395/361.

[25]   By the end of 1945, Chapman was able to report an even better
       position to Hugh Dalton in a letter of 8.12.1945, TWA,1762/7:
       'all the factories which according to the present arrangements
       are to be filled have been let and will provide employment for
       about 4,000'.

[26]   Cullingworth, J.B. 1970, p.112.

[27]   McCrone, G, 1971, p.111.

[28]   TWA,1395/45, internal note, Heyman (chairman of Company's
       successor) to Bevan (chief executive), 4.1.1972, shows that the
       Company initially resisted the handing over of the estate.

[29]   The figure is an estimate, computed from the approx. floor area
       occupied by the three immediate post-War tenants. No other
       information was found.

[30]   TWA,1762/9, schedule, 'NETE-managed factories which have been
       built or altered by Government Departments, the ownership in such
       buildings or alterations not having passed to the Estate Company
       or the Board of Trade', August 1947.

[31]   TWA,1762/9, Board of Trade, Directorate for Industrial Estates
       (Baylis) to Methven, 20.10.1947.

[32]   TWA,1395, Box 271, File 1826, typed copy, Sadler Forster to
       Methven, 'Ministry of Food Buffer Depots', 29.3.1947.

[33]   TWA,1395, Box 656, untitled File, Company to Board of Trade,
       Directorate for Industrial Estates, (Cook), 15.6.1948.

[34]   TWA,1395/3110 (New index). The sole information which has been
       found is an undated information sheet 'West Chirton', listing the
       tenants and the floor area they occupied as well as their
       products, ca. mid-1949. The total floor area of the wartime
       buildings was added in ink. By 1949, the total floor area of the
       estate - on both sides of the Coast Road - had grown to 875,602
       sq.ft.

[35]   BT 106/101.

PART V: THE POST-WAR YEARS TO THE END OF 1948

1 Factory construction after the war

It has been shown in II/3 that the role played by government-financed trading estates in pre-War Special Areas policy was an unforeseen one. The 1934 Act had made no provision for financing factories and there were, indeed, initial difficulties to overcome before it became possible to use the Special Areas Fund for this purpose. Furthermore, the government had serious doubts whether trading estates could succeed in the Areas, and the first one - in the North East - was authorised for reasons only partly related to the industrial needs of the region. The Commissioner's powers to build factories under the 1937 Act were conceded reluctantly and for a limited purpose.

Given the importance they would assume in the post-War world, it may also be recalled that the concept of government-financed factories arose outside the Establishment: it was proposed by an industrialist acting as a temporary Commissioner, who was convinced of the need to experiment with a new approach to the problems of the depressed areas.

The results of that experiment up to the beginning of the last War were evaluated in earlier chapters. An examination was made of the Team Valley Estate and - to a lesser extent, the outside sites - in the short period of their existence before the outbreak of the War: the tenants they attracted, the industries they were engaged in, their structural impact and the employment they created.

For the immediate post-War period, the focus must necessarily shift. The 1945 election manifesto of the Labour Party had promised 'full employment in any case, and if we need to keep a firm public hand on industry in order to get jobs for all, very well. No more dole queues, ... there must be no depressed areas in the New Britain'.

The election victory of the Labour Party would ensure the determined pursuit of Development Area policy. Government-financed factories would now assume a central role, because the aims of the Distribution of Industry Act could not be realised without an adequate number of factories available for rent.

The implementation of the 1945 Act poses important economic and political questions, some of which require a detailed examination in the context of this study: the background against which the government-financed factory programme was undertaken; the aims of the programme, the problems it encountered and how far the aims were achieved; the impact on the employment situation and on the industrial structure of the North East; the effectiveness of direct government control over the programme, and finally, the relationship between the government and the Company. The last four chapters of this study attempt to contribute to an understanding of these aspects of the 1945 Act.

There were two categories of factories the Board of Trade would finance under the powers it had acquired: those designed to the specific requirements of manufacturers and Advance Factories. In this chapter, the factory construction programme will be examined as a whole. Advance Factories will be discussed in the next chapter.

The task before the government appeared to be an awesome one: the number of those in the Services and in gainful employment had increased during the War from 18.5 to 21.2 million. 4.5 million people in the Services would have to be re-absorbed [1] and a large number of those engaged in War production would have to change their occupations. While the demand for goods and services was likely, for a time, to outstrip the availability of labour in the country as a whole, there would be local unemployment, particularly in those parts of the Development Areas where the dominant traditional industries might not be able to absorb all those seeking employment.

The sellers' market for factory space in the Development Areas immediately after the War appears to have been larger than anyone had foreseen. Odber [2] has given some reasons for this:-

Industry in general was in a particularly persuadable condition. Industrial building had been strictly controlled in wartime. Many firms were in old-fashioned and unsuitable premises; others, particularly in London, had suffered bomb damage and wanted to restart or expand production. Above all, business confidence was high.

Odber might have added that many firms were occupying requisitioned factories and feared eviction from their temporary homes after the end of the War. In a joint paper by the Ministry of Production and the Board of Trade of 9 June 1944, this was believed to be the reason why the Board of Trade had received 700 enquiries for factories in the previous six months [3].

At the same time, there was some anxiety that the demand for factory space was of a temporary nature. This was expressed by the Chancellor of the Exchequer in a letter to the chairman of the Company on 29 May 1946: 'this (sellers' market) will not last forever and, therefore, we must not miss the tide' [4].

Unexpectedly, the sellers' market lasted. It was not until 1954 that the Company was to note again - for the first time since before the War - that 'almost every conceivable argument has been used by some firm or other against transfer of part or all their production to, or the siting of any new capacity in a Development Area' [5].

But at the end of the War, the circumstances for the Development Areas were uniquely favourable: not only was the demand for factories on a scale never to be experienced again, but a government was in power which was committed to bring the pre-War distressed Areas to the same level of full employment and prosperity that it intended to maintain throughout the country. There was a Chancellor of the Exchequer who had insisted from the moment of his appointment in July 1945 that, so far as plans for the Development Areas were concerned, 'the Treasury was henceforth to be no longer a curb but a spur'[6]. In his Budget Speech in April 1946 Dalton had proclaimed:-

I have told my colleagues that I will find, and find with a song in my heart, whatever money is necessary to finance useful and practical proposals for developing these areas, and bringing them to a condition which they never had in the past, of full and efficient and diversified activity. I pledge my word that this job will not fall down for lack of finance.

By avoiding the concentration of any one incoming industry and by aiming for a spread of size and type of manufacture [7], the government hoped to achieve a better 'balance of industry'. But the concept was ill-defined. It is unlikely that the merits of the desired degree of diversification were examined in relation to a policy of limited specialisation, or that attempts were made to identify 'sunrise' industries. Firms with viable propositions of almost any kind had little difficulty in securing assistance, particularly if they were willing to establish their works in those localities where the government particularly wished to create new employment.

The need for employment in some of the smaller and less central places apart, there was now a powerful additional argument in favour of a policy of dispersion: building materials were in short supply and existing housing, schools, hospitals and other social amenities would have to be used to the full, as the 1944 White Paper had foreseen. Migration within the Development Areas from the smaller to the bigger places would be discouraged, except from some isolated villages where no basis for new industrial activity existed.

One aspect of the 1945 Act had a negative effect on the region. It neither enabled local firms in obsolete buildings to be rehoused - unless they could show a significant increase in employment - nor did it encourage new indigenous development, although Sir Stafford Cripps, as President of the Board of Trade, seemed to be in favour of it [8]. While the scope for such development was probably limited, the experience gained by firms and individuals during the War and the opportunities of the immediate post-War world represented a unique conjunction of favourable circumstances which might have been exploited more effectively. The expansion of a number of existing local firms on the Team Valley Estate (see Appendix 24) and the establishment of small new manufacturing concerns in obsolete buildings were tokens of local potential.

The large majority of the new government-financed factories would be occupied by branches of national or international companies, or by individual entrepreneurs from outside the region.

Because of the difficulties involved, no serious attempt has been made to establish how many of the new arrivals had moved their head offices into the region, but discussions with survivors of the Company's staff would indicate that the proportion was very small.

The opportunistic nature of some of the incoming branch ventures and the possible consequences for the region did not go unnoticed. Pepler and MacFarlane [9], for example, hoisted warning signals as early as 1948/49:-

> There is some doubt ... as to the future prospects of a number of concerns settled here since the War. Anxious to get into production to take advantage of the post-War demand for consumer goods, ... will they stay when the present inflated demand is satisfied, or are they likely once more to concentrate production at their headquarters elsewhere in Britain.

In future, they concluded, more regard would have to be paid to the type of industry coming in rather than 'clutch at any bits and pieces ... that seem to offer the prospect of additional work'.

While this observation provides a contemporary confirmation of the apparent lack of a structural policy, the problem of stability of employment in branch factories did not affect the region as a whole until more than 20 years later, although the withdrawal of a few large firms affected particular localities. Appendix 26 shows that the number of tenants in government-financed factories increased at least until 1960 - the last year for which detailed information is readily available. Furthermore, there is much evidence that the substantial employment growth until 1970 was achieved to a large extent by the expansion of existing tenants. Since the majority of the expanding tenants were branches, it is evident that the concerns of Pepler and MacFarlane were not justified in the medium term.

There were a number of factors which should have facilitated the factory construction programme immediately after the War: planning permission - as distinct from clearance with the Ministry of Town and Country Planning under the 1932 Act - was not yet required, as the comprehensive planning machinery under the Town and Planning Act 1947 did not come into force until 1948. Had that machinery existed in 1945, it would certainly not have been possible to conceive of a large, multi-site factory construction programme and implement it within the time available to achieve the government's objectives.

As for land acquisition - the other potentially lengthy procedure - a recent measure should have largely solved the problem: in order to speed up the procedure particularly for the housing programme, the Ministry of Health had sponsored a Bill which was passed by Parliament as the Acquisition of Land (Authorisation Procedure) Act in April 1946. Once a decision was reached to acquire a site by compulsory purchase (compulsory purchase powers as such were provided under the 1945 Act), the Board of Trade would be able to obtain powers under the new Act to enter the land seven days after certain formalites had been fulfilled. Negotiations with owners would follow later.

One cause of the delays experienced at this time was the serious understaffing of the District Valuer. Leases for factories could not be completed until he had fixed the rents. His difficulties were compounded by the extra work resulting from the government's policy to let factories on the basis of 1939 rentals.

This policy was adopted before the end of the War. The government was anxious that the disposal of the wartime factories - by letting or selling - should result in employment as soon as possible after they were no longer required for the production of munitions. The post-War demand for factory space appears to have been underestimated at the time and inducements were felt to be necessary to persuade manufacturers to establish works in Development Areas. The Treasury agreed to the policy because the wartime factories were erected at little more than 1939 costs [10]. But the same basis would also have to apply to rentals for new buildings, because their tenants could not be put at a disadvantage. The policy created many anomalies and distorted the rent structure to such an extent that the Company felt it necessary to remonstrate with the Board of Trade [11].

The policy appears to have been particularly inequitable to firms building their own factories at current costs, i.e. at approximately twice the 1939 costs. Tables 6 and 7 show that Development Area policy relied heavily on privately-financed factories. On the face of it, the cost disadvantage suffered by such projects should have operated against the policy objectives. Although private factory construction is outside the scope of this study, enquiries were made to establish whether there was any form of compensation, apart from possible tax advantages. None were found, if Treasury loans and grants under the 1945 Act were left out of account. This is justified because private factory construction could not have benefited more than marginally, given that the total sum involved in the years 1946 - 1949 was only £1 million [12]. Across-the-board grants for private factory construction in the Areas were introduced at a much later period (by the Local Employment Act 1960).

For reasons which will be discussed later in this chapter and the next, the construction of government-financed factories in the first two years after the War fell far short of the targets set by the government. Hugh Dalton was disturbed by the delays at an early stage, because Development Area strategy - in which he retained a strong interest - was seen to depend crucially on new factory space. By the spring of 1946, he could contain his impatience no longer: 'on March 29 we had a furious row at the Lord President's Committee over the slow progress made by the Board of Trade in the Development Areas ... After some tumult, Morrison suggested that I should be chairman of a Ministerial sub-committee to hustle things along' [13].

This was how the Chancellor became supremo of the factory construction programme in the Development Areas and why he began to encourage and cajole all concerned from his office at the Treasury: 'I am very disappointed to hear from the Board of Trade that the rate of new factory building in the North East is now tending to fall much behind the rate both in South Wales and in Scotland', Dalton wrote to the chairman of the Company on 29 May 1946. 'We are determined to do everything we can to cut out delays and indecision, and to infuse a sense of urgency into the handling of these problems' [14].

As for the the North East falling behind, it was true that work had
started on a larger number of projects in South Wales and Scotland in
1946, but more factories would be completed in the North East by 30
September 1947 than in the other regions (see Appendix 27).

The immediate reason for the pressure exerted by Dalton is revealed in
the same letter: 'my colleagues and I are all seriously concerned at the
serious growth in unemployment in the North Eastern Development Area'.
Was this anxiety justified?

The labour statistics for each employment exchange and office area in
the North East for the years 1945-1948 are given in Appendix 28. Except
for one or two places, they show very low rates of unemployment for July
1945, in spite of the fact that production for the War effort had slowed
down or stopped. By July 1946, the insured labour force had increased -
reflecting the effects of demobilisation (see Table 13 and Appendix 28)
- and the immediate post-War unemployment rose to a peak in all but
three places (where it peaked either in 1945 or 1947). In spite of the
continuing increase in the labour force, unemployment fell both in 1947
and 1948. But even in 1946, the peak unemployment exceeded the 10% level
in only eight out of the 67 exchanges or offices. It may be noted,
however, that these eight places suffered high unemployment rates in
1938 (compare the data in Appendixes 28 and 32).

Dalton's letter to the chairman of the Company was written a few weeks
before the labour statistics for July 1946 would be published. While
Dalton must have been aware that the figures would reflect the effects
of demobilisation, he evidently did not foresee the rapid decline in
unemployment in the following two years. Given the anxieties of the
government about local unemployment and the importance Dalton attached
to the government-financed factory programme, his frustration at the
slow progress can be understood.

The lack of progress of which Dalton complained was not due to delay
and indecision on the part of the Company. Indeed, it 'had always been
proud of its record for speed of operation', and, in spite of some
hesitation in expanding its staff in line with the task immediately
after the War, the chairman believed that the Company 'can still lay
claim to an equal efficiency despite the volume of work in hand and the
more complicated precedures necessary for its fulfilment under post-War
conditions' [15]. The delay in the government factory programme was
almost entirely due to the departments headed by some of Dalton's
colleagues and, perhaps, to the very involvement of government.

Dalton did not confine his interventions to memoranda and letters; he
visited sites and checked progress on the ground, particularly in his
constituency. In June 1946, he arrived at a site at Shildon just as the
builders were running out of bricks. The clerk of works told him that
50,000 bricks were needed before any further progress could be made.
Dalton was angry and dealt quite roughly with Allen, the Regional
Controller of the Ministry of Works. His annoyance was compounded when
he witnessed the delivery of a large quantity of bricks to an adjacent
housing site, a quantity evidently far in excess of immediate needs!

This episode illustrates one of the main problems which troubled the
factory construction programme in the years immediately after the War:
the shortage of building materials and the conflicting priorities in
their allocation.

The responsibility for materials - except for steel - rested with the Ministry of Works. Harold Wilson, the Parliamentary Secretary, was given the task to improve the supply. Slowe [16] has claimed that Wilson succeeded, with some difficulty, in meeting the demands of the factory building programme, after making administrative changes, including the appointment of a Director-General of Building Materials Production. Since the programme fell ever more behind the target (see below), this claim is difficult to test, because other factors played a part, for example, the shortage of building labour.

The supply position was not unforeseen, and there was a willingness to consider alternative materials, as the following example shows:

At the end of May 1946, the Assistant Controller of the Ministry of Works at Newcastle was instructed to go to Cornwall - with a representative of the Board of Trade acting as an observer - and to investigate the possibility of using concrete blocks said to be available there. They were to bring back samples, and if these were found to be useable, negotiations would be conducted with the contractors and the unions to deal with any problems which might arise out of the use of non-conventional materials. In the event, the emissaries found no concrete blocks, but a large amount of aggregate for manufacturing them. The idea that this material should be shipped into the Tyne and the blocks manufactured locally was strongly supported by the Company: the chairman seemed convinced that '£10,000 worth of machinery ... would solve the problem in the North East'. The idea was abandoned, but the example shows to what lengths it was considered necessary to go to ensure the supply of common materials.

The position was almost as difficult with structural steel. In a period of acute shortages, these difficulties were inevitable and even an improved allocation procedure might not have made much difference.

The priorities do not seem to have been clearly established or understood, perhaps because they varied in different parts of the country, depending on the relative local importance of employment and housing. The Regional Controller of the Board of Trade at Newcastle was certainly 'alarmed by a statement from the suppliers that they cannot supply bricks for factories in preference to the housing programme without a direct instruction from the Ministry of Works and although the Ministry of Works say that this attitude is not justified, the brick yards appear to be working rather rigidly on these lines' [17].

Apart from the apparent priority of the housing programme, the Development Areas also competed for materials with other parts of the country, where a considerable amount of industrial building continued to be licensed.

The other block to progress was the bureaucratic procedure, which involved at least three stages within the Board of Trade in London, (the Regional Distribution of Industry Committee, the Directorate for Industrial Estates and the Finance Division), the Regional Controller of the Board and the Regional Distribution of Industries Committee in Newcastle, which, in itself represented a variety of departmental interests. The final approval for a project came from the Board of Trade in London. The next step was Treasury authority. When this had been granted, building licences had to be obtained from the Board of Trade and building materials allocations, together with priority certificates, from the Ministry of Works. Further reference to procedure will be made in V/4 and an outline is given in Appendix 29. The contrast with the simple procedure available to the Company before the War could not have been greater.

As if this was not enough, the Board of Trade in London - unlike the Commissioner before the War - not only kept detailed financial control on building contracts but also on minor expenditure, even after the management - and often the Board of the Company - had scrutinised and agreed it. A list of items of capital expenditure of less than £100 for which the Company had to obtain sanction from the Board of Trade in London in 1948 is given in Appendix 30.

There was little control, on the other hand, of the Company's revenue expenditure. The temptation to speed up progress by using revenue for small items of capital expenditure must have been great.

The day-to-day control of the building programme exercised by the Board of Trade and its demands for information on a mass of apparently unnecessary detail caused much extra work to the Company's directors and staff and not a little resentment [18]. This was bound to affect the relationship between the Company and the Board of Trade (see V/4).

The widespread opinion that the procedure was one of the main causes of delay was largely confirmed by Harold Wilson in February 1947 in his capacity as chairman of a sub-committee of the Chancellor's committee on factory building progress. Wilson identified the most serious administrative block: the bouncing backwards and forwards between the regional office of the Board of Trade and Whitehall of decisions on location and, in the case of special projects - factories built to individual specifications - of allocations to tenants. Wilson proposed to solve this problem by devolving more of the decision-making process to the regional offices [19].

By the late spring of 1947, it became evident that matters could not continue as before: On 9 May, the President of the Board of Trade wrote to the chairman of the Company [20]:-

> The difficulties have recently increased ... to such an extent, that I have decided that there should be someone at Headquarters devoting his whole time to these problems. I have, accordingly, asked Air Vice-Marshal Hugh Fraser CB... to accept the appointment of Chief Progressing Officer ... It is my wish that he should spend as much time as possible in the Development Areas examining special difficulties ... and taking appropriate action at Headquarters where that is necessary. He has assured me that he has no illusions about the difficulties.

The appointment reflected the impatience of Ministers with the situation, but it is doubtful whether the introduction of yet another official - and the duplication of effort involved - actually improved matters.

The other main cause of delay identified by the Wilson sub-Committee was the attempt to do too much all at once. More realistic plans over shorter time spans would produce better results. But it was not until

Wilson became President of the Board of Trade in September 1947 that he was able to institute the reforms he had proposed earlier that year. By this time it would, in a sense, be too late: the country's economic circumstances made it necessary to put a halt to the building of new factories - special cases apart - and even to the completion of those which had not progressed very far (see V/3).

In the first year after the War, a comprehensive programme of government-financed factories evolved only slowly. It was not until the late summer of 1946 that a large programme was put forward by the Board of Trade. It was this programme which Wilson would later judge to be unrealistic.

The clearest statement of the 1946 programme available was given at conferences of representatives of local authorities in Newcastle upon Tyne and Durham on 2 October and in Middlesbrough on 3 October 1946 by Brazendale, the Regional Controller of the Board of Trade at Newcastle, in the presence of the Parliamentary Secretary to the Board of Trade J.W. Belcher. It is very likely that the programme included all the new factories and wartime factory conversions authorised since the beginning of 1945. A summary of the programme is given in Table 7. It may be noted, that the Treasury-financed schemes included both Advance Factories and special projects.

In order to facilitate the comparison between the targets set by this programme and the actual achievement discussed later in this chapter, the information in Table 7 is stated in an abridged form in Table 6.

Table 6
Abridged Summary of the
Factory Construction and Wartime Factory Conversion Programme 1946

	Treasury New Buildg. sq.ft.	Wartime Factories sq.ft.	Emplmnt.	Private Projects sq. ft.	Emplmnt.
Newcastle Area	3,133,200	1,500,000	42,700	2,989,485	7,500
Durham Area	1,202,000	1,500,000	22,500	638,000	2,050
Middlesbrough Area	1,440,000	435,000	18,200	3,300,000	17,000
TOTALS	5,775,200	3,435,000	83,400	6,927,485	26,550

TOTAL Government Factories: 9,210,200 sq.ft.
TOTAL Employment expected from the Programme: 109,950 jobs.

Source: Table 7.

Of the 83,400 jobs in government factories, 56,300 were expected in new Treasury-financed factories, and the rest in wartime factories and converted Royal Ordnance Factories. 47,500 jobs in government factories would be for females, representing a significant majority of jobs in the Newcastle & Durham Areas. By contrast, of the 26,550 jobs expected in private projects, only 8,650 would be for females.

Table 7
Factory Construction and Wartime Factory Conversion Programme 1946

	No.of Schemes	Area in sq.ft.	Expected Employment Male	Female	Total
NEWCASTLE CONFERENCE					
Treasury-Financed					
Approved	65	2,400,000	9,100	15,000	24,100
Under consideration	17	733,200	3,900	3,700	7,600
		3,133,200	13,000	18,700	31,700
Privately-Financed					
Approved	74	2,989,485	3,750	3,750	7,500
Total New Building		6,122,685	16,750	22,450	39,200
Wartime Govt. Factories	22	1,500,000	5,100	5,900	11,000
TOTALS		7,622,685	21,850	28,350	50,200
DURHAM CONFERENCE					
Treasury-Financed					
Approved	20	612,000	1,400	5,000	6,400
Under consideration	25	590,000	1,800	3,700	5,500
		1,202,000	3,200	8,700	11,900
Privately-Financed					
Approved	17	638,000	1,150	900	2,050
Total New Building		1,840,000	4,350	9,600	13,950
Wartime Govt. Factories		1,500,000	4,700	5,900	10,600
TOTALS		3,340,000	9,050	15,500	24,550
MIDDLESBROUGH CONFERENCE					
Treasury-Financed					
Approved	17	640,000	2,600	2,600	5,200
Under consideration	9	800,000	3,500	4,000	7,500
		1,440,000	6,100	6,600	12,700
Privately-Financed					
Approved	45	3,300,000	13,000	4,000	17,000
Total New Building		4,740,000	19,100	10,600	29,700
Wartime Govt. Factories	4	435,000	3,800	1,700	5,500
TOTALS	315	5,175,000	22,900	12,300	35,200

Source: TWA 1762/8, Minutes of conferences on 2 & 3 October 1947 at
Newcastle, Durham and Middlesbrough.

The low ratio of employment/factory floor area in the private schemes indicates a preponderance of capital-intensive projects. This conclusion is strengthened by the relatively small proportion of female employment expected, particularly in the Middlesbrough area, where the huge developments by Imperial Chemical Industries Ltd at Wilton on Tees would be included.

There is little doubt that the 1946 programme was meant to be a first programme only. This was implicit in the government's confirmation in November 1945 that it intended to continue to build Advance Factories as long as a demand existed (see next chapter).

In answer to a question at the Newcastle conference regarding the likely accuracy of the employment forecasts, Belcher agreed that the figures were estimates, but claimed that allowance had been made for any undue optimism.

As for the adequacy of the programme, Brazendale suggested that the expected employment should be seen against the unemployment in the region in August 1946. The figures quoted by Brazendale at the three conferences are given in Table 8:-

Table 8
Unemployment in the North East in August 1946

	Men	Women	Juveniles	Total
Newcastle Area	17,000	7,000	1,000	25,000
Durham Area	7,600	3,900	not stated *	11,500
Middlesbrough Area	3,500	4,000	not stated *	7,500
	------	------	-----	------
	28,100	14,900	1,000	44,000

* While at Newcastle Brazendale distinguished between men, women and juveniles, at Durham and Middlesbrough he referred to males and females.

Source: same as for Table 7.

Even if all those on the live register had been employable, the employment aims of the 1946 programme show that provision was made for an increase in the working population. Furthermore, and in spite of the pre-War experience that employment was needed particularly for male workers, the government factories would provide for a majority of female workers. The demands of light industries and the increasing female activity rate had evidently been taken into account.

An analysis of the employment targets of the 1946 programme in relation to the total insured population will be given in Table 19 in the Conclusions.

No information has been found on the completion targets for the programme as a whole. For the year 1 September 1946 to 30 August 1947, however, the programme of construction of the Treasury-financed projects is known. Since the figures in Table 9 were provided by the Estates

Company in connection with an application for materials for the ensuing 12 months and at the express request of the Board of Trade, it can be assumed that this was a definitive minimum programme - minimum, because no Advance Factory construction had been allowed for in the last quarter:-

Table 9
Construction Programme of the Company, 1.9.1946 to 31.8.1947

1946 / 1947	Sep-Nov sq.ft.	Dec-Feb sq.ft.	Mar-May sq.ft.	Jun-Aug sq.ft.	Total sq.ft.
Advance Factories	707,600	707,600	240,000	---	1,655,200
Special Projects	592,000	643,000	630,000	208,000	2,073,000
TOTAL					3,728,200

Source: TWA, 1395, Box 410, File GM 102/1.

The 1946 programme foresaw the construction of 5,775,200 sq.ft. (Table 6). Assuming the continuation of the rate of building indicated in Table 9, it might have been expected to complete the programme in 18 months.

The question how far the target was met is of great interest and importance for any conclusions about the effectiveness of the control of the programme by the Board of Trade. Table 10 records the progress made with new factory construction and also with the conversion of former Royal Ordnance and other wartime factories:-

Table 10
Progress Information on the 1946 Factory Programme

Treasury-financed factories in North East	31.08.1946 sq.ft.	30.09.1947* sq.ft.	31.08.1948 sq.ft.	31.08.1949 sq.ft.
UNDER COSTRUCTION Floor Area	1,893,331	3,410,899	1,185,914	489,211
COMPLETED Floor Area (Total)	191,463	1,094,318	3,354,019	4,434,750
CONVERSIONS **				
Completed	29,125	637,207	915,572	2,408,415
In progress	802,315	724,526	541,550	182,557
Floor Area occupied	n.a.	1,239,190	1,302,712	2,583,357

* the report for 31.8.1947 was not found.
** the figures for 1949 include wartime factories requiring no conversion.

Source: Appendix 27.

252

Table 10 shows that, 15 months after the end of the War in Europe, factories with a floor area of only 191,463 sq.ft. had been completed. The figures also confirm Wilson's conclusion that too much was being attempted all at once: the total factory floor area under construction on 31 August 1946 was 1,893,331 sq.ft.; some of this had been started several months before, yet little more than half would be completed 13 months later.

A comparison of the target in Table 9 with the completions actually achieved in Table 10 must lead to the conclusion that only 30% of the Company's target for the year to 30.8.1947 had been met.

The figures for the conversion to industrial use of the two Royal Ordnance and other wartime factories up to September 1948 are difficult to interpret, particularly if it is assumed that the some of the buildings at the Spennymoor complex and the Ministry of Food buffer stores required little conversion. Since at the end of August 1947 the floor area occupied was about twice as large as that which had been converted for industrial use, it is evident that conversion was proceeding while tenants were in occupation. The fact that they accepted the inconvenience underlines the great demand for factory space at the end of the War.

The next topic of interest are the sites of the government-financed factories. The rate at which these were being developed between the end of the War and 1948 was never to be repeated again. Table 11 shows the sites and number of tenants for July 1948 and March 1949. The significance of these dates will become apparent later in this chapter. The number of factories may be taken to have been the same as the number of tenants, because the post-War factories - unlike the 6,000 sq.ft. units at Team Valley before the War - appear to have been built for single tenants, a few exceptions apart.

By March 1949, there were 255 tenants (including a small number of service tenants and workshops for the disabled) on 30 separate sites. Only four of these had existed before the War, (Team Valley, Pallion, Tynemouth and St. Helen's Auckland, sometimes referred to as West Auckland). More than half the tenants were located at Team Valley and Aycliffe.

The 26 post-War sites varied in importance from single - often large - factory units to group sites and trading estates, although none of the latter would become as large as the Team Valley Estate. By the beginning of 1949, only the Aycliffe, Bede and West Chirton sites had gained any importance. The risks to continuity of employment involved in placing single factories in some of the smaller localities - to begin with, at least - seem to have been accepted.

The socio-economic criteria for selecting sites will be examined in the next chapter. Table 16 indicates - not unexpectedly - that the pre-War unemployment record of a locality seems to have been the main consideration.

Because the sites were spread over a large part of the region, four separate management areas were established by the Company, which, in turn, were supervised by Area Boards of Directors.

Table 11
Sites and Number of Tenants, July 1948 and March 1949

		Sites	Number of Tenants	
			8.7.1948	23.3.1949
PW	1	Team Valley Estate	87	81
	2	Aycliffe Estate	54	57
	3	Bede Estate	8	16
	4	Stockton, Bowesfield	1	2
	5	Hartlepool Estate	8	9
	6	Lanchester	1	1
	7	Langley Moor	2	2
	8	Stanners	1	2
	9	East Middlesbrough *	1	3
	10	Middlesbrough	1	2
PW	11	Pallion Estate	8	12
PW	12	Tynemouth **	1	1
	13	Sherburn Estate	5	6
	14	Skelton Estate	2	4
PW	15	St. Helen's Auckland Estate	5	8
	16	Spennymoor	3	3
	17	South Shields	3	3
	18	Sunderland	1	1
	19	West Chirton Estate ***	5	13
	20	Bedlington		2
	21	Southwick, Sunderland		1
	22	Palmer's Shipyard		3
	23	Blyth		1
	24	Chester le Street		1
	25	Houghton le Spring		4
	26	Stockton, North Tees Estate		7
	27	Crook		2
	28	Tow Law		1
	29	Shildon		6
	30	Guisborough		1
			---	---
	TOTAL		197	255

PW = Pre-War sites.

Sites are listed in the order in which they appear in the records.

* In the 1948 records, 9 and 10 were under a single heading. It is believed that 9 was later described as the South Tees Estate.
** This pre-War site is close to the West Chirton sites.
*** This comprised sites both south and north of the Coast Road. In July 1948, there were already one or two tenants in the former Ministry of Supply Depot, although the Company had not yet formally taken it over.

Source: TWA, 1395/3110, which also gives lists of tenants on each site and the industries they were engaged in.

There remain to be discussed the effect of the delays in factory construction on the employment target of the 1946 programme on the one hand, and the impact of the employment actually created, on the other.

Before attempting to estimate the employment in the post-War Treasury-financed factories at the end of 1948 or soon after, it is necessary to define the factories for which the Company was responsible.

According to the Company's annual report for the year to 31 March 1949, the factories for which it was responsible employed 'over 30,000 people' [21]. Since there were 255 tenants, the average employment per tenant, therefore, was more than 120 people. This compares with 50 employees per tenant on the Team Valley Estate at the end of 1939 [22], and with 136 at Slough in 1938 [23] - 15 years after that Estate was established.

The factories managed by the Company included the Team Valley Estate and the pre-War outside sites, the Royal Ordnance Factories at Aycliffe and Spennymoor and, from October 1947, the six reserve munitions factories.

There were, in addition, the Ministry of Food Buffer Depots and the West Chirton complex noted in the last chapter, and a number of other government-owned factories in the North East. A Board of Trade file [24] contains employment returns for all such factories for an earlier date, but they do not indicate those for which the Company was responsible.

For the purpose of arriving at a tentative estimate of the employment in new post-War Treasury-financed factories and extensions to 31 March 1949, the employment in the miscellaneous factories will be ignored, although this will lead to an over-estimate of the employment in the post-War factories.

The employment in the Buffer Depots and at the West Chirton complex has been estimated. The other figures in Table 12 are justified in a footnote [25].

Table 7 shows that the new Treasury-financed factories were intended to provide work for 56,300 people. If the assumption arising from Table 9 is accepted, the programme should have been completed by March 1948. Allowing for a lag of one year between the completion of the factories and the achievement of the planned production, the employment target should have been met by March 1949.

The employment actually achieved by March 1949 was only 11,200, or 19.9% of the target figure (see Table 12), and even this is likely to be overstated.

The employment figures in Table 12 prompt another reflection: Table 10 shows that 3,354,019 sq.ft. had been completed by 31.8.1948, i.e. 58.1% of the target, while only 19.9% of the employment target would be reached seven months later. Even allowing for a lag between factory completions and employment, the large difference between the percentage attainments of the targets implies that the completions shown for 31 August 1948 were recent and that a large proportion of these factories were not yet in production. The difference would be increased by further completions before March 1948.

This conclusion is supported by the rapid rise in the number of occupied sites and tenants after the summer of 1948: between 8 July 1948 and 23 March 1949, the number of post-War sites occupied increased from 15 to 26 and the total number of tenants from 197 to 255 (see Table 11). The conclusion is further confirmed by figures in a White Paper published in October 1948 [26].

Table 12

Computation of Employment in Treasury-financed Projects
1945 - 1949

Total employment in factories for which
the Company was responsible, 31.3.1949.   30,000

Employment

- at Team Valley at the end of
  the War, approx.,   7,000
- on pre-War Outside Sites
  at the end of the War, approx.,   2,500
- in six wartime reserve
  munitions factories,   2,800
- at Royal Ordnance Factories
  Aycliffe and Spennymoor,   5,000
- at former Food Buffer Depots, est.   500
- at West Chirton complex, est.   1,000

                                                  18,800

Employment in post-War Treasury-financed
projects (new factories or extensions)
on 31 March 1949:   11,200

An attempt is made in Table 14 to estimate the employment impact of the the immediate post-War government factories in the North East. The population figures and the employment in the three main industries in July 1948 are given in Table 13, while the employment in government factories at the end of March 1949 is taken from Table 12.

The conclusions from Table 14 must be that, for the region as a whole, the employment in all the factories under the control of the Company was small even as a percentage of the post-War increase in the insured population. The effect of the post-War Treasury-financed factories was almost negligible, even when using employment figures which are likely to be somewhat overstated. In relation to the employment in the three main industries, however, the employment in all the factories under the Company's control was beginning to be of some significance.

The foregoing conclusions ignored the strong probability that the impact of government-financed factories was more significant in some places than in others.

Table 13
Employment in the Main Industries and Insured Population
in the North East 1945 - 1948

	July 1945	1946	1947	1948
MAIN INDUSTRIES				
Coal Mining	147,460	151,710	158,650	172,410
Shipbuilding & Reprng.	50,480	49,820	46,310	50,730
Heavy Engineering	71,800	74,910	89,990	96,510
Totals	269,740	276,440	294,950	319,650
INSURED POPULATION				
Males	591,600	706,550	756,040	885,900
Females	252,220	233,660	244,740	331,930
Totals	843,820	940,210	1,000,780	1,217,830

Increases (Total 374,010)   96,390   60,570   217,050

Source: Appendix 31.

Table 14
Employment and Diversification Impact of Government Factories
in the North East 1948/49

A = Employment in all factories under the control
    of the Company, March 1949, (30,000).
B = Employment in post-War Treasury-financed
    factories, July 1948 (11,200).

As a percentage of:	A	B
total work force (1,217,830)	2.46	0.92
increase in the total working population 1945-1948, (374,010)	8.02	3.00
female work force (331,930), if 2/3 of employment in A and B was for females	6.03	2.25
employment in the three main industries (319,650)	9.39	3.50

In spite of the minimal impact of the Treasury-financed factory
programme and in the face of a sharp increase in the working population
(see Appendix 33 for some reasons), the unemployment figures had fallen
since 1946 in all but four of the 67 Employment Exchange and Office
areas of the Ministry of Labour in the North East (see Appendix 28).

The favourable employment trend was particularly notable in the
pre-War depressed industries. Employment in coal mining and shipbuilding

reached post-War peaks in 1949 and remained almost steady for the next six years (see Appendix 31).

An evaluation of the effect of the delays of the 1946 factory programme on the few places which suffered relatively high unemployment rates would not yield much additional insight. Appendix 28 reveals only four employment areas where unemployment was in excess of 5% in July 1948: Cockfield (6,5%), Hartlepool, but not West Hartlepool, (12.3%), South Shields (5.2%), Elswick, Newcastle upon Tyne (8.5%).

It may be observed, however, that - except in Cockfield - unemployment had steadily fallen since 1946 even in these places.

The first two places had insured populations of under 2,500, too small for any meaningful conclusions.

The last two were part of the Tyneside conurbation, so that travel-to-work patterns would affect any conclusions. The delay in the completion factories in South Shields and at Jarrow may have marginally affected employment prospects in that area. As for the ex-Armstrong-Whitworth (Vickers) workers at Elswick and Scotswood, they may have been marginally affected by delays in the completion of factories on the government-financed trading estate at Newburn.

A special role was assigned in the 1946 programme to Advance Factories: to steer new employment particularly into those parts of the region which had depended too heavily on a few, or even a single industry. These industries were depressed before the War and might be again when the boom was over. The history of Advance Factories and the role they were expected to play in the post-War economy of the North East are of sufficient interest to warrant a separate discussion.

2 The 1946 Advance Factory programme

Within the assumptions made by the government, Advance Factories were intended to become one of the principal instruments for implementing the full employment policy in Development Areas, particularly in those parts of the Areas which were less obviously attractive to industry, but where new economic activity was seen to be necessary. In a period of great demand for factory space, the early availability of factories would persuade some industrialists to go to places which they might not have considered otherwise.

The Advance Factory component of the 1946 construction programme is of interest for two reasons: firstly, because the floor area planned for a 12 month period was large when compared with the rate of building at Team Valley before the War; secondly, because the planning and execution of the programme would constitute a particularly good test of the proposition that the State could effectively intervene directly in Development Areas by becoming the principal developer and landlord of factories. The progress of factories built to the specific requirements of manufacturers would provide less conclusive evidence. Other factors apart, they could not be planned like Advance Factories because the demand for them could not be foreseen.

Advance Factories are of necessity standard factories, i.e. they are designed without reference to the needs of any particular tenants who, by definition, are not yet known. They cost less and can be constructed more quickly than special-purpose factories, particularly when several are built on the same site. These considerations led to the adoption at Team Valley of a limited number of standard designs before the War. The concept of standard factories was already well-understood by private factory estate developers in the 1920's and the early experience of the

Company had confirmed that a wide variety of industries could be accommodated. Special factories were necessary in only a few cases.

The origin of the term 'Advance Factory' is given in [12] below, but common usage shows much confusion in terms: 'stock', 'speculatively-built', 'standard', 'ready-made', 'advance', and even 'advanced standard' factory were alternatives used by executives of the Company, by Ministers and civil servants.

The term is also sometimes used too loosely. Slowe [1] has defined an Advance Factory as 'a factory built speculatively - in the hope of finding an occupant', yet he has applied the term to factories financed by the Commissioner at Pallion, Sunderland. It has been shown in III/5 that factory construction on the 'outside sites' sites - Pallion was one of them - could not begin until a tenant had signed a lease. If the term is to have any meaning, it must apply to factories which are at least in the course of construction before any tenants are found.

Before 1937, there were practically no small modern factories to rent in the North East. When the Team Valley Estate was established, the potential demand for factory space from light industry was unknown, so that the number of factories to build speculatively in order to achieve early availability could not have been estimated. Because of the absence of any measures limiting factory development in areas of the country believed by industrialists to be more favourable for business success, the uncertainty persisted for the period remaining up to the outbreak of the War.

References to 'stock' factories are to be found, nevertheless, in several early documents. In a letter to the Commissioner of 18 August 1936 accompanying the Scheme of Acquisition of the Team Valley site, the Company outlined its policy on speculative building: 'apart from the construction of a small number of factories for stock and nursery purposes ... it is not our intention to do anything but build factories as we are able to make arrangements with tenants to occupy them' [2]. This undertaking was confirmed and made more specific on a later occasion, when the Company assured the Commissioner that 'expenditure will not be incurred except for factories to be let as soon as erected, with the exception of an extra number of six to be kept in stock, available for tenants who may require immediate occupation' [3]. The evidence indicates, however, that the aim can only rarely have been achieved.

The building of factories for stock was suggested by the consultants of the Company, Sir Alexander Gibb and Partners. In their report of 13 March 1936, they had advised that 'it will as well be advantageous and, indeed, necessary to have empty factories available for immediate occupation' [4]. This advice was based on the experience of the private trading estate companies that immediate availability attracted tentants.

There is some evidence that the Commissioner was not convinced, to begin with, that stock factories were necessary. In his approval of the Team Valley Development Scheme on 16 November 1936, he agreed to the construction of six factories for stock on the understanding 'that any factory which has been in use by a tenant but has become vacant on the termination of the lease will be included in the total of six factories available in advance of actual requirement' [5]. The caution displayed by the Commissioner may well have been justified , but it confirmed that the provision of Advance Factories was not seen, initially, as an important policy tool in the Special Areas.

There were generally three reasons why factories became vacant again: agreed tenancies were not taken up, tenants failed, or, more positively, outgrew their first factories. As none of these events could be foreseen, the restriction imposed by the Commissioner would have made it difficult to administer the stock factory programme within the remit. For reasons discussed below, the problem did not often arise in practice.

Since standard factories varied in size from 6,000 sq.ft. to 24,000 sq.ft., it was necessary to define the Commissioner's concession more precisely. Following some discussion and correspondence, Methven obtained the Commissioner's agreement to his understanding of the remit: the Company would be allowed 'a maximum of six vacant factories of any standard sizes on the Estate as a whole' [6]. The agreement foresaw two vacant factories in each of the three blocks which were being developed in different parts of the 60 acres forming the initial development.

Up to November 1937, the monthly reports by the Company's general manager are the only source available on firms or individuals who had agreed to take space at Team Valley and were awaiting the completion of their factories.

The reports for December 1936, June 1937 and December 1937 also provide early information on the stock factory programme. At the same time, the names of prospective tenants are shown against most of them. The report for December 1937 [7], for example, indicates that the 6,000 sq.ft. factories intended for stock, suitably subdivided, had been spoken for by 12 tenants, although some space in these factories may still have been available.

The information in the reports of the general manager is incomplete. Nor is the record of leases in the Board minutes conclusive. Leases were often sealed long after legally non-enforceable undertakings to rent factories had been signed (see Appendix 14). Not all such undertakings were honoured. With this proviso, the Company appears to have obtained 47 tenants by July 1937, when only 13 factories were reaching completion (see Table 1). Even 14 months later, the backlog was not made up: for the period January to September 1938, the number of tenants waiting for factories to be completed varied between 41 and 55 (see Table in Appendix 14).

One of the difficulties in drawing conclusions from this information is due to the confusing practice of the Company and the Commissioner of equating 'a factory' at times with a building and at others with that part of a building occupied by a tenant. The question is further discussed in Appendix 14.

There is much evidence to suggest, at least until September 1938 - when special factors began to operate, including a war scare -, that the floor area under construction at any one time was generally less than the floor area let, if all those who had signed undertakings to rent factories had proceeded. Under these circumstances, there can only rarely have been available any factories at Team Valley for immediate

261

occupation, particularly in the sizes most in demand, i.e. from 1,500 - 6,000 sq.ft.

The Commissioner confirmed this position in a letter to the Ministry of Labour in March 1938. He claimed that the question of stock factories was 'a remote contingency', because the Company had '26 further tenancies agreed, for whom factories have not yet been started ' [8].

The conclusion must be that it was the concept of small, modern factories for rent and their situation in pleasant surroundings - in an area where almost no such factories existed - which stimulated new economic activity, rather than their immediate availability. In any case, factories were normally erected within a short time. An example was given in III/1.

The term 'Advance Factory' came into general use towards the end of the War. Yet as late as May 1946, - when a large Advance Factory programme was being discussed - the chairman of the Estates Company still referred to 'speculatively-built factories'.

But even with powerful government support and with the wartime experience and organisation which largely shaped the policy, the aim to have factories available in advance of requirement was only rarely achieved, if ever, in the immediate post-War period. Although for different reasons and under quite different circumstances, the position was strikingly similar to that which existed before the War.

In his evidence to the Select Committee on Estimates on 4 February 1947, Sadler Forster, the Director for Industrial Estates at the Board of Trade, explained why the Board was moving away from building factories in the Development Areas to tenants' specific requirements and was persuading industrialists to accept 'advanced standard type of factories'. He reported that the policy was meeting with a considerable measure of success, in that 'these advance factories have been let, that is to say accepted by tenants, before we have really started to build them ' [9].

This evidence confirms that there were, generally, not only no factories available in advance of requirement, but that their construction had often not even begun at the time when tenants signed leases.

Before examining the 1946 Advance Factory programme, a brief reference must be made to the first true Advance Factories, the construction of which had started during the last War.

Early in 1944, the Ministry of Production had proposed that ten factories should be built in Development Areas to a specification suitable both for wartime and post-War use. Details of the six factories allocated to the North East were given in IV/3. The idea, originally from Norman Kipping, the head of the regional division of the Ministry [10], was strongly supported by Hugh Dalton, the President of the Board of Trade. In his Memoirs , Dalton recalled that these factories 'would be a reserve against mishaps, due to enemy action in London'. As for their longer-term purpose, Dalton told the House of Commons on 7 June 1944 that 'these standard factories are being built in accordance with the principles ... of putting factories in places where it is most necessary to furnish a balanced and diversified employment after the War' [11]. It may be noted that the decision to build these factories coincided with the drafting of the 1944 White Paper on Employment Policy.

The factories were larger than any which had been built by the Company before the War. They were intended for the larger or large firms which were expected to be in need of - mainly branch - factories immediately after the end of the War. This forecast - which proved to be accurate in the event - was made possible by the close contacts established with industry by the Ministry of Production and the Control of Factory and Storage Premises Division of the Board of Trade during the War.

The term 'Advance Factory' was coined in relation to these reserve factories. In his Memoirs , Dalton described them as 'standard factories, empty but ready for immediate occupation. "Advance Factories" we called them, built in advance of demand, but, once built, soon tenanted' [12].

Reference has already been made to the conclusion by Booth [13] that the government departments involved in the War production effort played a key role in the development of the post-War location policy. The proposal by the Ministry of Production to site these wartime Advance Factories in Development Areas adds further support to his thesis.

Given their immediate purpose, the Company was not associated with the construction of these factories. They were built by the Ministry of Works, either on land owned by the Commissioner or on land requisitioned under wartime powers. Two of these factories (at St.Helen's Auckland in South West Durham and Pallion, Sunderland) were located on pre-War outside sites. It may be noted that those built on requisitioned sites at Tyne Dock (South Shields), Southwick (Sunderland), Hartlepool and Middlesbrough were sited at or close to places where government-financed factory sites or trading estates would be developed at the end of the War.

The great demand for factory space immediately after the War ensured that these factories were soon filled: three were occupied by 6 November 1945, two more by 1 March 1946, and the last one on 27 September 1946 [14]. The floor area of these six factories amounted to approximately 40% of the total space at Team Valley before the War and the employment they created is believed to have been proportionally greater. The Estates Company took over the full management of the reserve factories in 1947.

By the autumn of 1945, the government had crystallised its policy on Advance Factories and on the priorities in the siting of all categories of factories within the Areas. The policy was outlined to the chairmen and chief executives of the government-financed trading estate companies on 7 November 1945 at the Board of Trade, which had taken over authority for the estates from the Ministry of Labour. Although it had been foreshadowed in correspondence with the Company, it was at this meeting that the first small post-War Advance Factory programme authorised by the Treasury was announced: the total floor area would be 675,000 sq.ft., of which 200,000 sq.ft. would be built in the North East [15].

Sir Philip Warter explained the policy of the Board of Trade both on standard and Advance Factories; and although it is evident that neither the distinction between the two concepts nor the pre-War experience of the Company had been fully understood, the policy relied on the assumption that the success of the Team Valley Estate and other government-financed trading estates had largely been due to Advance Factories: 'experience has shown that the availability of ready-made factories was an important factor in determining the location of industrial undertakings' [16].

In siting these standard units, the Board of Trade 'would have to have regard to the special difficulties and needs within each Development Area, so as to give an impetus to the development of particular and otherwise "difficult" districts'.

The implication of this remark may not have been immediately appreciated by the companies' officers: it would not necessarily be possible to build where developed land was available, for example at Team Valley, even if the acquisition and development of the selected new sites would result in delay. This policy appeared to conflict with the need for speed which would be urged upon the Company by Ministers, particularly by the Chancellor.

The chairman of the Company pleaded for a more flexible policy. In a letter to the President of the Board of Trade on 10 January 1946, he wrote [17]:-

We would strongly urge that we be permitted to build some of these (authorised Advance Factories) on existing trading estates and not wait until single sites have been acquired in various parts of the area ... If we can put them up on existing trading estates we are sure they would be soon let, and then others could be built on the sites which may be in contemplation in various parts of the area after they have been acquired.

Sir Stafford Cripps replied that these factories were intended 'to open up areas in which there is, as yet, little or no development' [18].

At the meeting on 7 November 1945, Sir Philip Warter had emphasised the need for standardisation in factory design: this would speed progress 'by eliminating the time spent in discussing and agreeing specialised buildings which were not essential for the great majority of applicants'. Standardisation would also lead to economy both in labour and in materials.

The government-financed trading estate companies were well aware of the advantages of standard factory designs; each company had adopted its own from the beginning. The government now hoped that a countrywide standardisation would come about in the longer run.

While Warter was preaching to the converted, the Board of Trade, in its anxiety not to lose new industries in Development Areas, continued to accept requests for specialised buildings, if manufacturers were able to show that they could not be accommodated in standard factories.

Apart from land acquisition problems in the early stages of the factory programme, the Company saw 'the idiosyncrasies of industrialists having factories built to their own specification' as the main obstacle to progress [19]. In the draft letter to the Chancellor of Exchequer - from which the last quotation was taken - the chairman of the Company drew on recent experience and recalled that 'at Aycliffe, industrialists have been ready to accept the most unpromising buildings, but given a free hand, they become extremely particular and uncertain'.

In his evidence to the Select Committee on 4 February 1947, Sadler Forster explained both the original policy with regard to specialised factories and the reasons why the Board of Trade was moving away from it [20]:-

In the early days (after the War) ... in order to give (manufacturers) the maximum encouragement to make up their minds ... it was desirable to give them a certain element of choice in regard to the building that they required ... (later) we began to develop the idea in our minds that perhaps some of the manufacturers were having too many frills and fancies and their own whims considered, and therefore we have modified our policy in recent months.

Table 9 shows that more than half the floor area in Treasury-financed factories planned for the 12 months from 1 September 1946 was in specialised buildings. The policy to steer incoming industry into standard factories was evidently beginning to be implemented after the 1946 programme was published in October of that year, although Sadler Forster had referred to the change in policy as early as May 1946 (see [25] below).

Warter had assured the companies' officers on 7 November 1945 that the standard factory building programme 'was intended to be a continuous programme'. As the authorised quota of advance building progressed and the factories were let, 'authority should be sought to build further units'. The Board of Trade had in mind 'that the trading estate companies should maintain a stock of ready-made factories available for prospective tenants' [21]. It will be noted that Warter used three different terms for Advance Factories, and that he again confused 'standard' and 'advance' or 'ready-made' factories.

The policy was warmly welcomed by the the companies. Concern was expressed, however, on a number of matters, of which the availability of building labour was the most widely-voiced.

One result of the meeting was the setting up of a permanent forum, the Consultative Committee on Trading Estates. At its first meeting on 14 March 1946, the small Advance Factory programme was discussed in more detail [22]. A further Committee was set up, to be presided over by the President of the Royal Institute of British Architects, which would advise on alternative forms of factory construction - so as to avoid as far as possible the use of materials required for the housing programme - and on standardised factory design.

The demand was for larger standard factories than before the War. Two sizes were planned: 25,000 sq.ft. and 10,000 sq.ft. The latter would be made up of two 5,000 sq.ft. bays which could be let separately. Variations in design would be allowed so long as .the cost remained about the same.

The sites for the Advance Factories approved by the Treasury in November 1945 were not announced until some months later. By 2 April 1946, one 25,000 sq.ft. Advance Factory each had been allocated to sites at Guisborough, Blaydon, Houghton le Spring, Chester le Street, Dragonville (Sherburn, Durham), Bede (Jarrow), Hartlepool and Ashington, making 200,00 sq.ft. in all [23]. Although construction of some of these factories may have commenced, the programme was changed later and incorporated in a much larger programme, in which sites at Guisborough and Blaydon no longer featured (see Tables 15 and 16).

The large Advance Factory programme referred to above was discussed by the Consultative Committee on 11 April 1946 [24]:-

> It was ... decided that the estate companies, in conjunction with the Regional Controllers of the Board of Trade should prepare an estimate - first a twelve months programme, and finally a three years programme - of factory construction, and convert it into a list of all materials, heating and lighting plant, etc. required. When this has been done, it was hoped that the Board of Trade ... would place a bulk order for supplies to come forward at regular intervals over three years, against which contractors could draw, paying for the materials which they drew as though they were normal contractors' purchase.

On 2 May 1946 - soon after Dalton's Budget speech - Sadler Forster wrote to Brazendale, the Regional Controller of the Board of Trade in Newcastle, advising him that his Directorate intended to ask the Treasury for authority to proceed on a further Advance Factory programme. He requested information on the amount of building which might be put in hand at once 'on land already in our possession'. This would not rule out the possibility - also at an early date - 'of building, in advance of requirement, in other places where there are known employment needs'. He asked for the necessary applications for building licences to be prepared, which the Board of Trade 'would rush through'.

The object of the proposed programme would be not only to add greatly to the existing building programme, but also to simplify it by attempting to accommodate in Advance Factories of standard design many of the firms which might have preferred factories designed to their own specifications [25]. Furthermore, new single or group sites, as well as new industrial estates were to be considered, after consultation with the Regional Distribution of Industry Committee. Finally, Sadler Forster repeated that 'the Board of Trade was prepared to consider building in any of these areas in addition to those with which you are now dealing'.

Brazendale was well prepared; he replied on 4 May [26] and listed 31 sites in the North East, indicating those where the land was already owned by or on behalf of the Board of Trade. By including sites where land was not yet available, he was acting entirely within his remit from Sadler Forster, but these sites would cause some confusion a few weeks later.

The Company was asked to propose a programme immediately. Methven prepared a draft, which involved the construction of 200 Advance Factories within 12 months. On 7 May 1946, a copy of the draft programme was sent to the Chancellor of the Exchequer, but not, apparently, to the

Board of Trade. Dalton's connection with the factory construction programme has been explained in V/1, but the reasons for this curious procedure are not clear. It is possible that Dalton had asked for a first, confidential sight of the programme.

The briefing of Dalton introduced a delay of a few days before Methven sent a slightly amended programme to the Board of Trade on 14 May 1946. The delay caused Warter to telephone to express his annoyance that the North East had not yet formulated an Advance Factory programme for the following 12 months [27]. Yet Methven had produced a programme within four days after receiving a copy of Sadler Forster's letter to Brazendale!

The programme Methven had submitted on 14 May 1946 comprised 194 Advance Factories. In the accompanying letter to Brazendale, he explained his approach to the question of sites [28]:-

I have not strictly confined my placing of factories to sites which we actually own for two reasons: firstly, that we feel satisfied that we know pretty well the additional land needed to broadly satisfy the requirements of the Area and secondly, that being the case, I have relied on the new method of obtaining entry to ensure that we can make a start on all sites either in the first quarter or the second quarter after we receive the necessary licences etc. from the Ministry of Works.

'The new method of obtaining entry' to sites was a reference to the Acquisition of Land (Authorisation) Act briefly discussed in the last chapter. The 'requirements of the Area' undoubtedly meant the employment needs.

On 20 May 1946, the Regional Distribution of Industry Committee formally rejected the programme of 194 factories, but approved proposals for 93 factories - subject to certain modifications requested by the Ministry of Labour [29].

The Committee and the Company's officers met on 23 May 1946 at Team Valley. Brazendale instructed the Company to confine itself to sites which were already in its possession and 'thus limit our programme to 93 factories' [30], in spite of the fact that Methven had advised him that the Company owned land for only 62 [31]. The Regional Controller retorted that Sir Philip Warter wanted 93 built all the same!

Chapman - the chairman of the Company - complained that 'the Company had neither been consulted before the changes were made nor been given any reasons for them'.

It may be useful at this point to explain the basis on which the Treasury-financed factory programme appears to have been arrived at: first, the Ministry of Labour estimated the number of people in each locality likely to seek employment; there followed the assumption that about half the number available would be absorbed by privately-financed factories, leaving the rest to be employed in Treasury-financed factories, i.e. Advance Factories and special projects.

At the meeting of 23 May 1946, Hanham, for the Ministry of Labour, had explained why a programme involving 194 factories would have been too large: 'it was not purely a question of absorbing the unemployed in the Advance Factory programme, but that other considerations, such as privately financed schemes and specialised factories not covered by such a programme had to be borne in mind'.

Methven rejoined that the programme of 194 factories was based on the estimates of the labour available according to a report by Hanham himself, so that this number of Advance Factories would have absorbed 50% of the unemployed, leaving the other 50% to specialised Treasury and privately-financed factories. But Methven had misunderstood the policy: the privately-financed schemes alone were expected to absorb 50% of the available labour.

The changes which the the Ministry of Labour had required at the meeting of the Regional Distribution of Industry Committee on 20 May 1946 involved cuts of a total of 12 Advance Factories at Lanchester, Bishop Auckland and Crook. The effect of these cuts was to reduce the 93 factories proposed by Brazendale to 81. A programme based on this number was forwarded to London.

The Board of Trade reacted quickly: on 31 May 1946 [32], Sadler Forster gave the following list of Advance Factories and sites which the Board of Trade would submit to the Treasury for approval:-

Table 15
Advance Factory Programme, May 1946

St.Helen's Auckland Trading Estate	2	factories
Dabbleduck Site, Shildon	1	"
Crook Site	1	"
Dragonville Estate, Sherburn, Durham	4	"
Skelton, Cleveland	6	"
Portrack Grange, Stockton	10	"
South Teesside Site	6	"
Hartlepool Trading Estate	12	"
Houghton le Spring Estate	5	"
Pallion Trading Estate	6	"
Bede Trading Estate	12	"
Ashington Group Site	6	"
	--	
	71	factories

The factories would be of standard design, to be known later as Type 90 factories, with a floor area of approximately 25,000 sq.ft. each.

This programme was more modest even than that approved by the Regional Distribution of Industry Committee. Nevertheless, it involved about 1,775,000 sq.ft. of floor area.

It may also be noted that, in spite of the apparently confused discussions, the programme was agreed and ready for approval in less than four weeks.

The scheme allowed for the reduction in the number at any one site and the replacement by specially-designed factories, if tenants could not be accommodated in standard factories. But special projects could presumably be considered only before the construction of all the Advance Factories allocated to a particular site had commenced.

A comparison of the descriptions of the sites in Table 15 with those in Table 16 would indicate that some of the sites were later designated for Trading Estates.

Sadler Forster's letter of 31 May 1946 encouraged the Regional Controller in Newcastle to consider further developments - presumably for a period beyond the following 12 months - at Stanley, Anfield Plain and Consett, where the sites were of an unusual nature. 'You should not necessarily be discouraged from locating factories in those areas because of the heavier cost of earth works and underpinning'.

The same letter also contained a reference to the policy regarding the Team Valley Trading Estate: the Board of Trade was not prepared to build any Advance Factories there, because 'in terms of available labour we feel it is becoming too large. We are prepared, however, to review the position from time to time'.

The preparations for the implementation of the Advance Factory programme were set into motion by the Estates Company at once. A monthly programme of work was drafted. This kind of planning enabled the Company to react with great speed to instructions following authority and licence.

How fast the Estates Company was expected to react is illustrated by the following episode: the Chancellor announced that he would be visiting his constituency on Saturday, 20 July 1946. On Monday, 15 July, Sadler Forster telephoned the Company to say that he had sent off a written authority to start building two factories at St.Helen's Auckland, in the Chancellor's constituency. Sadler Forster asked for an immediate start of work on the site so that the Chancellor might see some activity during his visit [33]. In the event, the Chancellor was prevented from paying the visit, but one wonders whether such a prompt reaction would be possible today.

But no matter how efficiently the Company operated, the shortage of materials and the bureaucratic procedure would vitiate its efforts.

On 31 August 1946, the Board of Trade asked for an up-to-date list of materials in short supply for a realistically-phased requirement, including the basic materials not yet ordered for special projects [34]. The urgency of this matter was underlined by a telephone call from Sir Philip Warter on 3 September 1946, who was recorded as saying that 'unless we get a demand into the Ministry of Works forthwith, we may find that we receive no help on allocations'. The data in Table 9 was extracted from the information supplied by the Estates Company in response to this request. It is believed to be the only available information on the planned construction target of the Treasury-financed programme for the year from 1 September 1946.

The programme put forward by Sadler Forster at the end of May 1946 was to be only slightly increased later, but it did go through a number of modifications. Table 16 shows the probable final version of the 1946 Advance Factory programme and also an earlier one. The document is undated, but the internal evidence suggests - for example, the cancelling of six factories at Ashington - that the revision was made necessary by the emergency instructions in November 1947 following the economic crisis in that year (see next chapter).

Since the siting policy was likely to have taken into account the record of past local unemployment, the rates for the years 1938 and 1946 - the immediate post-War unemployment peak - have been set against the districts these sites are assumed to have served. The relatively low unemployment rates in 1946, in some districts at least, had evidently less influence on siting decisions than structural and employment concerns based on pre-War experience.

Table 16
Final List of Sites of Advance Factories and Floor Areas,
with Districts presumed to be served
and Unemployment Rates 1938 and 1946

Abbreviations: TE = site intended to be developed as a trading estate,
GS = group site, SS = single site.

Site	Floor Area Authorised sq.ft.		After Revision sq.ft.		District served	Unemployment % 1938	1946
Bede	375,000	TE	322,450		Jarrow	21.8	7.7
					S/Shields	30.0	8.3
Hartlepool	375,000	TE	327,150		Hartlepool	51.6	22.0
					W/H/pool	19.2	8.1
South Tees	150,000	TE	146,050		Middles/bro	26.6	5.3
Ashington	175,000	TE	24,400		Ashington	55.3	4.9
Knitsley	25,000	TE	250,000		Consett	8.7	2.5
Crook	25,000	GS	24,400		Crook	36.7	7.4
Shildon	25,000	TE	24,400		Shildon	29.0	7.4
W.Auckland	50,000	TE	48,800		W/Auckland & Bp/Auckld	37.8	11.9
Stanners	25,000	GS	24,400		Newburn	15.0	5.2
Dragonville	125,000	TE	121,650		Durham	22.5	7.2
Wingate	-	SS	30,000		Wingate	14.9	8.7
Chester/le/Str.	-	SS	24,400		Chester	17.3	7.7
					Birtley	13.8	9.0
North Tees	250,000	TE	156,410		Stockton & Thornaby	17.1	3.7
Houghton l/Spring	125,000	TE	143,090		Houghton	16.8	10.7
Pallion	150,000	TE	165,580		Pallion & W.Sund/ld	23.9	5.9
Skelton	150,000	TE	167,925		n.a.	n.a.	n.a.
Seaham Harbour	-	SS	24,400		Seaham & S/Harbour	10.5	5.5
	---------		---------				
TOTAL sq.ft.	2,025,000		2,025,505				

Sources: TWA, 1395, Box 410 File, GM 102/1,
Unemployment rates for 1938 & 1946 from Appendixes 32 & 28.

Most of the Advance Factories were allocated to sites designated as trading estates. The Knitsley (Consett) site was found to be unsuitable in the event, and the sites at Wingate and Seaham Harbour were not proceeded with, even if they survived the cuts in the programme in 1947 (see next chapter).

The revised programme was approved in principle only. Table 17 shows that only three quarters of the programme had been approved by the Finance Branch by 30 September 1947. The reasons for the freezing of the approvals after that date - at a lower level than that 'approved in principle' - will be discussed in the next chapter.

Table 17
Board of Trade Approvals of Advance Factories in the North East
with Progress Information 1946 - 1950

	Approved In Principle sq.ft.	Approved by Finance Branch sq.ft.	Area of Work Begun sq.ft.	Allocation of Space approved sq.ft.
31.8. 1946	n.a.	n.a.	250,755	n.a.
30.9. 1947	2,025,350*	1,543,163	1,434,119	904,019
31.8. 1948	2,025,350	1,553,556	1,444,665	1,272,389
31.8. 1949			1,444,665	1,387,577
30.6. 1950			1,443,523	1,443,523

Source: Appendix 27.

* note a small discrepancy with the figure in Table 16.

If allocations of factories to tenants can be taken taken to mean that the factories were ready for occupation, Table 17 shows that 904,019 sq.ft. of Advance Factories had been completed by 30 September 1947, compared with a target of 1,655,200 sq.ft. by 31 August 1947 (see Table 9), i.e. 55% of the target. But since Table 10 shows total completions under the Treasury-financed programme on 30 September 1947 to have been 1,094,318 sq.ft., the conclusion must be that only 190,299 sq.ft. of special projects had been completed, compared with a target of 2,073,000 sq.ft. shown in Table 9, i.e. 9% of the target. If the assumption is not right, the relative percentages achieved for Advance Factories and special projects must be adjusted.

It is evident from Table 10 that the rate of factory completions increased considerably in the two years to September 1949. Since - on the assumption made - only about 640,000 sq.ft. of Advance Factories remained to be completed under the curtailed programme after September 1947, completions of other kinds of Treasury-financed factories became more significant (see Table 10). These would have been, in the first place, the special projects which survived the 1947 cuts. The remainder were standard factories built on demand.

The distinction between Advance and standard factories has been examined at the beginning of this chapter. The delays in the construction of Advance Factories - coupled with the large demand for factories - meant that the Advance Factory programme had turned into a standard factory programmme, as Sadler Forster was obliged to admit to the Select Committee on 4 February 1947.

The Committee's report 'The Administration of the Development Areas' was published in May 1947 [35]. It drew attention to the exceptional difficulties faced by those having to implement the provisions of the Distribution of Industry Act. The Committee was impressed by the efforts made to overcome them and it made a special reference to the enterprise displayed in the Development Areas. Nevertheless, it felt that the progress made in factory construction gave cause for concern. While the Board of Trade had estimated that the planned Treasury-financed factories in the Development Areas would provide employment for 149,000 people, the factories completed by 31 March 1947 employed only 3,251.

The Committee appreciated the problems with the supply of building materials. It wondered, however, whether the use of progress officers both by the Board of Trade and the estates companies would not lead to a duplication of effort and suggested that the need was rather for decisions at Ministerial level to ensure that the production of materials was improved. The Committee also pleaded for an improvement 'in the planning of factories, suggesting a more realistic programme, for which materials should be given the 'highest, if possible, exceptional priority'.

Finally, the Committee referred the delays caused 'by the necessity for constantly referring matters, especially difficulties occasioned by increasing costs and such questions as tenants' alterations, to Headquarters for financial approval'. It had been put to the Committee that the devolution of financial responsibiliy would lead to more rapid decisions. The Committee was doubtful whether this would do much to reduce delays, but it suggested that the idea should receive careful examination.

The Committee's views on the more fundamental aspects of the control of government-financed factory construction will be examined in V/4.

By the middle of 1947, the delay in the construction programme was no longer the only concern of the Company. A new and unexpected problem arose in some parts of the region: tenants reported difficulties in recruiting labour for manning the factories actually completed.

The sum of the problems moved the Company to address an extraordinary letter to the President of the Board of Trade on 13 September 1947 [36], in which the cessation of any further building and new development work was suggested, except, perhaps, in a corner of North West Durham and for firms of great national importance.

This advice must have gone very much against the grain of the directors and officers, who had been so deeply involved in the industrial development of the North East, some of them for many years. The following arguments were adduced by the Company in support of its drastic proposal:-

First: the Board taking into account the present crisis in the Nation's affairs, doubt whether the demand of a further extended programme upon labour and materials can be justified at this time.

The crisis referred to was the so-called Dollar Crisis, which was to lead to emergency measures by the government a few weeks later. The background and the effect of these measures on the Company and the region will be discussed in the next chapter.

Second: because the building labour force is now spread so thin on the ground that all factory building is proceeding much too slowly as a result.

Third: the labour force does not appear to be as ready to enter industrial occupations as was expected at the end of the War, nor to the extent which is indicated in national percentages ... the need for factory space might originally have been somewhat exaggerated ... it was apparent that some firms were having difficulty already in recruiting the labour force even for the comparatively small percentage of factories completed and occupied ... there had already been a complaint of being misled with regard to the availability of labour.

The letter ended with the following recommendation: 'having in mind the list of factories erected or being erected and available for allocation as at 30 August (1947), we felt we should advise extreme caution in putting further work in hand until the present programme was considerably nearer completion'.

By anticipating the next chapter, it may be noted here that the government would act on these lines a few weeks later.

The problems highlighted in the Company's letter largely resulted from the government's failure to adjust Development Areas policy to the extent of the post-War boom.

But there was perhaps even more to the letter than objective advice to the government. The Company had always maintained that, given anything like its pre-War autonomy, it would have achieved any practical government objectives more readily than the Board of Trade. After battling with the government for two years on this issue, the Company had recently had to give up any remaining hope of recovering even a token of its former autonomy. Reading the letter in the context of the events described in V/4, the impression cannot be avoided that there was an element of 'I told-you-so' in the fact that the letter was written at all.

This impression is strengthened by the contents and tone of a further letter of the same day [37], in which the Company reiterated its disagreement with the government on a particular policy issue: the 1939 basis of costs for assessing rentals.

In the Company's view, the inducements used in the early days after the War to persuade manufacturers to establish themselves in Development Areas were no longer necessary, as conditions had changed materially since the 1939 basis was introduced. Building restrictions and labour shortages in many parts of the country made it 'no hardship but an advantage for a firm to be able to establish itself in one of the Development Areas'.

Rents based on 1939 costs effectively provided tenants in post-War factories with substantial and growing subsidies. The Company considered it inappropriate that such assistance should continue to be given to branches of some of the largest firms in the country. Furthermore, the 1939 basis made it more and more difficult to maintain a rational rent structure, particularly in view of the increasing, rather than the forecast reducing inflation. For all these reasons, the Company recommended an immediate return to rents related to current costs, although not necessarily in a single step for all tenants.

The post-War Advance Factory building programme had a short run: in November 1947 it was cut and frozen (see Table 17 and next chapter), a fate suffered temporarily by all other factory building except for priority cases. After the delayed completion of the reduced 1946 programme, no Advance Factories at all would be built for more than 12 years. When building was resumed, it was to be on a small scale.

The events which forced the Labour Government to halt a programme designed to play a key role in Development Areas policy will be described in the next chapter.

3 The economic crisis of 1947

The advice by the Company to halt the government-financed factory construction programme included a reference to the 'crisis in the nation's affairs'. All other considerations apart, it was the growing economic crisis which forced the government to take the advice.

It must be a matter of speculation how the government reacted to the other reasons advanced by the Company, but they would have merely confirmed what the government already knew: that too much was being attempted within the available resources.

The economic problems coming to a head in the summer of 1947 resulted from the fact that world trade had not yet recovered from the War. Representatives of the main trading nations had been assembled in Geneva for many months in order to work out a new, multilateral scheme for world trade, but the negotiations were making only slow progress.

For Britain, the key to the problem was the overseas balance of payments, particularly the balance with the Dollar countries. While Europe was struggling to rebuild its infra-structure and its industries - ravaged by six years of War -, the United States of America had emerged from the War with its productive capacity greatly increased. It was able to supply the food, the fuel and the raw materials as well as the manufactured goods eagerly sought by all. Its balance of payment surplus with the rest of the world was running at an annual rate of $13,000 million [1]. This unprecedented situation was to be largely resolved by the Marshall Plan, which would soon be launched.

In the meantime, the American Loan negotiated by Keynes and his team in the latter part of 1945 was running out fast, yet, under the terms of of the Loan Agreement, the Pound Sterling was to be made convertible on 15 July 1947.

The government found it necessary to take emergency action: convertibility was suspended again within a few days - on 20 July 1947; on 6 August, reductions were announced in purchases from hard currency countries affecting food, raw materials, films and other items; on 27 August, the basic petrol ration was abolished and private foreign travel was banned.

More fundamental measures were being put in hand: in the Debate on the Address on 23 October 1947, Sir Stafford Cripps, the Minister for Economic Affairs, announced that the domestic production of food - the largest single item in the Dollar import bill - was to be increased by any means, although it was not clear where the labour was to come from which would replace the 135,000 German prisoners of war recently repatriated; exports were to be encouraged intensively, and coal and steel - scarce commodities at home - would have to make further contributions to the export effort.

In the case of steel, this aim could not be achieved by increasing output alone; it was necessary to cut down the investment programme, both in the private and the public sectors, since there were no other sources from which steel could be diverted to export markets: 'the object of this curtailment of our capital construction programme is primarily to save steel, fuel and some dollar imports such as timber' [2]. At the same time, some deflation became necessary because of signs of price inflation [3].

The government laid down two immediate objectives: to finish off as much construction work as had already been started as quickly as possible, and to postpone only the less essential items of the programme.

As a first step, the government required a cut of £200 million from the annual expenditure on capital construction, encompassing all new building, plant, machinery etc. - whether government or privately financed. Sir Stafford Cripps promised to issue a White Paper, in which the various investment reductions would be set out in full, but, in the meantime, he proposed to reduce the supply of steel for factory construction by 120,000 per annum.

This was not going to be easy. In relation to the availability of steel, 'there are many more (factories) started than we have the resources to finish quickly. Some factories which have not yet got their steel will have to be stopped for the time being, unless they contribute to export or some other very special purposes' [4].

So far as the Development Areas were concerned, Sir Stafford Cripps promised to give them preference in the finishing of factories, on the assumption that labour was available and waiting to be taken up, an assumption that did not apply to all parts of the North East.

The gist of the statement by Sir Stafford Cripps of 23 October 1947 was communicated to the Consultative Committee on Trading Estates which, by chance, had met in London on the same day [5]. Pending the preparation of more detailed instructions, the Board of Trade confirmed the outline of the immediate action to be taken in a letter to the Company on 24 October 1947 [6]. So far as new works were concerned, the ruling was as follows:-

At least for the next six months (and probably longer), no new industrial building and extension to be started apart from exceptional cases where refusal will mean that the export drive will definitely suffer and where no other accommodation is available. In view of the very severe cut in the Board of Trade building labour ceiling and the sharp further reduction in the allocation of steel for industrial buildings, this export test will have to be very stringently applied ... This decision will mean a review of all projects on which building work has not yet started as well as projects still under consideration ... Any project which it is considered should, for exceptional reasons, go ahead, should be submitted to the Directorate for Industrial Estates.

The definition and identification of 'new works' proved to be relatively straightforward, even if the stringent export criterion - and the Dollar import-saving, which was later held to be equivalent - required further elucidation. The work-in-progress ruling, on the other hand, raised many, and sometimes, complicated questions:-

All factory building (including extensions) which has not yet reached the steel erection stage is to be reviewed with the object of postponing at least half. But in assessing the claims of particular schemes to be allowed to go ahead, the existing preferential treatment of the development areas within the reduced programme for completing industrial building projects already started is to be continued.

The Board of Trade was still considering the administrative arrangements for projects in this category. In the meantime, the Company was advised to 'concentrate their efforts particularly on jobs for which steel is already on site or in the hands of the fabricators'.

The emergency measures caused the Company's officers and staff a few weeks of troublesome work and not a little confusion.

At a meeting with the senior staff of the Company on 27 October 1947, Methven asked that lists be prepared of projects agreed but not yet in progress which, on the facts available, the Company could recommend to be stopped or reviewed. In the case of those already in progress, the test would be whether the steel erection stage had been reached or not. There would be no priorities and no exceptions. Methven gave his staff 24 hours to prepare draft proposals [7].

On 30 October 1947, the Board of Trade announced the cancellations of the following Advance Factories [8]: Ashington (6), North Tees (6), Houghton le Spring (2), Skelton (1) and Wingate (2). The cancellations added up to 334,000 sq.ft. at this stage. It is evident from a comparison of the floor area approved in principle with that approved by the Finance Branch (see Table 17) that further cuts were made later (see also below). In addition, some Advance Factories were re-sited, but the records are difficult to interpret.

At the same time, the Board of Trade issued a priority list of special projects which 'should be entitled to the first refusal of the structural steel that has been fabricated, or is now in the course of fabrication ... for Advance Factories which have been cancelled' [9]. This kind of switch proved to be difficult in practice because the steelwork ordered for the cancelled Advance Factories was not always suitable for priority projects.

The cancellation of so many projects raised other problems: professional fees for work done would have to be paid; contractors and sub-contractors would have to be advised of cancellation of contracts or changes of locations; some contractors would not be able to service the new locations. Even more difficult, the decision to cancel projects had to be communicated to the firms concerned. Given the policy issues involved, what exactly were they to be told?

At a meeting on 29 October 1947, Rhodes, the new Regional Controller of the Board of Trade at Newcastle 'did not think it would be advisable to write to firms and say their propositions had been abandoned' [10]. He thought that the letter should merely say that they had been postponed for six months or longer. Tenants would want an assurance that the Board of Trade would build when conditions were more favourable. Methven, on the other hand, insisted that 'requests for such assurances would have to be refused. Projects stopped now would be "killed" and they would have to begin again from the beginning at some future time if circumstances changed'.

Methven tested his views in this matter with the Directorate for Industrial Estates in a letter of 4 November 1947 [11]. While the reply is missing from the file, it appears that Methven's view prevailed, although an instruction was issued by the Directorate that letters to tenants were to be most carefully phrased.

In an internal memorandum of 29 October 1947 on the legal liability of the Company [12], the fear was expressed that the Company might be involved in breach-of-contract litigation if it cancelled some projects and not others, unless the government made an order imposing a selective ban on building. The author of the memorandum was in favour of telling prospective tenants that their propositions had been postponed indefinitely, because 'those who will be likely to suffer the greatest loss will probably then try to withdraw from their agreements themselves'.

The problems involved in deciding which projects should be stopped were forecast by Sir Stafford Cripps on 23 October 1947: 'the House may imagine, it is fairly difficult to determine priorities when there are such good arguments in favour of every item' [13].

The Company drew up several alternative lists of special projects to be cancelled [14]. Each one, no doubt, would have been discussed at length.

Given the alternative uses of steel from cancelled Advance Factories and special projects, the difficulties in tracing the outcome of cases under review and the continuing discussion of priority cases, it has been found impossible to establish the actual cuts in special projects decided by the Board of Trade.

But even if the cuts could have been estimated, it would not be possible to weigh their effect on the special projects unless the number and size of those added or removed from the 1946 programme were known and taken into account.

The problem is aggravated by the fact that a number of projects were cut - including some substantial ones - which were in a preliminary stage but had already been allocated a Board of Trade factory number. Some of these projects had been intended to open up sites additional to those shown in Table 11: at Ferryhill, Howden le Wear, Darlington, Castleside (all in County Durham) and Wallsend on Tyne.

By contrast, the cuts made in the Advance Factory programme can be established with accuracy: it is evident from Table 17 that the programme was reduced from 2,025,350 sq.ft. to about 1,444,000 sq.ft., a reduction of 581,350 sq.ft. i.e. 28.7%. It is likely that the Advance Factory Programme suffered a smaller, perhaps a much smaller percentage curtailment, than the special projects. At the same time, Table 10 shows that the relatively small part of the programme oustanding was not completed until 1950.

In the opinion of the Board of the Company, the cuts did not go far enough: in a letter of 4 November 1947 to the Regional Controller of the Board of Trade in Newcastle - which included the Company's first recommendations in accordance with the instructions -, Methven reported that the Board of the Company 'do not and cannot recommend pressing forward with all the schemes (remaining) on these lists in view of the economic position in which the country finds itself' [15].

Odber [16], on the other hand, has drawn attention to the severity of the cuts: 'insofar as the Development Areas had been getting the lion's share of ... (industrial) building, it was understandable that they should suffer most. In point of fact, the Areas suffered a much greater percentage cut in industrial building than did the rest of Britain'. The evidence for this conclusion is provided by the Second Report of the Select Committee of the Session 1955/56 [17]: in the years 1945 - 1947, the Development Areas had received 51.1% of all industrial building, although they contained only 19.9% of the population. In the following three years, they would receive slightly less than their share of the population.

It may be seen from Table 10 that the floor area of completions increased sharply in the year the cuts were introduced, from 1,094,318 sq.ft. in 1946/7 to 3,354,019 sq.ft. in 1947/8. The figures confirm that the policy of concentrating on completions was a wise one.

The promised White Paper was published in December 1947 [18]. It provided a wide-ranging analysis of the investment situation in Britain, and it showed how far public and private development objectives had outstripped national resources, particularly in the light of the problem of the balance of payments.

The ban on new construction was gradually lifted. This is evident from the post-1948 reports by the Directorate for Industrial Estates [19] and the continuing growth - although at a much slower rate than in the years 1945-1949 - in the number of the Company's tenants (see Appendix 26).

The enforced retrenchment embarrassed the government. The cuts came at a time when the Town and Country Planning Act 1947 had just been passed and the ad hoc arrangements for locating industry under the wartime building licensing system would come to an end. From the summer of 1948, the Act would make possible a true location of industry policy in Britain for the first time. At this precise moment, the curtailment in factory construction would make it more difficult for the government to exert pressure on manufacturers to move their works to the Development Areas.

4 Policy and the changing role of the company, 1944-1948

The War had set into motion profound changes and the Company could not have expected to start again at the end of hostilities where it had left off in 1939. If this had not been fully understood before May 1944, the White Paper on Employment Policy would have left it in no doubt that, in comparison with the pre-War Special Areas policy, Development Areas policy would occupy a far more central position in the government's plans. The crucial role assigned to government-financed factories in the attempt to modify the location of industry and the overall control of the policy by the Board of Trade would have far-reaching consequences for the Company.

This chapter will be devoted to an examination of these consequences and the attempts by the Company to maintain its original functions in the face of the new circumstances. The period covered encompasses the events which occurred between the publication of the 1944 White Paper on Employment Policy and 1 May 1948, when the Company lost the last vestiges of its autonomy.

Reference has already been made to the equivocal position of the Company from its inception: it was established to perform a public service and, at the same time, expected to operate as a commercial business. Within these - sometimes conflicting - remits, the Company had looked upon itself as the principal development agency in the Special Areas of the North East. In pursuit of finding tenants, it had created interest in the region at home and abroad. It had worked in partnership with the Commissioner and in parallel with the local development agencies, even if the collaboration with some of them was not always easy. While the activities of other agencies were limited to promotion and research, the Company not only promoted the region but made available factories for rent and was able to offer or procure at least some inducements to firms it particularly wished to attract. No other agency in the region had the powers or the means to perform all these functions.

Given the Company's self-image, it was natural that it should have concerned itself almost from the beginning with issues beyond those related directly to the development and management of industrial estates.

This concern was particularly evident in the last 18 months of the War, when the Company gave serious thought to the industrial policies it should adopt in the post-War world. This in itself confirms that the Company expected to retain some responsibility for regional industrial policy. Methven, at least, appears to have assumed this until the end of October 1944 (see [13] below). The notion may now appear somewhat naive, but neither Methven nor the Board seem to have been aware of the direction in which post-War policy was developing before the 1944 White Paper, nor of the full implications for the Company after it was published.

The following example is an indication of the Company's interest in the wider issues:

Early in 1944, the Company was invited to contribute an article to a newspaper concerning its future in the economy of the North East. In a letter to Appleyard of 3 February 1944 [1], Methven wondered 'what should be your message today'? Even if the heavy industries were able to continue to offer employment to those engaged in them during War, Methven did not believe they could absorb more than a few of the men who would return home after demobilisation. He was by no means alone in this erroneous forecast of the post-War employment prospects in the traditional industries of the region.

Methven posed some pertinent questions: was it wise to attract consumer industries? Would the Estates Company and the region prosper if they acquired 'a heterogeneous mass of sundry and unrelated industries'? Should the Company sponsor research into the possible benefits of interconnected businesses which might form a section of industry, economically self-supporting and based upon indigenous raw materials?

He feared that a heterogeneous collection of firms 'might be blown into liquidation by a strong wind of adverse trade conditions'. This view was strengthened by information obtained from tenants 'on the various disadvantages they suffer as to their isolation', although it is not clear whether isolation from related industries was meant or from markets, or both. With pre-War attitudes in mind, Methven also foresaw that industry outside the Development Areas would dislike the idea of a clearly identifiable industrial sector being established in the North East.

In the same letter, Methven examined the relative importance of the proximity of markets and of raw materials. He concluded that the proximity of firms in the same or in ancillary trades was the most important factor and he was to be very concerned with what he called 'industrial linkages' for the the next few years. He anticipated - in an intuitive and undeveloped way - the work of Perroux on growth poles by

282

some ten years. McCrone [2] has stated the basic idea of the concept in a simple form: -

> The production of goods is essentially a joint process between a variety of firms and industries, the output of one being the input of another. The ability of any one firm to face competition from competitors in other areas is, therefore, not simply a matter of its own efficiency, but of the efficiency of the complex of related industries to which it belongs.

Methven's conclusions led him to propose the following post-War strategy: 'we should determine what branch of industrial activity is most suitable to diversify industrial occupation in the North East, most likely to succeed there and most likely to contribute to the nation's future prosperity' [3].

Although he was probably unaware of it, Methven had defined in these few words the objectives of a true location of industry policy appropriate to the circumstances of his time. One reason why the government policy makers had failed to give more weight to such considerations was suggested in IV/2: the means for implementating the post-War Development Area policy were formulated under the pressure of time. It was only when concern began to be felt - unwarranted in the event - about an early subsiding of the post-War boom that questions about 'a heterogenous mass of industries' were asked again, for example, by Pepler & MacFarlane [4].

The years between 1944 and 1948 saw an almost continuous examination by the Company of its role, requests to the government to have this role re-defined and pleas to confirm its autonomy. As the Labour Government of 1945 would attach such great importance to employment creation in the formerly depressed areas and given the scale of industrial development it would consider necessary to prevent a recurrence of serious unemployment, it was a forlorn hope that the execution of so important a policy would be delegated to a small Public Utility Society.

This period of the Company's history began with the publication of the White Paper on Employment Policy in May 1944. There is no evidence that the Company was ever consulted during the months before publication. But it must have sensed that the policies outlined in the White Paper would have incalculable effects on its future activities.

By the end of the summer of 1944, the Company decided to attempt to influence the further development of policy, at least so far as it affected government-financed factories.

The apparent trigger for the approach to the government was a report from Methven which alerted the Board of the Company to the possibility, not to say danger, that the local authorities in the area would attempt to compete for the available mobile industry after the War. The Board considered that this would be most unfortunate. Accordingly, it resolved on 1 September 1944 that

> the Company should offer its services to be the government agents for all government industrial property, built, building or to be built ... the Company must be prepared to do any practical work in connection with the location of industry that

was reasonably required of it for any part of the old Special Areas, whether by way of research, development or otherwise [5].

The implication is clear: the Board proposed that the Company should be charged with the implementation of Development Area policy in the North East region.

In pursuit of this aim, Methven drafted a letter which, after some changes suggested by the available directors, was addressed to the President of the Board of Trade and the Minister of Labour on 10 October 1944 [6]:-

This Company has gathered a great deal of experience in estate development, building for light industry, seeking new industries and assisting them to establish themselves in the North East. This activity has not been confined to the Company's Estate at Gateshead, and my Directors' objective has always been the diversification of industrial activity over the whole North East Area. My Board feel that this highly specialised experience might well be of service to you in putting into effect the government's intentions as outlined in the White Paper on Employment, and would be glad to place their knowledge at your disposal.

Dalton responded by inviting representatives of the Company to meet him on 29 November 1944. Bevin did not reply presumably because the White Paper foresaw a transfer of the responsibility for the Development Areas from the Ministry of Labour to the Board of Trade.

In the meantime, the Company had to face challenges to its post-War ambitions from two local organisations which had recently been established. At a meeting on 20 October 1944, the directors were shown a paper by the Northern Industrial Group (see Appendix 11), containing tentative suggestions for diversifying the industrial base of the North East. The paper envisaged the setting up of an organisation which, it appeared, would operate in parallel with the Company. The directors felt that 'it would be a very great pity if our own organisation were duplicated for fear we became competitive with the rest of the Area' [7].

Accordingly, they confirmed their readiness to help any organisation operating on behalf of the North East by any means in their power. To this end, they agreed that individual servants of the Company might render assistance to such organisation, in the hope that

by making this offer, the Northern Industrial Group, the recently-established North East Development Association (see Appendix 11) and the local authorities throughout the area might be persuaded to abandon any feeling erroneously held that his Company was solely or too greatly interested in the prosperity of Team Valley, and hence, (was) unduly favouring Gateshead.

The association by local interests of the Company almost exclusively with the Team Valley Estate would be a handicap to the realisation of the Company's post-War aims. But this handicap would be more serious in London. An aide-memoire drafted by Methven to serve the directors in their discussions with Dalton confirmed his concern that the Company might appear to have been associated too closely with the policy of concentration at Team Valley, a policy which would not only not commend itself to Hugh Dalton, but which was contrary to the policy outlined in the White Paper.

The memorandum was couched in somewhat apologetic terms and it moved Sir George Martin to comment: 'if I may criticise, I think we are trying to defend ourselves. We have no need to do that. I think we have done a jolly fine piece of work, and if the President (of the Board of Trade) does not .wish to take advantage of our services, it will be quite alright with us' [8]. In his reply to Sir George Martin, Methven justified the 'very suppliant attitude' of the draft: 'I see our position in much the same light as that of a man seeking a position with a new master who does not yet know his capabilities nor appreciate his past achievements' [9]. The memorandum attempted to correct this position [10]:-

> The first Commissioner agreed that, in order to succeed with its first task, it was essential to concentrate the Company's effort and to create a centre which, by its size and scale, would command attention. The Financial Agreement entered into with the Commissioner embodies this idea, and, in effect, by its scheme, confined our activities to Team Valley. The second Commissioner somewhat altered the emphasis and called for the creation of outside sites, notwithstanding the fact that the Company was then embarked on a course involving considerable government expenditure, which might be endangered by this self-competition. After putting forward its views, the Company loyally followed the second Commissioner's lead, even accepting the application of inducements to the outside sites which were not applied to Team Valley.

It was a piece of bad luck for the Company that the chairman of the Labour Party Commission on the Depressed Areas - which had objected to the concept of the Team Valley Estate - was now effectively responsible for the formulation of post-War Development Area policy. Methven could only hope that Dalton had forgotten that he was received with minimal courtesies when the Commission visited the Company at the end of 1936 [11].

Before the meeting with Dalton took place, Methven received from Appleyard a copy of a document, which appears to have outlined how the government intended to implement the White Paper proposals. The plans put paid to the Company's ambitions [12]. This prompted Methven to write to Appleyard on 24 October 1944 [13]:-

> It does look, doesn't it, as though the government had determined to do the job for which you created our specialist organisation. It is sad, because with the experience which we have at the back of us in research and in talking to new industries, I really believe today we could make concrete suggestions which, boldly carried to fruition, might almost solve the area's problems at one stroke. Maybe my geese are swans or my swans .are geese, but with the keenness I have for finding a solution, the present feeling of frustration is not easy to bear.

The profound disappointment revealed in these lines not only confirms that Methven had expected the Company to play the leading role in the post-War industrial development of the North East but also shows how far he was personally committed to this task, the magnitude of which he almost certainly underestimated.

The meeting with the President of the Board of Trade on 29 November 1944 marked a turning point in the Company's history. The directors came face to face with those who would take over before long from the Commissioner. They would have to learn an entirely new set of objectives and rules. Neither the self-image of the Company as the principal regional development agency, nor its record - least of all its aim to create employment for 40,000 people at Team Valley - would count for much from now on. In future, government-financed factories would serve the aims of high politics.

The discussion started well enough; Dalton remarked that the Trading Estate Movement was important and that Team Valley had served an excellent purpose. But he went on to say that 'the Estate had probably nearly reached its optimum size' and proposed that eight or nine new small estates should be created [14].

The directors of the Company, supported by a representative from the Commissioner's office, advanced the view that some expansion at Team Valley might still be desirable, particularly because of the availability of a substantial area of developed land. This would enable existing tenants to grow and serve large prospects from outside the region.

A consensus was arrived at on this occasion that further small estates were required and that a certain expansion at Team Valley would occur through natural growth and the individual preference of new prospects. The principle should be to oblige them rather than risk losing them. When at a later date the government developed clearer policy objectives within the region, the principle enunciated here was largely put aside. This was one of the reasons why the further development of the Team Valley Estate would remain contentious for some years.

Contrary to the views previously held within the Company [15] - and perhaps, to show their flexibility -, the directors proposed single factories in places where larger schemes would not be feasible and the President concurred.

It was agreed that the Company should take over the administration of all factories and estates in the North East which would be transferred to or created by the Board of Trade, and that preliminary steps to this end should be taken by the Company even before the necessary legislation was enacted.

In this connection, the directors mentioned the reserve factories being built by the Ministry of Works referred to in IV/3 and V/2. The President had an open mind on this matter. He seemed disposed to include these factories with the trading estates after they were handed over to the Board of Trade, but 'he was so anxious to see buildings erected that he did not want to raise questions of administration while the Ministry of Works building programme continued'.

As to the continuation of the independent position of the Company, it was considered desirable by all those present, but the President felt it advisable to strengthen the Board.

Dalton appointed additional directors in the spring of 1945 [16]. They were: Lt.Col. R.A. Bartram, chairman and managing Director of Bartram & Sons Ltd, Shipbuilders, Sunderland, J.R. Bradshaw, engineer, manager, secretary and director of the Hartlepool Gas and Water Company, Dr. Alexander (later Lord) Fleck, a director (later chairman) of Imperial Chemical Industries Ltd, Norman Mascall, director, J. & R. Mascall Ltd, Bishop Auckland, Middlesbrough and Darlington. Major Richard Miles, managing director, Head, Wrightson & Company Ltd, Thornaby on Tees, Alderman J.W. Mitchell, Mayor of South Shields 1944/45, an official of the Amalgamated Engineering Union, and Col. Methven. Methven apart, the new directors were associated with parts of the region where new trading estates and smaller sites would be developed.

Soon after the passing of the Distribution of Industry Act in June 1945, Sir Philip Warter formally invited the Company to assist the Board of Trade in carrying out the functions it had assumed under the Act in the Development Areas [17]. Regarding the role of the Company, Sir Philip announced

> that we regard your Company as the normal instrument for carrying out those functions which you had previously undertaken for the Ministry of Labour under the Special Areas Act, together with similar additional duties undertaken by the Board of Trade under the Distribution of Industry Act.

In the view of the Board of Trade, 'the government-financed trading estate companies will play an increasingly important part in the industrial revival of the Development Areas'.

Warter looked forward 'to a happy and fruitful collaboration between the Board of Trade and your Company' and he noted that a procedure for cooperation between the Company's officials and the regional officers of the Board of Trade 'is being smoothly worked out in practice'.

The letter informed the Company that Sadler Forster had been appointed to the new post of Director for Trading Estates in the Distribution of Industry and Regional Division of the Board of Trade and that he would take up his duties in August 1945.

In his reply of 25 July 1945 [18], Chapman, the chairman of the Company, welcomed the role assigned to North Eastern Trading Estates Ltd. In order to demonstrate that the Company was getting down to work quickly, he reminded Warter that plans for a trading estate at West Hartlepool were already in the hands of his department and advised him that proposals for an estate at South Shields would soon be ready. He also mentioned that 'we have placed one of our senior men at Aycliffe, and we are in touch with proposals at Spennymoor (Royal Ordnance Factory), Langley Moor, Sherburn and other places'.

But things did not go as smoothly as the Company had hoped. The machinery of Whitehall started to grind only slowly into action and, in the opinion of the Company, caused many avoidable delays.

The visit to the North East on 22 September 1945 by Sir Stafford Cripps - who had succeeded Hugh Dalton at the Board of Trade - enabled the Company to put to him some of its concerns and to make a plea for 'greater responsibility and freedom of action in carrying out the policy of the Board of Trade' [19].

In the Company's recent experience, land purchase and associated problems represented the most serious obstacle to the rapid establishment of new industries in the North East. Other matters raised with the President included the acceptance by the Board of Trade of too many requests for specialised factories, the administrative problems arising from the many single sites being proposed and the delays caused by the overburdened and understaffed District Valuer, who had taken over from the Company the responsibility for fixing rents.

The Company's proposals for overcoming delays relied on being allowed to purchase land in estate lots as soon as possible; to prepare standard lease agreements for such land; to erect standard factories 'speculatively' (i.e. to build Advance Factories); to fix fair rents on the basis of 1939 costs and to erect executive housing for some 5% of the anticipated number of employees.

According to the notes of the meeting [20], Cripps 'listened sympathetically, proclaiming himself in favour of decentralisation'. The events related in this chapter would indicate that the President's view was not shared by his department.

Sir Stafford hoped that the new Directorate for Industrial Estates would improve the procedures, but he was prepared to receive written suggestions from the Company.

He promised speedy action but warned that the Treasury might take a little longer if changes were proposed in financial control. This caveat implies that the Company had requested such changes and that the President had at least agreed to consider them.

The Company also pleaded for 'equal priority to be given to local small industries wishing to expand and occupy new premises'. The President 'immediately expressed his sympathy with the principle of assisting local industries and especially small local industries to expand, provided this principle was not allowed to prevent sound new industrial processes being introduced to the North East'.

In the event, the wish of the President did not prevail. This was largely because the Board of Trade chose to interpret its powers under the 1945 Act in a narrow sense. But it may also have been the government's view - implied in the reference to the need for new industrial processes - that indigenous enterprise could not make a significant contribution to the regeneration of its own region. Whatever the reason, it was not until the Industry Act 1972 that local industries generally were put on an equal footing with inward-moving industries and became fully eligible for regional aid.

The Company's written suggestions for greater freedom of action were sent to Cripps on 26 September 1945 [21]. They will be examined below in the context of the reply by the Board of Trade.

Cripps's offer to receive written representations from the Company had been tied to a highly political stipulation: that a copy be sent to the Regional Board for Industry (see Appendix 11).

The comments of the Regional Board were damaging to the Company's case and would have confused the Board of Trade [22]. They included the view that the 'the Company indicated a desire to usurp the functions of the Board of Trade', and the fear that 'the Company's proposals, if accepted, would have the effect of cornering all building labour'.

The background of the Company's proposals to Sir Stafford Cripps appears not to have been understood by the Regional Board - in spite of Lord Ridley's membership of both organisations. There were few dissenting voices when one member insisted that 'central control should not be taken out of the hands of government departments'. A situation was evidently developing where the Company pleaded for more decentralisation and the Regional Board for less.

This was not the only example indicating that local bodies preferred to put their trust in central government rather than in the Company. In a letter to Sadler Forster of 31 January 1946, the Regional Controller of the Board of Trade at Newcastle reported that he had attended a meeting of the Durham County Council at which the Trading Estate Company was referred to. He was somewhat alarmed to find that 'in addition to viewing this concern with considerable distrust, there was a strong impression, which I found difficult to dispel ... that the Trading Estate Company is an important factor in determining the location of incoming industrial concerns' [23].

This misunderstanding was sadly ironic: the Company no longer had any influence on location decisions. This had been made clear in the reply by the Board of Trade on 24 October 1945 [24] to the Company's proposals for greater freedom of action.

The reply opened with a statement of the basic aim of the government in Development Areas, which was 'to take the work to the workers'; in order to achieve this, 'development in the North Eastern Region during the next three years should take the form of individual sites plus the fullest development of trading estates already planned'.

The Company had proposed that it should select and suggest to the Board of Trade 'a further four or five sites in Northumberland, Durham and North Yorkshire of sufficient size and rightly situated to serve all available workers without their having to travel more than half an hour each way daily'. This concept was not in accordance with government policy and the Company's wish to 'discuss freely with local authorities all site proposals' in search of such sites had become irrelevant.

Apparently not yet aware of all the implications of government policy, the Company had also proposed that it should be the first body to meet industrialists visiting the North East, so that it could 'successfully locate them on a pre-chosen site and with some linkage, also to see that the terms of the lease were made clear to them from the start'.

This proposal was not acceptable to the Board of Trade. In order to ensure the proper distribution of industry, the policy was 'to steer industrialists not only to development areas but to those parts of the development areas where there is the greatest need'. 'There had been a tendency in the past', the Board of Trade observed with an implied criticism,

> for considerable development to take place in those parts of the region which were adjacent to the large towns - for example at Team Valley - and for the more remote parts to be neglected. It was for this reason that industrialists would be sent, in the first instance, to the Regional Controller of the Board of Trade.

Regarding the industries to be encouraged in particular locations, the Board of Trade 'welcomes suggestions from the trading estates companies as to the type of industrial activity necessary for each site and gives the fullest consideration to the view of the Estates Company in carrying out the government's distribution of industry policy'.

As for the Company's suggestion that it should take over from the Valuation Department the responsibility for land pricing, rentals and conditions of leases, the Board of Trade regretted that it could not depart from the established procedure, but agreed that an expansion of the District Valuer's staff was necessary to deal with the increased volume of work.

Some of the Company's other suggestions, however, were accepted and clarified: the Board of Trade welcomed the submission of development schemes for trading estates already approved and it agreed to the procedure proposed by the Company for the financial estimates for such development schemes. The practice of the Board of Trade would be to approve plans for development in principle and sanction expenditure in stages; within the framework of approved schemes, the Company would have full autonomy, but individual site schemes would have to be approved by the Board of Trade.

The meeting of the chairmen and chief executives of the trading estates companies at the Board of Trade on 7 November 1945 has already been referred to in V/2. Methven appears to have returned from the meeting in low spirits. The official record of the proceedings [25] does not reveal any particular grounds for this. In his own report [26], Methven complained that the chairman - Sir Philip Warter - had made everyone feel subordinate except Sir Gerald Bruce, the chairman of the Welsh trading estates company, with whom he seemed to have a good understanding. The officers of the other companies either had agreed with everything Warter had said or had remained silent, so that Methven 'was put in the position of being the only protagonist'. In a letter to his chairman - who was present at the meeting - Methven noted that 'we, as a Company, were very much out of favour', and he advanced the extraordinary opinion, 'that our Board has to take a decision on a rather serious issue, namely how far they are prepared to oppose the Board of Trade on all sorts of questions, large and small' [27].

Methven's hint at rebellion pointed to a disturbing state of affairs. While the early relations between the Company and the Board of Trade - in the last months of the War - were not free from mutual irritations, the real difficulties began to develop within a few months after the end of the War. Initially, they revolved around the delays in obtaining decisions from London. The Company continued to act as if it, rather than the Board of Trade, was responsible for progress. The reluctance to accept its new and subordinate role was at least partly due to Methven, whose powers were rapidly being taken away from him. His response to this situation did not augur well for the future of the Company.

Methven might well have come away with new hope from the first meeting of the Consultative Committee on Trading Estates on 14 March 1946. The President of the Board of Trade personally addressed the meeting and informed those present that the government looked upon the estates companies as 'one of the main instruments of the Cabinet's full employment policy' [28]. The companies would assume an increasing importance, because 'they were now developers of whole areas rather than of particular trading estates'. In so far as it overstated the scope available to them, this remark may have misled the officers of the companies.

Some of the matters discussed at the meeting have already been examined in V/2. One item on the agenda may be mentioned here, because it is relevant to the difficulties developing between the Company and the Board of Trade: Sir Philip Warter had proposed that the companies should be renamed 'industrial' estates companies. The change was accepted by all the companies except North Eastern Trading Estates Ltd. The latter believed that its existing name 'carried with it a certain reputation and goodwill' [29]. While the Board of Trade would later agree to defer 'to meet the Company's views and convenience' [30], the Company had once again strained the patience of its masters.

In the meantime, the delays continued. Land acquisition problems prevented a start of construction of the trading estates at West Hartlepool and Jarrow (Bede), and of a large factory at Sunderland. Chapman wrote to the President of the Board of Trade on 10 January 1946, asking him to intervene [31]. In his reply of 29 January, Cripps wrote of 'the complex nature of many cases and the large number of interests who have frequently to be consulted', but assured the chairman that 'we are sparing no effort to bring the cases to completion' [32].

This particular problem would be eased after the passing of the Acquisition of Land Bill, but there were other occasions when the blocks in the system would require intervention at the highest level, indicating that something was wrong either with the administrative machinery or with the ambitions of the government, or - as it turned out - with both.

In a letter of 26 August 1946, the Board of Trade claimed that some of the administrative problems had arisen because

> we have all been dealing with Treasury-financed building projects under conditions of extreme pressure and in many respects the procedure has had to be built up in the light of experience, with the result that there has been no very clear definition of the information required at headquarters ... This has led to ... delays in particular cases [33].

The draft procedure appended to the letter extended to six closely-typed pages. It attempted to codify the ad hoc practices which had been built up during the first post-War year. The proposed procedure was so complex that it would be necessary to simplify it later.

In his reply to the Board of Trade of 8 October 1946, Methven commented that the draft

> did not meet with any enthusiastic reception, in fact, rather the reverse, for it struck my directors that the whole procedure sounded cumbersome. I was asked to point out that if a responsible body, such as the Board of this Company, satisfied itself in detail from all points of view with regard to the financial prospects on an intended new industry; if they are allowed to arrange the rental of the building on a basis which shows the Treasury a sound return on the capital investment, and if the (Regional) Distribution of Industry Panel (Committee) is satisfied ... from the viewpoint of employment that the district location is correct, then my Board should not be called upon to supply a great amount of detail for submission to the Treasury and only during the present period of shortage bottlenecks should it be necessary to supply much detail to the Production Department concerned [34].

The Company had not only become impatient with the bureaucratic shackles on progress, it no longer minced its words in saying so. Nevertheless, it was willing to operate the procedure until arrangements were made which were, in its view, more sensible: 'pending a full discussion of this Company's remit, we are prepared to use our best endeavours to carry it out, but we would not like this willingness to work in accordance with this procedure to be construed as endorsement of it'.

Early in October 1946, the Board asked Methven to prepare a memorandum containing 'suggestions for fundamental points for submission to the President of the Board of Trade', in case there were opportunities to raise them during the two planned meetings with him during the month - one of which was to be in the North East. Methven's memorandum [35] included the following concerns:-

> Our functions are no longer those defined for us by the Commissioner ... we have no clearly defined functions except at Team Valley, Pallion, West Auckland and at Tynemouth ... at Team Valley, our autonomy has decreased by the control imposed on us in capital expenditure, and at other sites the control of rental assessments has been removed.

He went on to ask 'whether we are intended to play any part in attracting new industries, to suggest plans for the diversification of industry in the Area, to administer properties placed in our care so as to ensure a percentage return to government and, if so, what percentage, to be responsible for locating an industrialist within a district defined by the Regional Distribution of Industry Committee ...'.

Summing up what he considered to be the heart of the matter requiring discussion with the President, Methven expressed it in a simple question: 'what is our remit'?

It was certainly true that no formal change in the Company's pre-War remit had ever been agreed or even discussed. Nevertheless, some of the questions raised in Methven's memorandum - for example the role of the Company in locating particular firms within the Area - had been answered by the Board of Trade a year earlier (see [24] above). The conclusion cannot be avoided that Methven persisted in asking the same questions because he did not like the answers the Company had received on previous occasions.

There was much discussion within the Company in the autumn of 1946 on the question of autonomy and how far attempts should be pushed to obtain more. The correspondence between Methven and Dr. Fleck - one of the new directors - shows that opinions on this question were divided.

Fleck had written to Chapman on 11 September 1946 (the letter is missing) and Methven had replied on 8 October, noting that there was 'a wide difference between us' [36]. Fleck appears to have been in favour of limiting the Company's objectives to those 'which certain officials in the Board of Trade ascribe to us', while Methven was 'looking at (the objectives) in the light of what they were and what they should be perhaps be in the future'. He pinned his hopes on the fact that those who had indicated these functions so far 'were not those in the highest positions in the Board of Trade'.

Methven's long letter rehearsed once again the arguments in favour of the original _modus operandi_ . There was a strong implication that the Company had all the virtues; it would interpret correctly the policies of the government and implement them efficiently; it was better equipped for the task than the Board of Trade.

The ideas which were eventually agreed within the Company were embodied in draft Heads of Agreement [37]. In anticipation of a meeting with the President of the Board of Trade òn 31 October 1946, the draft was sent to the other estates companies in the hope that it would be accepted and that, as a result, it would be possible to present a united front to the government.

This was not to be, mainly because the Welsh estates company would not cooperate. This was made only too clear in a letter from Bruce on 24 October 1946 [38]:-

> As to the Heads of Agreement ... I am sorry that I cannot agree, not so far as this estate is concerned, to what you asked for. I do not think that the request would be met, nor do I think it is an opportune time to ask for so much ... I do not wish in any way to spoil your case, but I think that you should know beforehand that I do not feel that I can go all the way with you.

There is no record of any discussions on the Heads of Agreement with the officers of the other companies on 31 October 1946, which would have taken place outside the Consultative Committee, but as the meeting on the same day with the Sir Stafford Cripps was cancelled, the matter had become immediately less pressing.

Cripps paid another visit to the North East on 10 December 1946. He seemed to have struck up a personal friendship with Chapman, because only dense fog prevented him from dining at the chairman's home that evening. The following day, Chapman addressed a letter to Cripps, from which it may be concluded that the discussions had been frank: 'though you may have been disappointed in apparently slow progress in places, I think you are fully aware of the causes ... I look forward to hearing shortly from your department on the question of more autonomy for us. I am sure it would save manpower and time and lead to a speed-up' [39].

Cripps had evidently asked Chapman a question - rather a curious one from a Minister, but indicating the kind of relationship he had established with Chapman: would a reduction in staff at headquarters help to improve matters? Chapman replied with some hauteur: 'I do not think that a reduction in numbers now would lead to a speed-up and it would have disadvantages that would outweigh advantages; it would be better to allow attrition to reduce numbers in due course' [40].

Chapman wrote an 'official' letter to Cripps on 9 January 1947 in which he returned to the main issue [41]: 'when you visited this area last month you intimated that you had under consideration some further decentralisation of responsibility for the industrial development of the area and some greater autonomy for our Company'. At the same time, Chapman enclosed the Heads of Agreement which were 'to form the basis of a finance agreement along the lines somewhat similar to those operative before the National War Emergency ... we feel confident that they would serve to save staff and speed up the work we have in hand for you'.

It may have been the receipt of the Heads of Agreement that prompted the Board of Trade to put the Company's finances in order and to take the opportunity to bring its remit up to date. But it is evident from the reaction to the draft of a new finance agreement (missing from the files) that the Company's proposals had been ignored.

Irvine, the Company's resident legal adviser, found the draft completely unacceptable. While ostensibly intended to deal with the financial past and to put the future expenditure at Team Valley on a proper footing, 'it alters the original conception of an Approved Scheme to cover, with a cloak of legality and formality, the interminable and detailed everyday correspondence we have with the Board of Trade on every single project and (would) perpetuate the very system and procedure from which we are trying to shake clear' [42]. Campling, the Principal Secretary of the Finance Branch of the Board of Trade, had tried to convince the Company that 'the execution of the Agreement will not prejudice the revision of the present arrangements', but Irvine thought that such a view would 'seem to bespeak complete ignorance in regard to the legal implications of the draft'.

The Company's senior management was evidently becoming exasperated with the Board of Trade. The contents of yet another letter to Sir Stafford Cripps from Chapman on 5 May 1947 reflected this feeling: 'I am getting very anxious about the position which seems to be arising between your department and my Company, and would be very grateful if you could give me an opportunity of discussing the position privately' [43].

Cripps replied on 13 May 1947, asking for details of what was in Chapman's mind, as 'I am not aware of any changes in the relationship between my department and your Company' [44].

Chapman, frustrated by the evident impossibility of communicating with Cripps without interference from his staff had asked for the private conversation 'to enable him to appreciate more thoroughly the basic principles on which you want my Company to operate, and remove the doubts expressed by some of my colleagues on the Board as to whether they are performing any really useful function for you' [45].

In his reply of 28 May 1947, Cripps referred to the recently published Report of the Select Committee [46] and asked for time to consider 'some matters touching the relationships of the Board of Trade and the industrial estates companies'. But he had no doubt as to the basic function of the estates companies, which was 'to erect as soon as practicable the factories which it has been decided to build' [47].

Chapman wrote once more, on 2 June 1947 [48]. He agreed 'that one of the basic functions of our Company for building operations is not in doubt', but wondered 'what other functions you attribute to this Company and its Directorate; some of these functions, we feel, may also be basic'.

But there was nothing in Cripps's letter of 28 May that might have given Chapman the slightest justification for adding: 'I am glad that you do not ascribe our building function as our sole basic function'. The addition reflected the dawning realisation by the Company that, in the government's view, it had no other. Indeed, Campling's draft - according to Irvine - had defined the Company's sole function as 'the provision of industrial premises'.

It was nearly the end of the road. Chapman's letter of 2 June appears to have been the last communication with Cripps on the autonomy question. The meeting with him never took place. A few months later, he was moved to another department in order to deal with problems of a much more pressing nature (see previous chapter).

Some comments of the Select Committee on the delays in the factory construction programme have already been examined in V/2. In the context of the strained relationship between the Company and the Board of Trade, the Committee's observations on the causes of the difficulties are of particular interest.

The Committee recognised that the problems arose mainly from 'the sharing of the administration of the Distribution of Industry Act between the Board of Trade and the Company, and from the resulting division of responsibility' [49]. While efforts had been made to define the division of functions, some overlap remained. 'Moreover', the report of the Committe continued,

> the character and original purpose of the estates companies must be borne in mind. The present form of administration may tend to be regarded as irksome by the companies and may fail to provide them with sufficient scope for enterprise and initiative. This cannot be helpful to efficient and economical administration.

The urgency of getting on with the task might preclude immediate steps being taken towards the unification of the administration, but 'the possibility should not be overlooked and in any case, its eventual desirability should be accepted'.

The Committee made two alternative proposals for simplifying the administration: one was to revert substantially to the system operated by the Commissioners for the Special Areas before 1939, a system involving block grants and leaving the companies a wide discretion, with the Board of Trade determining policy. This approach was justfied by the likely future tasks of the companies: after the completion of the large post-War building programme, their main function would be to manage the estates and factories. This task would be on a much larger scale than before. In order to ensure proper departmental supervision, the structure of the companies would have to be changed. The chairmen should give their full time and be reasonably remunerated; the Boards of Directors should be reconstituted and the Board of Trade should have the power to appoint and remove directors. The Boards of the companies should be smaller, the object being to create compact executive bodies with each member taking an active part in the direction of his company.

The Committee was obviously impressed by the evidence from Chapman and Methven on 27 February 1947. Their arguments may have influenced the Committee to propose, within the first alternative, a measure of local autonomy going far beyond the building of factories:-

> Thus reconstituted, the estate companies would have the duty of encouraging the industrial development of their Areas and would largely determine the location of individual industrial projects. The members of the Regional Distribution of Industry Panels (Committees) should act in an advisory capacity to the Boards of the estates companies. Such reorganisation would do much to ensure local cooperation, to encourage local confidence and to eliminate avoidable delays.

The effect of the Select Committee's first alternative would have been to return most of the decision-making and control of the implementation of the government's plans to the regions; and within the regions, to reverse the roles of the companies and the Regional Distribution of Industry Committees.

This prescription might almost have been written by the Company, but although the Committee had provided for the appointment of the directors by the Board of Trade, was it likely that the government would accept either block grants or the degree of local autonomy envisaged?

The Committee evidently had some doubts: 'if the suggestion of a block grant is unacceptable, the whole of the administration should be brought directly under the Board of Trade'. In that case, however, the Committee was anxious that the advantages of independent advice and direction 'which have proved themselves of such value' should not be lost. It suggested either a Regional Committee with its own secretary and staff, or an extension of the terms of reference of the Regional Boards for Industry. The Regional Committee would be responsible for the location of industry.

The Select Committee appreciated the difficulties in conducting an administrative reorganisation under the given circumstances, but it deemed it possible 'to revise the functions and strengthen the character of the estates companies without undue interference with present activities', and for this reason it recommended 'that the first alternative should be adopted as soon as possible'.

The questions raised by the Select Committee do not appear to have been discussed during the summer of 1947, when the government was occupied with more serious matters. It was not until the autumn that Harold Wilson, the new President of the Board of Trade, considered a response. A meeting with the trading estate companies was scheduled for 23 October. The Consultative Committee would meet on the same day, the day on which Sir Stafford Cripps announced the cuts in the factory programme. As Chapman was unable to attend, the Company was represented by Sir George Martin and Lord Westwood. Methven again prepared briefs for the directors, but they contained nothing new, except, perhaps, a note of desperation [50].

According to a report of the meeting by Sir George Martin [51], the President appeared to accept the solution preferred by the Select Committee - and, no doubt, by the Company: he was in favour both of block grants and local autonomy; but since he had to answer to Parliament for the expenditure incurred by the Company, he felt that he should have the power to appoint the directors, as the Select Committee had proposed. This power had alread been written into the Articles of the recently-established North Western Industrial Estates Company Ltd.

The meeting soon showed up the strained relations between the Company and the Board of Trade; while the President had no criticism to make of the Scottish or Welsh companies, he seemed to go out of his way to show displeasure with North Eastern Trading Estates Ltd: its Board 'was composed of too many high-ranking Army officers and savoured too much of the old school tie'. Sir George Martin rejoined that, while the original directors had been appointed by the Commissioner, the new directors had been selected by Hugh Dalton!

Martin had formed the impression that Wilson was reading from a brief which he believed to have been drafted by Calder, the Deputy Secretary in the Regional Division of the Board of Trade. Martin made this assumption as a result of a short conversation with Calder before the meeting, when it became apparent to him that 'Calder knew very well what the President was going to refer to'.

According to Martin's report, the only decision made at this meeting was that the chairmen of the companies would meet the President again within three months.

Wilson wrote to the Company on 10 November 1947 [52], requesting it 'to amend the Articles of Association so as to bring them in line with those of North Western Industrial Estates Ltd'. The effect of the amdendments would be to empower the Board of Trade to appoint the directors.

Wilson assured Chapman that there was nothing personal in the proposal and that he fully recognised and appreciated 'the admirable work of the companies'. But 'their activities now covered a very much wider field than was contemplated when when they were formed ... and their relationship with my department must necessarily be very different from that current in the days of the Commissioners for the Special Areas'.

The Company consulted with the Scottish estates company. Sir Stephen Bilsland, its chairman, and another director had made it plain 'that they are not going to accept the proposals without a fight and went so far as to say that the resignation of the whole Board my be involved'. Bilsland was reported to have insisted that 'unless a greater measure of autonomy is granted, it is futile for the present Board to carry on' [53]. The question of the amendments to the Articles had evidently become entangled with the quite separate issue of autonomy.

The indication that the Scottish estates company would take a hard line may have emboldened the Board of the Company to reply to Wilson with a last defiance: 'we have given careful consideration to those Articles of North Western Industrial Estates Ltd to which you directed our attention, but your suggestion ... does not commend itself to us and we are not willing to agree to your proposal' [54]. The Company was prepared to discuss the Amendments 'in an endeavour to meet the changed conditions and to meet your wishes', but it insisted 'that the stability and continuity of direction should not be interfered with'.

A few days later Bilsland wrote to Chapman and enclosed the draft of a letter he proposed to address to Wilson. This contained points of complaint very similar to those advanced by the Company and almost identical reasons for rejecting the changes in the Articles of Association. Bilsland's letter, however, introduced one new argument: 'if we are to carry on, then we consider that we should have the same status as such bodies as the National Coal Board ... and, clearly, it is one of much greater autonomy than we at present enjoy' [55].

The next meeting with Wilson took place on 19 February 1948. The Company delegation included Chapman, Methven, Bradshaw - one of the new directors - and Appleyard, who was still a director.

In his report of the meeting, Methven noted that the 'the President and his officers met us in a most friendly spirit and were fully prepared to discuss rather than dictate' [56].

All the same, Wilson made it clear from the start that 'while he hoped they would reach agreement ... should they fail, it would not be difficult to introduce legislation ... The House would be very willing to pass legislation, as the Select Committee had recommended that he should appoint the directors'.

It turned out that the objections of the Company to the proposed changes in the Articles did not raise much discussion. Most of the changes were of a purely legal nature; for example, whether the directors were to be appointed by the Board of Trade or the President and who would appoint the auditors. Wilson proved to be flexible, but he insisted that 'all the Articles of the various companies should be in conformity'.

When the amended Articles were available, the Board would resign and Wilson would appoint a chairman, a vice-chairman and one of the present directors. He was unwilling to discuss the names of any others he had in mind to appoint, but he stressed that he, too, placed great importance on continuity and that 'he would very carefully consider the claims of members of the existing Board'.

Appleyard then introduced a discussion on procedure after the reappointment of the Board and the President invited Methven to speak.

Methven attributed the friction which had occurred between Board of Trade officers and the Company 'to the lack of any clear indication where the ultimate authority lay'.

At this point the discussion took an unexpected turn: Appleyard observed that 'a good deal of friction had arisen in connection with Team Valley', and although this was true in the sense that the Company had found the control of the Board of Trade over its 'own' Estate particularly irksome, the unanimous agreement of the meeting to Appleyard's proposition must be considered very surprising: all the Company's letters and memoranda indicate that the differences covered a much wider ground.

Methven - who must have had Board authority - took up the point: if Appleyard was right, there was an easy solution: 'to put Team Valley on "all fours" with the rest of the property, surrendering the freehold etc.'. This proposal 'obviously intensely surprised the civil servants present, and they were delighted at the suggestion, but said they thought we would never have conceded it'.

Methven replied that 'if the ultimate authority was the Board of Trade's, there would no longer remain any obstacle to this transfer'. As the 'ultimate authority' had been written into the Distribution of Industry Act 1945 more than two and a half years earlier, Methven's diplomatic exit would indicate that his directors had come to the conclusion that the Company might achieve its objectives more readily by eliminating all causes of friction with the Board of Trade.

The retreat was almost certainly agreed and rehearsed by the Board of the Company beforehand, although there is no indication in the Board minutes to this effect. It is inconceivable that Appleyard - who had not actively participated in the Company's affairs since the beginning of the War - would have rendered his final service without the full agreement, or even at the request of the directors. He had certainly attended the Board meeting on 2 February 1948. He gave advice on that occasion from which it was clear that he had made contact at the highest level. He was 'strongly of the opinion that complete autonomy would not be conceded because the President of the Board of Trade under the Act is responsible for the Company's expenditure' [57]. At the same time 'Mr. Harold Wilson's personal view was that if the Board of Trade had a chosen instrument, they should trust it; if it failed, they should change it'. Appleyard warned, however, that this was not necessarily the Treasury's view'.

On the same occasion, the directors had discussed possible reasons why the Board of Trade was so reluctant to concede a degree of autonomy equivalent to that enjoyed by the National Coal Board. Appleyard appears to have convinced the directors that the one obstacle to greater autonomy was the Company's refusal to alter its Articles and that 'if the the directors were to agree that their appointment should be made by the President, a substantial measure of autonomy would be given'.

Although some of the directors may have considered it risky to rely on Appleyard's advice, they evidently accepted it, but how and when they decided to go even further is not known. In any event, only a few of the directors would be members of the new Board which might enjoy the greater autonomy hoped for.

On 2 March 1948, Methven wrote to Sadler Forster [58]: 'whilst in some ways the termination of twelve years regime of decentralised authority cannot be but sad in that it is the break-up of many old-standing conditions, yet I am satisfied that it is a thoroughly sensible move'.

There was irony in these words, because the change was to become a personal tragedy for Methven. It could not have been otherwise, for the new executive chairman would, in effect, replace him as chief executive of the Company. The fact that it would be Sadler Forster was probably not yet known to Methven, but it would make his own demotion no easier to live with. Nevertheless, he stayed on for another seven years, retiring in 1955. He died in November 1962. Percival, the Company secretary, left in 1956 to start his own business. He had found the control by the Board of Trade increasingly intolerable [59].

Methven never received any official recognition for his pioneering work in the North East. Chapman was knighted in 1950, but his may have been in recognition of his many services to the Community and to the Territorial Army. He received a Baronetcy in 1958.

The Board retired on 29 April 1948 and Sadler Forster took over as chairman of the Company on 1 May. Of the original Board, Chapman, Lord Ridley and Walton were reappointed. The leader in the North Mail , Newcastle upon Tyne, of 30 April 1946, had this to say about the dropping of Bradshaw, the director representing the Hartlepools area (who would be reappointed later), but the sentiments were intended to have a more general relevance:-

In this as in certain other branches of civic and industrial administration a policy of increasing centralisation is continuing to decimate the personal contacts and local influences which hitherto have served to foster local interest and pride, beside maintaining a sound standard of efficiency and enterprise.

At a dinner on 29 April 1948 to mark the retirement of the Board, one of the guests was Sir Malcolm Stewart. He recalled that 'there were many Jeremiahs when the experiment was launched', but team work had produced a permanent memorial to every person engaged in it. 'Here was the free gift of free enterprise not only to a district, but to a nation'. He regretted the break-up of an efficient team and advised the government that 'it should lay down high policy, but the administrative details should be left to those with practical knowledge and practical experience to carry them out. I respectfully ask the government to think again' [60].

There remains to examine briefly how far the new arrangements were in line with the recommendations of the Select Committee.

The executive chairman had been appointed and the President of the Board of Trade had exercised his powers under the revised Articles to appoint a new Board.

But the draft of the Finance Agreement, tabled at the first meeting of the new Board on 11 May 1948, fell far short of expectations. Walton expressed the general view 'that the draft was a completely negative document confining itself ... to saying what the Company was not to do and giving little indication of any constructive functions which a responsible Board of Directors should exercise'. While Sadler Forster hoped that arrangements would be made for more freedom ... under the heading of 'finance', he held out no hope that the Company would be permitted 'to handle policy matters relating to the distribution of industry which Ministers had decided should be determined by their departmental officials'.

The final version of the Agreement was tabled at the Board meeting on 8 November 1948. Chapman observed that the Agreement failed to give the Company either the promised block grants or any autonomy. Sadler Forster explained why 'it was administratively impossible for the Board of Trade to give block grants under present conditions' [61].

The government had substantially failed to adopt the solution preferred by the Select Committee, although the brake on new factory construction under the economic emergency measures adopted a year earlier would have made block grants of little immediate importance.

The arrival of Sadler Forster should have brought with it a number of benefits: he had a long record of commitment to the welfare of the North East; he had worked for the Board of Trade since 1943 and his knowledge of the civil service machinery and mentality, as well as his many contacts, should have succeeded where the Company's officers had failed. But his appointment did not solve the outstanding problems between the Company and the Board of Trade.

If anything, the Board of Trade increased its grip on the Company's activities. The control of small items of expenditure is an extreme example of this; the schedule in Appendix 30 shows items of less than £100 in value for which spending authority had to be sought in London in the year Sadler Forster was appointed. He would eventually feel as frustrated as the Company's officers had been under the old regime [61].

Although the last vestiges of its independence had been removed, North Eastern Trading Estates Ltd continued to exist for another 12 years before it disappeared altogether in a further, more extensive reorganisation of the administration of government-financed factories in Development Areas. But the first day of May 1948 marked the end of an era.

REFERENCES AND NOTES

V/1.   Factory Construction after the War

[1]   Central Statistical Office, 1952, Table 127, p.108. The total personnel in the Armed Forces in June 1945 was 5.9 million. 3.06 million of these had been demobilised by June 1946.
[2]   Odber, J. Alan, 1965, p.338.
[3]   BT 106/24, Ministerial Sub-Committee on Industrial Problems, 9.6.1944.
[4]   TWA,1762/8, Chancellor of the Exchequer (Hugh Dalton) to Company chairman (Chapman), 29.5.1946.
[5]   TWA,1752/11, memorandum by Whitehouse, 'General Arguments used against Location of Industry in Development Areas with some Counter-Arguments', 12.5.1954.

[6]   HC Deb 421, 1807.

[7]   HC Deb 428, 307, outline of the rationale of the policy by Sir
      Stafford Cripps: 'we have attempted to avoid concentration upon
      any particular size and type of industry and to give as large a
      spread as possible so far as type and size of manufacture is
      concerned'. On the other hand, Allen, E. et al., 1957, p.30, have
      pointed out: 'we know of no definition of "a balanced structure
      of industry": indeed, the phrase taken by itself is meaningless'.

[8]   TWA,1762/7, undated 'Note of a Meeting with Sir Stafford Cripps at
      the Registered Offices of the Company on Saturday, 22nd September
      1945.'

[9]   Pepler, G. & McFarlane, P.W., ca.1949.

[10] BT 105/54, 'Note of a meeting held on 20 December (1944) to
      discuss factory building under the Special Areas Acts', and
      correspondence, Control of Factory and Storage Premises Divison,
      Board of Trade (Jay) with Treasury (Proctor), January and
      February 1945.

[11] TWA,1762/9, Chapman to Board of Trade (Calder), 13.9.1947.

[12] McCrone, G., 1971, p.114.

[13] Dalton, Hugh, 1962, p.107.

[14] Op.cit.[4].

[15] TWA,1762/8, Chapman to Hugh Dalton, 6.5.1946.

[16] Slowe, Peter M., 1981, p.17.

[17] TWA,1395, Box 410, File GM 102/1, Regional Office, Board of Trade
      to Directorate for Industrial Estates, Board of Trade (Sadler
      Forster), 17.8.1946.

[18] The Company refused to supply information at least on one
      occasion: in response to a request by the Directorate for
      Industrial Estates for details of building contract tenders
      (asked for by the Treasury), the Company's reply contained the
      following: '(my directors) do not welcome proposals for placing
      burdens, however small, on the staff which are apparently
      unproductive and it is for this reason that they decided that in
      this particular instance your request should not be acceeded to'.
      TWA,1762/9, Company Secretary to Board of Trade (Miss Mocatta),
      31.1.1947.

[19] Op.cit.[16].

[20] TWA,1762/9, Cripps to Chapman, 9.5.1947.

[21] EIE, Annual Report for 1948/1949.

[22] TWA,1762/4, General Managers' report, 'The Activities of the
      Company from September 1938 to December 1939', 20.2.1940, p.5.

[23] RCDIP, 1940, p.283.

[24] BT 106/100. The file also provides employment figures at Team
      Valley, the pre-War outside sites and at the former ROFs Aycliffe
      and Spennymoor.

[25] For Team Valley, the data nearest to the end of the War was found
      in BT 106/100, 'North East Development Area, Numbers on Payroll
      in Government Financed Factories and Trading Estates', 23.3.1946.
      At that date, 7,729 people were employed on the Estate. There
      will have been a run-down in War production and a change-over to
      civilian employment. For the computation in Table 12, it was
      assumed that the increase in employment at Team Valley and the
      outside sites was created by new construction between 1945 and
      1948. On balance, the assumed figure for the employment at the
      end of the War can be justified. Employment in the six wartime
      factories on 30.3.1949 is not known and has been estimated on the
      basis of relative floor area, i.e. 40% of that at Team Valley at

the end of the War. This method is likely to lead to an underestimate. The employment at Aycliffe and Spennymoor on 30.9.1948 is known from a handwritten note in BT 106/101.

[26] White Paper, 1948, Appendix 7, p.48, claims that 9,246 people were employed in new government and privately-financed factories and extensions over 5,000 sq.ft. in the North East on 30.6.1948. There are grounds for believing that the employment credited to new government-financed factories in Table 12 is an overestimate. This would further strengthen the conclusions.

V/2.   The 1946 Advance Factory Programme

[1]   Slowe, Peter, M., 1981, p.3.
[2]   TWA,1762/2, Appleyard to Commissioner, 18.8.1936.
[3]   TWA,1762/2, Company Secretary to Commissioner, 15.10.1936, p.4.
[4]   TWA,1762/2, report by Sir Alexander Gibb & Partners, (e), p.8, 13.3.1936.
[5]   TWA,1762/2, Commissioner to Company secretary, 16.11.1936.
[6]   Ibid.
[7]   TWA,1762/2, General Manager's report for December 1936.
[8]   BT 104/28, Commissioner (Boyd) to Min. of Labour (Ayres), 3.3.1938.
[9]   Select Committee on Estimates, 1947, para. 79, pp.10 & 11.
[10]   Booth, Alan, 1982, p.12.
[11]   HC Deb 400, 1392.
[12]   Dalton, Hugh, 1957, p.440.
[13]   Op.cit.10.
[14]   TWA,1762/9, 'Details of Wartime Factories', dated August 1947.
[15]   TWA,1762/7, 'Trading Estate Companies', minutes of meeting on 7.11.1945.
[16]   Ibid.
[17]   TWA,1762/8, Chapman to Cripps, 10.1.1946.
[18]   TWA,1762/8, Cripps to Chapman, 29.1.1946.
[19]   TWA,1762/7, undated draft, ca. December 1945, Chapman to Hugh Dalton.
[20]   Op.cit.[9], pp.10,11.
[21]   Op.cit.[15]. The intentions were confirmed in Select Committee on Estimates, 1947, para.47, p.xv: 'the Board of Trade decided to erect a number of standard factories in advance of demand, in order to provide read-made premises, as an inducement to manufacturers wishing to get into production quickly'.
[22]   TWA,1762/8, minutes of 1st meeting of Consultative Committee on Trading Estates, 14.3.1946, pts.5 & 6.
[23]   BT 104/70.
[24]   TWA,1762/8, notes, probably by Methven, on 2nd meeting of Consultative Committee, 11.4.1946, p.3.
[25]   TWA,1762/8, Sadler Forster to Board of Trade, Regional Office (Brazendale), 2.5.1946.
[26]   TWA,1762/8, Brazendale to Sadler Forster, 4.5.1946.
[27]   TWA,1762/8, Methven to Brazendale, 14.5.1946.
[28]   Ibid.
[29]   TWA,1762/8, this is evident from the 'Notes of a meeting held at Team Valley', 23.5.1946.
[30]   Ibid.
[31]   Op.cit.[27].
[32]   TWA,1762/8, Sadler Forster to Brazendale, 31.5.1946.

[33] TWA,1762/8, internal note from Methven to Perry, 15.7.1946.

[34] TWA,1395, Box 410, File 102/1, Distribution of Industry and Regional Division, Board of Trade (Bowden) to Company (Methven), 31.8.1946. The Company (Progress Manager) replied to Board of Trade on 5.9.1946.

[35] Op.cit.[9].

[36] TWA,1762/9, Chapman to Board of Trade (Calder), 13.9.1947.

[37] TWA,1762/9, separate from [36], Chapman to Board of Trade, (Calder), 13.9.1947.

V/3.   The Economic Crisis of 1947

[1] HC Deb 441, 1657, Hugh Dalton quoted US imports as $ 8 billion and exports as $21 billion.

[2] HC Deb 443, 277.

[3] Central Statistical Office, 1952, p.302: between 1946 and 1947 the wholesale price index (old series) rose from 172.7 to 189.1 (1943 = 160.4).

[4] HC Deb 443, 280.

[5] The papers of the Consultative Committee on Trading Estates are in BT 177/18.

[6] TWA,1762/9, Board of Trade (Calder) to Methven, 24.10.1947.

[7] TWA,1762/9, notes of a meeting of the Company's staff, 27.10.1947.

[8] TWA,1762/9, Board of Trade, Regional Office (Ashwanden) to Company (Perry), 30.10.1947.

[9] Ibid.

[10] TWA,1762/9, minutes of a meeting between Methven and Rhodes, 29.10.1947.

[11] TWA,1762/9, Methven to Directorate for Industrial Estates, Board of Trade (Miss Mocatta) 4.11.1947.

[12] TWA,1762/9, internal note on the legal liability for abandoning agreed factory projects, Smith to Methven et al, 29.10.1947.

[13] HC Deb 443, 278.

[14] The recommendations (believed to be the final ones) are in TWA,1762/9. The full record is in TWA,1395, Box 573, File M 1831.

[15] TWA,1762/9, Methven to Board of Trade, Regional Office (Rhodes,) 4.11.1947.

[16] Odber, J. Alan, 1965, p.339.

[17] Quoted in McCrone, G., 1971, p.112.

[18] White Paper, 1947.

[19] The (incomplete) reports up to 1952 are in TWA,1762/11.

V/4.   Policy and the Changing Role of the Company

[1] TWA,1762/6, Methven to Appleyard, 3.2.1944, p.1.

[2] McCrone, G., 1971, p.215.

[3] Ibid.

[4] Pepler, G. & MacFarlane, P.W., ca.1949.

[5] EIEB, minute 1423, 1.9.1944.

[6] TWA,1762/6, Methven to Hugh Dalton and Bevin, 10.10.1944.

[7] EIEB, minute 1431, 1.9.1944.

[8] TWA,1762/6, Martin to Methven, 21.11.1944.

[9] TWA,1762/6, Methven to Martin, 23.11.1944.

[10] TWA,1762/6, undated memorandum by Company (Methven) 'President of

the Board of Trade'. This must have been sent before 29.11.1944, the date of the meeting with Dalton.

[11] TWA,1395, Box 590, File M 1811, note of a telephone conversation Methven/Forbes Adam regarding the visit by Dalton and 'his Commission', from which it emerges that he was to be afforded the minimum courtesies.
[12] RO Circular 1/29 referred to in [13] below. The circular itself has not been found.
[13] TWA,1762/6, Methven to Appleyard, 24.10.1944.
[14] TWA,1762/6, Methven's notes (Memorandum) of the meeting with the President of the Board of Trade, 30.11.1944.
[15] TWA,1762/3, unsigned and undated memorandum to Methven, headed 'Outside Sites', almost certainly by Whitehouse, sales representative (later Sales Manager) of Company, ca. August 1937. Related to a memorandum by Percival, Company Secretary 'Sites outside the Team Valley Estate' 16.8.1937 in the same file.
[16] EIEB, minute 1538, 11.5.1945.
[17] TWA,1762/7, Warter to Chapman, 20.7.1945.
[18] TWA,1762/7, Chapman to Warter, 25.7.1945.
[19] TWA,1762/7, undated memorandum (retyped), 'Visit of the President of the Board of Trade to the Team Valley Estate, Gateshead, proposed for September 22nd 1945'.
[20] TWA,1762/7, undated 'Note of Meeting with Sir Stafford Cripps at the Registered Offices of the Company on Saturday, 22nd September 1945'.
[21] TWA,1762/7, memorandum, headed North East Development Area, Diversification of Industrial Activity, entitled 'North Eastern Trading Estates Ltd request greater liberty of action in performing its function of "Instrument of Government"'.25.9.1945.
[22] TWA,1762/7, minutes of a meeting of the Northern Regional Board on 1.10.1945, attached to a letter of 19.10.1945 by Redpath, the Regional Controller of the Board of Trade at Newcastle. The quotations show that the regional officers of at least two government departments were against more autonomy for the Company.
[23] BT 106/57, Brazendale to Sadler Forster, 31.1.1946.
[24] TWA,1762/7, Cripps to Methven, 24.10.1945, with the attachment of a memorandum from Warter to Cripps, 19.10.1945.
[25] TWA,1762/7, minutes of meeting, 'Trading Estate Companies', 7.11.1945.
[26] TWA,1762/7, Methven's notes of the meeting on 7 November in London with Warter and other government trading estate executives, attached to his letter to Chapman, 8.11.1945.
[27] From letter in op.cit.[26].
[28] TWA,1762/8, minutes of 1st meeting of Consultative Committee on Trading Estates, 14.3.1946, point 20.
[29] TWA,1762/8, Company Secretary to Sadler Forster, 4.7.1946.
[30] TWA,1762/8, Sadler Forster to Company (Percival), 9.7.1946.
[31] TWA,1762/8, Chapman to President of the Board of Trade, 10.1.1946.
[32] TWA,1762/8, Cripps to Chapman, 29.1.1946.
[33] TWA,1762/8, Board of Trade, Directorate for Industrial Estates (Moat) to Methven, 23.8.1946.
[34] TWA,1762/8, Methven to Directorate of Industrial Estates, Board of Trade (V.I.Chapman), 8.10.1946.
[35] TWA,1762/8, Methven to Chapman, 4.10.1946.
[36] TWA,1762/8, Methven to Fleck, 8.10.1946.

[37]   TWA,1762/9, A copy of the undated Heads of Agreement are attached
        to a letter from Chapman to Cripps, 9.1.1947.
[38]   TWA,1762/8, Bruce to Chapman, 24.10.1946.
[39]   TWA,1762/8, Chapman to Cripps, 11.12.1946.
[40]   The letter is referred to in op.cit.[37].
[41]   Ibid.
[42]   TWA,1762/9, internal memorandum, Irvine to Methven, 13.3.1947.
[43]   TWA,1762/9, Chapman to Cripps, 5.5.1947.
[44]   TWA,1762/9, Cripps to Chapman, 13.5.1947.
[45]   TWA,1782/9, Chapman to Cripps, 19.5.1947.
[46]   Select Committee on Estimates, 1947.
[47]   TWA,1782/9, Cripps to Chapman, 28.5.1947.
[48]   TWA,1762/9, Chapman to Cripps, 2.6.1947.
[49]   Op.cit.[46], para.59, p.xix.
[50]   TWA,1762/9, 'Notes for Meeting with President of the Board of
        Trade', probably by Methven, 20.10.1947.
[51]   TWA,1762/9, 'Report of Sir George Martin's meeting with the
        President on 23.10.1947'.
[52]   TWA,1762/9, Harold Wilson to Chapman, 10.11.1947.
[53]   TWA,1762/9, handwritten note from a private address, signature
        unreadable, to Methven, 21.11.1947, probably by secretary of the
        Scottish estates company.
[54]   TWA,1762/9, Sir Steven Bilsland (chairman of Scottish estates
        company) to Chapman, 15.12.1947.
[55]   TWA,1762/9, Chapman to Harold Wilson, 4.12.1947.
[56]   TWA,1762/10, notes by Methven, 'Meeting with the President of the
        Board of Trade ... , London, ... 19th February 1948'.
[57]   EIEB, minute 2036, 2.2.1948.
[58]   TWA,1762/10, Methven to Sadler Forster, 2.3.1948.
[59]   Personal interview with Col. Percival, February 1984.
[60]   EIE, Journal of Events, newspaper cutting, believed to have been
        the North Mail , Newcastle upon Tyne, 30.4.1948.
[61]   EIEB, minute 2184, 8.11.1948.
[62]   Personal discussion with Sadler Forster in the spring of 1972. He
        had ceased to be executive chairman on reaching the age of 65 in
        1965, but continued as non-executive chairman until September
        1970. He died on 24 June 1973.

Conclusions

This study has shown that government-financed factories were the main tools of regional policies applied within the Areas, both in the pre-War period and in the immediate post-War years. The aim of this final chapter is to attempt a critical examination of some aspects of the policies, their implementation and the impact they made on employment in the North East. The chapter will end with a brief look beyond 1948.

The most significant political outcome of the pre-War depression was the belated recognition by the government that market forces alone would not make an adequate contribution to the solution of the problems of the depressed areas within a tolerable time span. A modest level of intervention was eventually accepted, but it was looked upon as an exceptional departure for a limited period. When unemployment declined - as it did continuously between 1934 and the autumn of 1937 (see Appendix 19) - the Cabinet was initially in favour of terminating the Special Areas legislation, although the decline was not the result of any structural improvement. But there was little interest in structural questions; the government looked for solutions to the problems of the depressed areas - and claimed achievements - almost wholly in terms of a reduction in unemployment.

Any conclusions about the Team Valley experiment in the pre-War period must be tentative, because only two years elapsed between the occupation of the first factories in September 1937 and the onset of the War. By that time, the factories in the Estate employed between 3,000 and 4,000 people (see Appendix 14).

At first sight, this employment may seem significant in relation to the unemployment in the Gateshead area given in Table 18.

Table 18

Live Register of Wholly Unemployed People in the Gateshead Area
10 July 1939

Labour Exchange or Employment Office	Men	Boys	Women	Girls	Totals	Women, Boys & Girls
Gateshead	4,845	112	635	189	5,781	936
Dunston *	617	-	-	-	617	-
Felling	1,393	21	89	49	1,552	159
Chester-le-Street **	1,025	98	42	188	1,353	328
Birtley *	449	-	27	-	476	27
	8,329	231	793	426	9,779	1,450

* No figures are available for juveniles (and women at Dunston)
  but given the relatively small male unemployment figures,
  the number is likely to have been small.
** includes figures from the Juvenile Employment Bureau

Source: TWA, 1762/20.

But as the large majority of the 3,000 people employed at Team Valley
in the summer of 1939 were women and juveniles under the age of 18 -
perhaps as many as 2,100 (70%) [1] -, it must be concluded from Table 18
that a large proportion of these workers either came from other places
in the area or there was an increase in the female activity rate, or
both. Table 18 also shows that even if all the approximately 900 men
employed at Team Valley had come from the Gateshead area, it would not
have had a significant effect on the unemployment registers.

As for the structural impact of the industries at Team Valley, Table 4
and the discussion in III/6 show that it was negligible.

How successful was the Team Valley Estate before the War in attracting
industries from outside the region? Apart from the employment created on
the Estate, this is the most interesting question.

The intensive public relations effort resulted in a significant number
of enquiries - including some from large firms -, but only 21
manufacturers from outside the region took up tenancies in the event
(see Appendix 21).

An examination of the background of these firms shows that only a
minority appear to have made locational choices in the usual sense (see
Appendix 22). There were only eight branch plants, and one of these was
an expansion scheme of a branch already established in the area (No.94).

All but two of the eight new firms from outside the region (Nos.83 &
84) involved individual entrepreneurs, for whom the availability of
small factories and the hope of loans may have been the main reason for
coming to Team Valley (in one case, No.80, the presence of family played
a part, and in another, No.82, a local partner). Factories and the
possibility of loans appear to have influenced at least two of the five
small firms to move existing businesses to Team Valley (Nos.86 and 87),

Refugees apart, only a single firm from abroad has been identified (No.95).

Given the limited amount of serious interest from significant companies on the one hand, and the need to retain the interest and commitment of the government on the other, the Company had little latitude in the choice of tenants.

While the proviso made earlier must be borne in mind, a few conclusions may, nevertheless, be drawn with some certainty.

The availability of small modern factories for rent - in an area that was still depressed - encouraged at least some new local initiatives. This, in itself, was a significant discovery.

As important, the experience of manufacturers had shown that adult labour was adaptable, that juvenile labour was quick to learn, and that the supporting structure and services were adequate to permit light manufacturing to be carried on successfully. Fogarty [2] believed that this was a demonstration British industry needed in order to change its attitude to the North East, a part of the country that was widely considered to be suitable only for heavy industries.

Had it not been for the War and the fear of War - and given a reasonably stable economic environment -, it is likely, therefore, that more firms from outside the region would have rented factories at Team Valley, perhaps even at an increasing rate.

Not the least important aspect of the Team Valley experiment was the character of the organisation which built and managed the Estate. Public Utility Societies had previously been used for housing and land settlement. At Team Valley, this type of organisation is believed to have been used for the first time for industrial development.

The Estate represented a large public works project (see Appendix 15). It was carried out under initially difficult weather conditions and in the face of a severe shortage of steel. Yet barely three years had elapsed between the arrival of the contractors on the swampy 700 acre site and the time when more than 100 tenants were in occupation, including 76 manufacturing firms. This was a considerable achievement, which owed much to the fact that the Estates Company was run like an entrepreneurial private business.

While no performance targets seem to have been set, both the government and the Commissioner were surprised and pleased that factories were apparently being let as fast as they were being built: 'the Team Valley Estate has surpassed all our expectations' wrote the Minister of Labour in June 1938 [3]. A more careful analysis might have caused some anxieties when lettings fell off at the end of 1937 (see Table 2), even if refugees partly made up for this later.

Neither the government nor the Commissioner seem to have had any views on the relevance of tenant industries to the structural needs of the region. Apart from employment creation, the achievement of commercial viability of the Estate was the main concern.

It is probable that the results obtained by the Team Valley Estate were overestimated before the War. Yet it was precisely the _apparent_ success of this and the other pre-War government-financed trading estates that influenced the post-War policy makers, as Jay has confirmed [4]. But the role and character of the companies set up to develop the estates was not fully appreciated. If this had been understood, the post-War organisation for the construction of government-financed factories might well have been structured differently.

Because of their small size and the nature of their locations, no conclusions are being attempted about the outside sites up to the War.

In contrast with the pre-War situation, the post-War planners were not faced with the need to reduce unemployment. Their task was to develop practical policies to prevent it, both in the transition period from war to peace - which was expected to be difficult for some localities in the North East - and in the longer-term, when the expected post-War boom would come to an end.

Although the government's aim was to achieve a better balance of industry in the region, the policy was really employment-directed. In practice, it appears to have been assumed that any kind of viable industry moving into the North East and other Development Areas would contribute to permanent structural change.

The first doubts on this issue were raised by Methven early in 1944, when he asked whether the region would prosper 'if it attracted a heterogeneous mass of sundry and unrelated industry'. [5]. Whatever the intention was - and a rationale for selecting industries for particular locations certainly existed [6] -, the list of the Company's tenants for July 1948 does not reveal any particular structural intentions [7].

The policy - like its pre-War predecessor - 'did not rest on any considered judgment about the right location of industries up and down the country', but was based largely on a desire 'to attract any sort of industry into areas in which there was an evident shortage of jobs' [8]. Diversification was aimed at, but in a purely local and limited sense.

When the policy was devised - in the War years 1943/1944 -, there might not have been enough time for such considerations, but it can be argued that the failure to consider structural aspects more seriously was inherent both in the origins and aims of Development Areas policy; the government departments and individuals who formulated the implementation of the policy had successfully organised production in the Areas during the War. On the basis of that experience, the planners would look upon the prevention of unemployment largely as a problem of putting men and women into _production_ ; Booth [9] believes that they saw the solution to unemployment largely in terms of moving industries in search of labour to places where labour would be available.

Given the pessimistic assumptions made by most of those concerned with post-War planning about the medium-term employment prospects of the region, a policy to create the maximum employment rather than to change the industrial structure of the region was defensible for the immediate post-War period; the error was to continue the policy unchanged when the assumptions proved to be erroneous.

Although there were individual entrepreneurs from outside ·the region, the implementation rules of the 1945 Act resulted in the establishment mainly of branch factories of national and foreign firms, i.e. of production units. They would demand and create few of the new skills the region needed. It was feared at the time that this would limit 'spin-off' - the continuous creation of new indigenous economic activity. While this fear proved to be apparently justified for a generation, the business recession starting in the mid-1970s and the withdrawal of many branch factories resulted, in fact, in the establishment of a substantial number of successful new manufacturing businesses by former managers and specialists from such factories.

For critics of the branch factory economy, the doubts expressed about the reliance on such factories in other than boom times [10] presented even greater - although, in the medium-term, largely unjustified concerns.

In contrast with the pre-War period, the attraction of industries did not prove to be a problem in the years immediately after 1945. The demand for factory space and labour was so great that manufacturers would go wherever they would find them.

The government was in almost total control of industrial location through the building licensing system. Insofar as this was used as a 'negative' control, it was applied outside the Areas , but it would be effective only if manufacturers were able to rent or build factories as soon as possible within the Areas .

It is appropriate, therefore, to consider how effectively the government-financed factory programme - the main form of government action under the 1945 Act within the Areas [11] - was carried out, particularly the programme of new construction.

The first observation must be that the programme started too late to have any effect on the most difficult period after the War. Of the 5.09 million men and women in the Services in June 1945, 3.06 million had been released by June 1946 [12]. Although the construction of government-financed factories in the North East had begun before that date, only five factories with an estimated employment for 470 people had been completed by 30 August 1946. Even 13 months later - for reasons outlined in V/1 and V/2 -, only 30% of the construction target for the period was reached.

There can be little doubt that the late start and the failure to complete the programme on time was largely due to the fact that it was planned and directed by central government.

The 1944 White Paper had proposed 'that there should be a single channel through which government policy on the distribution of industry can be expressed', but it was taken for granted that no single department could conveniently undertake the responsibility for administering the policy [13]. Superimposed on the inter-departmental decision-making process was an involved procedure within the Board of Trade, which assigned too little initiative to the organisations in the regions. The process of planning and constructing factories and matching industries to particular locations, therefore, was bound to be a much more complex process than before the War, even if the building licensing and materials allocation procedures are left out of account.

Given the complexity, the evident errors in planning - both on the demand and supply sides of labour and materials - were probably unavoidable. On the other hand, the problems arising out of the control by the Board of Trade of almost all aspects of the implementation of the programme were not: the Select Committee on Estimates had concluded that the 1945 Act would permit a return to the pre-War system of block grants [14], which the Commissioners for the Special Areas had operated successfully. Such a system would have kept the effective control of the programme in the hands of the Company.

The downgrading of the role of the Company to that of land and building agent for the government cannot have been conducive to efficiency, particularly at a time when a great deal of improvisation was necessary.

These observations must lead to the paradoxical conclusion that a policy measure unforeseen in the 1934 Special Areas Act was carried into effect by an efficient organisation - the Company -, while the implementation of a crucial part of post-War Development Area policy was subjected to the full rigours of bureaucratic, and therefore, inflexible and time-consuming control.

A 1948 White Paper [15] gave some indication of the assumptions made in 1945 of the additional job opportunities needed to provide full employment in the Development Areas, but the 1946 factory construction programme (Table 7) provides the only clear indication of the government's plans for the North East in the immediate post-War period.

Table 19 shows the intentions in relation to the insured population. The figures are global ones for the region. It is evident from Table 7 that the ratio of male/female employment expected to result from the 1946 factory programme differed in the three programme areas. The averages do not, therefore, fully describe the position. With this proviso, it can be seen that, for the region as a whole, the male employment expected to result from government-financed factories was relatively small, while that for females foresaw a greatly increased activity rate.

If the government's forecasts of the employment needs of the region had proved to be right, the delay in the completion of factories would have resulted in the loss of opportunities to locate manufacturers in the North East, particularly in the smaller single-industry places.

But in spite of the sharp increase in the insured population since 1939 (see Appendix 31) and the relatively small contribution to employment made by the government-financed factories and wartime factory conversions up to 1948 (see Table 14), the North East enjoyed full employment.

This satisfactory situation owed much less to the distribution of industry policy than to other policies of the government and the recovery in world demand.

Full employment caused a shortage of labour in a few localities in the North East and some manufacturers who had moved into the region were unable to fill all their vacancies.

The delayed completion of the government-financed factory programme and the cuts made in 1947 effectively re-phased the 1946 programme in line with the realities of the supply of materials and labour.

Table 19

Employment expected from the 1946 Factory Programme
as a Percentage of the Insured Population in 1946 and 1948

Type of Projected Factories	Insured Population Males	Females
Treasury- financed New and Conversions	35,900	47,500
Privately-financed	17,900	8,650
	------	------
	53,800	56,150
	------	------
Male Insured, 1946,	706,550	
Female Insured, 1946,		233,660
Male Insured, 1948	885,900	
Female Insured, 1948		331,930
% Contribution to Employment by the 1946 Factory Programme	1946 7.6%	24.0%
	1948 6.1%	16.9%

Sources: Table 7 and Appendix 31.

The government's overestimate of the employment needs of the North East was largely due to its anxiety to prevent a recurrence of serious unemployment. Dennison, who had worked throughout the War in the Economic Section of the War Cabinet Secretariat (and had become Chief Economic Assistant), had warned in October 1945 that 'the conditions of the 1930s are a bad guide to future policy' [16], but the outlook of the Labour Government remained profoundly influenced by the experience of that decade.

Economists, on the other hand, had overestimated the distortions in the economy resulting from the distribution of industry policy, and from the 'black-spot' policy within Development Areas. With hindsight, it can be seen that such fears were not justified: the total amount of money spent by the Board of Trade between 1946/47 - 1948/49 in all the Development Areas scheduled under the 1945 Act - almost wholly in the form of investment in factories - was £29.2 million, while Treasury loans in the same period totalled only £1 million [17].

Male unemployment in the Northern Region remained at very low levels for almost 15 years after the War. Between 1948 and 1950, the rate was 2.8%, declining continuously to 1.4% in 1956 (see Appendix 34).

313

In striking contrast with the inter-War years, the rate differed little from the national average. From 1956 - 1958, the difference was only 0.2%. Moreover, the low male unemployment rates were achieved in spite of the fact that many of the incoming industries provided employment mainly for females.

Since the traditional industries of the region continued to prosper, the need for restructuring appeared to be not only less pressing but also less feasible because there would not have been the labour to sustain it. 'Governments may perhaps be excused for supposing during this period that the regional problem was virtually solved' wrote McCrone [18], but the boom had merely masked the underlying problems and postponed the time when they would have to be faced. In the meantime, too high a proportion of the men and boys in the region were employed, once again, in those industries which had suffered serious decline before the War and might do so again in the future.

If these conclusions were to end here, they would be incomplete and misleading. Just as the real significance of the Team Valley experiment rested in its longer-term influence, so the post-War government-financed factories would make a considerable impact on the economy of the North East many years later. This delayed effect was largely due to the fact that the period of post-War prosperity lasted so much longer than expected. The figures in Apendix 31 show that the decline in employment in the coal mining industry did not begin until 1957. The decline of the shipbuilding and ship repairing industry started in 1959, but employment in the heavy engineering industries in the North East continued to grow for at least 25 years after the end of the War.

When the long period of post-War prosperity enjoyed by the traditional industries finally came to an end, the light industries which the distribution of industry policy had brought to the North East in the years before and after 1948 and the government-financed factories which continued to be built - although at a much slower rate than during the immediate post-War years - began to make a significant impact on the the industrial structure of the region. This is clearly indicated in Table 20.

It may be concluded, therefore, that the distribution of industry policy came into its own just when it was beginning to be really needed, - about 20 years after the end of the War - and that the government-financed factories then played their intended role. Although there was still no real structural policy and the location policy was pursued less firmly, the increase in employment in new industries and the decline of the traditional ones resulted, in effect, in an improvement in the industrial structure of the North East.

Nor was this the sum total of the positive changes resulting from the policy: the diversified employment achieved in government factories not under the control of the Company or its successor organisations and in the privately-financed projects must be added. An indication of the employment expected from such projects in the 1946 factory programme is given in Table 7. Later figures are not readily available, but the 1960s saw the inward movement of many important firms.

Table 20
Structural Impact of Government-Financed Factories 1948 and 1970

Employment in	Coal Mining	3 Basic* Industries	In Company's** Factories	% of Mining	% of 3 Basic Industries
1948	172,410	319,650	30,000	17.40	9.38
1970	72,400	263,400	94,678	130.77	35.94

  * Coal Mining, Shipbuilding and Repairing, Heavy Engineering
** In 1970, the Company's successor organisation is meant here

Sources: Appendixes 26 and 31.

The availability of - mainly small - advance factories of standard design, usually grouped on industrial estates or smaller sites, was now widely seen to be an important factor in economic development, particularly when supported by a variety of inducements. Other bodies concerned with industrial development and employment began to offer factories for rent: New Town Corporations, local authorities, and when the tax regime made it apparently profitable, even private developers. By the end of 1984, it was estimated that less than half of the modern factories available for rent in the North East had been financed by central government [19].

Given the reluctance of private developers to invest in industrial estates in the North East in the inter-War years, the Team Valley Estate can now be seen to have fulfilled an essential role: it demonstrated that factories available for rent were commercially viable prerequisites for industrial development in economically depressed peripheral areas with a background of mining and heavy industry.

Sir Malcolm Stewart's 'Novel and Unorthodox Proposal' of more than 50 years ago has long been adopted in orthodox practice. It has had a powerful and lasting effect not only on the North East and similar regions in Britain, but on countries in widely varying stages of industrial development.

REFERENCES AND NOTES

[1]   The Company's reports to the Commissioner gave the total number of employees without analysis. Fogarty, M.P., 1945, p.178, claims that half the workers at Team Valley at the outbreak of the War were girls under the age of 18. Adding women and boys, this would mean that something like 65% - 70% of the workers were females and boys. Appleyard, K.C., 1939, (p.862, reply to Dr. Paterson) claimed that half the workers in June 1939 (i.e. about 1,500) were boys and girls under the age of 18 and that of the adults, the majority were men, i.e., the share of male employment would be more than 25%.

[2]   Fogarty, M.P., 1945, p.179.

[3]   CAB 37/578, DA (34) 16, memorandum by Minister of Labour, 13.6.1938.

[4]   Jay, D., 1980, p.112.

[5]   TWA,1762/6, Methven to Appleyard, 3.2.1944.

[6]   For an outline of the rationale, see Sir Stafford Cripps,
      HC Deb 428, 307, quoted in [7], p. 302.

[7]   TWA,1395/3110,'List of Tenants in Occupation as at 8 July 1948'.
      This coveres all tenants in factories under the control of the
      Company, with products made or services provided.

[8]   Cole, G.D.H., Introduction to Fogarty, M.P., 1945, p.xxxi.

[9]   Booth, Alan, 1982.

[10] For example, Pepler, G. & McFarlane, P.W., ca.1949.

[11] McCrone, G., 1971, p.114.

[12] Central Statistical Office, 1952, p.108.

[13] White Paper, 1944, para.30, p.13.

[14] Select Committee on Estimates, 1947, para 16, p.xix.

[15] White Paper, 1948, para.56, p.19.

[16] CAB 124/218, memorandum by S.R.Dennison to Lord President,
      23.10.1945, commenting on a memorandum by the Minister of Labour,
      CP.(45) 228.

[17] Op.cit.[11].

[18] Op.cit.[11], p.116.

[19] The research group at the Department of Trade & Industry at
      Newcastle (ref. E. Stringer, July 1985) was not in possession of
      any list covering all government-financed factories in the
      region, nor of those owned by local authorites, New Town
      Corporations or private estates companies and other investors. In
      an interview on 30 August 1985, K. John, the secretary of the
      English Estates Corporation, believed it was probable that the
      Corporation now owned less than half the number of factories in
      the region available for rent. On the basis of sqare footage ,
      however, the position may be different because the other
      providers of such factories have built mainly small or very small
      factories. The position may be different again if occupied square
      footage is considered, given that at the time of the interview
      some of the largest factories owned by the Estates Corporation
      were unoccupied. Government-financed factories subsequently sold
      to tenants add a further complication.

Sources and bibliography

I. PRIMARY SOURCES

1. The Papers of North Eastern Trading Estates Ltd.

The Company and its successor organisations have been absorbed by the English Industrial Estates Corporation (St. George's House, Kingsway, Team Valley, Gateshead NE11 ONA). The papers used are of four kinds:-

a. The Files of the Company.

In 1982, the files were transferred to the Tyne & Wear Archives (Blandford House, Blandford Street, Newcastle upon Tyne NE1 4JA). They are available under accession number 1395.

Copies of most of the material used have been deposited at the Tyne and Wear Archives under accession number 1762. They are available under the following numbers:-

1762/2,	files for the year(s)	1936
1762/3,	"	1937
1762/4,	"	1938
1762/5,	"	1939
1762/6,	"	1940-1944
1762/7,	"	1945
1762/8,	"	1946
1762/9,	"	1947
1762/10,	"	1948
1762/11,	"	post-1948

317

Papers used but not copied are in 1395, followed by the old box and file numbers (where file numbers existed), and, in a few cases, by the new file numbers.

The study was begun before the documents were transferred and re-catalogued by the Tyne & Wear Archives. The catalogue became available only shortly before the study was completed. The staff of the Archives are able to correlate the old references with the new ones.

b. The Minute Books of the Boards of Directors of the Company

These have been transferred to the Tyne & Wear Archives early in 1987. Typed abstracts of relevant items made by the author have been placed in TWA,1762/12.

c. A Microfilm File

This contains the correspondence with the early tenants. The file was transferred to the Tyne & Wear Archives early in 1987.

d. A Variety of other Documents relating to the early Years.

Those consulted include the Rent Book from 1 August 1938 (the earlier one having been lost), a Journal of Events, 1939 to 1956, Annual Accounts and Reports, and promotion material. These documents are being retained by the Corporation. Some pictorial material, however, has been transferred to the Tyne & Wear Archives.

Progress Information

Copies of the correspondence between the Company and the Commissioner and the available progress returns from 1937 - 1941 have been placed together in TWA,1762/13. Copies of the relevant progress reports for the immediate post-War period from the Directorate for Industrial Estates at the Board of Trade have also been placed in this file.

2. Documents at the Public Record Office,
   Ruskin Avenue, Kew, Richmond, Surrey TW9 4DU.

The principal groups of documents used were in the following Classes:-

The Cabinet Minutes and Conclusions in CAB 23 constitute the core documents on policy during the years 1919 to 1939; they contain the references to all the papers put before the Cabinet in arriving at its conclusions. These papers are in CAB 24. The Cabinet Minutes and Conclusions for the period 1939-1945 are in CAB 65, and those from 1945 onward in CAB 128. Copies of the Cabinet Minutes and Conclusions made available under the 30 year rule of the Public Records Act 1967 are displayed on open shelves in the reading room.

The papers of the Cabinet Committee on the Reports of the Investigators and of the Commissioners for the Special Areas, as well as those of the Inter-departmental Committee attached to the Cabinet Committee, are in the following Classes:-

CAB 27/577 Proceedings & Memoranda (some also in CAB 24).
CAB 27/578 Meetings, with some material from CAB 27/577.
CAB 27/579 Draft Reports from Investigators.

The key documents relating to the Company are in the files of the Commissioner for the Special Areas of England and Wales, BT/104. The files relating to the formation and development of the Company are in BT 104/23 - 31. The Class also contains the files relating to the North East Development Board (1) and some of the files of the Directorate for Industrial Estates (70 - 79), i.e. those relating to Advance Factories, leases, land acquisition etc.

The papers of the Ministry of Labour on the Special Areas from 1934 - 1946 are in LAB 23. Employment figures for (post-1945) government-owned factories are in BT 106/100.

The principal Treasury papers on pre-War policy are in T 172/1827 & 1828 (Special and Distressed Areas).

Documents on the formation of post-War policy are in the following Classes:

Reconstruction Problems: CAB 87/ 1-3, February 1941 - October 1943.
Reconstruction Priorities: CAB 87/12-13, January 1943 - November 1943
Reconstruction: CAB 87/ 5-10, November 1943 - May 1945.
Control of Factory and Storage Premises: BT 106.

Other main documents relating to both pre- and post-War events, are in the following Classes:

BT 64, Board of Trade, Industries & Manufacture Division.
BT 177, Board of Trade, Distribution of Industry & Regional
        Division, which also contains some papers of the
        Directorate for Industrial Estates.
BT 171 Proceedings of the Regional Boards for Industry.
BT 208 Lists of government-owned factories.
CAB 58 Economic Advisory Council.
CAB 66/43
        War Cabinet Memoranda (WP & CP), 1943.
CAB 124/218
        Employment Policy, October 1945.

Additional Classes and Files used in this work are indicated in the References.

It was originally intended to photocopy every item from the Public Record Office used, but this did not prove to be feasible. Nevertheless, a considerable number of essential documents have been copied and these have been deposited at the Tyne & Wear Archives under the following numbers:-

                1762/14 material for 1934 - 1939
                1762/15   "   1940 - 1944
                1762/16   "   post - 1945

The material is identified, however, by Public Record Office references.

3. Regional Labour Statistics.

The Manpower Services Commission (Training Division), Newcastle upon Tyne, has made available to the author the departmental information of the Ministry of Labour on insured persons and unemployment for every Employment Exchange, Employment and Branch Office in the North East for the periods 1936 - 1939 and 1945 - 1965. A copy of this material has been deposited at the Tyne & Wear Archives under number 1762/20.

4. Newspapers and Periodicals.

Of the newspapers of the period, The Times was the most frequently consulted, not least because it played a key role in the early events related in this study. The Economist , too, commented on every Parliamentary occasion relating to the problems of the depressed areas. The North Mail , the Newcastle Journal (the two papers merged in 1939), and the Evening Chronicle - all published in Newcastle upon Tyne - provided much information, as did several national newspapers, including the Daily Telegraph ,the Manchester Guardian and the News Chronicle , as well as a number of local newspapers, for example, the Evening News , North Shields. The periodicals consulted included Business , June 1937 and the Architectural Journal , 20 May 1937.

The files of the Company and of the Commissioner for the Special Areas of England and Wales contain many press cuttings and reprints of articles on the Team Valley Estate.

5. Local Documents

Books, Pamphlets and Reports published by local Organisations:-

Allen, E. et al, 1957, Allen, E., Odber, A.J., & Bowden, P.J., Development Area Policy in the North East of England , Newcastle upon Tyne, North East Industrial and Development Association.
Daysh, G.H.J. et al., 1936, A Survey of Industrial Facilities of the North East Coast , Newcastle upon Tyne, North East Development Board.
Forster, Sadler S.A., ca. 1965, An Introduction to Industrial Estates , Gateshead, Industrial Estates Management Corporation For England, (now English Industrial Estates Corporation).
Goodfellow, David M., 1940, Tyneside: The Social Facts , Cooperative Printing Society, Newcastle upon Tyne.
Grenfell Baines, 1948, Aycliffe: Master Plan , Grenfell Baines & Partners, Preston, Lancs. Available at Aycliffe & Peterlee Development Corporation, Newton Aycliffee, Co. Durham DL5 6AW.
Production Engineering Ltd, 1960, Inquiry into Means for Promoting Industrial Development in the North East , Newcastle upon Tyne, North East Industrial and Development Association.
Tyneside Industrial Development Board, 1950, Tyneside Story, Cheltenham & London, E.J. Burrow.

Various items at Gateshead Central Library, Local Studies Section:-

Newcastle & Gateshead Chamber of Commerce Journal, 1929, North East Coast Exhibition Supplement.
North East Development Board, 1936, Executive Committee, 1st Report , 7 February.

Oxberry, J., Collected Press Cuttings (without references to sources),
   'Beginning of the Team Valley Trading Estate, 1936 - 1939'.
Tyneside Industrial Development Board, 1936, 1st Annual Meeting,
   Proceedings , 2 October.
Tyneside Industrial Development Board, 1937, 2nd Annual Meeting,
   Proceedings , 27 May.

At the Tyne & Wear Archives:-

TWA, 589, Newcastle upon Tyne City Council, 1932, Trade and Commerce
   Committee, Report , 5 October.

6. Political Tracts

Joint   Election   Manifesto,   1935,   by   the   Leaders   of   the   National
Government,
   A Call to the Nation , London, Conservative Central Office
   Library, 1035/107.
Labour Party, January 1937, Commission on the Distressed Areas,
   A Programme of Immediate Action , Interim Report,
   Labour Party Library, 529 (Lab).
Labour Party, April 1937, Final Report on Durham and Tyneside ,
   Labour Party Library, 329 (Lab).
Labour Party Election Manifesto 1945, in Craig, F.W.S., Editor, 1975,
   British General Election Manifestos, 1900 - 1974 ,
   London, The Macmillan Press.

II. GOVERNMENT REPORTS AND OTHER PUBLICATIONS

Armstrong   College,   1932,   Industrial   Survey   of the North East Coast ,
   prepared for the Board of Trade, 51-194, London, HMSO.
Balfour   Committee, 1925 , Committee on Industry & Trade, Report , Vol.1,
   Survey of Overseas Markets, London, HMSO.
Board   of   Trade, 1936, Surveys of Industrial Developments , 1933 - 1935,
   51-203-33 & 51-203-35, London, HMSO.
Central   Statistical Office, 1952, Annual Abstracts of Statistics   No.88,
   1938-1950, London, HMSO.
Commissioner for the Special Areas of England & Wales, Reports ,
   CSAEW, 1935, 1st Report, July   , Cmd.4957, London, HMSO
   "   1936, 2nd Report, February , Cmd.5090,   "   "
   "   1936, 3rd Report, October , Cmd.5303,   "   "
   "   1937, 4th Report, November , Cmd.5595,   "   "
   "   1938, 5th Report, December , Cmd.5896,   "   "
Department   of   Employment,   1971, British Labour Statistics , Historical
   Abstract, 1886 - 1968, London, HMSO.
Hansard   Parliamentary   Reports,   5th   Series,   Debates   in   the House of
   Commons and House of Lords.
Industrial Transference Board, 1928, Report , Cmd. 3156,
   London, HMSO.
Macmillan Committee, 1931, Committee on Finance & Industry, 1931,
   Report , Cmd.3897, London, HMSO.
Ministry of Labour, 1932, Report for 1931 , Cmd. 4044,
   London, HMSO.
Ministry of Labour,   Gazette , December 1932,
   London, HMSO.

Northern Regional Strategy Team, 1975, Evaluation of the Impact of
    Regional Policy on Manufacturing Industry in the North East Region
    Appendix A to Technical Report No.2, London, HMSO.
Pepler, G. & MacFarlane, P.W., ca. 1949, North East Area Development
    Plan , Interim Report,
    London, Ministry of Town and Country Planning.
The Public General Acts , 1934, 1936, 1937, 1945, 1947,
    London, Council of Law Reporting.
RCDIP, 1940, Royal Commission on the Distribution of the Industrial
    Population, Report , Cmd. 6153, London, HMSO.
RCDME, 1937 - 1938, Minutes of Evidence for RCDIP,
    London, HMSO.
RIDT, 1934, Ministry of Labour, Reports of Investigations into the
    Industrial Conditions in certain Depressed Areas , II, Durham and
    Tyneside, Cmd. 4728, London, HMSO.
Royal Commission on Local Government in England, 1969, Vol.I,
    Report , Cmnd. 4040, London, HMSO.
Royal Commission on Local Government in the Tyneside Area, 1937,
    Report , Cmd. 5402, London, HMSO.
Royal Commission on the Poor Laws, 1909, Report , Cd. 4499,
    London, HMSO, also the Separate Report , often referred to as the
    'Minority' Report.
Select Committee on Estimates, 1947, Second Report, together with
    Minutes of Evidence taken before Sub-Committee C, The Administration
    of Development Areas , Session 1946 - 1947, London, HMSO.
White Paper, 1929, Memorandum on Certain Proposals Relating to
    Unemployment , Cmd. 3331, London, HMSO.
White Paper, 1937, Statement Relating to the Special Areas ,
    Cmd. 5386, London, HMSO.
White Paper, 1944, Employment Policy , Cmd. 6527,
    London, HMSO.
White Paper, 1947, Capital Investment in 1948 , Cmd. 7268,
    London, HMSO.
White Paper, 1948, Distribution of Industry , Cmd.7540,
    London, HMSO.
White Paper, 1951, Town & Country Planning, 1943 - 1951 ,
    A Progress Report, Cmd. 8204, London, HMSO.
White Paper, 1963, The North East , A Programme for Regional
    Development and Growth, Cmnd. 2206, London, HMSO.

III. PUBLISHED BOOKS

Addison, Paul, 1975, The Road to 1945, British Politics and the Second
    World War, London, Jonathan Cape.
Armstrong College, 1935, Staff of the Department of Economics,
    The Industrial Position of the North East Coast, London, P.S. King.
Boothby, R. et al, 1927, Boothby, R., MacMillan, H., Loder, John de V.
    & Stanley, Oliver, Industry and the State, A Conservative View,
    London, Macmillan.
Bredo, W., 1960, Industrial Estates , Glencoe, California,
    USA, Free Press.
Brown, A.J., 1972, The Framework of Regional Economics in the UK ,
    London, Cambridge University Press.
Bullock, Alan, 1967, The Life and Times of Ernest Bevin , Vol.2,
    London, Heinemann.

Crump, Norman, 1947, <u>By Rail to Victory</u> , The Story of the L.N.E.R
in Wartime, London, London and North Eastern Railway Company.
Cullingworth, J.B., 1970, <u>Peacetime History</u> ,
Vol.3 Environmental Planning, London, HMSO.
Dalton, Hugh, 1957, <u>The Fateful Years</u> , Memoirs, Vol.2, 1931-1945,
London, Frederick Muller.
Dalton, Hugh, 1962, <u>High Tide & After</u> , Memoirs, Vol.3, 1945-1960,
London, Frederick Muller.
Daysh, G.H.J. & Symonds, J.S., 1953, <u>West Durham: A Problem Area</u>
<u>in North East England</u> , Basil Blackwell, Oxford.
Dennison, S.R., 1939, <u>The Location of Industry and the Depressed Areas</u>
London, Oxford University Press.
Feiling, Keith, 1970, <u>The Life of Neville Chamberlain</u> ,
Hamden, Conn., USA, Archon Books.
Fogarty, M.P., 1945, <u>Prospects of the Industrial Areas of</u>
<u>Great Britain</u> , London, Methuen.
Goldring, D. 1938, <u>A Tour in Northumbria</u> ,
London, G.Allen & Unwin.
Hannington, Wal, 1976, (re-issue), <u>The Problem of the Distressed Areas</u> ,
Wakefield, EP Publishing.
Hansen, Alvin H., 1953, <u>A Guide to Keynes</u> ,
London, McGraw-Hill.
Harris, Kenneth, 1982, <u>Attlee</u> ,
London, Weidenfeld & Nicholson.
House, John W., 1969, <u>The North East</u> ,
Newton Abbot, David & Charles.
Howson, S., & Winch, D., 1977, <u>The Economic Advisory Council 1930-1939</u>
A study in Economic Advice during Depression and Recovery,
London, Cambridge University Press.
Jay, Douglas, 1980, <u>Change and Fortune</u> , A Political Record,
London, Hutchison.
Keynes, J. M., 1936, <u>The General Theory of Employment, Interest</u>
<u>and Money</u> , London, Macmillan.
Law, Christopher M., 1980, <u>British Regional Development</u>
<u>Since World War 1</u> , London, Methuen.
Lewis, W.,Arthur, 1963, <u>Economic Survey 1919 - 1939</u> ,
London, G. Allen & Unwin.
Manners, G. et al., 1972, Manners, G., Keeble, D., Rodgers, B.
and Warren, K., <u>Regional Development in Britain</u> ,
London, John Wiley & Sons.
McCord, Norman, 1979, <u>North East England</u> , The Region's Development,
1760 - 1960, London, Batsford Academic.
McCrone, G., 1971, <u>Regional Policy</u> ,
London, G.Allen and Unwin.
Mess, Henry, A., 1928, <u>Industrial Tyneside</u> , A Social Survey,
London, Ernest Benn.
Mowat, C.L., 1955, <u>Britain Between The Wars</u> ,
London, Methuen.
Odber, Alan J., 1965, contributor, 'Regional Policy in Great Britain',
from <u>Area Redevelopment Problems in Britain and the Countries of</u>
<u>the Common Market</u> , a report prepared for the Area Redevelopment
Administration of the U.S.Department of Commerce by the Institute
of Industrial Relations, University of California at Los Angeles.
Peden, G.C., 1979, <u>British Rearmament and the Treasury, 1932-1939</u> ,
Edinburgh, Scottish Academic Press.
Percival, Geoffrey, 1978, <u>The Government's Industrial Estates In Wales</u> ,
<u>1936-1975</u> , Welsh Development Agency.

Percy of Newcastle, Lord, 1958, Some Memories ,
London, Eyre & Spottiswode.
Pilgrim Trust, 1938, Men Without Work ,
Cambridge, Cambridge University Press.
Pimlott, Ben, 1985, Dalton ,
London, Jonathan Cape.
Pinder, John, (Ed.), 1981, 50 years of Political and Economic Planning
London, Heinemann.
Political & Economic Planning, 1939, Report on the Location
of Industry , London, Political & Economic Planning.
Pollard, Sidney, 1969, The Development of the British Economy ,
1914-1967, London, Edward Arnold.
Priestley, J.B., 1977, (re-issue), English Journey ,
Harmondsworth, Penguin Books.
Richardson, Harry, W., 1967, Economic Recovery in Britain, 1932-1939 ,
London, Weidenfeld & Nicholson.
Richardson, Harry, W., 1970, Regional Economics ,
London, Macmillan.
Segal, N. 1979, 'The Limits and Means of "Self-Reliant" Regional
Economic Growth', in D. MacLennan and J. Parr (Eds.), Regional
Policy : Past Experience and New Directions, Oxford, Martin Robinson.
Skidelsky, Robert, 1967, Politicians and the Slump ,
London, Macmillan.
Slowe, Peter M., 1981, The Advance Factory in Regional Development
Aldershot, Gower.
Stevenson J. & Cook, Chris, 1977, The Slump ,
London, Jonathan Cape.
Stilwell, Frank J.B., 1972, Regional Economic Policy ,
London, Macmillan.
Times Newspapers Ltd, 1952, History of the Times , Part II,
Chapters XIII - XXIV, 1921- 1948, London, The Office of The Times.
The Next Five Years Group, 1935, An Essay in Political Agreement ,
London, Macmillan.
Vaizey, John (Ed.), 1975, Economic Sovereignty and Regional Policy ,
(Symposium), Dublin, Gill and Macmillan.
Wiener, Martin J., 1982, English Culture and the Decline of the
Industrial Spirit, 1850-1980 , Cambridge, Cambridge University Press
Wilkinson, E., 1939, The Town that was murdered :
The Life Story of Jarrow, London, Victor Gollancz.
Williams, Philip M., 1979, Hugh Gaitskell ,
London, Jonathan Cape.
Winch, Donald, 1972, Economics and Policy , A Historical Study,
London, Collins Fontana.
Wrench, Sir Evelyn, 1955, Geoffrey Dawson and our Times ,
London, Hutchinson.

IV. PUBLISHED PAPERS AND AN UNPUBLISHED THESIS

Appleyard, K.C., 1939, 'Government-sponsored Trading Estates'
Journal of the Royal Society of Arts , June 30.
Booth, Alan E., 1978, 'An Administrative Experiment in Unemployment
Policy in the Thirties', Public Administration , Vol.56, Summer.
Booth, Alan, 1982, 'The Second World War and the origins of modern
regional policy', Economy and Society , Vol.11, No.1, February.
Booth, Alan, 1983, 'The "Keynesian Revolution" in Economic Policy-
Making', The Economic History Review , Vol. XXXVI, No.1, February.

Boyd, C.H., 1937 'The Special Areas of England', Some Technical Aspects
of the Commissioners' Work, Institution of Chemical Engineers,
Transactions , Vol.15.

Chinitz, B., 1961, 'Contrasts in Agglomeration: New York & Pittsburgh'
American Economic Review , Vol.51.

Heim, Carol E., 1983, 'Industrial Organisation and Regional
Development in Interwar Britain', Journal of Economic History ,
Vol.XLIII, No. 4.

Heim, Carol E., 1984, 'Limits to Intervention: The Bank of England and
Industrial Diversification in the Depressed Areas',
The Economic History Review , Vol.XXXVII, 4 November.

Loebl, H., 1978, 'Government-financed Factories and the Establishment
of Industries by Refugees in the Special Areas of the North of
England, 1937-1961, unpublished M.Phil. Thesis in the
University of Durham.

Lonie, A.A. & Begg, H.M., 1979, 'Comment: Further Evidence of the Quest
for an Effective Regional Policy 1934 - 1937', Regional Studies ,
Vol.13, pp. 497-500.

Peden, G.C., 1983, 'Sir Richard Hopkins and the "Keynesian" Revolution
in Employment Policy, 1929-45', The Economic History Review ,
Vol.XXXVI, No.2, May.

Peden, G.C., 1984, 'The "Treasury View" on Public Works and Employment
in the Interwar Period', The Economic History Review ,
Vol.XXXVII, No.2, May.

Pitfield, D.W., 1978, 'The Quest for an Effective Regional Policy,
1934-37', Regional Studies , Vol.12, pp.429-443.

Index to appendixes

Appendix 1: Employment in the expanding Industries of the North East 1924 - 1934

Industry or Service	1924 Males	Females	Total	1934 Males	Females	Total	Increase Males	Females	Total Number	%
Fishing	970	--	970	1,300	10	1,310	330	10	340	35.1
Mining (Stone, Clay etc.)	3,360	40	3,400	4,210	30	4,240	850	(10)	840	24.7
Non-Metallifrs.Mining Prods.	1,240	60	1,300	1,540	70	1,610	300	10	310	23.8
Brick, Tile, Pipe Making	3,290	680	3,970	4,870	460	5,330	1,580	(220)	1,360	34.3
Glass Trades	1,510	530	2,040	1,700	850	2,550	190	320	510	25.0
Chemicals etc.	7,080	1,320	8,400	14,630	1,910	16,540	7,550	590	8,140	96.9
Metal Manufacture	100	30	130	470	10	480	370	(20)	350	269.2
Engineering etc.	8,940	690	9,630	11,530	890	12,420	2,590	200	2,790	29.0
Vehicles, Constr. & Repair	2,100	230	2,330	3,100	300	3,400	1,000	70	1,070	45.9
Metal Trades	7,780	670	8,450	10,070	1,090	11,160	2,290	420	2,710	32.1
Textile Trades	60	60	120	130	80	210	70	20	90	75.0
Clothing Trade	2,250	4,450	6,700	2,070	5,020	7,090	(180)	570	390	5.8
Food,Drink & Tobacco	4,490	4,970	9,460	5,960	6,000	11,960	1,470	1,030	2,500	26.4
Saw Milling, Furniture	5,030	630	5,660	7,210	990	8,200	2,180	360	2,540	44.9
Printing & Paper Trades	3,240	2,130	5,370	4,480	2,210	6,690	1,240	80	1,320	24.6
Building & Public Works	33,380	360	33,740	71,060	500	71,560	37,680	140	38,820	112.1
Other Mfg. Industries	310	210	520	480	270	750	170	60	230	44.2
Transport & Communications	20,540	1,030	21,570	34,700	1,440	36,140	14,160	410	14,570	67.5
Distributive Trades	33,490	33,540	67,030	54,880	42,120	97,000	21,390	8,580	29,970	44.7
Miscellaneous Trades	22,550	13,900	36,450	41,240	19,490	60,730	18,690	5,590	24,280	66.6
All Expanding Industries	161,710	65,530	227,240	275,630	83,740	359,370	113,920	18,210	132,130	58.2
All Industrs. in North East	622,970	80,120	703,090	622,010	94,960	716,970	(960)	14,340	14,340	2.0

Source: Daysh, G.H.J. et al., 1936, pp. 98,99, quoting Ministry of Labour figures.

329

Appendix 2: Population Statistics for Durham & Northumberland
1931 - 1935 and Outward Migration 1921 - 1935

	Durham	Northumberland
POPULATION (estimated)		
Mid-1935	1,473,400	766,400
Mid-1931	1,490,920	757,080
Change	- 17,520	+ 9,320
NATURAL INCREASE		
Mid-1931 to Mid-1935		
Births	109,467	50,462
Deaths	71,985	37,787
Increase	37,482	12,675
OUTWARD MIGRATION		
1921 - 1931	163,128	43,546
Mid-1931 to Mid-1935	55,002	3,355
Total 1921 - 1935	218,130	46,901

Source: CSAEW, 1936, 3rd Report, Appendix II, p. 171.

Appendix 3: Summary Comparison of Employment in the
23 fastest-growing Industries * 1923 - 1937,
in London & the Home Counties and Northumberland & Durham

	London and Home Counties	Northumberland and Durham
Number of the 23 industries found in each area in 1923	23	23
Total insured population in the 23 industries in 1923	1,342,270	139,300
Percentage of total population of these areas in the 23 industries in 1923	55.5	22.5
Total insured population in the 23 industries as % of total insured in the same industries in Great Britain:-		
1923	33.3	3.5
1937	32.9	3.7
Increase in the 23 industries 1923 - 1937 as % of total increase in Great Britain in those industries	31.2	4.1 **

* The 23 industries included 7 'local' industries such as Distributive Trades, Tramway & Bus services, Laundries, Building, etc., and 16 'basic' industries, such as Motor Vehicles, Cycles and Aircraft, Silk and Artificial Silk, Electric Cables, Apparatus, Lamps, Electrical Engineering, Hotel, Public House and Restaurant services, etc.

** Of the seven areas or regions analysed by the Ministry of Labour in their evidence to the Barlow Commission, only the Glamorgan and Monmouthshire region showed a lower increase than Northumberland and Durham.

Source: RCDIP, 1940, p. 39. Crown Copyright.

Appendix 4: Number of insured Workers and Unemployed in the Basic Industries and in all Industries in the North East 1929 - 1934

At end of June	Insured				Unemployed			
	1929	1930	1932	1934	1929	1930	1932	1934*
BASIC INDUSTRIES								
1.Coalmining	207,990	207,190	199,320	188,360	27,626	46,159	75,000	39,359
2.Iron-ore, Coke, Iron & Steel	43,780	43,310	38,340	36,360	6,096	10,933	17,501	8,478
3.Engineering **	60,660	62,170	57,250	52,570	8,894	13,525	28,360	25,048
4.Shipbuilding	54,350	54,710	45,890	36,820	14,511	19,855	36,455	25,048
5.Chemicals	16,460	15,950	12,230	13,430	763	2,370	3,632	1,880
6.Shipping	28,110	26,920	31,480	27,310	7,567	9,725	14,912	11,801
	411,350	410,250	384,510	353,850	65,457	102,573	176,115	103,381
OTHER INDUSTRIES	278,280	291,050	337,180	362,120	34,865	49,887	91,994	103,631
ALL INDUSTRIES	689,630	701,300	721,690	716,970	100,322	152,450	268,089	207,012

* Mid-December
** General, Electrical, Marine and Constructional Engineering

Source: Armstrong College, 1935, p.53, quoting Ministry of Labour figures.

Appendix 5: Note on the official Unemployment Statistics

Unemployment alone is not a complete indicator of economic activity. Some unemployment may be due an increase in productivity. This was certainly an important factor in the coal and steel industries in the North East in the depression years. But it is generally considered to be the best indicator available, particularly if it persists over a number of years in a particular area or country.

The official unemployment figures were based until 1948 on the statistics of Unemployment Insurance supplied by the Ministry of Labour; they were almost a by-product of these statistics. The principal group of workers excluded from insurance were those engaged in agriculture, in private domestic service and all under 16 and over 64 years of age. (For the situation after 1947/1948 see Appendix 33).

The Unemployment Insurance Act 1934 lowered the age of entry for boys and girls from 16 to 14. Until then, the majority of school leavers had been excluded from the statistics for the first 2 years of their working lives. Since a larger proportion of young people stayed at school beyond the age of 14 in the more prosperous parts of the country, the omission from the statistics up to September 1934 of those between the ages of 14 and 16 resulted in an over-optimistic comparison between the unemployment in the North East and the national average.

Similarly, the lower than average activity rate in the North East of girls above the age of 16 and women led to an understatement of the unemployment position relative to the national average.

Dennison [*] drew attention to the fact that the South of the country had a larger proportion of employed than insured workers, while in the depressed parts of the North East - and in other depressed areas of the country -, the position was reversed. This was simply another way of stating that in the South, the employment situation was better than suggested by the official figures, while in the depressed areas it was worse.

But the most serious problem of comparability of the local and national figures was posed by migration and transference - migration assisted by official bodies.

The Table in Appendix 2 shows the outward migration figures for the years 1921 - 1935. These figures include those transferred under official schemes from 1928 to 1935.

There is no way of adjusting the official figures to allow for this large net outflow of people, but it must be borne in mind in any consideration of the real extent of the unemployment problem of the North East.

[*] Dennison, S.R., 1939, p.142

Appendix 6: Notes on Land Settlement and Transference

While neither land settlement nor industrial transference are of direct interest in relation to the main topic of this work, both continued to be important regional policy components for some years after the passing of the Special Areas Act 1934.

At a distance of more than 50 years, the political consensus in the country - reflected in the debates on the Reports of the Investigators, on the Address and on the Bill leading to the 1934 Act - on land settlement as a significant element in any solution of the problems of the depressed areas needs some explanation.

On the face of it, the agricultural industry - which was itself in a depressed state at the time - did not seem to offer much opportunity for the unemployed of the North East. Even if the problems of suitable land and working capital could have been solved, there remained the questions of viability, of an entirely different way of life from that of the industrial worker and, perhaps most important, of the lack of skill to wrest a living from the land.

Employment in the industry had been falling ever since the beginning of the century and the process seemed both to continue and to be unstoppable. Why was it, then, that the Investigator for Durham and Tyneside, the government and politicians of the main political parties all believed in the importance of land settlement?

A number of reasons can be discerned for this, some of which were at least arguable, while others have to be looked for in cultural preferences.

McCrone has pointed out that 'being the first nation to industrialise, it paid Britain to buy her primary products overseas ... and to specialise in the production of industrial exports in which, initially, she had no competition' [1]. Indeed, he traces the origin of the regional problem in the industrial areas to the collapse of this long-established policy.

One of the consequences of the policy was the decline of the agricultural work force which, by the early 1930's, had fallen to 3.6% of the total labour force [2]. A larger percentage of the working population was looking for employment in industry than in any other country.

The views of those who argued for the need to reverse the trend was well expressed in the debate on the Third Reading of the 1934 Act [3]:-

A great many people have been investigating the (unemployment) problem for years, but have found no alternative employment for the surplus population of the country except the bringing of this country on to a level with other countries in the percentage of its population that is employed on the soil.

In parts of the coal fields of the North East, a particular opportunity seemed to exist: the land sterilised by coal mining operations had become available for other purposes when mining had ceased. In this connection, Wallace had observed that 'no comprehensive survey of the conditions of the Durham coalfield can avoid the conclusion that the ultimate destiny of a large part of the county, now industrialised, must return to agriculture' [4].

Those imbued with the axioms of the orthodox economy seemed to find it inconceivable that any of these places would ever be able to sustain a process of industrial diversification, and the Investigator was no exception: 'the most optimistic forecast could hardly anticipate the possibility that new industries, capable of employing even a reasonable proportion of the inhabitants, could be established in such communities'.

The other body of explanations for the importance assumed by land settlement is to be found in the deep culture of Britain. Wiener has shown that important elements in British society had never accepted the consequences of the industrial revolution, which was seen as a historical mistake [5]. According to this view, it was Britain's destiny to remain a 'green and pleasant land'. It was, therefore, not surprising - as McCord has pointed out [6] -, that in periods of economic and social stress, there was often an almost instinctive reaction to look to the land for solutions. He quotes the Chartists' land schemes and Joseph Chamberlain's Land League ('3 acres and a cow') as examples.

Ramsay McDonald summed up the attitude of the times when he said, - somewhat facetiously: 'the great new industry that we all seem to strain after is the new industry of going back to the land' [7].

After the passing of the 1934 Special Areas Act, the Commissioner for the Special Areas of England and Wales was under considerable pressure to initiate a major land settlement programme. From the beginning, however, he was more than cautious in his judgment of the possibilities: 'many people have assured me that land settlement would provide a cure for unemployment. They simplify the problem by assuming that the transit of the unemployed to the land is just an easy walk-over' [8].

In a further observation, he realistically forecast the very limited role which land settlement would play in the solution of the unemployment problem of the Special Areas: 'the relief which will accrue from my schemes will indeed appear diminutive compared with the anticipation created by some colossal figures quoted' [9]. Indeed, he pointed out that, if large numbers could, in fact, readily be settled on the land, the economic consequences and the reactions from the existing agricultural work force would make the effort inadvisable [10].

This view was supported a few months later in a study by Orwin and Darke which spelled out some of the dangers of transferring large numbers of industrial workers to the land: it would 'depress the agricultural workers' standard of living, contract the market for the produce of existing growers, add nothing to the demand for manufactured goods and depress the level of prices and thereby the standard of living for all producers' [11].

It would go too far to recite the various public and private schemes which had been in existence when the Commissioner came on the scene, or to describe the several quite distinct schemes which he supported. These are fully recorded in the five Reports of the Commissioner. Only an outline of the Commissioner's support is recorded here, and a rough assessment is given of the results of his land settlement schemes. A comparison of the costs and the results obtained with those of the Team Valley Trading Estate is given in [12].

The well-intentioned but uncoordinated attempts to settle unemployed people on the land were put on a more systematic basis by the establishment of the Land Settlement Association in the summer of 1934, some months before the first Special Areas Act. The purpose of the Association was to carry out experiments and to pass on any experience gained. A Welsh Land Settlement Society was established early in 1936.

By February 1936, the Commissioner reported that he had approved a programme 'which should enable 2,000 families from the Special Areas (of England and Wales) to be established on grouped smallholdings within 18 months - mostly in groups of about 40 families' [13]. Although the Durham County Council was participating in land settlement schemes financed by the Special Areas Fund and there was some settlement in Northumberland, the majority of the places in which people from the North East would be settled were far away from home.

Even though this programme could not make any significant impact on the unemployment problem in the Areas, it was a very large undertaking. The Commissioner noted the novelty of this experiment: 'never before in this country has there been a systematic attempt to settle on the land, with the aid of public funds, men who not only have little or no experience in its cultivation but are not in a position to contribute any of the capital required' [14].

Not all the people transferred to the land succeeded, but in spite of cases of lack of aptitude - after careful screening -, of homesickness, integration problems in the host areas and poultry disease, the experiment developed, initially, in a modestly successful way.

The cost of settling a family, which was originally estimated at £860 [15], rose to £1,250 [16]. This would later prove to be a considerable under-estimate.

When the second Commissioner for England & Wales assumed office in November 1936, he found that three-quarters of the first programme was well on the way to completion. He decided that a second programme should be initiated, but on a more modest scale. Accordingly, he authorised schemes for the settlement of a further 1,000 families [17].

By the end of 1937, circumstances changed. In spite of the onset of a cyclic decline but fuelled by the rearmament programme, the employment market in the North East improved. The rate of recruitment for the Land Association's schemes dropped off very substantially. A large number of settlers relinquished training and either took up employment in the locality in which they found themselves or returned home [18]. The Commissioner was forced to reduce the second programme and he informed the Land Settlement Association that no further estates should be acquired for schemes assisted by the Special Areas Fund. On 27 July 1938 the Commissioner set up a Committee to enquire into the working of land settlement schemes for unemployed men in England and Wales [19].

When the Commissioner last reported - on 30 September 1938 -, 729 families from the North East - involving 3,654 people - had been settled by the Land Association and the Durham County Council. Of these, 200 families, involving 922 people, had been settled in Durham and in Northumberland [20].

The outcome of the experiment disappointed the many people who had seen in land settlement an important contribution not only to the solution of the unemployment problem in the Special Areas, but also to a better balance in employment between industry and agriculture. It is notable that no serious proposals were made for settling people on the land during the economic crisis which started in the late 1970's, when the unemployment rate in the North East was once again among the highest in Britain.

By contrast, the policy of Industrial Transference - publicly assisted migration - was much more successful, at least in terms of numbers.

Reference has already been made to the migration of people from the North East since the end of the first world War. From 1928 on, assisted migration of unemployed people - particularly coal miners - to districts offering better prospects of employment was stimulated by the Industrial Transference Board funded by the Ministry of Labour. It has already been noted that the establishment of this Board has been seen by some as the first regional policy measure in Britain. Retraining in new skills was an essential part of the scheme.

In addition, specific schemes financed by the State and administered by local authorities were introduced to facilitate the removal of households (in 1928), and of whole families (in 1935).

The necessity to face migration in order to earn a living must always be a matter of sorrow for those living in tightly-knit communities and the Commissioner recognised this: 'a man puts down his roots in the place where he works and lives. He has his family and friends and associations in that place. It is a hard thing to tear up these roots. It is one of the finest characteristics of mining communities that their personal associations, their communal life, is strong' [21].

There were two categories of people, however, for whom Transference appeared to offer the only prospect of ever finding work: the able-bodied men and youths in the mining villages where the pits had closed, and a large proportion of young people in many other localities in the North East.

Unemployment in some of the smaller places in the Durham coal field had for some years amounted to almost three-quarters of the employable population. Nobody believed that there was the slightest chance of attracting industrial enterprises to such places. While there had always been a tendency to abandon pits which had become uneconomic in favour of new areas with untapped coal deposits, the process had normally been spread over a number of years, and 'the disinherited population (had) less difficulty in becoming absorbed in other places' [22]. It was the tragedy of the people of the mining areas of Durham that the decline of the coal industry and the closure of pits since 1926 were telescoped into relatively few years.

Unemployment among young persons was considered the most serious aspect of the problem. In the spring of 1934, the Ministry of Labour had estimated that in Durham and Tyneside, there would be approximately 16,600 boys between the ages of 14 and 17 surplus to requirement in that year, a figure which would rise to 31,500 in 1937. The Unemployment Insurance Act 1934 contained provisions which, if fully applied, would have dealt with this problem from the time they left school up to the age of 18. While this would have postponed the problem for many, there were not, in fact, sufficient places for them after they left the Junior Instruction Centres.

'I am alarmed when I think of the future of those unemployed youths, whose disastrous start in life is to be consigned to idleness and who are consequently early enmeshed in its attendant evils', wrote the Commissioner for England and Wales in November 1936, and concluded that 'unless there was a marked and unforeseen revival of trade in the Special Areas, I remain convinced that the best prospects for most of these young men will be in transference to more prosperous districts' [23].

The total number of people from all the depressed areas in each category (men, women, boys, girls, household and family transfers) assisted under the official schemes are given in Table 21:-

Table 21
People and Households/Families transferred
under the main official Schemes 1928 - 1938

	Men	Women	Boys	Girls	Total Number of Persons	Households/ Families
1928 *	3,600	360	1,840	n.a.	n.a.	--
1929	36,843	2,239	2,622	1,994 **	43,689	2,850
1930	28,258	1,752	1,313	1,1708	33,031	2,100
1931	17,889	2,631	868	1,986	23,374	1,680
1932	8,359	2,651	628	2,502	14,140	990
1933	5,333	4,038	1,117	2,955	13,443	605
1934	6,282	4,420	1,661	3,512·	16,421	1,308
1935	13,379	6,350	5,376	4,684	29,752	3,718
1936	20,091	8,008	9,449	5,958	43,506	10,025
1937	24,000		7,657	6,450	38,125	7,673
1938	18,000		4,131	5,496	27,627	4,000

Totals 1929 - 1938   238,118   34,749
(from all depressed Areas ***)

   *   Part of year only.
  ** Women and girls transferred after training. No records exist of other female transfers in this year.
*** The Transference Schemes covered a wider range of depressed areas than those that were designated Special Areas.

Source: Pitfield, D.W., 1978.

No complete separate data appear to exist for the depressed areas of the Northern Region.

The figures for 1929 (the first complete year of the scheme) were the highest for the 10 years recorded. The sharp reduction in the numbers in 1930 and 1931 was due to the increasing grip of the business slump. As a result, the incoming workers from the North East were seen to take away scarce jobs from people in previously relatively prosperous parts of the country, which now also suffered levels of unemployment never before experienced. This led to social tensions in the receiving areas. Mr. Lansbury (Lab., Poplar), for example, reported 'vehement protests from people in East London about giving job assistance to people transferred from the North East' [24].

The 1934 Special Areas Act enabled the Commissioners to promote an increase in official Transference and this was reflected in the rise in the numbers after 1934. 1936 was a new peak year, in which the numbers were almost as high as in 1929. With the improvement in the employment market in the North East, - already noted in connection with land settlement -, the Ministry of Labour Gazettes for 1937 and 1938 show that the numbers declined.

The Transference policy had many critics. Mr.Greenwood (Lab., Wakefield) described it as 'asking the working classes of this country to share the burden of unemployment among themselves' [25]. In the same vein, Keynes had made the point that in the absence of policies which would stimulate the aggregate demand, transference would merely distribute unemployment more equitably around the country. Since this was perceived to be happening in some of the reception areas, the Commissioner for England and Wales addressed himself to this criticism: he drew attention to the fact that, in spite of a rapid increase in the working population in the London area, unemployment there was lower than in any industrial area of the country. For those who were not persuaded by this view, the Commissioner had an answer ready, which confirmed the views of Greenwood and Keynes by implication:-

Even if, under the present conditions, the transfer of men and women from the depressed areas to the prosperous areas would for a time appear to deprive some of the persons in the prosperous areas of the opportunities of employment, and, at the worst, this can only be for a time, then I think that in the national interest, the issue should be faced ... it is a choice between a rather more intermittent employment for certain groups of workpeople in prosperous areas, and the virtual condemnation of whole communities to complete idleness [26].

Another argument against Transference of skilled men was that it would 'enable the South to compete more effectively with the Special Areas and act as a deterrent to the establishment of new industries' [27]. There was also the question of the sheer survival of the mining villages: 'many villages and hard-pressed country areas are being depleted of their youth and energy. In many instances only the sick and infirm are left and these ... will become a permanent charge on the local authorities concerned [28].

Finally, there were those who believed that, since Transference generally involved the most able and venturesome, their loss would would make it more difficult for the depressed areas to recover.

In conclusion, it may be observed that without Transference and unassisted migration the unemployment figures for Durham and Tyneside would have been much higher. Migration was the safety valve which prevented serious social unrest. The government was well aware of this and continued to see Transference as one of the two main policy options for several years after the passing of the 1934 Act.

REFERENCES AND NOTES

[1]   McCrone, G, 1971, p.16.
[2]   Ibid.
[3]   HC Deb 296, 601.
[4]   RIDT, 1934, para 65, p.96.
[5]   Wiener, Martin J., 1982.
[6]   Discussion with Professor N. McCord.
[7]   HC Deb 309, 1042.
[8]   CSAEW, 1935, 1st Report, para.210, p.82.
[9]   Ibid.
[10]   Ibid.
[11]   Quoted in CSAEW, 1936, 2nd Report, para.171, p.48.
[12]   By 30.9.1938, the Commissioner had committed a total of £3,238,000 on land settlement schemes in England and Wales (see Appedix 12). By the same date, he had committed £4,005,000 on trading estates and outside sites. The first programme, intended to settle 2,000 families, was three quarters completed before the second programme involving 1,000 families was started (CSAEW, 4th Report, 1937, para.552, p.138). When the second programme was halted, land for a total of approx. 1,900 families had been acquired (CSAEW, 5th Report, 1938, para.286, p.70). Since on 30.9.1938 only 1,108 remained (source last quoted), almost half did not proceed or left the land, either returning home or taking jobs locally. For this reason, and because of serious under-estimates of the cost of training and working capital requirements, the cost to the Commissioner per family remaining had gone up to £2,922. If it is allowed that work for two people was provided per family remaining on the land, i.e. a total of 2,216 jobs, the commitment figure means that the cost per job was £ 1,461 . By comparison, it was concluded in III/4, p.150 that the cost per job at Team Valley was of the order of £220. This means that the cost to the public purse per job created through land settlement was more than six times greater than one in a government-financed factory. Moreover, with the onset of the War 11 months after the Commissioner last reported, it is likely that more families would have left the land, never to return again.
[13]   CSAEW, 2nd Report, para.168, p.47.
[14]   Ibid, para. 170, p.47.
[15]   CSAEW, 3rd Report, 1936, para.320, p.96. £ 750.- was the Commissioner's contribution.
[16]   CSAEW, 4th Report, 1937, para.554, p.139.
[17]   Ibid, paras.552,553, pp.137,138.
[18]   CSAEW, 5th Report, 1938, para.293, p.71.
[19]   Ibid, para.294, p.72.
[20]   Ibid, para.286, p.70.
[21]   CSAEW, 1st Report, 1935, para.165, p.65.
[22]   Ibid, para.163, pp.64,65.
[23]   CSAEW, 3rd Report, 1936, para.424, p.120, and para.432, p.123.

[24]   HC Deb 293, 2004.
[25]   "   , 2077.
[26]   CSAEW, 1st Report, 1935, para.167, p. 66.
[27]   HC Deb 309, 1242.
[28]   "   , 1286.

Appendix 7: Extent and Cost of Unemployment in Durham & Tyneside 1934

Abbreviations: IP = Insured Population on 1 July 1933
LR = Number of Unemployed on Live Register on 4 June 1934
UE = Unemployed
UY = Unemployed for more than one year
UB = Unemployment Benefit
TP = Transitional Payments
PA = Public Assistance
SC = Cost of TP + PA per Head of Population

	IP	LR	% IP UE	% IP UY	S C (£)	In receipt of UB	% of LR In receipt of TP	Others (Incl. PA)
CO. DURHAM, S.WEST								
Bishop Auckland	10,697	5,722	50.4	80.0	5.3	8.6	79.0	12.4
Cockfield	2,244	838	35.8	78.7	3.4	8.7	83.7	7.6
Crook	9,684	3,807	35.9	79.2	5.7	8.9	85.3	5.8
Spennymoor	10,974	3,367	26.2	69.3	6.2	12.7	74.8	12.5
Stanhope	1,763	197	9.8	34.5	1.5	36.0	61.9	2.1
Wolsingham	527	144	26.4	51.4	2.2	20.8	76.4	2.8
Shildon	4,004	1,951	47.4	81.7	7.4	6.7	84.0	9.3
Totals	39,893	16,026	37.0	76.3	5.4	9.7	80.2	10.1
CO. DURHAM, EAST								
Sunderland	56,302	28,545	41.0	47.2	5.6	13.7	69.0	17.3
Haswell	3,639	689	16.0	55.3	3.4	17.7	70.7	12.3
Houghton le Spring	14,760	3,166	20.2	60.2	3.4	19.1	70.0	10.9
East Boldon	3,525	2,208	27.5	29.7	2.4	12.5	30.7	56.8
Seaham Harbour	15,422	6,113	23.3	38.3	4.4	17.0	42.6	40.4
Hartlepool	5,074	2,866	44.5	42.3	6.3	14.3	64.5	21.2
West Hartlepool	20,394	7,361	29.8	42.2	4.8	20.7	72.0	7.3
Horden	11,038	1,060	9.7	24.6	1.9	14.5	82.2	3.3
Wingate	9,170	5,063	23.2	31.5	5.7	9.1	36.8	54.1
Totals	139,324	57,071	30.7	43.7	4.6	16.7	57.3	26.0

	IP	LR	% IP UE	% IP UY	S C (£)	In receipt of UB	% of LR In receipt of TP	Others (Incl. PA)
CO. DURHAM, N.WEST								
Consett	10,869	1,190	10.3	61.3	1.7	21.8	61.5	16.7
Chopwell	4,988	752	14.9	86.0	2.0	9.4	67.2	23.4
Lanchester	3,348	1,267	30.6	52.3	5.2	12.5	68.2	19.3
Durham	15,087	4,113	24.2	69.6	4.5	13.0	72.6	14.4
Chester le Street	11,831	2,582	20.5	64.3	3.6	17.6	72.6	9.8
Birtley	4,645	1,276	26.6	62.6	3.5	13.8	78.2	8.0
Washington	7,026	1,379	16.8	56.6	2.7	21.8	67.4	10.8
Stanley	16,927	7,179	27.8	37.7	4.3	23.5	40.0	36.5
Totals	74,721	19,738	21.6	55.0	3.5	18.4	59.6	22.0
TYNESIDE								
Newcastle*	116,738	26,285	20.8	53.2	4.0	22.0	61.3	16.7
Newburn	5,255	1,301	20.8	40.5	2.9	20.8	62.7	16.5
Wallsend	13,333	5,173	26.2	49.0	5.3	19.2	60.4	21.4
Willington Quay	4,149	2,232	40.6	41.8	6.8	15.6	68.5	15.9
North Shields	15,515	5,575	27.3	29.4	3.5	26.0	61.0	13.0
Blaydon	7,633	2,707	24.5	54.3	3.5	16.7	68.9	14.4
Dunston	5,486	1,367	24.5	43.6	3.6	20.6	65.5	13.9
Felling	9,164	3,131	30.5	70.1	5.6	12.1	71.0	16.9
Gateshead	28,906	11,939	36.0	47.5	4.0	22.1	58.1	19.8
Hebburn	8,863	3,447	29.8	51.1	6.9	11.2	63.7	25.1
Jarrow	9,191	6,385	56.8	58.5	9.6	11.6	72.0	16.4
South Shields	31,682	13,005	30.9	33.2	4.0	30.2	63.0	6.8
Totals	255,915	82,547	27.0	47.7	4.4	21.5	62.7	15.8
Totals Survey Area	509,853	175,382	27.2	49.8	4.4	18.5	62.3	19.2
Totals Gt. Britain	12,62M	2,09M	16.1	23.3	2.0	39.0	44.0	17.0

* including Gosforth & Benton.

Source: RIDT, 1934, pp. 116, 117.

Appendix 8: Summary of the Principal Recommendations
of the Investigator for Durham & Tyneside,
July 1934

1. Unification of coal-mining royalties.

2. Formation of an Industrial Development Company for Tyneside.

3. Some measure of unification of Local Government authorities on Tyneside to be considered.

4. (a) Appointment of Commissioners to administer ordinary outdoor relief in the administrative County of Durham.

   (b) An Exchequer Grant to reduce the cost of Public Assistance in the county to the average for the whole country.

5. Application of proposal 4 (b) to the County Boroughs of Sunderland and West Hartlepool.

6. Removal of all financial obstacles to the most effective prosecution of a policy of Industrial Transference.

7. (a) A land settlement scheme, on the lines at present in operation under the Durham County Council, to be financed by the Exchequer.

   (b) Financial Assistance to Durham County Council for drainage schemes.

8. (a) Jarrow Slake Scheme to receive consideration, with a view to grant aid.

   (b) Scheme for a road tunnel under the Tyne between North and South Shields to be considered for a grant aid.

   (c) Clearance of derelict factory sites, either by the Government or through the Development Company referred to in Recommendation 2.

   (d) Provision of playgrounds and other amenities by a scheme of voluntary work for Transitional Payments plus working clothes, a midday meal and a small sum of pocket money.

9. Promotion of special housing schemes.

10. The appointment of a Commissioner to co-ordinate all activities in connection with Government schemes for the rehabilitation of the area.

Source: RIDT, 1934, Section VIII, p.109.

Appendix 9: Brief Biographies

MEMBERS OF THE FIRST BOARD OF DIRECTORS OF THE COMPANY.
(with periods of office).

Appleyard, Major General Kenelm Charles, 1936-48 (see also p.81)

Born 25 March 1894; TD 1912; OBE 1937; CBE 1940; apprenticeship with
C.A. Parsons & Co Ltd 1912, later with Sir W.G. Armstrong Whitworth
as a Production Manager; General Manager and Managing Director of
the Birtley Company Ltd 1919-47; Member of Durham County Council
1922-25; Member of several Engineering Institutions; played leading
roles in local and national Employers' Organisations; Vice Chairman,
Cty. Durham Unionist Association 1923-30, Northern Director of
S.A.R.A 1936-48; Military Member, Durham Territorial and Air Force
Association 1922-51, Lt. Col. Royal Engineers (TA) and CRE 60th
(Northumbrian) Division 1931-36; Member of Advisory Committee,
Industrial Estates Ltd Nova Scotia, Canada; Col. 1937, Brigadier
1939, local Major General 1940; Chief Engineer, Field Force
Component BEF 1939-40 (mentioned in despatches); Director of Labour
Supply and International Labour Branch, Ministry of Labour 1940-41;
lent to Ministry of Works as Director of Emergency Works 1941;
Director of Opencast Coal Production 1942-45, adviser on regional
organisation 1945-46. Died 20 December 1967.

Chapman, Col. Sir Robert, 1936-60

1st Bt 1958; KT 1950; born 1880; CB 1940; CMG 1918; DSO 1916; Legion
d'Honneur; TD; DL Cty. Durham 1946-58; JP Cty. Durham and South
Shields; BA London; Chartered Accountant; War service in Royal
Artillery 1914-18 (wounded, mentioned four times in despatches);
Volunteer and Territorial Artillery, Col. 1900-50; MP (Nat U) Durham
Houghton-le-Spring 1931-35; High Sheriff of Cty. Durham 1940-41;
Councillor and Alderman of South Shields Town Council 1921-1952;
Chairman, Durham Territorial Association 1941-46; President,
Chairman and Member of many local, national, statutory, civic,
sporting and charitable bodies and organisations; Director of a
number of companies. Died 31 July 1963.

Martin, Sir George William, 1936-48

KBE 1935; born 24 June 1884; LLD (Leeds) 1951; Chairman, Wilkinson &
Warburton Ltd; Lloyd's Underwriter; Chairman, Leeds Music Festival
1942-54; Chairman, Vice-chairman and member of many national and
local, statutory, civic and charitable bodies. Died 13 October 1976.

Micklem, Commdr. Sir (Edward) Robert, 1936-46

KT 1946; born 5 June 1891; CBE 1942; Royal Navy 1903-19; served in
European War as Lt. Commdr., incl. two years in Submarine Service;
joined companies associated with Vickers Ltd in 1919; Chairman and
Managing Director of Engineering Works and Shipyards, Vickers
Armstrong Ltd; Chairman, Regional Board Northern Area, Ministry of
Production 1942; lent to Ministry of Supply 1942; Chairman, Tank
Board and Armoured Fighting Vehicle Division, Ministry of Supply,
1942-44. Died 15 May 1952.

Ridley, Lord, 1936-49

Mathew White Ridley, 3rd Viscount (1900), 4th Baron Wensleydale (1900), Bt (1756); born 16 December 1902; CBE 1938; TD; Hon. DCL Dunelm; DL Northumberland 1939; Hon. Col. Northumberland Hussars TA 1962; Chairman, Northumberland County Council 1940-46 and 1949-52; JP; Landowner; Regional Controller for the North, Ministry of Production 1942-49; Director of Producer Gas Vehicles, Ministry of Transport 1942. Died 25 February 1964.

Sisson, Henry Arnott, 1936-48

Born 31 October 1886; OBE; MA; FCA; Chartered Accountant; served in European War 1914-18 in a field company of the Royal Engineers; later Deputy Assistant Director of Gas Services, GHQ France; joined family firm of accountants in the mid-1930s, senior partner in successor firm Winter, Robinson Sisson and Benson, which later became part of Deloitte Haskins and Sells; Director of a number of companies, particularly associated with Farrar Boilerworks Ltd, Newark; Director, Northern Gas Board. Died 20 July 1963.

Walton, Brigadier Sir George (Hands), 1936-60

KBE 1958; date of birth unknown; CBE 1937; CB 1953; TD 1942; DL Cty. Durham; JP Northumberland; Chartered Accountant; Chairman, Newcastle Board, Commercial Union Assurance Company Ltd; served in European War 1914-18 and in Territorial Army between Wars; commanded 50th Divisional Signal Regiment 1930-36; Col. 1934; Deputy Chief Signal Officer Northern Command 1937-39; Chief Signal Officer throughout the War of 1939-45, Northern Command, York; saw other active service (mentioned twice in despatches); Brigadier 1942; four years in Middle East Command; seconded by Army in 1943 to serve as Director on the Middle East Board of United Kingdom Commercial Corporation, a British Government War organisation. Died 25 November 1976.

Westwood, Lord, 1936-48

William Westwood, 1st Baron 1944, of Gosforth; born 20 August 1880; started work at age of 10 in a jute mill in Dundee; later apprenticed in a shipbuilding yard; for many years Secretary of Dundee Labour Representation Committee and Labour Political Agent; Chairman, Scottish Labour Advisory Council 1918-19; Supervisor of Shipconstructors and Shipwrights Association 1913-29; General Secretary 1929-45; Principal Labour Adviser to the Board of Admiralty 1940; Director of Contract Labour, Admiralty, 1941-42; Chief Industrial Adviser to Board of Admiralty 1942-45; a Lord-in-Waiting to HM the King 1945-46; Chairman, Minerals Development Committee under the Ministry of Fuel and Power 1946; Member of Northumberland County Council 1937-47; President, Engineering and Shipbuilding Trades Federation 1933-36; President, Confederation of Shipbuilding and Engineering Unions 1936-39; Director of a number of companies. Died 13 September 1953.

GENERAL MANAGER OF THE COMPANY 1936-55

Methven, Col. Malcolm David, (Director 1945-48)

Born 1892. The following has been taken from the CV accompanying his application for the position of General Manager of the Company (BT 104/30): obtained a degree in mechanical engineering at Cambridge; immediately afterwards went to work in Burma until the outbreak of the first world War; As a Territorial, joined up at once in the Royal Flying Corps, where he was commissioned. After service in France and Britain, was sent on a technical mission to Canada, where he was promoted to Lieut.Colonel. Recalled in 1918 to take charge of Kidbrooke Depot with a staff of 8,000. On return to civil life joined an engineering firm but soon moved to a chemical company where he became Managing Director. After six years with this firm, joined a large toilet article manufacturer as Director and General Manager; eventually set up his own business in a similar field. This was successful, but 'as a process of self-analysis showed', felt that his best work 'had been accomplished as an executive and administrator where the responsibility had been largest'. For this reason, he welcomed an opportunity to dispose of his business and to look for employent 'where a big opportunity for organising and administrative work is offered'. Died 1962. One son was the late Sir John Methven, Director-General of the CBI.

COMMISSIONERS FOR THE SPECIAL AREAS OF ENGLAND AND WALES

Stewart, Sir (Percy) Malcolm

1st Bt 1937; born 1872; OBE 1918; DL Beds; JP; Hon. LLD (Manchester); Life President (formerly chairman), London Brick Co Ltd; President, Associated Portland Cement Mftrs. Ltd, British Portland Cement Mftrs. Ltd, Cement Makers Federation, Cement Makers Statistical and Technical Bureau; among first employers to introduce profit-sharing schemes and welfare benefits for retired employees; Chairman, National Council of Social Service; Director for the Ministry of Munitions of the Government Rolling Mills at Southampton 1917-19; High Sheriff of Beds.; associated with a number of charities; Commissioner 1934-36. Died 27 February 1951.

Gillett, Sir George Masterman

Kt 1931; born 1870; JP; Member of Finsbury Borough Council 1900-06, London County Council 1910-22; Alderman 1922-34; MP (Lab) Finsbury 1923-31, (Nat Lab) 1931-35; Parliamentary Secretary, Ministry of Transport 1930; Commissioner 1936-39. Died 10 August 1939.

Price, Sir James (Frederick George)

KBE 1938; born March 1873; CB 1927; entered Civil Service in 1888, served in various Government Departments; Deputy Secretary, Ministry of Labour 1936-38; retired 1938; Commissioner 1939-45. Died 1 June 1957.

OFFICERS OF THE BOARD OF TRADE

Dalton, Lord

Edward Hugh John Neale Dalton, Baron of Forest and Frith, County
Palatinate of Durham; Life Peer 1960; born 1887; PC 1940; MA Cantab;
DSc London; DSc Sydney; LLD Manchester; DCL Durham; MP (Lab)
Camberwell (Peckham Div) 1924-29, Durham (Bishop Auckland Div)
1929-31 and 1935-50; Research Student, London School of Economics
1911-13; Barrister-at-Law, Middle Temple 1914; Hon. Bencher 1946;
War service 1914-1919; Lecturer, London School of Economics 1919;
Reader in Commerce, University of London 1920-25; Reader in
Economics, University of London 1925-36; Chairman, National
Executive of Labour Party 1936-37; Parliamentary Under-Secretary,
Foreign Office 1929-31; Minister of Economic Warfare 1940-42;
President, Board of Trade 1942-45; Chancellor of the Exchequer
1945-47; Chancellor of the Duchy of Lancaster 1948-50; Minister of
Town and Country Planning 1950-51. Died 13 February 1962.

Forster, Sir (Samuel Alexander) Sadler

Kt 1966; born 1900; CBE 1956; Hon. DCL Dunelm; Chairman, North
Eastern Trading Estates Ltd 1948-60, English Industrial Estates
Corporation (incorporating North Eastern Trading Estates Ltd)
1960-70, Malta Development Corporation 1968-71; Chartered
Accountant; Industrial Manager, Welwyn Garden City Ltd 1936-41;
Regional Controller at Newcastle upon Tyne, Control of Factory &
Storage Premises 1942-45; Director for Industrial Estates, Board of
Trade 1945-48; Member, Peterlee (New Town) Development Corporation
1950-55; Member, Executive Council North East Industrial and
Development Association 1952-61, Vice President 1957-61; Member,
Northern Advisory Committee for Civil Aviation 1964-72; Member,
Northern Economic Planning Council 1965-69; associated with other
local, national and professional organisations and statutory bodies.
Died 24 June 1973.

Jay, The Rt. Hon. Douglas Patrick Thomas

PC 1951; born 23 March 1907; Fellow, All Souls College, Oxford
1930-37 and since 1968; on the staff of The Times 1929-33 and the
Economist 1933-37; City Editor, Daily Herald 1937-41; Ass.
Secretary, Ministry of Supply 1941-42; Principal Ass. Secretary,
Board of Trade 1944-46; Personal Assistant to the Prime Minister
1945-46; MP (Lab) Battersea North 1946-74, Wandsworth, Battersea
North 1974-83; Economic Secretary to the Treasury 1947-50; Financial
Secretary to the Treasury 1950-51; President, Board of Trade
1964-67; Chairman, Common Market Safeguards Campaign 1970-77, London
Motorway Action Group 1968-80; Director, Courtaulds Ltd 1967-70,
Trades Union Unit Trust 1967-79, Flag Investment Co 1968-71.

Warter, Sir Philip Allan

Kt 1944; born 31 December 1903, Director of Warehousing, Ministry of
Food 1940-42; Controller of Factory & Storage Premises, Board of
Trade 1942-45; Adviser on Industrial Estates, Board of Trade
1945-46; President, Associated British Picture Corporation Ltd;
Chairman, Thames Television Ltd, Thomas Cook & Son Ltd and other
companies. Died 14 April 1971.

OTHER EMINENT PERSONS APPEARING IN THIS STUDY

Dennison, Professor Stanley Raymond

Born 15 June 1912; CBE 1946; Hon. LLD Hull 1980; Lecturer in
Economics, Manchester University 1935-39; Professor of Economics,
University College of Swansea 1939-45; Chief Economic Assistant, War
Cabinet Secretariat (Economic Section) 1940-46; Member, Scott
Committee on Land Utilisation in Rural Areas (Minority Report) 1942;
Lecturer in Economics, University of Cambridge 1945-58; Fellow of
Gonville and Caius College; Professor of Economics 1958-61, Queen's
University Belfast 1958-61; Professor of Economics, University of
Newcastle upon Tyne 1962-72, Pro-Vice-Chancellor 1955-72;
Vice-Chancellor and Hon. Professor, University of Hull 1972-78, now
Emeritus Professor; Member, University Grants Committee 1964-78;
Chairman of Wages Councils; Member of a number of committees and
review bodies dealing with matters of public concern. Associated
with local charitable and educational organisations.

Holford, Lord

William Graham Holford, Baron of Kempton Town; Life Peer 1965; born
22 March 1907; Kt 1953; RA 1968; FRIBA; FRTPI; BA Architecture,
University of Liverpool; Hon. DCL Dunelm 1960; Hon. LLD Liverpool
1961; Hon. DLitt Oxon 1964; American Scholar of Society of Arts and
Sciences New York 1929; Rome Scholar in Architecture 1930; Florence
Bursar of RIBA; Professor of Town and Country Planning, University
College London 1948-70; Director, Leverhulme Trust Fund since 1972;
President, RIBA 1960-62; Member of many bodies connected with the
Arts and Architecture; closely concerned with the drafting of the
Town and Country Planning Act 1947; Consultant Architect to North
Eastern Trading Estates Ltd since 1936; Died 17 October 1975.

Montague-Barlow, The Rt. Hon. Sir (Clement) Anderson

1st Bt 1924; KBE 1918; born 28 February 1868; PC 1922; LLD; MA; FSA;
Barrister-at-Law; sometime Lecturer, Law Society and London School
of Economics; Examiner in Law, London University; Director and
Chairman, Sotheby Ltd 1909-28; Member, London County Council (East
Islington) 1907-10; MP (Con), South Salford, Dec 1910 - Dec 1923;
Parliamentary Secretary Ministry of Labour 1920-22; Minister of
Labour with seat in Cabinet, October 1922 - January 1924; Chairman,
Royal Commission on the Distribution of the Industrial Population
1937-39; Chairman of a number of governmental committees and Senior
Government Representative at International Labour Conferences
1920-1922. Died 31 May 1951.

LOCATION OF FACTORIES

Trading Estates

To The Editor of The Times .

Sir,

Mr. P. Malcolm Stewart, the Commissioner for the Special Areas of England and Wales discusses in his first report a number of interesting reasons which appear to hinder the establishment of factories in the special areas. I wish to add a further reason.

The greater part of the post-War development has occurred in the lighter industries, and a very large number of undertakings which have been established have been set up on the trading estates at Slough, Welwyn, Letchworth, St. Albans, Acton, Trafford Park, &c. These estates companies have placed at the disposal of the smaller manufacturers services which are very similar to those offered by the speculative builder to "the man in the street". The convenience of being able to rent or buy a ready-made factory with supplies of gas, water. electricity &c., already arranged is one which. is now widely appreciated. Obviously, the smaller manufacturer is not going to waste time buying and draining land, building a factory, negotiating for the essential services if he can obtain a factory as easily as he can secure a house. The manufacturer is enabled to commence production almost at once. What possible counter-advantage can the older areas offer against such facilities?

I have received very many enquiries from small firms, and in every case they have asked for a ready built factory of stated floor area. Practical experience has proved that it is useless offering them the out-of-date types of buildings which exist in the older areas. They want the kind of services which exist on the trading estates and which advertisements have made known to them.

The trading estate has proved successful in many ways. It shows how industry can be carried on in healthy, pleasing surroundings, enabling town planning to proceed on 'garden city' lines, and I consider that this is the way in which light industrial development will continue. The need for these trading estates in the older areas is, in my opinion, definitely proved. To establish them would provide employment and bring into existence useful assets.

After receiving the report of a survey made by experts the Government should assist with the necessary finance or guarantee the establishment of several trading estates situated in various parts of the country, having regard to existing unemployment and to the encouragement of industrial enterprise, given favourable conditions.

Certain specified trades should not be permitted to commence business except within such industrial estates. Town-planning authorities would thus be considerably assisted in their duties.

A national planning board of industrial development should be set up, the purpose of which, <u>inter alia</u> , would be to spread development more equitably over the country by encouraging new works to be set up on these trading estates.

In every district a great deal of employment is provided in connection with food, clothing, distribution, and transport, and the normal development of each area in these trades could be encouraged to take place on the estates.

Such a scheme as I have briefly outlined would, in my opinion, assist very considerably the older industrial area. The social advantages of development planned in this way are obvious.

Yours Faithfully,

S.A.Sadler Forster, Secretary
Tees District Development Board, County
Chambers, Marton Road, Middlesborough

Appendix 11: Brief Notes on Government Agencies, local and
other Organisations mentioned in this Study

1   Control of Factory and Storage Premises
2   Board of Trade, Regional Organisation at Headquarters
3   Board of Trade, Organisation in the Regions (Development Areas)
4   Regional Boards for Industry
5   Northern Industrial Group
6   North East Development Association
7   Public Utility Societies
8   Political and Economic Planning

The origins and functions of the following organisations have been given
in I/5 (pp.33-37): North East Development Board, Tyneside Industrial
Development Conference and Tyneside Industrial Development Board.

1   CONTROL OF FACTORY AND STORAGE PREMISES.

During the second world War, the bombing of the ports made it necessary
to remove industries and stocks of food and to find inland premises. The
Control was set by a Committee of the Lord President of the Council and
attached to the Board of Trade. Its task was to allocate factory and
storage premises for government departments and to control the
acquisition of premises by private firms. The object was to ensure that
national resources in premises were employed to the fullest advantage
and that new building was reduced to a minimum. The authority of the
Control over private firms was based on the Location of Industry
(Restriction) Order 1941. By a Cabinet decision, the same control
procedures were applied to government premises.

   The Control set up a register of all factories where space was likely
to be available. Factories employing less than 10 persons were left out.
Premises of firms engaged in essential War production such as
engineering and steel were not included, as it was assumed that these
were fully employed.

   In addition, the Control undertook the work of guiding new production
into suitable areas where premises were available and collated the
information regarding the supply of labour, billeting facilities, gas
electrical power, coal, transport etc. from the relevant government
departments. Premises in areas where demand for labour outstripped
supplies were used for storage premises.

   Source: Index to BT 106.

2. BOARD OF TRADE (REGIONAL ORGANISATION AT HEADQUARTERS).

A Distribution of Industry and Regional Division was set up with the
responsibility to implement the Distribution of Industry Act 1945. The
Distribution of Industry Committee of this Division was an
Inter-departmental Committee, operating in two 'Panels'. Panel A dealt
with new factory construction and Panel B with the conversion, sale or
leasing of wartime government factories. The Directorate for Industrial
Estates operated within this Division.

352

3. BOARD OF TRADE (ORGANISATON IN THE REGIONS)

The Board of Trade had no formal representation in the regions until 1945, when the offices of the Control of Factory and Storage Premises became the regional offices of a newly constituted Board of Trade. This was set up mainly to enable the Board to discharge the functions it acquired under the Distribution of Industry Act 1945 and from the merging of the Board with the Ministry of Production. The regional offices provided intelligence on all matters concerning the regions and carried out certain duties delegated from headquarter departments, especially those related to the distribution of industry, export promotion and services.

When the Board of Trade absorbed the Ministry of Production in 1945, it acquired responsibility for servicing the Regional Boards. The Regional Boards were converted into advisory bodies and their scope was extended to cover the whole range of productive industry. They were renamed Regional Boards for Industry (see 4. below)

The Regional Inter-departmental Committees on the Distribution of Industry, established by the Control of Factory and Storage Premises in the autumn of 1944, were later attached to the Regional Boards for Industry.

Sources: Indexes to BT 106 & BT 177

4. REGIONAL BOARDS FOR INDUSTRY

Initially known as Area Boards, they were set up by the Ministry of Supply in January 1940 to promote maximum War production in each civil defence region and to coordinate the activities of government agencies concerned with essential stores. While they were mainly concerned with industrial capacity, their function and the controlling government departments changed several times during the early part of the War.

Until August 1940, they were composed entirely of government officials. Thereafter, representatives of employers and trade unions were added. The Boards were renamed Regional Boards in May 1941. When a Minister of Production was appointed in February 1942, their function was investigated by the Citrine Committee and clear terms of reference were established. In July 1942, the Board came under the control of the Ministry of Production.

The wartime Regional Boards were dissolved in September 1945, to be re-established in eleven areas in October 1945 as Regional Boards for Industry under the control of the Board of Trade. Independent part-time chairmen were appointed and three representatives each of employers and trade unions, together with senior Regional Board representatives of government departments concerned with industrial production: the Board of Trade, the Admiralty and the Ministries of Supply, Labour, War Transport, Fuel and Power, Works and Town and Country Planning.

In Development Areas, the regional Inter-departmental Committees on the Distribution of Industry became committees of the Regional Boards because the relevant government departments were already represented there. The further history of the Regional Boards is complicated, but of no relevance to this study.

Source: BT 107 & 170.   353

5. NORTHERN INDUSTRIAL GROUP

Early in 1943, a few people met privately under the chairmanship of Lord Ridley to consider the post-War position of the North East and what might be done to prevent a recurrence of the conditions which developed after the first world War. The group set out its views in a memorandum, which was submitted to industrialists and trade union leaders.

Following a series of meetings, a report was drawn up, the signatories constituting themselves as the Northern Industrial Group. The aims of the Group and the list of members was published ('Northern Industrial Group', 1943, available at Newcastle Central Library, Class L 338, Acc.No. Cr.35344). Members served in their personal capacity, not as representatives of any interests.

The Group aimed to promote the development and prosperity of existing industry in the North East, to encourage commercial, technical and industrial research, and to advise and co-operate with government and local bodies in any initiatives which would maintain a high level of employment in the region. The organisation of the Group comprised an executive and an investigation committee, and technical panels covering 15 industries. The members of these panels were 'the most competent people in the region in their respective spheres'.

The lobbying by the Group in the formative period of the 1944 White Paper on Employment has been referred to in several places in this study.

The Group published a number of papers, some of which are available in Newcastle Central Library. The Group continued to be active for many years after the formation of the North East Development Association (see 6. below) - which it strongly supported.

In view of the favourable post- War employment situation in the region, the Group concluded in 1953 that it had completed its task. But members felt strongly that a regional body of some kind was needed. Accordingly, the Group merged with the North East Development Association (NEDA, see 6. below) to form the North East Industrial and Development Association (NEIDA). The constitution of the new body reflected the aim to attract a wider membership than NEDA.

6. NORTH EAST DEVELOPMENT ASSOCIATION

This body was formed in 1944 by the local Authorities in the region, to continue some of the work of the pre-War North East Development Board, to which several references have been made in this study. In view of the formation of the Northern Industrial Group the year before, the constitution of the Association did not provide for members from industrial or commercial firms. The work of the Association was seen to be complementary to that of the District Development Boards, some of which were re-activated towards the end of the War. The Association aimed to deal with matters of broader principle affecting the region as a whole. The merger with the Northern Industrial Group in 1953 has been referred to in 5. above.

Source: Annual Reports, Newcastle Central Library.

7. PUBLIC UTILITY SOCIETY

The term was used by officials when the problem of establishing government-financed trading estates companies within the 1934 Act was discussed, as also by the Daily Telegraph on 13 March 1936 (see II/4, p.85).

Mr. I.S. Stephenson, lecturer in Company Law at the University of Newcastle upon Tyne, has been good enough to advise that the term is unknown to him.

The form of organisation appears to have been a non-profit-making company, possibly always limited by guarantee. The societies met with in this study were involved in Housing and Land Settlement. The Welsh Land Settlement Association Ltd was referred to as a model for the Estates Company. It was the means by which the government funded organisations with a public purpose, but with a remit to operate commercially in due course.

The Daily Telegraph article mentioned above implied that the use of this form of organisation for industrial purposes was novel. It also saw it as a compromise between private enterprise and Socialism. This view seems to have been shared by a Board of Trade official who observed that the Estates Company was 'respectably cloaked as private enterprise, supported by government funds'.

It was clearly an arrangement which was intended to enable governments to intervene at arms length in order to avoid being accused of State trading.

8. POLITICAL AND ECONOMIC PLANNING (PEP)

This private research institute enjoyed much prestige almost from its inception. The Commissioner invited Mr. Israel Sieff of Marks and Spencer to become the government appointee on the Board of the Company largely because he was chairman of PEP at the time.

PEP was founded in 1931 - in the depth of the world business recession - to find out the facts on a wide range of burning issues and to propose policy directions which would correct the evident malfunctioning of the economic system and the government machine. Its work quickly attracted support from leading men and women in many fields and members of all political parties.

The information obtained was published in the form of 'broadsheets'. PEP reported on regional development in 1935 (Nos. 53 & 59), the location of industry in 1936 (No.87), regionalism and trading estates in 1938 (Nos.122 & 129), and on relevant topics ever since.

Evidence is provided in the source quoted below that the policy proposals by PEP influenced government thinking.

On 31 March 1978, PEP merged with the Centre for Studies in Social Policy to form the Policy Studies Institute.

Source: Pinder, John, (Ed.), 1981.

Appendix 12: Commissioner for the Special Areas of England and Wales:
Expenditure and estimated Commitments to 30 September 1938

INDUSTRY   £

    Harbour and Quay Developments   554,000
    Clearance & Improvements of Sites   412,000
    Trading Estates & Individual Sites   4,005,000
    Development Councils   34,000
    Inducements   100,000
    Miscellaneous   47,000

                                                           5,152,000

HEALTH

    Hospitals, Welfare Centres   3,023,000
    District Nursing & Ambulance Services   67,000
    Baths   98,000
    Water Supply   175,000
    Sewerage & Sewage Disposal   2,277,000
    Street Works   400,000
    Miscellaneous   72,000

                                                           6,112,000

HOUSING

    North East Housing Association Ltd   1,145,000
    Miscellaneous   17,000

                                                           1,162,000

AGRICULTURE

    Small Holdings Schemes, incl.
    Coop. Farms and Cottage Homesteads   3,082,000
    Group Holdings Schemes   133,000
    Assisted Allotments Schemes   23,000
    Land and Filed Drainage   22,000

                                                           3,260,000

MEASURES OF SOCIAL IMPROVEMENTS
AND MISCELLANEOUS   1,084,000

                                                        £ 16,770,000

Source: CSAEW, 1938, 5th Report, p.92.

Appendix 13: Map of the Team Valley Trading Estate ca.1969

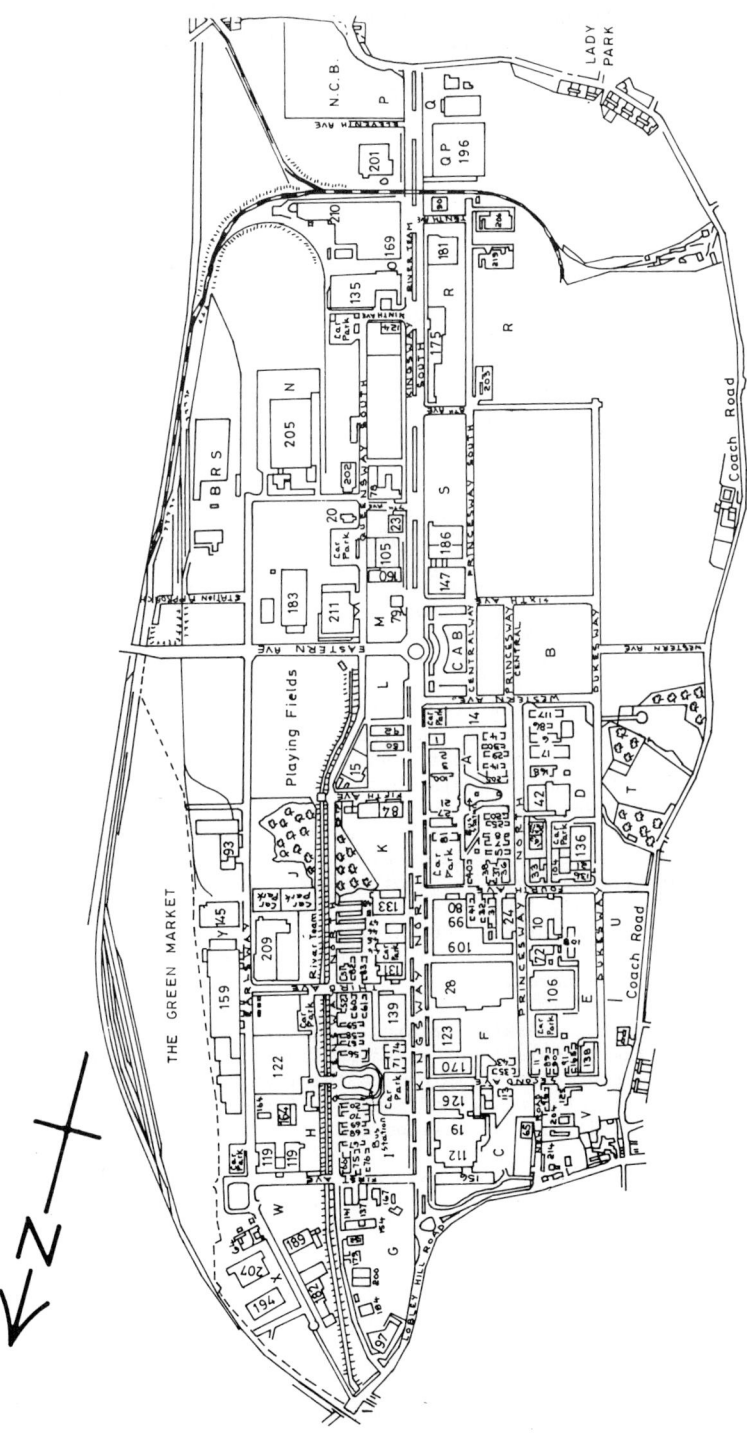

Appendix 14: The Team Valley Trading Estate:
Progress Information in the pre-War Period

The monthly reports of the General Manager for the first half of 1937 contain information on the planned start of building particular factories but little more than forecasts of completions. Until almost to the end of 1937, the available information is incomplete.

Until then, progress information was supplied to the Commissioner only in response to specific requests, initially for inclusion in his monthly reports to the Minister of Labour (see Table 1, p.117).

It was not until 2 November 1937 that the Commissioner asked the Company to provide regular progress returns 'on the first of each month ... under headings attached, in order to enable him to supply the necessary material for answers to Parliamentary questions'. The information was also used by the Commissioner for his Press statements and for his - by now - annual Reports. The first return by the Company - for November 1937 - was made on 7 December.

Questions were asked in the Commons even before any factories had been completed. For example, Mr. Shinwell (Lab., Durham, Seaham) asked the Minister of Labour on 24 May 1937 whether any factories had yet opened at Team Valley and how many workpeople were engaged in them. A similar question was asked by Mr. Stewart (Lab., Durham, Houghton-Le-Spring) on 24 June 1937. Parliamentary interest in the Team Valley Estate and the outside sites continued right up to the War.

These questions caused the Company a good deal of work. Employment figures for those engaged in construction had to be obtained from the building contractors and their sub-contractors. After the occupation of the first factories, tenants were ased to provide their employment figures. These was readily supplied at first, but tenants became less cooperative after a few months and the Company found it increasingly difficult to collect the information. 'We will, however, do our utmost to obtain reliable figures', wrote Methven to the District Commissioner on 4 November 1937, 'and, if all else fails, we shall be forced to make inspired guesses'. Later, the information was provided by the District Office of the Ministry of Labour, which computed the required figures from the insurance cards.

There were no separate returns, initially, for the outside sites. Thus, when the Commissioner asked for confirmation that the figures in the first return referred solely to the Team Valley Estate, Methven had to explain that the number of tenants listed as awaiting completion of factories included those at Pallion and South West Durham.

The format of the returns changed several times at the request of the Commissioner, the last time in April 1939. In October 1941, all written reporting ceased for the duration of the War.

NOTES ON PROGRESS INFORMATION

1. Definition of 'Factory' and 'Tenant'

a) There was some initial confusion in regard to the 6,000 sq.ft.
buildings, which the Commissioner regarded as the smallest factory
units, but which could be tenanted by up to four firms. The Company
seems to have defined the floor area of a factory as the total area of
the number of (normally) adjoining 1,500 sq.ft. sub-units units occupied
by any one tenant. The problem of definition did not arise with the
larger factories, which were always occupied by a single tenant.

b) The Company considered anyone a tenant who had signed - over a
sixpenny stamp - an undertaking to rent a factory. Such undertakings
were not enforceable in law and - the special circumstances in 2.e)
below apart - a few were not honoured. More binding agreements could not
be executed at this stage, however, because the exact details of the
factories to be completed or built were normally not yet known.

c) In May 1940, the Company had 21 tenancy agreements with the following
five rapidly expanding tenant firms: John Barran, two; Colmore
Adhesives , five; Sigmund Pumps, seven; North Eastern Aircraft
Components, two. For record purposes, the Company equated the number of
tenants with the number of tenancies rather than tenant firms.

2. The Summaries of the Progress Returns

a) The construction of factories at Team Valley started in April 1937.
The available information up to the end of that year is given in Table
1, p.117. On the other hand, the information after the end of 1939 is of
little interest, because construction effectively ceased after the
completion of the factories in progress at the end of 1939. For these
reasons, summaries of the returns are given only for the years 1938 and
1939.

b) Up to April 1939, the conclusion that factories were generally not
available in advance of requirement (pp. 261, 262) relies on a
comparison of the figures in column 5 (number of factories in progress)
and those in column 9 (number of tenants waiting for factories). On the
assumption that the factories completed but not occupied (column 3) had
either been let or were unsuitable for waiting tenants, it is clear that
the number of those waiting was always greater than the number of
factories in progress.

From April 1939, the information on the number of tenants waiting was
discontinued. Instead, the number of factories let but not yet in
progress (column 7) was given, together with their total floor area
(column 8). Again, the number of factories let was always greater than
the number in progress. The same applied to the floor areas, except,
inexplicably, in May and June 1939.

c) Up to and including February 1939, the returns included the outside
sites. This introduced a slight distortion in the figures. The removal
of these sites from the returns is reflected in the drop in completions
between February and March 1939.

SUMMARIES OF THE PROGRESS RETURNS FOR 1938 AND 1939

	(1)	(2) sq.ft.	(3)	(4) sq.ft.	(5)	(6) sq.ft.	(7)	(8) sq.ft.	(9)	(10) sq.ft.	(11)
1938											
January	28	n.a.	2	n.a.	25	n.a.	n.a.	n.a.	51	n.a.	825
February	33		2		26				55		900
March	40		2		30				52		950
April	42		2		35				53		975
May	43		2		45				52		1,000
June	57	455,000	2	12,000	38	400,000			44		1,100
July	64	483,000	4	21,500	30	363,850			41		1,570
August	64	484,103	4	29,350	32	285,394			41		1,800
September	71	519,603	13	65,267	20	232,334			27		1,500
October	83	584,288	12	50,000	12	174,341			24		1,600
November	85	619,463	14	60,500	11	185,591			22		1,700
December	89	745,029	14	62,000	6	34,200			18		1,840
1939											
January	92	742,259	9	50,770	11	69,700			24		2,150
February	98	774,199	9	40,500	7	49,700			19		2,310
March	94	700,992	10	50,650	5	47,200			18		n.a.
April	97	727,992	8	18,000	6	53,285	15	72,335		871,602	2,600
May	99	740,142	7	13,500	9	81,260	14	63,440		898,342	2,525
June	98	738,642	17	55,264	13	109,684	18	102,290		1,005,880	2,640
July	102	784,742	15	46,264	11	78,799	18	97,800		1,007,605	3,010
August	103	799,666	19	68,764	6	67,375	26	155,820		1,091,625	3,320
September	111	827,600	12	40,764	6	67,375	26	155,820		1,091,559	n.a.
October	115	844,266	9	27,464	7	89,305	22	100,140		1,061,175	n.a.
November	114	855,841	12	34,964	6	80,430	21	98,640		1,069,875	4,170
December	117	867,841	9	22,964	6	80,430	21	98,640		1,069,875	4,330

(1) = number of factories completed and occupied
(2) = total floor area of (1)
(3) = number of factories completed but not occupied
(4) = total floor area of (3)
(5) = number of factories in progress;
(6) = total floor area of (5)
(7) = number of factories let but not yet in progress
(8) = total floor area of (7)
(9) = number of tenants waiting for factories
(10) = (2) + (4) + (6) + (8)
(11) = number of people employed by tenants

Sources:

the correspondence referred to in this Appendix and the available progress returns from 1937 to September 1941 are in TWA,1762/13. Lists of Team Valley tenants from June 1939 to October 1941 are in TWA,1395/3106.

d) Between August 1938 and the end of the year, there was a sharp drop in the number of tenants waiting for factories and in the number of factories in progress. This was the consequence of the decline in enquiries leading to lettings which had begun in the last quarter of 1937 (see Table 2, p.176).

e) The returns for November and December 1939 (and in January 1940) showed 21 tenants still waiting for factories but only six factories in progress. This prompted the Commissioner to ask the Company in a letter on 21 February 1940 'to report on the position in these cases in relation to the limitation of factory erection during War time'. In his reply of 21 February 1940, Methven explained:-

> To be perfectly honest with you, these are a number of foreigners and other cases who have signed on the dotted line that they are going to take factories ... but who, for one reason or another, have failed to come up yo scratch. Quite frankly, I do not fancy the chances of any of them.

The records show that the majority of those who did not take up their tenancies were would-be refugees who had failed to get out of the domains of the Nazis before the start of the War had barred their admission to Britain. The question must be asked whether the presence of this relatively large number in the lists of tenants waiting for factories affects the conclusions referred to in 2.b) above.

f) The observation in 2.d) indicates that the majority of refugee firms had not yet entered the lists of tenants waiting for factories at Team Valley at the end of 1938 (three of the four refugee firms on the outside sites had occupied their factories by December 1938). Indeed, it is clear from the internal evidence that it was only in the spring and summer of 1939 that factories were being built for the majority of the refugees who had arrived. Most of the 21 refugees and others who were unable to take up their tenancies would have made contact with the Company only in the summer of 1939. At most, they would have featured in the lists of tenants waiting for 2 - 3 months before October 1939.

The conclusions referred to in 2.b) above are not vitiated, therefore, by the phantom tenants waiting for factories.

g) It has already been observed that the reporting format changed several times. The summaries have been so drawn that the information resulting from the last change in format could be accommodated. Items reported at an earlier stage, including the number of lease negotiations in progress, the contractors' labour (divided into local and outside labour) and the division of tenants' labour into male and female and boys and girls - which no longer figured in the return after March 1939 - have been omitted.

Appendix 15: Scale of the Team Valley Trading Estate
as a Public Works Project

Although only part of the site would be used in the first phase,
the final lay-out of the Estate was planned from the beginning.

The engineering development for the whole of the area
authorised was almost completed by the end of September 1938, 23
months after the start of work on the site.

A measure of the scale of the project may be gained from the
following civil engineering data and the number of men engaged
in construction and building:-

Roads built	11.5 miles
Drains laid	27 miles
Kerbing	21 miles
Paving	6 miles
Railway Track	6 miles
Water Mains	8 miles
New Channel for the River Team	2 miles
Bridges	5
Earth removed from Estate	575,000 tons
Stone fill brought from Pit Heaps	1,720,000 tons
Number of Men employed in Construction and Building (at peak)	1,500

Sources: civil engineering data : TWA 1762/4, Report on the
Activities of the Company during the Year to the
30th September 1938, p.2. Employment figure: from
undated Notes for the Minister of Labour ca. May
1938, TWA,1762/13. The civil engineering data
given in the two sources differs. The later
information has been used.

Appendix 16: Financial Assistance from S.A.R.A, Nuffield Trust and Treasury Fund to Firms in Durham and Tyneside, May 1936 - 31.1.1938

Abbreviations: NT = Nuffield Trust, TF = Treasury Fund
SA = S.A.R.A., Special Areas Reconstruction Association Ltd
OC = Other New Capital, EJ = Estimate of Jobs arising
* = Firms at Team Valley, ** = Firms on Outside Sites

1. CASE ASSISTED BY NUFFIELD TRUST, TREASURY FUND & S.A.R.A.

	NT	TF	SA	OC	Total	EJ
Perga	15,000	15,000	10,000	–	40,000	126

2. CASES ASSISTED BY NUFFIELD TRUST & TREASURY FUND

	NT	TF	SA	OC	Total	EJ
Modern Fuels	30,000	20,000	–	40,000	90,000	300
Jarrow Metal Industries	60,000	40,000	–	100,000	200,000	355
Jarrow Steel	310,000	300,000	–	400,000	1,010,000	400
E. Rosenthal	20,000	10,000	–	20,000	50,000	350
Standard Pulverised Fuel	17,000	25,000	–	–	42,000	100
	£437,000	£395,000	–	£560,000	£1,392,000	1,505

3. CASES ASSISTED BY NUFFIELD TRUST & S.A.R.A.

	NT	TF	SA	OC	Total	EJ
Sunderland Engineering Equipment	2,000	–	6,000	1,700	9,700	80
* Jayess Clothing	3,000	–	5,000	2,000	10,000	143
Armstrong Whitworth (Pneum.Tools)	25,000	–	10,000	35,000	70,000	350
** Kings (Sunderland)	6,000	–	8,000	2,200	16,200	300
F.Turnbull	10,000	–	10,000	–	20,000	200
** Ernest & Henry	2,500	–	5,000	–	7,500	55
Chas. Crofton	15,000	–	10,000	–	25,000	100
British Wiredrawers	10,000	–	10,000	10,000	30,000	67
	£73,500	–	£64,000	£50,920	£188,420	1,295

4. CASES ASSISTED BY NUFFIELD TRUST ALONE

	NT	TF	SA	OC	Total	EJ
John Spencer & Sons (1928)	17,000	–	–	–	17,000	50
High Toft Hill Colliery	500	–	–	–	500	12
J.G.T. & E.W. Ray	1,250	–	–	450	1,700	12
Newburn Cordage	12,000	–	–	–	12,000	30
N.Shields Herring Merchants.Ass.	2,250	–	–	–	2,250	50
English Lead Mines Exploration	10,000	–	–	10,000	20,000	50
Douglas Coal	300	–	–	–	300	30
Woodhouse Close Colliery	2,066	–	–	–	2,066	40
J.W. Philipson	600	–	–	–	600	6
Dryers	6,000	–	–	–	6,000	45
Sunderland Mantle & Gown	2,000	–	–	–	2,000	88
Northern Bedding	10,000	–	–	–	10,000	60
Tyne Plywood Works	30,000	–	–	–	30,000	300
T.J Smith (Flashamea)	1,250	–	–	–	1,250	12
Welsh & Son	14,125	–	–	–	14,125	50
** Alligator Leather	30,000	–	–	10,000	40,000	450
L. Pistol	2,750	–	–	2,750	5,500	20
Ventners Hall Colliery	4,000	–	–	–	4,000	70
	-------			------	-------	-----
	£146,091	–	–	£23,200	£169,291	1,335

5. CASES ASSISTED BY TREASURY FUND ALONE

	NT	TF	SA	OC	Total	EJ
British Periclase	–	50,000	–	50,000	100,000	75
Jarrow Tubes	–	50,000	–	100,000	150,000	300
		-------		-------	-------	---
	–	£100,000	–	£150,000	£250,000	375

365

6. CASES ASSISTED BY S.A.R.A. ALONE

	NT	TF	SA	OC	Total	EJ
Novo Radio	-	-	900	1,150	2,050	11
St. Peter's Foundry	-	-	400	-	400	3
T.B.Pearson & Sons	-	-	1,000	-	1,000	5
Ryans (Newcastle)	-	-	3,000	-	3,000	21
Joseph Cook	-	-	6,000	-	6,000	60
* Fibreboard Boxes	-	-	10,000	9,500	19,500	60
Ward & Davidson	-	-	5,000	-	5,000	50
Scud Models	-	-	1,000	-	1,000	30
Tin Boxes	-	-	5,500	4,000	9,500	24
* Houghton & Hall	-	-	3,000	1,650	4,650	58
Tynecraft Industries	-	-	5,000	-	5,000	50
* Exeau Products	-	-	3,000	-	3,000	100
Donald Brown (Engineers)	-	-	10,000	-	10,000	50
Wearside Boatbuilding	-	-	2,000	-	2,000	10
Sentinel Instruments	-	-	3,000	-	3,000	15
Scoby Scaur Sand & Gravel	-	-	10,000	500	10,500	6
Geo. Dunn & Brothers	-	-	2,000	1,000	3,000	53
Elwine's Steel Stamping	-	-	10,000	5,000	15,000	30
* Bushboard	-	-	1,000	-	1,000	6
F.G. Denton	-	-	300	-	300	-
John F. Fife	-	-	200	-	200	-
* Square Grip Reinforcements	-	-	3,000	2,500	5,500	40
* Hugh Wood	-	-	10,000	15,000	25,000	150
* Celluware Supply	-	-	1,000	-	1,000	58
* Wilden Furniture	-	-	500	-	500	10
Hill's Construction	-	-	2,000	-	2,000	27
Watts Hardy	-	-	3,000	-	3,000	30
Pelton Brick	-	-	8,000	4,000	12,000	28
T. Toward (1932)	-	-	8,000	-	8,000	50

continued ...

	NT	TF	SA	OC	Total	EJ
P. Josephs	-	-	1,500	-	1,500	80
** Great Northern Knitwear	-	-	5,000	10,000	10,000	100
Ludwig Mueller	-	-	1,500	1,000	2,500	10
* Havmor	-	-	2,000	500	2,500	32
J.J. Thompson - Fell End Colliery	-	-	350	-	350	13
Artificial Stone	-	-	1,000	-	1,000	16
J. Fieldman	-	-	500	-	500	20
J. Stevens	-	-	50	-	50	5
Tynewear	-	-	5,000	1,000	6,000	200
Thirlwell Sling Lock	-	-	1,000	750	1,750	18
British Vacuum Flasks	-	-	10,000	20,000	30,000	135
Luther Wales	-	-	2,500	-	2,500	30
			------	------	-------	-----
			£153,200	£72,550	£225,750	1,743
Totals	£771,091	£510,000	£227,200	£856,670	£2,265,461	6,379

Total lent by three Funds in Durham and Tyneside to 31.1.1938: £1,508,291
= 30% of total Funds available for all Special Areas

Source: CAB 27/578, Report by Lord Portal to the Prime Minister, 9.3.1938

Appendix 17: Rent Concessions to Tenants
at the Team Valley Trading Estate 1937 - 1939

Name of Firm	Concession	Total Value of Concession
Havmor Ltd	£125 for 3-1/2 years	£ 436.50
J. Barran & Son Ltd	£262.50 for 2 years	525
J. Barran & Son Ltd	£245 for two years (appprox.period)	490
Jayess Clothing Co. Ltd	£66 for two years (approx. period)	132
Hugh Wood & Co Ltd	£80 for three years	240
Holland Coachcraft Lt	£100 for two years £50 for one year	250
Fancy Crepe Paper Mills Ltd	1st year £70 2nd " £50 3rd " £20 4th " £10 5th " £10 6th " £10	170
Team Valley Brush Co Ltd	£56 per annum for six months	28
R.M. Chamberlain	£154 per annum for six months	77
Tevaclo Ltd	£250 for 1st year	250
J. Heller & Co Ltd	£13.50 for 1st six months	13.50
		£ 2,612.00

This list does not appear to include the tenants receiving
concessionery rents for nursery units of £1.- per week (except,
possibly, J. Heller & Co.Ltd). Since unrebated rents for 6,000
sq.ft. factories (on 21 year leases) were of the order of £ 6.-
per week (£ 312.- per annum), the unrebated rent of a 1,500
sq.ft. nursery unit would have been approximately £1.50 per week.

Source: TWA,1762/5, undated.

Appendix 18: Employment in Refugee Industries
at Team Valley and on the Outside Sites
1940, 1963 & 1974

The list does not comprise all refugee firms in the region in 1939 (see [26], p.190), nor did all the surviving firms on the list remain on the Team Valley Estate until 1974. By contrast, the refugee firms (or their successors) on the outside sites still occupied their original sites in 1974.

		Employment			
		1940	1963	1974	Notes
Team Valley					
1	Alsco Cardboard Boxes Ltd	13	57	44	
2	Appetiser Co.Ltd	8	-	-	a)
3	Julius Bernet Ltd	11	20	60	
4	Burrell & Maurice Ltd	11	136	400	
5	Builders Chemicals Ltd	3	9	5	
6	Belts & Trimmings Ltd	10	25	-	b)
7	Chemika Ltd	-	-	-	c)
8	J. Heller & Co. Ltd	12	50	100	
9	Loblite Ltd	13	100	65	
10	Mellolite Ltd	-	-	-	d)
11	Metal Paper Works Ltd	7	13	18	
12	Fancy Crepe Paper Mills Ltd	39	200	550	e)
13	Norbrit Alloys Ltd	2	-	-	f)
14	Period Furniture Ltd	14	-	-	c)
15	J. Salomon Ltd	10	-	-	g)
16	Sigmund Pumps Ltd	325	1,300	1,830	
17	Sundox Products Ltd	3	-	-	h)
18	Team Valley Brush Co. Ltd	29	200	390	i)
19	Team Valley Weaving Inds. Ltd	15	60	160	
20	Tevaclo Ltd	41	100	120	k)
21	Toilet Goods Mfg.Co.Ltd	9	25	100	
Outside Sites					
22	Alligator Ltd (WA)	107	148	125	
23	Ernest & Henry Ltd (WA)	67	267	200	
24	Great Northern Knitwear Ltd (NS)	60	71	100	
25	West Auckland Clothing Ltd (WA)	444	675	550	
		1,253	3,466	4,817	

Abbreviations: WA = West Auckland, NS = North Shields

Notes

a) business absorbed by local firm.
b) business taken over by London firm and removed from area.
c) founder was interned and did not return to Newcastle.
d) failed before 1940.
e) taken over by Matador Ltd, another refugee firm, which is treated here as a successor firm.
f) went out of the type metal business, continued as a shoe manufacturer in Newcastle.
g) closed down in 1940 because of lack of materials.

h) business acquired by Tynebrand Ltd, a local firm.

i) the figures include those for the Lion Brush Company Ltd, which resulted from a split of this family business.

k) the firm was acquired and removed from the area, but the two founding brothers had previously divided the business between them. Distinctive Clothing Company Ltd, the resulting new business, effectively became ,the successor firm in the area.

Source: Loebl, H., 1978.

Appendix 19: Number of registered Wholly Unemployed Persons in Durham & Tyneside, December 1934 - September 1938

	Durham	S.W.Durham	Tyneside	Totals
17.12.1934	65,585	13,236	85,400	164,221
24.06.1935	63,760	12,736	78,329	154,825
21.10.	65,007	13,383	81,266	159,656
16.12.	61,330	13,335	77,608	152,273
24.02.1936	60,715	13,136	78,410	152,261
27.04.	55,137	12,613	72,417	140,167
20.07.	51,229	11,380	60,710	123,319
21.09.	48,784	11,462	61,739	121,985
23.11.	47,303	11,089	59,946	118,338
22.02.1937	45,690	11,042	59,904	116,636
19.04.	42,710	10,745	55,886	109,341
26.07.	36,584	9,898	51,038	97,520
13.09. *	35,799	9,078	50,039	94,916
15.11.	34,681	8,836	51,830	95,347
14.02.1938	38,231	9,100	53,352	100,683
04.04.	37,135	8,811	49,611	95,557
18.07.	36,659	9,663	45,799	92,121
12.09.	40,055	10,810	48,858	99,723

* Approximate date of occupation of the first 10 - 20 factories at Team Valley.

Sources: CSAEW, Five Reports, Appendices, see Bibliography.

Appendix 20: Alphabetical List of industrial Tenants
of the Team Valley Trading Estate and the Outside Sites,
from the Beginning to 31 December 1939,
with Dates of first Contacts

For Team Valley tenants, dates of first contacts with the the Estates
Company were found in the early correspondence. Tenants on the outside
sites were much more likely to have had their first contacts with the
Commissioner rather than with the Company and they have not been
investigated; they are marked OS.

A summary of the dates and numbers of first contacts of tenants is
given in Table 2, p. 176. The reference number is given to assist in
identifying tenant firms in Appendix 21.

	Ref.No.	Tenant Firm	First Contact
1	38	Alligator	OS
2	17	Alsco Cardboard Boxes	01.06.1938
3	42	Anglo-Scottish Trading	01.12.1937
4	43	Geo. Angus & Co.	25.06.1937
5	18	Appetiser	03.11.1937
6	44	Atlas Woodworkers	03.03.1937
7	92	John Barran & Sons	01.01.1937
8	100	Betta Biscuits	31.08.1937
9	45	J.M. & J. Bartlett	03.06.1939
10	19	Belts & Trimmings	01.07.1938
11	20	Julius Bernet	25.06.1938
12	16	Bond Moulding & Engraving	OS
13	46	Bradforth	31.05.1937
14	101	British Jeffrey Diamond	04.08.1938
15	21	Builders Chemicals	21.10.1938
16	22	Burrell & Maurice	27.05.1937
17	47	Bushboard	01.12.1936
18	102	Cadbury Brothers	17.09.1936
19	91	Cardinal Cabinets	OS
20	86	Celluware	24.03.1937
21	48	Central Upholstery	14.11.1937
22	78	R.M.Chamberlain	18.11.1938
23	23	Chemika	27.08.1937
24	61	Thomas Clegg	OS
25	1	Coach Confectionery	10.12.1936
26	79	Colmore Adhesives	28.01.1937
27	103	Consolidated Pneumatic	07.02.1938
28	87	Cottage Bakery	26.07.1937
29	70	E. Crawford	23.04.1937
30	2	Dandy Confectionery	08.07.1937
31	104	Danish Bacon	24.10.1938
32	3	Darlington Engineering	25.11.1936
33	71	Geo. Davidson	20.04.1937
34	4	Deason Chemical	28.06.1938
35	5	Denburn Firelighter	24.01.1938
36	80	Durham Steelwork	08.11.1938
37	49	Dynworks	06.02.1937

	Ref.No.	Tenant Firm	First Contact
38	39	Ernest & Henry	OS
39	93	Exeau Products	10.01.1937
40	24	Fancy Crepe Paper Mills	12.05.1938
41	81	Fibreboard Boxes	18.12.1935
42	6	T.M. Francis	15.08.1938
43	68	Garlick,Burrell & Edwards	08.09.1937
44	40	Great Northern Knitwear	OS
45	50	Mary Harris Gowns	01.0?.1938
46	51	Havmor Pies	12.08.1936
47	72	Thomas Hedley	01.06.1938
48	25	J. Heller	15.05.1939
49	105	Hills Patent Glazing	25.09.1936
50	88	Holland Coachcraft	15.12.1936
51	109	Home Office (HM Off.of Works)	15.01.1937
52	82	Houghton & Hall	25.07.1936
53	94	Hunters The Bakers	04.03.1937
54	106	Imperial Chemical Industs	07.10.1936
55	7	Jayess Clothing	17.11.1936
56	52	Jones (Potato Crisp)	18.06.1937
57	95	Kavli	19.05.1939
58	62	Kings (Sunderland)	OS
59	110	Labour,Ministry of	29.09.1936
60	89	Landauer	14.09.1937
61	8	Lawson Beck	01.04.1938
62	83	Laypak Battery	12.05.1939
63	26	Loblite	20.10.1938
64	107	J.Mackintosh	28.03.1939
65	96	J.F. Marriott	30.08.1938
66	64	D.R. Maxwell	09.07.1937
67	9	Medical Supplies (N/C)	03.05.1939
68	27	Mellolite	12.02.1937
69	28	Metal Paper Works	04.11.1938
70	65	B. Morton & Son	27.05.1938
71	10	Neotechnika	01.10.1937
72	29	Norbrit Alloys	11.10.1939
73	53	N.E.Aircraft Components	06.10.1939
74	54	North East Wires	19.01.1939
75	97	Northern Beverage	12.04.1938
76	73	Northern Plumbers Supplies	27.04.1937
77	55	Northern Wire Works	09.06.1937
78	69	Orrell & Brewster	20.08.1936
79	56	Patterson Lamp	15.10.1939
80	84	Perga	17.07.1937
81	30	Period Furniture	17.01.1938

	Ref.No.	Tenant Firm	First Contact
82	11	Photocrafts	10.09.1937
83	66	Ravensworth (Printers)	08.09.1938
84	74	Rickman & Thomas	05.01.1939
85	31	J. Salomon	11.01.1939
86	63	Saturn Oxygen	OS
87	32	Sigmund Pumps	26.08.1937
88	57	F.S.Slater	10.03.1937
89	98	Square Grip Reinforcements	17.08.1936
90	33	Sundox Products	07.10.1937
91	67	Samuel Talbot	20.09.1937
92	34	Team Valley Brush	28.02.1938
93	75	Team Valley Cold Storage	11.02.1938
94	35	Team Valley Weaving Inds.	26.08.1938
95	36	Tevaclo	Oct. 1938
96	37	Toilet Goods Mfg.	15.10.1938
97	12	Tyne Brush	03.12.1938
98	13	Vallee	15.11.1937
99	90	Variety Wafers	26.07.1938
100	58	Vestric Lamp	17.01.1938
101	85	Vulcan Welding Products	24.10.1938
102	76	Henry Walker (Refrigeration)	22.02.1938
103	14	Welburn (Radio)	26.04.1938
104	41	West Auckland Clothing	OS
105	15	Wilden Furniture	10.12.1936
106	59	James White (Shopfitters)	03.03.1937
107	60	Hugh Wood	02.10.1936
108	77	Wm. Wright & Campbell	24.08.1937
109	108	Sir Wm. Armstrong Whitworth	02.04.1937
110	99	A. Wyman	04.03.1937

Source: EIEM.

Appendix 21: Tenants at Team Valley and the Outside Sites
to the End of 1939, categorised by Origins, with Addresses, Products,
first Floor Areas and Areas occupied at the End of 1939

(For alphabetical list of tenants and date of first contact with the
Estates Company, see Appendix 20. For brief notes on the background of
tenants, see Appendix 22).

Sources: EIE, Rent book of the Company from 1.8.1938 and EIEM.

GENERAL NOTES

1. In principle, the leases sealed at Board meetings should make it
possible to build up a complete list of tenants and of the factories
they occupied. In practice this is not so. With some early exceptions,
leases were often sealed a considerable time after occupation had begun,
in some cases two years later. For this reason, firms which occupied
factory space for short periods only may not have signed any leases. The
rent book from the start to 31.7.1938 has been lost, so that tenants who
paid rent are known only from 1.8.1938. It is unlikely, however, that
more than a few short-term tenants have been omitted.

2. The monthly lists of tenants compiled from July 1939 onwards provide
another source of information (TWA, 1762/5). Until October 1939,
however, they included firms which had agreed to take space but did not
proceed. From November 1939, however, the reports show 'tenants in
occupation'.

3. The information in this Appendix, therefore, lists all those firms
which were recorded in the rent book after 1.8.1938, and, again, in the
list of tenants in occupation in December 1939. The floor area of
tenants' first factories is given here, as also the area occupied at the
end of December 1939, which may have been in more than a single factory
unit.

4. Firms which no longer appear in the list for December 1939 had left
the Estate or gone out of business. The number of these was surprisingly
small.

5. The total first floor area occupied by the industrial tenants listed
was 735,674 sq.ft. By 31.12.1939, this had increased to 863,751 sq.ft.
As the occupied office space, (including the temporary occupation of
parts of nursery factories by the Company's contractors) was
approximately 11,000 sq.ft., the total floor area occupied was
approximately 875,000 sq.ft. The progress record for 1939 in Appendix 14
shows the floor area completed and occupied as 867,841 sq.ft. The two
figures, arrived at in different ways, are less than 1% apart. There
were also 22,954 sq.ft. of floor area completed but not yet occupied.

NOTES ON THE TABLES IN THIS APPENDIX

1. Some firms were temporarily housed in small units until the factories
being built for them were ready. This becomes apparent when a firm was
shown to have moved after a few months from a small unit to a much
larger one. The Tables in this Appendix record the actual position at
the end of December 1939.

2. It is not clear why the size of some factories was reported to the
nearest square foot (e.g. 9,712), while others were rounded off (e.g.
1,500, or 6,000), particularly as it is known that there were small
variations in the size of these standard factories, depending on the
site.

3. Firms which were already in business in a small way before coming to
Team Valley are treated as new starts.

4. The small number of firms which rented factories on the outside sites
were attracted by special factors. They are shown separately in order to
permit statistics for Team Valley alone to be compiled.

5. When tenants of a particular origin were located both at Team Valley
and on an outside site, this is clearly indicated in the Tables. Where
no indication is given, a location at Team Valley is implied.

6. The files do not always provide enough information to permit the
allocation of tenants to particular categories of origin with complete
certainty. In a few cases, a judgment had to be made on the facts
available. The brief notes on the origins of the manufacturing tenants
in Appendix 22 indicates the level of information available.

7. The list of the office tenants is provided because the Estates
Company treated such tenants like industrial tenants for statistical and
public relations purposes. In addition to office tenants in the Central
Administration Building, the consulting engineers for the Estate
occupied two offices in factory K49 D during the construction phase of
the Estate. Two contractors of the Company used factory space as offices
and stores: H.E.Pitt Ltd, building contractors (A4) and Buell Combustion
Ltd (K61 D).

8. The addresses of factories start with the letter of the block in
which they were located (see map in Appendix 13). The 6,000 sq.ft. units
were subdivided into sections A,B,C & D.

ABBREVIATIONS

AD = Address,
FA = first floor area occupied, sq.ft.,
LA = floor area occupied on 31.12.1939, sq.ft.
WA = West Auckland,
NS = North Shields,
PA = Pallion, Sunderland,
IS = total floor area occupied by tenants in their first
   factories at Team Valley.

A. MANUFACTURERS

a) New Firms Apparently Started By Local Individuals

Team Valley				AD		FA	LA
1	1	Coach Confectry.	Confectionery	A 8	D	1,500	1,500
2	2	Dandy Confectry.	Confectionery	A 8	A+B+C	4,500	6,000
3	3	Darlington Engrg.	Engineering	I56	A	1,500	3,000
4	4	Deason Chemical	Glucose Drinks	A 5	A+B+C	4,500	4,500
5	5	Denburn	Fire Lighters	K46	D	1,500	1,500
6	6	T.M. Francis	Marble Processing	I67	D	1,500	1,500
7	7	Jayess Clothing	Clothing	A36		13,700	13,700
8	8	Lawson Beck	Electric Fuses	K46	A	1,500	1,500
9	9	Medical Supplies	Medical Products	K46	C	1,500	1,500
10	10	Neotechnika	Tennis Trainer	A38	C	1,500	-
11	11	Photocrafts	Photogrs.& Prec.Engs.	A40	C+D	3,000	3,000
12	12	Tyne Brush	Rd. Sweepg. Brushes.	I57	D	1,500	1,500
13	13	Vallee	Confectionery	I60	A	1,500	1,500
14	14	Welburn Radio	Domestic Radio Accss.	I67	A	1,500	-
15	15	Wilden Furniture	Fancy Furniture	A 5		6,000	-
						------	------
				6.35% IA		46,700	40,700

Outside Sites

16	1	Bond Moulding	Unknown	WA 3		6,300	6,300

b) New Firms Started By Refugees

Team Valley							
17	1	Alsco	Cardboard Boxes	I60	C	1,500	3,000
18	2	Appetiser Co.	Spec1ty. Food Prods.	K45	C+D	3,000	3,000
19	3	Belts & Trimmings	Leather goods	K49	C	1,500	1,500
20	4	Julius Bernet	Needlework Boxes	I69	C	1,500	1,500
21	5	Builders Chemcls.	Chemcls.Buildg.Trade	I57	C	1,500	1,500
22	6	Burrell & Maurice	Quilts	I58	C+D	3,000	3,000
23	7	Chemika	Chemcls.Buildg.Trade	I60	(part)	1,500	-
24	8	Fancy Crepe Paper	Toilet & Crepe Paper	F13		8,000	10,200
25	9	J. Heller & Co.	Braces & Suspenders	I68	D	1,500	1,500
26	10	Loblite	Electrc. Accessories	K83		6,000	6,000
27	11	Mellolite	Spec1ty. Lampshades	F32	(part)	3,000	-
28	12	Metal Paper Works	Metallised Paper	K44	C+D	3,000	6,000
29	13	Norbrit Alloys	Type Metal	I57	C	1,500	1,500
30	14	Period Furniture	Reprod. Furniture	F32	A	1,500	3,000
31	15	J. Salomon	Mattresses	K82	D	1,500	1,500
32	16	Sigmund Pumps	Fire Fighting Pumps	A 2		20,000	77,680
33	17	Sundox Products	Spec1ty. Food Prdcts.	I56	C	1,500	1,500
34	18	Team Valley Brush	Artists' Brushes	I69	D	1,500	1,500
35	19	T.V. Weaving Inds.	Furnishing Fabrics	D86		6,000	6,000
36	20	Tevaclo	Clothing	K51		9,712	9,712
37	21	Toilet Goods Mfg.	Fancy Goods	I68	C	1,500	1,500
						------	-------
				10.84% IA		79,712	141,092

Outside Sites

38	22 Alligator	Hndbgs. & Lther. Gds.	WA 1	22,000	24,300
39	23 Ernest & Henry	Buttons & Bttn.Mchry.	WA 2	10,000	10,000
40	24 Gt.Nthrn.Knitwear	Speciality Knitwear	T 1	8,000	8,000
41	25 W.Auckland Clothg.	Clothing	WA 5	29,000	29,000

Notes on Refugee Firms

18 A firm called Julius Nussbaum has been omitted as Mr.J. Nussbaum was a co-owner with his brother of the Appetiser Co. and occupied the same premises.

20 The firm was in existence in a small way in Newcastle, before two refugees bought it and used it as the base for their manufacturing business.

32 This firm has been classified as a refugee firm for reasons explained in Loebl, H., 1978.

34 The records show that the Team Valley Brush Co.and a Mr. M. Lion each occupied 1,500 sq.ft., but according to the information available, M.Lion joined Team Valley Brush Co. Ltd, forming one business.

39 This firm had started production in a small way in London before coming to West Auckland.

c) New Manufacturing Activities Or Expansion By Local Firms

Team Valley

			AD	FA	LA
41	1 Anglo-Scottish	Roof Tiles	C65	10,950	11,707
43	2 Geo. Angus	see note 43	K46 C	1,500	1,500
44	3 Atlas Woodworkers	Packing Cases	A38 A+B	3,000	3,000
45	4 J.M. & J. Bartlett	Blackout Blinds	I58 A+B	3,000	3,000
46	5 Bradforth	Quilts	K48	6,000	6,000
47	6 Bushboard Co.	Veneered Panels	A 4	4,589	4,589
48	7 Central Upholstery	Upholstery	A 3	6,000	-
49	8 Dynworks	Bicycle Dynamos	A 7 D	1,500	-
50	9 Mary Harris Gowns	Dresses	K84	9,712	9,712
51	10 Havmor	Pie Baker	A 1	9,000	9,000
52	11 Jones Pot.Crsps.	Food Products	A25 A+B	3,000	3,000
53	12 N.E.Aircraft	Aircraft Components	A81	9,712	9,712
54	13 North East Wires	Copper Wire Insulatn.	A29 (part)	3,000	6,000
55	14 Northern Wire Wks.	Wire Products	I59 A+B	3,000	3,000
56	15 Patterson Lamp	Miners' Oil Lamps	E91	6,000	6,000
57	16 F.S.Slater & Co.	Electrical Enginrs.	A34	5,595	5,595
58	17 Vestric Lamps	Lamp Mftrs.& Distrs.	A40 B	1,500	-
59	18 James White	Joinery Works	A27	6,100	13,300
60	19 Hugh Wood	Mining Machinery	C19	36,000	36,000
				-------	-------
			17.56% IA	129,158	131,115

Outside Sites

61	1 Thoms.Clegg (S'ld)	Unknown	P 4	10,640	10,640
62	2 Kings (S'land)	Unknown	P 2	13,200	13,200
63	3 Saturn Oxygen	Gas Products	P 1	17,300	26,300

```
B. TRADES                                       AD          FA       LA

64   1 D.R. Maxwell      Glaziers            A25 C        1,500    1,500
65   2 B. Morton         Sound Engs.& Agnts. K45 A        1,500    1,500
66   3 Ravensworth       Printers            K49 A+B      3,000    3,000
67   4 Samuel Talbot     Plmbs. & Heatg.Engrs. A39 A      1,500    1,500
                                                          -----    -----
                                          1.02% IA        7,500    7,500

C.ROAD TRANSPORT

68   1 Garlick Burrell & Edwards            M79          8,875    8,875
69   2 Orrell & Brewster                    C12          9,000   10,144
                                                         ------   ------
                                          2.43% IA       17,875   10.019

D. DISTRIBUTIVE TRADES (WHOLESALERS, DISTRIBUTORS & STORAGE)

70   1 E. Crawford       Groceries           F41          6,000    6,000
71   2 Geo. Davidson     Glass Storage       I56 D        1,500    1,500
72   3 Thomas Hedley     Soap Store          I74         12,215   12,215
73   4 N.Plmbrs. Suppls. Building Materials  A38 D        1,500    1,500
74   5 Rickman & Thomas  Bakers Sundries     I67 C        1,500    1,500
75   6 T.V. Cold Storage Cold Stores         E72         12,000   12,000
76   7 Henry Walker      Refrigeration       K47          6,000    6,000
77   8 Wright & Campbell Italian W'housemen  A39 B        1,500    1,500
                                                         ------   ------
                                          5.74% IA       42,215   42,215


                II. FIRMS FROM OUTSIDE THE REGION

A. MANUFACTURERS

a) Setting Up A New Business

78   1 R.M.Chamberlain   Engineering         I68 A+B      3,000      -
79   2 Colmore Adhesives Glass Laminators    A 7 C+D      3,000    7,000
80   3 Durham Steelwork  Constrctnl. Enginrs. Y93        16,800   16,800
81   4 Fibreboard Boxes  Cardboard Cases     E10         15,000   16,500
82   5 Houghton & Hall   Glass Bottle Mftrs. F13          6,000      -
83   6 Laypak Battery    Dry Batteries       I75          6,000    6,000
84   7 Perga             Waxed Paper Cartons D42         26,700   38,400
85   8 Vulcan Welding    Welding Rods        I70 C+D      3,000    3,000
                                                         ------   ------
                                         10.81% IA       79,500   87,700

b) Moving And Expanding An Existing Business

Team Valley

86   1 Celluware         Table Mats          F31          9,712    9,712
87   2 Cottage Bakery    Biscuits            K45 B        1,500    1,500
88   3 Holland Coachcraft Coachbuilders      D17         30,814   36,000
89   4 Landauer          Food Packers        D33         13,300   13,300
90   5 Variety Wafers    Biscuits/Ice Cream  I52          9,712    9,712
                                                         ------   ------
                                          8.84% IA       65,038   70,224
```

91	1 Cardinal Cabinets	Radio Cabinets	WA	unknown	

c) Setting Up A Branch Plant

			AD	FA	LA
92	1 John Barran	Clothing	A21	21,000	44,325
93	2 Exeau Products	Doors	F24	18,000	18,000
94	3 Hunters	Plant Bakers	F28	80,000	80,000
95	4 Kavli	Food Products	E90	6,000	6,000
96	5 J.F.Marriott	Mattress	I59 C+D	3,000	3,000
97	6 Northern Beverage	Cola Bottlers	I70 A+B	3,000	3,000
98	7 Square Grip	Concr.Reinfrcng.Bars	D 6	8,000	16,000
99	8 A. Wyman	Clothing	A 30	6,000	30,885
				-------	-------
			19.71% IA	145,000	201,210

B. DISTRIBUTIVE TRADES

100	1 Betta Biscuits	Distr. Depot	I61 A+B+C	4,500	4,500
101	2 Brit.Jeffrey Dmd.	Sales/Service	I76 A+B	3,000	3,000
102	3 Cadbury Brothers	Distr. Depot	M23	28,416	28,416
103	4 Consol. Pneumatic	Sales/Service	I67 A+B	3,000	3,000
104	5 Danish Bacon	Distr. Depot	K46 B	1,500	1,500
105	6 Hills Pat.Glazing	Distr. Depot	I66	9,712	9,712
106	7 Impl.Chem.Indsts.	Distr. Depot	E11	11,000	11,000
107	8 J.Mackintosh	Distr. Depot	E89	3,000	3,000
108	9 Armstrong Whitwrth	Service	F35	8,554	8,554
				------	------
			9.88% IA	72,682	72,682

Notes

100 Betta Biscuits were part of Meredith & Drew Ltd
108 Servicing Armstrong Saurer commercial vehicles.Although represented
in the region by Sir W.G. Armstrong Whitworth & Co.(Engineers)
Ltd, the Armstrong Saurer Company had its head office in London.

III. GOVERNMENT TENANTS

109	1 Home Office	Gas Masks Store	A14	34,656	34,656
110	2 Min. of Labour	Training Centre	L15	15,638	15,638
				------	------
			6.83% IA	50,294	50,294
				------	------

TOTAL OCCUPIED INDUSTRIAL FLOOR AREA AT TEAM VALLEY

	First factories	735,674
		sq.ft.
	31.12.1939	863,751
		sq.ft.

IV. OFFICE & SERVICE TENANTS

As at 31.12.1939. All Tenants were located at the Central Administration Building.

110	1	Barclays Bank	
112	2	Chipchase, Wood Short	Accountants
113	3	Lloyds Bank	
114	4	London & N. Eastern Railway	
115	5	Martins Bank	
116	6	Northern General Transport	Bus Operators
117	7	Post Office	
118	8	Percy F. Ward	Accountants

Appendix 22: Notes on the Origins of the manufacturing Tenants
of the Team Valley Trading Estate listed in Appendix 21

I. FIRMS FROM WITHIN THE REGION

a) New Firms Apparently Started By Local Individuals

1   Coach Confectionery Ltd
    Founded by a Mr. Brett. Appleyard noted in an undated speech, that
    Brett's fiancee refused to marry him until he had his own
    business, which he started in a garage at the back of the former
    Black's Regal Cinema in High Street, Gateshead.

2   Dandy Confectionery Ltd
    This firm had been producing confectionery in a room in the
    founder's home at 1, Norwood Gardens, Low Fell, Gateshead.

3   Darlington Engineering Co. Ltd
    The founder was a Mr. Kirkup who was believed to have been an
    engineer's agent, operating from an office in Pilgrim Street,
    Newcastle.

4   Deason Chemical Co. Ltd
    This firm developed from a Chemist's shop at 133, New Bridge
    Street, Newcastle, later traded as Barluze Ltd.

5   Denburn Firelighters Ltd
    The founder was a Mr. Dent, of Church Road, Low Fell, Gateshead.
    The firm was later taken over by Cook Industrial Supplies Ltd of
    30, St. Mary's Place, Newcastle.

6   T.M. Francis Ltd
    Mr. Francis was a small builder at Consett, Co. Durham, where he
    started to deal in and process marble and granite as a sideline.
    He imported the marble from Italy.

7   Jayess Clothing Co.Ltd
    The founder was a Mr. J. Smith, a local businessman, who joined
    two or three people with suitable experience to form this new
    business.

8   Lawson Beck Ltd
    The firm (later, Lawson Fuses Ltd) was formed by a Mr. Beck, a
    Newcastle businessman and a Mr. Lawson, who was previously
    employed by A. Reyrolle & Co.Ltd, Hebburn on Tyne.

9   Medical Supplies (Newastle) Ltd
    This firm existed in a small way at Bell's Court, Pilgrim Street,
    Newcastle. It was owned by a Mr. Astin, who developed new ethical
    products which he supplied in small quantities to local doctors.

10 Neotechnika Ltd
    Founded by a Mr. Ayers, of Glendale Ave., Gosforth, Newcastle. The
    product was a tennis trainer devised by a relative, the Rev. J.A.
    Appleton of Norfolk. The main objective of this firm appears to
    have been job creation.

11 Photocrafts Ltd
Founded by Mr. Carlisle Stewart, who operated a photographic shop
at 155, Barras Bridge, Newcastle. He developed photographic
processing and diversified into precision engineering components
during the War. It is believed that this activity was carried on
through an associated firm, the White Fox Instrument Company.

12 Tyne Brush Co.Ltd
Founded by a Mr. Purdy, 17, Guelder Road, Heaton, Newcastle and a
Mr. E. O'Connor. The firm produced road sweeping brushes.

13 Vallee (Newcastle) Ltd
Founded by a Mr.Clark and a Mr.Swallow, believed to have been
local, because the business was incorporated by a Newcastle firm
of solicitors, Bell and Allan.

14 Welburn (Radio) Ltd
Founded by a Mr. Brown, of 74, Benton Road, Newcastle, for his
son, who was a graduate (and PhD) of King's College, Newcastle.
The object was to manufacture an anti-fading accessory for
domestic radio receivers invented by Dr. Brown.

15 Wilden Furniture Ltd
The originator, a Mr. Holden, had produced samples of furniture
made from barrels and casks and had shown them at the Northern
Exhibition of Inventions at Newcastle in November 1936 (supported
by the Commissioner), where they aroused much interest. As Mr.
Holden had no capital of his own, a number of prominent local
citizens joined him to form the company.

b) New Firms Started By Refugees

A case history for each firm is given in Loebl, H., 1978.

c) New Manufacturing Activities Or Expansion By Local Firms

42 Anglo-Scottish Trading Co.Ltd
Producers of concrete tiles and agents for tile-making machinery.
The firm, which had operated from offices at 8, St.Mary's Place,
Newcastle, was connected with Mr. David Adams, Labour MP for
Consett, Co. Durham and his sons Ronald and McGregor, who were to
become involved in a number of enterprises at Team Valley later
(for a pre-War example, see 53 below).

43 Geo. Angus & Co.Ltd
This old-established local firm had operated a tannery behind
Grainger Street in the centre of Newcastle which caused a
nuisance. The firm planned to move the works to Team Valley and
instal a modern plant. As the space initially occupied was small
(1,500 sq.ft.), it is not clear whether this factory was actually
used for tanning.

44 Atlas Woodworkers Ltd .
Set up as a new activity by Mawson & Swan Ltd, Newcastle. The firm
manufactured packing and tin-lined cases.

45 J.M. & J. Bartlett Ltd
    This established builders' merchant in Newcastle decided to
    manufacture blackout blinds - a new activity - in anticipation of
    wartime demand.

46 Bradforth & Co.Ltd
    The firm, owned by a Mr. Renolds, appears to have been in
    existence in Low Fell, Gateshead. It manufactured quilts and later
    Board of Trade standard marine life jackets.

47 Bushboard Ltd
    Founded by Mr J.P. Law and Mr. F. Kerr, who had worked at the
    Bushing Co. Ltd, Hebburn, a firm which produced electrical
    insulators by winding and cementing layers of bakelised paper
    around circular formers. Law and Kerr hit on the idea of slitting
    the tubes made in this way and to flatten them, creating what is
    believed to have been the first plastic laminate for wood
    surfaces. Bushboard later became the largest laminator in the UK
    (information kindly supplied by Mr. G. Harrison).

48 Central Upholstery Co. Ltd
    This firm was originally established in Sunderland; its life at
    Team Valley was short.

49 Dynworks Ltd
    A new activity by the Newcastle firm of engineer's agents,
    J.Graham Parmley, backing a German refugee engineer, Dr. H. Walz.
    The first product is believed to have been a dynamo for bicycle
    lighting.

50 Mary Harris Gowns Ltd
    The business, founded by Mrs. Mary Harris, had previously operated
    in small premises in Westgate Road, Newcastle.

51 Havmor Ltd
    This firm, owned by a Mr. Wilkinson, had produced pies on a craft
    basis in the West end of Newcastle. The move to Team Valley was
    intended to introduce an industrial type of production. The firm
    is said to have occupied the first completed factory (A1) on
    Kingsway.

52 Jones (Potato Crisps) Co.Ltd
    The firm owned by a Mr. Jones had operated in a very small way in
    South Shields.

53 North Eastern Aircraft Components Ltd
    This firm was formed by Mr. James White (see 59 below) and a
    member of the Adams family (see 42 above) at the beginning of the
    War to produce precision wood and sheet metal components for War
    planes.

54 North East Wires Ltd
    The founder, a Mr. Saunders, had operated from an office at 12,
    St. Mary's Place, Newcastle. He appears to have manufactured
    insulated copper wire or heavy conductors before he came to Team
    Valley, but no details have been found.

55 Northern Wire Works Ltd
    The firm was owned by a Mr. Kelly; it had existed for some years
    at Akenside Hill, Newcastle.

56 Patterson Lamp Co. Ltd
    This apparently substantial firm had been located at Felling on
    Tyne; the move to Team Valley was necessitated by the destruction
    of its works at Sunderland Road by fire.

57 F.S. Slater & Co. Ltd
    A repairer of electrical and other machinery, the firm had
    operated from offices at Baltic Chambers, Sunderland. One of the
    directors was R.W. Gregory, senior partner in a well-known
    Newcastle firm of consultant engineers, which also acted for the
    Estates Company.

58 Vestric Lamps Ltd
    The firm had offices at 31, Ridley Place, Newcastle. The managing
    director was a Mr. Cook. The firm manufactured specialised
    double-filament 60W electric lamps and imported a range of cheap
    lamps. A list of 500 customers is in the file.

59 James White (Shopfitters) Ltd
    A joinery and cabinet-making business which had operated from 107,
    Pilgrim Street, Newcastle (see also 53 above).

60 Hugh Wood & Co.Ltd
    This firm of agents for mining machinery had operated from offices
    at Sun Buildings, Newcastle. The company also designed equipment
    and had it produced by sub-contractors. It became one of the
    largest employers at Team Valley.

II. FIRMS FROM OUTSIDE THE REGION

a) Setting Up A New Business

78 R.M.Chamberlain Ltd
    Mr. Maitland Chamberlain originated from Southampton, where he had
    been involved with a small sheet metal works. He intended to make
    steel air raid shelters. He appears to have paid the rent for some
    months, but vacated his factory, apparently before starting
    production, and moved to Low Fell, Gateshead.

79 Colmore Adhesives Ltd
    This firm was established to exploit a new process for laminating
    glass. The letter of intent to rent premises at Team Valley was
    signed by a Mr. Williams, of 77, Muncaster Road, London S.W.11.
    The name of the firm arose from the address of their solicitors in
    Colmore Row, Birmingham.

80 Durham Steelwork Ltd
    This firm was founded by Mr. Murray Buxton, of Holywell near
    Woking, Surrey. He had been a director of a firm of structural
    engineers, H. Young & Co. Ltd, Nine Elms Steel Works, London
    S.W.1. Mr. Buxton had family a connection in the area. He cam to
    Team Valley because he expected capital help from SARA and the
    Nuffield Trust.

81 Fibreboard Boxes Ltd
    The founder was a Mr. Nichols, of the Old School House, Trent, Sherbourne, Dorset. He set up the business at Team Valley in expectation of capital help from SARA and the Nuffield Trust.

82 Houghton & Hall Ltd
    Mr. Houghton was works manager of a glass bottle manufacturing business at Walkden, Manchester. Mr. Hall appears to have been connected with the Gateshead glass manufacturers Geo. Davidson & Co.Ltd (see 73 in Appendix 21).

83 Laypak Battery Co.Ltd
    The contact with the Estates Company was made by a Mr Proudlock, the chairman of the Acton Battery Co. Ltd, London. The company produced a novel type of battery for War equipment. The general manager was Mr. Laszlo Torday, a Hungarian refugee, who was one of the co-founders of the Tyneside Chemical Company Ltd, Gateshead at the start of the War (see [26], p.190). This business could not support two partners. After the War, he formed an electroplating company in North Shields which became an important business.

84 Perga Ltd
    A subsidiary of Rappings Ltd, waxed paper manufacturers in Sydenham, London. It is believed that Perga Ltd was a new business, although it may have existed in a small way before coming to Team Valley.

85 Vulcan Welding Products Ltd
    The founder, a Mr. Lindsay, originally came from Giffnock, Glasgow. Before starting his own business on Tyneside, he occupied a position with the Service Welding Company, College Ave, Newcastle.

b) Moving And Expanding An Existing Business

86 Celluware Ltd
    The owner, Mr. Will George, had operated in Cowley Mill Road, Uxbridge, Middlesex. The Uxbridge works are believed to have been closed.

87 Cottage Bakery Ltd
    This firm, owned by a Mr. Shaw, had existed in Great Ouseburn, N. Yorkshire. The Great Ouseburn bakery was closed.

88 Holland Coachcraft Ltd
    Owned by a Mr. Holland, the firm had operated at 95, Bath Street, Glasgow C.2. At Team Valley, production was commenced of caravans and trailers. The Glasgow garage is believed to have been disposed of.

89 Landauer Ltd
    This importer and exporter of dried fruit, nuts, canned goods, cereals and raffia had its headquarters at Golden Bough House, 39, Eastcheap, London E.C.3. Little is known about this firm, but it is possible that this was their first packing operation. If another existed, the Team Valley unit should be treated as a branch factory.

90 Variety Wafers Ltd
    This firm had originally operated at Bostock Works, Henley on
    Thames. The owner, a Mr. Fosschi, appears to have been connected
    with Mr. M. Reay, a Newcastle ice cream manufacturer, who may have
    become a partner. It is possible that the Henley business
    continued under different ownership.

c) Setting Up A Branch Plant

92 John Barran & Sons Ltd
    This Leeds-based firm set up a branch at Team Valley because of
    labour shortages at Leeds.

93 Exeau Products Ltd
    The headquarters of this building component firm were at 221, Lea
    Bridge Road London, E.10. The ready availability of a factory and
    the desire to produce nearer to the northern market seem to have
    been the reasons for setting up a branch at Team Valley. By March
    1938, the weekly production of flush doors had reached 1000
    (Timber Trade Journal, 19.3.1938).

94 Hunters The Bakers Ltd
    An earlier plant had existed at East Street, Gateshead. Believed
    to have been a branch of Allied Bakeries Ltd.

95 Kavli Ltd
    This Norwegian firm is believed to have continued production at
    its main plant up to the War at least.

96 J.F.Marriott & Co.Ltd
    The headquarters of this firm were at Liversedge, Leeds. The
    reasons for setting up a branch at Team valley are not known.

97 Northern Beverage Co.Ltd
    This appears to have been a Coca Cola bottling plant. Negotiations
    were carried out by Brown, Harriman and Co. Ltd, a division of the
    Investment Banking Corporation, 17, St. Helen's Place, London,
    E.C.3. Since the transaction was handled entirely by this firm,
    the name of the franchisee - if there was one - has not been
    found.

98 Square Grip Reinforcements Ltd
    This branch of the London-based Company was set up in order to
    exploit the opportunity of manufacturing on site all the
    reinforcements required by the contractors of the Estates Company.
    The firm has been in contact with the Estates Company as early as
    August 1936. It was the first firms to sign a lease with the
    Company (in March 1937), probably the first tenant to occupy a
    factory at Team Valley and the first to order an extension to the
    original building.

99 A. Wyman Ltd
    This Leeds waterproof clothing manufacturer was operated by the
    Michaelson family. The reasons for setting up a branch at Team
    Valley are believed to have been the same as for 92 above.

Appendix 23: Floor Areas occupied at Team Valley
by Industry Sectors with greater than Average Rates of
Expansion in Employment 1923 - 1937, represented both in
London & the Home Counties and Northumberland & Durham

The floor area occupied by industrial tenants in their first factories
was 685,380 sq.ft. (see Table 3, p.179). This analysis covers 72
(72.73%) of the 99 industrial tenants at Team Valley and 547,118 sq.ft.
of floor area, i.e. 79.83% of the first floor area they occupied.

Manufacturing		Area each Firm sq.ft.	Total Area Sector sq.ft.	% Total Ind. Area
1 Electrical Engineering				
57	F.S.Slater	5,595	5,595	0.82
2 Electric Cable, Lamps, Apparatus				
8	Lawson Beck	1,500		
15	Welburn Radio	1,500		
26	Loblite	6,000		
49	Dynworks	1,500		
53	N.E. Wires	3,000		
77	Vestric Lamps	1,500		
83	Laypak Battery	6,000	21,000	3.06
3 Motor Vehicles, Cycles, Aircraft				
53	N.E.Aircraft Components	9,712		
88	Holland Coachcraft	30,814		
108	Armstrong Whitworth	8,554	49,080	7.16
4 Miscellaneous Metal Goods				
55	Northern Wire Works	3,000		
56	Patterson Lamp	6,000		
85	Vulcan Welding	3,000		
98	Square Grip	8,000	20,000	2.92
5 Furniture Making, Upholstery				
16	Wilden Furniture	6,000		
31	J.Salomon	1,500		
48	Central Upholstery	6,000		
96	J.F.Marriott	3,000	16,500	2.41
6 Metal Manufacture (other than Iron & Steel)				
29	Norbrit Alloys	1,500	1,500	0.22
7 Paper & Paper Board				
24	Fancy Crepe Paper Mills	8,000	8,000	1.17

8 Miscellaneous Food Industries

1	Coach Confectionery	1,500		
2	Dandy Confectionery	4,500		
3	Vallee	1,500		
18	Appetiser	3,000		
33	Sundox	1,500		
51	Havmor	9,000		
52	Jones Potato Crisp	3,000		
89	Landauer	13,300	37,300	5.44

9 Glass & Glass Bottles

79	Colmore Adhesives	3,000		
82	Houghton & Hall	6,000	9,000	1.31

10 Cardboard Boxes, Stationery, Paper Bags

17	Alsco Cardboard	1,500		
81	Fibreboard Boxes	15,000	16,500	2.41

11 Chemicals, incl. Oils, Paints, Soap, Ink, Explosives

5	Denburn Firelighters	1,500		
21	Builders Chemicals	1,500		
23	Chemika	1,500	4,500	0.66

12 Leather & Leather Goods

19	Belts & Trimmings	1,500		
25	J. Heller	1,500	3,000	0.44

13 Dressmaking & Millinery

50	Mary Harris Gowns	9,712	9,712	1.42

14 General Drink Industries

4	Deason Chemical	4,500		
97	Northern Beverage	3,000	7,500	1.09

15 General Engineering

3	Darlington Engineering	1,500		
32	Sigmund Pumps	20,000		
60	Hugh Wood	36,000		
78	R.M. Chamberlain	3,000	60,500	8.83

16 Printing, Publishing & Bookbinding

66	Ravensworth Printers	3,000	3,000	0.44

17 Bread, Biscuits & Cakes

87	Cottage Bakery	1,500		
90	Variety Wafers	9,712		
94	Hunters The Bakers	80,000	91,212	13.31

18 Tailoring, Clothing

8	Jayess Clothing	13,700		
36	Tevaclo	9,712		
92	J. Barran	21,000		
99	A. Wyman	6,000	50,412	7.36

Non-Manufacturing

19 Distributive Activities

Firms from Within Region
Nos. 70 - 77 incls.   42,250

Firms from Without Region
Nos. 100 - 108 incl.   72,682   114,932   16.77

20 Road Transport, except for Buses & Trams

68	Garlick Burrell & Edwards	8,875		
69	Orrell & Brewster	9,000	17,875	2.61

                                                -------   ------
                                                547,118   79.85%
                                                sq.ft.   of 685,380
                                                              sq.ft.

Appendix 24: Factories authorised by North Eastern Trading Estates Ltd
in the Months before and immediately after the last War

BEFORE THE END OF THE WAR

Board meeting on	Company	Site	Floor Area sq.ft.
12. 2.1945	Charles Twigg	Pallion	50,000
	Shaffer Aircraft	S.Shields	50,000
	Sigmund Pumps	Team Valley	115,000 (Ext.)
	Tyneside Safety Glass	Team Valley	9,000 (Ext.)
12. 3.45	Mary Harris Gowns	Team Valley	10,000 (Ext.)
	Fibreboard Boxes	Team Valley	65,000
	Woodhouse & Smith	Langley Moor	25,000
23. 4.1945	Perga	Team Valley	19,300 (Ext.)
	A. Wyman	Pallion	73,000
	W. Auckland Clothing	West Auckland	61,500 (Ext.)
	Price's the Tailor	Sunderland	80,000

			557,800 sq.ft.

At Team Valley: Extensions 153,300 sq.ft.
                   New Factory 65,000   "

                   218,300 sq.ft., all for exsting tenants

IMMEDIATELY AFTER THE END OF THE WAR

Board meeting on	Company	Site	Floor Area sq.ft.
11. 5.1945	Hirst & Thackray	Langley Moor	30,100
	Leyland Motors	Team Valley	16,000
8. 6.1945	Huwood	Team Valley	47,250
	J. & S. Bickley	Sherburn	20,300
	Jules Coppe	Team Valley	8,000
	Curry & Co	n.a.	27,500
	John Binns & Sons	Darlington	32,000
	" " "	Ferryhill	30,000
	M. Jackson & Sons	Team Valley	80,000

			291,150 sq.ft.

At Team Valley: New Factories 104,000 sq.ft. for new tenants
                New Factory   47,250   "   " an existing tenant
                               ----
                151,250 sq.ft.

Total at Team Valley: 369,550 sq.ft. out of a total of 848,950 = 43.5%

The Company is believed to have authorised only one more factory. After
the passing of the Distribution of Industry Act 1945 on 15 June 1945,
the authorisation of factories became a matter for the Board of Trade
(see Appendix 29 for the outline procedure).

Source: EIEB.

Appendix 25: Unanimous Recommendations of the Royal Commission on the
Distribution of the Industrial Population

The Commission unanimously accepted the following nine conclusions:-

(1) In view of the nature and urgency of the problems before the Commission, national action is necessary.

(2) For this purpose, a Central Authority, national in character and scope, is required.

(3) The activities of this Authority should be distinct from and should extend beyond those within the powers of any existing Government Department.

(4) The objectives of national action should be:-

(a) Continued and further redevelopment of congested urban areas, where necessary.
(b) Decentralisation or dispersal, both of industries and industrial population, from such areas.
(c) Encouragement of a reasonable balance of industrial development, so far as possible, throughout the various divisions or regions of Great Britain, coupled with appropriate diversification of industry in each division or region throughout the country.

(5) The continued drift of the industrial population to London and the Home Counties constitutes a social, economic and strategical problem which demands immediate attention.

(6) The Central Authority, whether advisory or executive, should, in pursuance of objectives 4 (b) and (c), examine forthwith and formulate the policy or plan to be adopted in relation to decentralisation or dispersal from congested urban areas in connection with the following issues:-

(i) In relation to what congested urban areas is decentralisation or dispersal desirable.

(ii) In cases where such decentralisation or dispersal is found desirable, how far should the following be encouraged or developed:-

a) Garden cities or garden suburbs.
b) Satellite towns.
c) Trading Estates.
d) Further development of existing small towns or regional centres (provided adequate planning schemes are applicable thereto).
e) Other appropriate methods.

In all cases, adequate provision must be made:-

(a) For the requirements of industry (i.e. in respect of labour supply, markets, transport and power), and for the social and amenity needs of the communities.

(b) That the risk of unnecessary competition is avoided.

(c) That strategical considerations are given due weight.

(iii) The time factor is important in developments under (ii). Without excluding activities of private enterprise, such as authorised associations under the Town and Country Planning Act 1932, municipalities (which have special facilities in respect of housing, roads and other social services) should be encouraged to undertake such development, and:-

(a) Where considered necessary, they should be given opportunity for dealing with the problem, so far as found desirable, on a regional rather than on a municipal basis.

b) In cases approved and to the extent approved by the Central Authority, financial assistance should be available for the municipalities from Government funds, especially in the early years.

(7) The Central Authority should have the right to inspect all existing, and future Planning Schemes under current Town and Country Planning legislation, whether regional or local, and to consider, where necessary, in co-operation with the Government Departments concerned the modification or correlation of existing or future plans in the national interest.

(8) The general problem of unemployment lies outside the Commission's Terms of Reference; and the problem of the Special and Depressed areas is only covered by those Terms in so far as those areas represent disadvantages arising from the concentration of industries or the industrial population in large towns or particular areas.

The Special Areas legislation and the work of the Commissioners appointed thereunder will afford increasingly valuable experience. The Central Authority, whether advisory or executive should in the light of this experience study the location of industry throughout the country with a view to:-

(i) Anticipating cases where depression may probably occur in the future (e.g. the armament industries when normal peace conditions are again definitely secured), and encouraging before a depression crisis arises the development in such cases, so far as possible, of other industries, or public undertakings.

(ii) Pursuing the plan laid down in 4 (c) above.

(9) The Powers of the Authority should also include:-

(a) Collection and co-ordination of information relating to location of industry, now in the possession of the various Government Departments.

(b) Research; and collection of information as to the various natural resources - land, agriculture, amenities, etc. - that may be affected by industrial location.

(c) Advice to Government, local authorities and industrialists as to problems of location.

(d) Publicity and Annual Reports.

Source: RCDIP, 1940, para.428, pp. 202,203.

Appendix 26: Number of Tenants 1939 - 1960 and Employment 1939 - 1980
in Government-financed and wartime Factories in the
North East under the Control of the Company,
with a Comparison of Employment in Coal Mining

	Employment	Number of Tenant firms	Employment in Coal Mining
end of 1939 *	5,000	110	
mid-1945 *	9,500	n.a.	145,460
31 March			
1947 **	18,000	n.a	
1949	30,000	250	
1955	49,000	308	
1957	52,750	300	167,280
1960	58,000	326	
1963	64,484		
1964	70,535		
1965	76,440		113,000
1966	83,884		
1967	83,879		
1968	87,470		
1969	90,678		
1970	94,678 Peak Year		72,700
1971	92,398		
1972	89,360		
1973	93,308		
1974 **	87,916		
1974 ***	93,000		
1975	80,593		
1976	74,658		
1977	73,909		
1978	70,658		
1979	70,850		
1980	71,543		**** (1981) 35,559

    * Employment and tenant numbers include the outside sites.
    ** The Aycliffe Trading Estate was handed over to the New
Town Corporation in May 1973. The employment at Aycliffe
was removed from the Company's figures.
    *** This is the figure with the Aycliffe employment added
back.
**** There was no labour census in 1980.

Sources: employment and number of tenants, EIE, Annual Reports
of the Company. Employment in coal mining up to 1970,
see Appendix 31. Employment in coal mining 1981,
Mr. K.G. Hodgson, Manpower Services Commission,
Newcastle upon Tyne.

Appendix 27: Progress Information on Factory Construction & Conversions
from the Directorate for Industrial Estates, Board of Trade

NEW FACTORY CONSTRUCTION : (NF = number of factories)

| | 31.8.1946 | | 30.9.1947 | | 31.8.1948 | | 31.8.1949 | | 30.6.1950 | |
	NF	sq.ft.	NF	sq.ft.	NF	sq.ft.	NF	sq.ft.	NF	sq.ft.
NORTH EAST										
Under Construction	53	1,893,331	111	3,410,899	35	1,185,914	14	489,211	10	363,107
Completed	5	191,463	31	1,094,318	110	3,354,019	144	4,443,750	157	4,687,314
SCOTLAND										
Under Construction	62	2,093,938	149	4,856,206	44	4,002,883	39	1,591,380	13	1,028,850
Completed	0	0	38	540,661	107	2,050,206	195	4,594,914	228	5,678,124
WALES & MONMOUTHSHIRE										
Under Construction	62	2,260,641	110	4,034,395	69	2,783,542	21	966,574	19	626,252
Completed	0	0	28	777,316	82	2,275,142	138	4,258,645	158	4,950,775
WEST CUMBERLAND										
Under Construction	12	318,386	8	317,568	6	182,993	0	0	3	113,500
Completed	1	13,982	14	383,678	19	554,817	26	751,149	25	745,375
NORTH WEST										
Under Construction	0	0	4	256,100	8	390,100	7	134,114	7	251,852
Completed	0	0	0	0	1	10,000	8	380,100	13	474,807

CONVERSIONS OF ROYAL ORDNANCE & OTHER WARTIME FACTORIES

NT = number of Tenants

	31.8. 1946		30.9. 1947		31.8. 1948		31.8. 1949		30.6. 1950	
	NT	sq.ft.	NT	sq.ft.	NT	sq.ft.	NT	sq.ft.	NT	sq.ft.
NORTH EAST										
Completed		29,125		637,207		915,572		2,408,415		2,579,849
In Hand		802,315		724,526		541,550		182,557		57,286
Not yet Started		319,250		105,107		0		7,200		85,725
Totals		1,150,690		1,466,840		1,457,122		2,598,172		2,722,860
Occupied	n.a.	n.a.	56	1,239,190	57	1,302,712	79	2,583,357	89	2,677,675
SCOTLAND										
Completed		0		395,132		1,069,530		1,344,184		2,080,159
In Hand		294,400		2,438,496		2,762,002		2,652,336		1,987,555
Not yet Started		455,200		67,520		41,520		41,520		124,195
Totals		749,600		2,901,148		3,873,052		4,038,040		4,191,909
Occupied	n.a.	n.a.	13	1,539,839	30	3,590,572	34	3,681,554	37	3,984,497
WALES & MONMOUTHSHIRE										
Completed		4,274		1,375,222		2,258,587		3,000,131		3,578,107
In Hand		1,306,857		903,617		233,535		495,046		298,534
Not yet Started		288,228		151,000		126,600		222,630		104,886
Totals		1,599,359		2,429,839		2,618,722		3,717,807		3,981,525
Occupied	n.a.	n.a.	135	2,178,830	137	2,342,122	156	3,700,389	163	3,959,379

Source: TWA,1762/13

Notes on Appendix 27

NEW FACTORY CONSTRUCTION

1. The format of the progress reports changed slightly after 1946.

2. The progress reports defined completed factories as 'either 100% or so near that tenants have been able to move in'; factories 'ready for occupation' were presented separately. Notes in the reports for 1948,1949 and 1950 stated that some components were still missing even for factories in this category.

   It is not clear why a distinction was made between these two categories, since the factories appear to have been in a similar state of completion. For the purpose of the Appendix, Factories Ready for Occupation have been added to Factories Completed. Given the provisos in the reports, it is likely that the resulting figures for completions are somewhat overstated.

3. The figures for factories under construction include the floor areas of factories for which site work only had been commenced.

CONVERSIONS OF ROYAL ORDNANCE AND OTHER WARTIME FACTORIES

4. The completion figures in the reports for 1949 and 1950 include wartime factories which did not require any adaptations.

5. In addition to the conversions in the North East, Scotland and Wales & Monmouthshire, the progress report of 6.6.1950 shows that 113,500 sq.ft. had been converted for four tenants in West Cumberland.

Appendix 28: Labour Statistics for the North East 1945 - 1948
(collected in July in each year)

IP = Insured Population, UE = Unemployment.

Employment Exchange or Office	1945 IP	% UE	1946 IP	% UE	1947 IP	% UE	1948 IP	% UE
1 Alnwick	5,538	0.2	6,135	1.0	6,102	0.6	7,980	0.6
2 Amble	2,745	1.9	3,162	4.5	2,872	4.1	3,453	1.4
3 Ashington	15,152	2.1	15,939	4.9	17,140	2.8	18,884	1.5
4 Barnard Castle	1,696	0.8	1,783	2.0	2,500	1.2	2,782	1.0
5 Bedlington Stn.	7,143	5.8	8,291	4.8	9,040	2.4	10,167	2.7
6 Berwick	4,760	1.1	5,445	3.3	5,914	2.1	7,683	1.2
7 Birtley	14,429	0.6	9,591	9.0	9,160	5.9	10,122	2.4
8 Bishop Auckland	10,826	3.7	9,913	11.9	10,876	4.6	12,136	3.9
9 Blaydon	7,867	4.6	9,766	10.7	10,028	6.5	10,028	4.4
10 Blyth	10,456	2.5	11,186	7.5	12,070	4.3	13,320	3.2
11 Chester le Street	11,849	1.3	14,241	7.7	10,978	4.6	12,222	3.7
12 Chopwell	1,017	11.0	1,236	20.1	2,941	4.5	3,340	1.9
13 Cockfield	1,564	4.5	1,860	9.8	1,841	1.7	2,106	6.5
14 Consett	15,268	0.8	16,870	2.5	14,471	1.3	16,435	0.8
15 Crook	7,855	4.2	10,636	7.4	8,837	5.6	10,127	3.3
16 Darlington	48,759	0.2	45,735	2.0	36,105	1.0	46,104	0.8
17 Dunston	5,993	1.0	7,148	2.8	8,330	1.9	8,061	2.3
18 Durham	13,590	5.9	15,006	7.2	20,009	3.3	24,348	2.0
19 East Boldon	1,235	3.1	1,670	7.2	4,996	1.9	5,650	1.5
20 Elswick	21,850	3.7	17,588	15.9	17,504	10.7	19,504	8.5
21 Felling	6,500	2.3	7,705	8.8	7,963	4.8	7,350	4.4
22 Gainford	526	0.2	557	2.7	563	1.2	810	0.5
23 Gateshead	30,433	3.3	37,553	9.0	28,343	5.1	43,176	4.7
24 Guisborough	1,104	0.5	1,424	3.9	1,700	2.6	1,986	2.1
25 Haltwhistle	1,513	1.2	1,772	4.2	1,865	2.5	2,454	1.6
26 Hartlepool	1,680	10.7	2,368	22.0	2,197	18.0	2,287	12.3
27 Haswell	3,794	2.9	3,974	7.0	4,158	4.7	4,296	3.3
28 Haverton Hill	4,420	0.6	5,328	5.3	6,301	4.8	7,004	1.5
29 Heaton	17,438	2.4	18,676	7.3	22,208	4.0	24,885	3.3
30 Helmsley	1,548	0.0	1,692	0.2	1,810	3.3	2,661	0.6
31 Hexham	5,217	0.7	6,018	2.1	6,878	1.5	9,680	0.8
32 Horden	10,341	3.1	11,900	5.3	11,229	3.2	13,312	2.1
33 Houghton le Spr.	11,200	3.9	14,308	10.7	13,855	6.5	14,996	4.1
34 Jarrow & Hebburn	22,904	2.2	23,011	7.7	22,627	6.1	25,198	4.4
35 Lanchester	2,233	3.7	2,764	4.5	3,419	2.3	3,860	0.9
36 Loftus	3,363	1.0	3,660	2.4	3,602	1.5	4,408	1.0
37 Middlesborough	30,675	1.5	38,780	5.3	38,263	3.1	54,232	2.1
38 Morpeth	5,304	0.8	5,667	3.3	6,068	1.7	8,663	1.3
39 Newburn	4,975	2.1	5,847	5.2	5,912	2.6	6,376	2.1
40 Newcastle / Tyne	76,938	1.2	91,313	2.7	84,309	2.2	100,085	1.8
41 North Shields	11,121	2.9	15,639	6.1	17,727	11.1	21,593	3.7
42 Pallion	18,321	2.1	20,357	5.9	20,734	4.7	20,824	3.9
43 Prudhoe	4,567	1.2	4,858	3.4	3,991	2.1	4,829	1.3
44 Redcar	2,299	1.5	3,141	4.8	6,726	1.2	7,707	0.9
45 Saltburn	1,405	0.3	1,947	5.5	3,462	0.7	4,406	1.5
46 Seaham	12,892	2.3	14,591	5.5	15,313	2.8	17,018	1.8
47 Seaton Delaval	7,797	1.1	8,323	2.8	6,645	1.1	7,557	1.0
48 Sedgefield	3,026	0.8	3,079	2.3	3,032	1.2	4,049	0.7
49 Shildon	n.a.	-	4,697	7.4	4,494	2.7	5,587	3.0

Employment Exchange or Office	1945 IP	1945 % UE	1946 IP	1946 % UE	1947 IP	1947 % UE	1948 IP	1948 % UE
50 South Bank	19,605	0.4	21,041	1.9	18,501	0.7	20,916	0.5
51 South Shields	26,200	3.6	31,928	8.3	29,817	6.4	35,488	5.2
52 Southwick	7,277	1.1	7,714	7.6	7,360	5.1	8,033	3.4
53 Spennymoor	17,412	4.9	17,643	7.1	12,788	3.7	14,967	3.0
54 Stanhope	1,115	2.2	1,244	5.7	1,177	4.9	1,569	2.9
55 Stanley	12,522	2.1	14,397	7.4	14,123	4.2	15,553	2.6
56 Stockton & Thby.	40,549	0.7	44,216	3.7	45,761	3.2	52,056	2.3
57 Stokesley	1,028	1.0	1,288	2.0	1,415	1.3	2,123	0.8
58 Sunderland	33,984	3.0	39,738	3.1	41,300	5.6	47,057	4.4
59 Walker	10,627	1.8	11,552	5.0	11,155	4.8	11,264	4.7
60 Wallsend	17,744	0.7	19,202	10.9	18,781	2.7	20,453	1.3
61 Washington Stn.	5,888	1.5	6,652	7.4	6,227	3.8	7,291	1.6
62 West Hartlepool	21,034	2.7	26,009	8.1	27,543	6.2	31,194	3.4
63 West Moor	n.a.	-	2,307	11.0	2,790	5.2	3,114	3.4
64 Whitley Bay	6,458	2.5	8,348	5.3	8,332	3.6	10,403	2.3
65 Willington Quay	3,428	0.7	3,665	5.7	3,905	3.7	4,331	2.2
66 Wingate	7,865	3.4	9,423	8.7	8,794	4.6	9,196	3.7
67 Wolsingham	873	0.0	914	1.3	811	1.6	994	0.2

Source: computed from Ministry of Labour records, TWA,1762/20.

Appendix 29: Outline Procedure for Government-financed Factories
before the Start of Construction of Special Projects.

The procedure for Advance Factories is not covered here, but there were
common features in the early stages.

In practice, the following outline procedure was complicated by a set of
sub-procedures.

                            B o T = Board of Trade

B o T (Regional Office)   selects site conforming to the
                                 Distribution of Industry policy, with the
                                 the advice and cooperation of local
                                 authorities. The estates companies provide
                                 details on ownership, basic services and
                                 a plan of the area.

                                 When site is approved,

B o T (Regional Office)   obtains clearance from the Ministries
                                 involved, i.e. Town & Country Planning,
                                 Health, Works, Agriculture, Fuel & Power.

                                 After receipt of clearance,

B o T (Regional Office)   instructs District Valuer to start
                                 negotiations with owners

Applicant for factory   is interviewed by B o T at Regional Office
                                 or in London. Arrangements are made for
                                 him to visit the most appropriate estates
                                 company.

Applicant for factory   discusses his financial position, space
                                 and labour needs with the estates company
                                 selected; the company explains the terms.

                                 If and when agreement is reached,

Applicant for factory   makes application either to the estates
                                 company or to the Board of Trade. If to
                                 the company, application is forwarded to
                                 the Regional Office of the B o T.

                                 If Regional Controller is satisfied,

B o T (Regional Office)   sends application, with comments, to the
                                 Board of Trade in London.

B o T (Distribution   Panel A of the Distribution of Industry
of Industry & Regional   Committee considers the application and
Division), London   obtains reports from the Production
                                 Departments on

                                   i) requirements for goods to be made
                                  ii) availability of raw materials
                                 iii) availability of required machinery.

	if project is approved, it is forwarded to
B o T (Regional Office),	which submits it to the next fortnightly meeting of the local Regional Distribution of Industry Committee. Approval or refusal are transmitted to the B o T Regional Office.
B o T (Regional Office)	forwards the approved project to the estates company.
Estates Company	applies to B o T (Regional Office) for building licence, submitting plans, costs, tenants extras etc.
B o T (Regional Office)	applies for financial approval to B o T London.
B o T (Regional Office) or Estates Company	receives approval and applies to the Ministry of Works for a building materials licence and a priority certificate.

Provided no unforeseen delay occurred, the average time which elapsed from the date on which the details of any project had been agreed with a manufacturer to the issue of a building licence was stated to be about eight weeks.

Source: abstracted from Select Committee on Estimates, 1947, paras. 40, 41, p.xiv.

Appendix 30: A 1948 Schedule of Items of Capital Expenditure of less than £100
requiring Authority from the Board of Trade in London

No.	Site	Project	Amount	Date	Reference	Details
1	Team Valley	C.113 Northumbrian Transport Services	£95.10	13.11.48	DIR 4978/46	Partition Walling
2	-do-	-do-	£4	20.12.48	B/B 257	Additional to (1) above
3	E. Gateshead	Development	£15	9. 1.48	DIR 400/46	Repairing gaps in wall
4	-do-	-do-	£50.13	16.12.48	DIR 400/46/3	Investigation etc.
5)	Team Valley	E.91 Warden Farm Dairies	£30	8. 7.48	DIR 4513/46	Installation of 2 water meters
5)	-do-	-do-	£26	6.10.48	DIR 4513/46	Extra on water meters above
6	Team Valley	A.20 Canteen	£35	6.10.48	CBL 115/46	Fitting heavy duty iron windows
7)	Team Valley	F.109 A. Wyman	£42	6. 4.48	CBL 822/45	Glazing to ground floor offices
7)	-do-	-do-	£78	8. 9.48	CBL 822/45	Extra on above
8	-do-	-do-	£64	8. 9.48	CBL 822/45	Alteration of switch gear
9	Team Valley	K.49 Belts&Trimmings	£43.10	21. 8.48	DIR 2754/48	Removing sliding door etc.
10	Ashington	BT21/2 G.T. Culpitt	£50	20. 3.48	B/PWE/BFG.104	Travelling expenses, painter
11	North Tees	BT20/16 David Hughes (Leeds Ltd)	£60	12. 1.48	B/PEW/53/BDG	Transport of Boiler Sections

Source: TWA, 1395, Box 272, File M.1802 (a).

Appendix 31: Insured Population in the North East 1937 - 1939,
Employment in Basic Industries and Insured Population 1945 - 1965, 1970

	Coal Mining	Ship/Bldg. & Reprng.	Heavy Enging.	Total 3 Inds.	Insured Population		
					Male	Female	Total
1937					723,560	140,750	864,310
1938					734,000	152,140	886,140
1939					699,730	150,270	850,000
1945	147,460	50,480	71,800	269,740	591,600	252,220	843,820
1946	151,710	49,820	74,910	276,440	706,550	233,660	940,210
1947	158,650	46,310	89,990	294,950	756,040	244,740	1,000,780
1948	172,410	50,730	96,510	319,650	885,900	331,930	1,217,830
1949	172,950	50,840	100,570	324,360	884,880	335,100	1,219,980
1950	171,090	47,930	99,720	318,740	897,930	344,390	1,242,320
1951	170,280	45,360	102,950	318,590	887,010	351,590	1,238,600
1952	171,070	44,750	107,670	323,490	881,120	355,550	1,236,670
1953	169,350	45,600	109,260	324,210	889,960	359,000	1,248,960
1954	168,850	45,340	110,850	326,040	894,160	364,000	1,258,160
1955	168,120	45,810	114,880	328,810	892,100	370,000	1,262,100
1956	168,420	47,300	116,200	331,920	907,050	378,000	1,285,050
1957	167,282	48,120	118,170	333,572	906,980	381,000	1,287,980
1958	166,110	46,560	121,320	333,990	914,960	386,000	1,300,960
1959	162,390	46,500	117,850	326,740	911,050	389,000	1,300,050
1960	151,460	43,710	120,500	315,670	905,240	398,000	1,303,240
1961	143,520	41,220	119,770	304,510	898,260	406,000	1,304,260
1962	136,400	39,200	119,000	293,600	871,900	404,400	1,276,300
1963	127,700	33,300	114,300	275,300	851,700	408,000	1,259,700
1964	118,600	32,700	120,700	272,000	853,400	418,900	1,272,300
1965	113,500	34,200	131,600	279,300	865,000	436,000	1,301,000
1970	72,700	41,100	149,600	263,400	850,000	476,000	1,326,000

Source: Ministry of Labour Records, TWA,1762/20.

Appendix 32: Labour Statistics for the North East, July 1938

Some Labour Exchanges and Employment Offices included in their reports the figures for juvenile unemployment. These are shown without comment. The figures for the number of unemployed suffixed

IC   include figures obtained from separate juvenile employment office reports.

+J   indicate that no juvenile unemployment figures were available under the name of the Exchange or Office listed.

IP = Insured Population, NU = Number of Unemployed

	Employment Exchange or Office	IP	NU		% IP	
1	Alnwick	3,350	244		7.3	
2	Amble	3,160	477		15.1	
3	Ashington	14,920	8,250		55.3	a
4	Barnard Castle	1,030	177	+J	17.2	
5	Bedlington Station	8,630	544		6.3	
*6	Berwick	-	-		-	
7	Birtley	5,320	733	+J	13.8	
8	Bishop Auckland	10,580	3,972	IC	37.8	
9	Blaydon	10,300	1,849	IC	18.0	
10	Blyth	11,100	1,657		14.9	
11	Chester le Street	12,250	2,125	IC	17.3	
12	Chopwell	2,030	387	+J	19.1	
13	Cockfield	2,000	750	+J	37.5	
14	Consett	15,710	1,373	+J	8.7	
15	Crook	8,630	3,171	IC	36.7	
16	Darlington	31,470	2,431		7.7	
17	Dunston	5,320	789	+J	14.8	
18	Durham	17,050	3,698	IC	22.5	
19	East Boldon	3,080	1,344	+J	43.6	
20	Elswick	23,140	3,763	+J	16.3	
21	Felling	9,270	1,527		16.5	
22	Gainford	340	115	+J	33.8	
23	Gateshead	30,370	6,404		21.1	
24	Guisborough	1,360	389		28.6	
25	Haltwhistle	1,600	334		20.9	
26	Hartlepool	3,090	1,594		51.6	
27	Haswell	3,580	2,100	+J	58.7	
28	Haverton Hill	3,180	364	+J	11.4	
29	Heaton	17,740	3,558	+J	20.1	
*30	Helmsley	-	-		-	
31	Hexham	4,020	379		9.4	
32	Horden	11,150	6,149	+J	55.1	a
33	Houghton le Spring	13,000	2,186	IC	16.8	
34	Jarrow & Hebburn	19,300	4,205		21.8	
35	Lanchester	3,820	780	+J	40.8	
36	Loftus	3,820	755		19.8	
37	Middlesborough	36,980	9,850	IC	26.6	
38	Morpeth	3,950	484		12.3	
39	Newburn	5,280	790		15.0	
40	Newcastle upon Tyne	79,930	5,805		7.3	b
41	North Shields	13,370	3,807	IC	26.5	c

Employment Exchange or Office		IP	NU		% IP	
42	Pallion	16,700	3,995	+J	23.9	
43	Prudhoe	3,450	416		12.1	
44	Redcar	3,680	820		22.3	
45	Saltburn	2,440	583		23.9	
46	Seaham Harbour	14,660	1,546	IC	10.5	
47	Seaton Delaval	7,370	727		9.9	
48	Sedgefield	2,890	173	+J	6.0	
49	Shildon	3,880	1,128	+J	29.0	
50	South Bank	19,230	2,243		11.8	
51	South Shields	32,920	9,740		30.0	
52	Southwick	6,570	1,969	+J	30.0	d
53	Spennymoor	9,950	2,625	IC	26.4	
54	Stanhope	1,220	282	+J	23.1	
55	Stanley	14,840	5,134		34.6	
56	Stockton & Thornaby	33,910	5,806	IC	17.1	
57	Stokesley	790	185		23.4	
58	Sunderland	40,380	9,949	IC	24.6	
59	Walker	8,720	1,766	+J	20.3	
60	Wallsend	16,400	1,850		11.3	
61	Washington Station	6,670	792	+J	11.9	
62	West Hartlepool	23,980	4,594		19.2	
63	West Moor	7,720	403		5.2	
64	Whitley Bay	4,640	651		14.0	
65	Willington Quay	3,600	1,069		29.7	
66	Wingate	7,870	1,173	+J	14.9	
67	Wolsingham	730	103	+J	14.1	

* Not yet included in the North East returns

Notes:

a. The very high unemployment figures were due to a large proportion of men being stopped temporarily.

b. The figures for juvenile unemployment were reported by the Employment Exchange and separately by the juvenile employment bureau at the Exchange. The figures do not correlate and have been ignored.

c. The figures from the juvenile employment bureau at Tynemouth have been used; no figures were given in the return from the North Shields Exchange.

d. This area was probably covered by the juvenile employment bureau in Sunderland and the unemployment figures may have been included in the return for that Exchange area.

Source: computed from Ministry of Labour records, TWA,1762/20.

Appendix 33: Note on the Labour Statistics from 1947

The Labour statistics for 1947 and later years were affected by two important social changes.

The first was the raising of the school leaving age in 1947 from 14 to 15 years. The effect of this was to postpone by one year the entry into the labour market of juveniles who would have left school in 1947.

A more significant change occurred in 1948. Up to July of that year, the labour statistics (usually referred to as manpower statistics after the War) were based primarily on the number of unemployment books issued under the Unemployment Insurance Acts. This information was later called 'old series'.

These Acts were replaced on 5 July 1948 by the more comprehensive schemes under the National Insurance and National Insurance (Injury) Acts. A new series of manpower statistics began on that date, based on the number of contributors under these schemes. The new and broader base for the statistics widened the scope of those included in the figures.

The new series covered men of 65 and over and women aged 60 and over together with private indoor domestic servants, who had been omitted from the old series. In further contrast, part-time workers were now counted as one unit each because they were insured under the new Acts. The change made it no longer possible to distinguish between part-time and full-time workers. This accounts, in part, for the rapid and continuous rise in the female labour force shown in Appendix 31.

The effect of the new basis for the collection of manpower statistics was that they now included all persons aged 15 and over at work or available for work.

The change largely accounts for the 21% increase in the insured population between 1947 and 1948 shown in Appendix 31.

The new basis for the collection of manpower data and the use of the Standard Industrial Classification in the analysis of the industrial totals make it impossible to relate the information in the new and old series.P

Source: Central Statistical Office, 1952, p.107.

Appendix 34: Male Unemployment in the Northern Region* 1948 - 1962

	Great Britain Per cent	Northern Region Per cent	Difference Per cent
1948	1.7	2.8	1.1
1949	1.7	2.8	1.1
1950	1.6	2.8	1.2
1951	1.2	2.1	0.9
1952	1.7	2.1	0.4
1953	1.6	2.0	0.4
1954	1.3	2.0	0.7
1955	1.1	1.6	0.5
1956	1.2	1.4	0.2
1957	1.5	1.7	0.2
1958	2.3	2.5	0.2
1959	2.4	3.6	1.2
1960	1.8	3.1	1.3
1961	1.7	2.7	1.0
1962	2.4	4.3	1.9

* The North East contained approx. 90% of the insured
   population of the Northern Region, which included
   the counties of Cumberland and Westmorland.

Source: White Paper, 1963, p.43.

Index

Engineering in North East (cont.)

fall in employment, inter-War
23-4
Evening Chronicle , Newcastle
90, 169
Evening News , N.Shields 172

Fabian Society: Tract on Full
Employment 220
Federation.of British Industries
(FBI) 64, 77, 123
Fisher, Sir Warren 136, 137
Fleck, Sir Alexander (later Lord)
287, 293
Fletcher, L. 122
Fogarty, M.P. 309
Forster, S.A. Sadler (later Sir
Sadler) 204, 266, 267, 269, 272
287, 300, 301, 348
on Advance Factories 262, 265
letter to the The Times ,1935,
350-51
promotion of Trading Estates
62-3, 68, 78

Gateshead Corporation 115,116
land owned at Team Valley
109, 113
unemployment, 1939, 308
Gibb & Partners, Sir Alexander
91, 107, 111, 158, 197, 260
reports on possible sites for
North Eastern Trading Estates
91-7
Gillet, Sir George 124, 153, 193,
347
on Sir Malcolm Stewart 141
on Special Areas (Amendment) Act
1937, 141
see also Special Areas,
Commissioners for England and
Wales
Goldring, Douglas: A Tour of
Northumbria 168
Great Britain
Dollar Crisis, 1947, 273, 275-6
electoral reasons for authorising
trading estate 74-5
Gold Standard: abandonment, 1931
10; return to, 1925, 6, 8, 18
government attitude to
intervention over industrial
decline 1-4 passim , 8-9
government's task re remployment,
1945, 242

male unemployment, 1948-62, 407
post-War building problems 244-6,
247-9
rearmament programme, from 1936,
174-5
recession of 1930s, 16
recovery from recession, 1930s,
41, 127
Greenwood, Arthur 51, 53, 131, 339

Halifax, Earl of 43
Hanham, F.G. 267, 268
Hannon, Sir Patrick 129
Hartlepool
reserve munitions factory 232,
236, 263
trading estate 204, 205, 287, 291
Headlam, C.M. (later Sir Cuthbert)
51, 214
Heim, Carol E. 64, 147, 148, 149
Henson, Dr. L, Bishop of Durham 133
Herbert, Major J.A. 153
Hertfordshire County Council,
adopts villages in Co. Durham,
1930s, 32
Hillington trading estate 118
Hobson, J.A. 7
Holford, W.G. (later Lord)
114, 166, 204, 349
Holmes, Stanley 35
Hopkins, Sir Richard 8
Hutchinson, Lord 54

Imperial Chemical Industries (ICI)
Ltd 251
Industrial Transference Board 5
32, 337
Irvine, W. 294

James I, King 46
Jarrow 50, 91, 93, 98, 258
closure of Palmer's shipyard 23
Jarrow Slake 49, 89, 90, 93
march of Jarrow men to London
23, 133
unemployment, 1930s, 23, 44
Jarvie, J.G. 145
Jarvis, Sir John 32
Jay, Douglas 211, 212, 222, 310,
348
role in industrial reconstruction
and employment 212-13, 218, 220
Jenkins, W.A. 130
Johnstone, Harcourt 53

411

Morrison, Herbert 245

North Eastern Trading Estates Ltd (cont.)

progress in assigned role (cont.)
prepares programme for Advance Factories, 1946, 266-7, 269-70; question of sea access, 90, 91, 92; retirement of Board, 1948, 300; suffers post-War Board of Trade bureaucratic delays 247-8; suggests suspension of building, 1947, 272-3; takes over former wartime factories 230-4
proposes itself as agent for government industrial property and location of industry in NE, 1944, 283-4
self-image 281-2, 286
tenants numbers, 1939-60, 394
thoughts on post-War strategy 282-3
views on Advance and specialised factories 264, 265
see also Team Valley Trading Estate
North East Industrial and Development Association 284
North Mail , Newcastle 85, 90, 98 99, 173, 300
articles criticising Team Valley Estate 119-20, 121, 122
Northern Industrial Group 201, 214, 216, 284, 254
Northern Industries Development Co. Ltd 36, 64, 145
North East region defined xvii-xviii
Northern Regional Production Board 199, 200, 289, 296, 352, 353
North Western Industrial Estates Ltd 297
Nuffield, Lord 147
Nuffield Fund for Special Areas, 1936, 147, 148, 149, 152, 154, 161, 170
financial assistance to firms in NE, 1936-8, 364-367

Odber, J. Alan 242
on Dollar Crisis cuts, 1947, 279
Orwin, C.S. and Darke, W.F. 335

Pallion outside site, Sunderland 119, 149, 158-61 passim , 253, 260, 292

reserve munitions factory 232, 255, 263
Park Royal trading estate 62, 91, 92
Peden, G.C. 8, 83, 228
Pelaw Main Collieries Ltd 109, 112
mineral rights under Team Valley Estate 108
Pepler, G. and McFarlane, P.W. 230, 244, 283
Percival, Ronald M. 84, 97, 159, 194, 300
on outside sites 156
Percy, Lord Eustace 54, 57, 75, 146, 208
Perroux, F. 123, 282
Pigou, A.C. 7, 8
Pilgrim Trust: on unemployment, 1938, 28
Pimlott, Ben 220, 225
Hugh Dalton 211
Pitfield, D.W. 55, 74, 228, 338
Political and Economic Plannning (PEP) 82, 207, 355
Portal, Lord 68, 125, 126, 128, 148, 149, 150, 154
Price, Sir James 193, 347
Priestley, J.B. 27
Public Utility Society 355

Ravensworth, Lord 110
Redcliffe-Maud Report 52
Regional Board for Industry see Northern Regional Production Board
Regional policy
defined 5-6
question of concentration or dispersion 123, 124
Rhodes, J.G. 278
Richardson, Harry W. 61
Ridley, Lord 68, 79, 80, 81, 90, 132, 140, 199, 200, 201, 214, 289, 300, 345,
Rose, Sir Arthur 50
Royal Commissions
on Distribution of the Industrial Population, 1940,
see also Barlow Commission
on Local Government on Tyneside (Scott), 1937, 52
on Poor Laws, 1909, 7
Runciman, W. (Viscount) President of Board of Trade, 34
Runciman, W.L. 80

Unemployment (cont.))

inter-War 6, 16, 25, 44
Means Test 29
moralistic attitudes over 7
official statistics 333
public works and 8, 9
'Treasury View', 1929, 8-9
later modification 9
Unemployment Act, 1934,
29
Unemployment Assistance Board 43
134, 142, 169

Wallace, Capt. D. Euan 57, 61
recommendations 46-7, 52, 344
work as Investigator for Durham
and Tyneside, 1934, 44-8, 64,
145
conclusions 45-6
Wallsend sites 89, 90, 95, 97
Waltham Royal Gunpowder Factory 227
Walton, Col. G.H. (later Brig. Sir
George) 81, 82, 85, 300, 346
War Damage Act 1941, 197
Warter, Sir Philip 220, 221, 264,
267, 269, 290, 291, 348
on post-War factory building 265
on role of NE Trading Estates 287
Waterhouse, Capt. C. 224
Watkinson, L. (later Sir Laurence)
216
Wedderburn, Scrymgeour 66, 67, 68
Welsh and Monmouthsire Industrial
Estates Co. Ltd 300
Welwyn trading estate 62, 92
West Auckland site
see St. Helen's Auckland
outside site
West Chirton outside site
see Tynemouth outside site
Ministry of Supply clothing depot
233
Westwood, W. (later Lord) 80, 81,
85, 97, 297, 346
Whitburn site, Sunderland 90, 95,
97
Whitehouse, H.J. 155, 171, 194
Wiener, Martin J. 335
Wilkinson and Marshall, solicitors
84
Wilkinson, Ellen 23, 115, 116
Willis, F.A. 168
Wilson, Harold 252
as President of Board of Trade
297, 298, 299
attempts to deal with
bureaucratic delays 248-9

attempts to deal with
bureaucratic delays 248-9
work on post-War factory building
programme 247
Winch, Donald 7, 8
Winchester, Bishop of 27
Wimpey Ltd (George) 115
Withers, Sir John 131
Wolmer, Viscount 128, 136
Wood, Sir Kingsley 213
Woolton, Lord 215
Woolwich Royal Gunpowder Factory
227